FRUITS OF VICTORY

FRUITS OF VICTORY

THE WOMAN'S LAND ARMY OF AMERICA IN THE GREAT WAR

ELAINE F. WEISS

Potomac Books, Inc.
Washington, D.C.

Published in the United States by Potomac books, Inc. All rights reserved. No part of this book may be reproduced in any manner whatsoever without written permission from the publisher, except in the case of brief quotations embodied in critical articles and reviews.

Library of Congress Cataloging-in-Publication Data
Weiss, Elaine.
  Fruits of victory : the Woman's Land Army of America in the Great War / Elaine F. Weiss. — 1st ed.
    p. cm.
  Includes bibliographical references and index.
  ISBN 978-1-59797-273-4 (hardcover : alk. paper)
  1. Women's Land Army of America—History. 2. World War, 1914-1918—Women—United States. 3. World War, 1914-1918—War work—United States. 4. World War, 1914-1918—Participation, Female. 5. World War, 1914-1918—Food supply—United States. 6. World War, 1914-1918—Economic aspects—United States. 7. Women farmers—United States—History—20th century. I. Title.
  D639.W7W45 2008
  940.3'73082—dc22

                                2008042104

Printed in the United States of America on acid-free paper that meets the American National Standards Institute Z39-48 Standard.

Potomac Books, Inc.
22841 Quicksilver Drive
Dulles, Virginia 20166

First Edition

10 9 8 7 6 5 4 3 2 1

CONTENTS

ACKNOWLEDGMENTS

I once knew a real farmerette of World War I, and I first encountered the Woman's Land Army in her farmhouse in the hills of Vermont. Her name was Alice Holway, and she was nearly eighty years old when I met her. Still working on the land, she was quite a character, or a real spunky gal, as she might say. As I sat in a lopsided chair in her parlor she regaled me with stories of her youthful service in the WLA's Nauhlahka Unit, near Brattleboro, and she was very proud of having "done her bit" in service to her nation. Her participation in the Land Army changed the course of her life, and she, in turn, touched and shaped mine. This book honors the memory of Alice Holway, and all of her fellow farmerettes.

Attempting to restore the farmerette to her rightful place in the American saga was a team effort, and I am profoundly grateful for the support of two smart and savvy women of letters. My literary agent, Whitney Lee, of the Fielding Agency, has been my loyal counselor and champion. Her unshakable belief in this project fortified me, and her fierce optimism kept me buoyant. My talented and tenacious editor, Elizabeth Sherburn Demers, is the fairy godmother of this book. She has carried it with her on her journeys, protected it, promoted it, and with a skillful wave of her green pen, shaped it into a finer work.

The task of reconstructing the history of the Woman's Land Army, scattered and buried for nearly nine decades, was a grand adventure in archival archeology, and I have many to thank for their assistance in the digging. So many archivists and librarians, across the country and across the Atlantic Ocean shared with me their knowledge and enthusiasm as well as the treasures of their collections. I am especially indebted to Donald Glassman and Astrid Cravens at the Barnard College Archives; Wilma Slaight and Ian Graham at the Wellesley College Archives; Dean Rogers at the Vassar College Archives; Sydney Roby at the Goucher College Archives; Patricia Albright at the Mount Holyoke College Archives; and Nanci Young at the Smith College Archives, as well as Amy Hague and Maida Goodwin at the Sophia Smith Collection. Eileen Kearing at the Kroch Library of Cornell University was enormously helpful, as was Betty Carter and

Carolyn Shankle at the University of North Carolina–Greensboro Archives and Jonathan Schmitz at the Chautauqua Institution in New York.

The marvelous Schlesinger Library of the Radcliffe Institute at Harvard holds many essential records of the Woman's Land Army, and it was my privilege to spend hours there in happy research. I extend my thanks to Ellen Shea and Diana Carey at Schlesinger for all their assistance.

State and local archives also held rich deposits of documents for me, and I must especially thank Greg Cox at the Illinois State Archives in Springfield; Tim Rives at the National Archives and Record Administration's Central Plains Region office in Kansas City, Missouri; and Tomas Jaehn at the Museum of New Mexico in Santa Fe for finding such gems. Carol Harbison Samuelson at the Southern Oregon Historical Society in Medford was extraordinarily helpful, as was Michelle Stahl of the Peterborough (New Hampshire) Historical Society and Harriet Taylor of the Wilton (Connecticut) Library Association's History Room. Pamela Edwards and Legard Waldrop were most generous with their time and attention during my visit to the New Milford (Connecticut) Historical Society, and Beverley Cook at the Museum of London made my research foray there pleasant and productive.

This book has been enriched by the insights of Melissa Fitzgerald, Edith Diehl's great-niece, who allowed me to visit Diehl's house in Brewster, New York, and explore her library. The ability to touch Miss Diehl's Woman's Land Army insignia buckle was a true thrill. I am appreciative of the research of Debbie Rafferty-Oswald on the life of Diehl and of Virginia McLaughlin's writings on the Land Army service of her aunt Daisy Day.

I want to extend a special thanks to Dr. Jessica Elfenbein, historian and friend, for her contributions and Dr. Jill Jonnes, historian, author, and friend, for her good counsel. My devoted cheerleaders, kind critics, and eagle-eyed readers, Samuel and Natalie Babbitt, have been by my side for nearly four decades, providing guidance and inspiration—and swift kicks when necessary. My gratitude for their faith in this scrivener. And I, along with ten thousand other artists over the past century, owe a sweet debt to the MacDowell Colony in Peterborough, New Hampshire, where the gift of a fellowship and a cabin allowed me to write early versions of Alice Holway's stories.

Over the course of this project's long road, many friends, near and far, offered sympathetic ears, helping hands, advice, and succor to keep me on track and in balance. Writing is a solitary task, but I'm lucky to have a patient and loving family surrounding and supporting me. My mother, Jeannie, and mother-in-law, Bess, strong women born in the era of Great War, have waited expectantly for this book to finally arrive. My husband, Julian Krolik, and children, Teddy and Abby, graciously tolerated my long hours at the desk and short stints in the kitchen, cheerfully accepting the invasion of the Woman's Land Army into our household for an extended stay. Their daily encouragement sustained me. And Julian, my lodestar, made it all possible.

Prelude: Liberty Day

To do her bit she's ready,
Of work she's not afraid,
She's waiting for the summons,
In fitting garb arrayed;
She'll grasp the tools of labor
And never pine nor fret,
But do her stunt appointed,
The plucky farmerette.

For soldiers sore are needed,
And as to camp they go,
To take the place now vacant
Of the man behind the hoe,
The woman steps out bravely;
She's never failed us yet;
She'll not make a beginning
With the sturdy farmerette.

The toil is hard and novel,
But it is there to do;
This is not play, but earnest,
And the new recruit is true
To country and to duty;
She will have no regret,
And so we hail and bless her,
The patriot farmerette.

The New Recruit
Wall Street Journal
June 24, 1918

On a sunny afternoon in October 1918, President Woodrow Wilson marched down Fifth Avenue in the Liberty Day Parade, the largest war processional New York City had ever seen. Smiling and tipping his tall silk hat, the president marched with twenty-five thousand fighting men from twenty-two Allied nations, from Belgium to Brazil. Forty marching bands kept the beat along the three-mile parade route, pausing by an "Altar of Liberty" set up at Madison Square. Police estimated almost a million people lined the sidewalks.

Reports from the trenches of the American Expeditionary Force hinted that the Hun was finally on his knees, exhausted and starving, so the crowd was in a celebratory mood. Still there was an air of urgency about raising the $6 billion needed from the American public's pockets to pursue the war to its conclusion. So this Liberty Day Parade, initiating the Fourth Liberty Loan campaign, was not only a tribute to military might, but also an homage to the national will—its resolve, sacrifice, and service.

Playing George M. Cohan's wartime favorite "Over There," John Philip Sousa's Great Lakes Naval Training Station Band led off the parade, followed by the colorful Allied military divisions. The commander in chief took his place at the head of the American military forces, a massive column of army khaki and navy blue. Some of the marching doughboys were wounded veterans with a uniform sleeve or trouser leg pinned up, signifying a missing limb. Some marched wearing their gas masks, others with their bayonets fixed. Some spectators were also wearing protective face masks, as the deadly influenza epidemic was sweeping the nation. Airplanes swooped overhead, tipping their wings in salute, while huge floats carried planes and boats in the parade, with the men of the factories and naval yards waving from atop their creations.

And parading just in front of the president, the American women war workers were cheered wildly by the crowds. Red Cross nurses marched, their capes flapping in the breeze. Women of the Motor Corps, in their snappy khaki uniforms, stepped lively; women in blue Police Reserve uniforms walked in perfect formation; and women in munitions makers' baggy costumes kept pace. Members of the Camouflage Corps, the telephone operator "Hello" Girls, the National League for Women's Service, Young Women's Christian Association (YWCA) canteen workers, Red Cross medical supply workroom volunteers, elevator operators, and street car conductor ladies—all marched to the beat.

"The service of women in the struggle," the *New York Times* reported, was "vividly illustrated" in the parade. Called the "Girls Behind the Guns," they were the heroines of the home front. Their likes had never been seen before. And within the ranks of those women war workers on parade, striding smartly in uniforms of khaki bloomers, belted jackets, and broad-rimmed hats, marched a regiment of the Woman's Land Army of America. These "farmerettes" paraded with hoes over their shoulders, pushing wheelbarrows, or carrying wicker baskets of fruit. They were the female Soldiers of the Soil, the Girls with the Hoe, the plucky "Patriot Farmerettes" in America's fields, and they sparked a roar of approval from the sidewalk crowd.

While President Wilson used the rallying cry "Food will win the war," the Woman's Land Army organized in forty-two states and mobilized more than twenty thousand farmerettes to live in hundreds of "unit" camps spread across the country. The volunteer corps recruited women of all ages and social classes to do the farm labor of the men called away to fight, bringing city workers, society women, teachers, artists, business professionals, and college students to the rural home front to do men's work while dressed in men's clothing. The farmerette in her "bifurcated garb of toil" became a popular icon of American womanhood serving Uncle Sam. She was the toast of Broadway, the darling of the smart set, and the star of the wartime cinema newsreel. Victor Herbert and P. G. Wodehouse wrote songs about her, Rockwell Kent drew sly pictures of her, Charles Dana Gibson created posters for her, Theodore Roosevelt championed her, major American newspapers and magazines wrote editorials about her, and Flo Ziegfeld put her in his follies.

And then she disappeared. For ninety years the farmerette of the Great War has been lost, totally and inexplicably forgotten, wiped from the national memory. This book is the chronicle of the Woman's Land Army of America, those farmerettes who marched so proudly on Liberty Day. Their story has been lost for too long.

It begins across the sea, with another parade.

Part One

The Girl With a Hoe
Behind the Man With a Gun

1

THE RIGHT TO SERVE:
A BRITISH LAND ARMY

On a rain-soaked and chilly July afternoon toward the end of the first year of the Great War, tens of thousands of British women took to the streets of London. Marching behind the fiery suffrage leader Emmeline Pankhurst, they demanded "the right to serve" their nation during wartime.

They formed a mighty river of women, thirty thousand strong—many dressed in pure white, others draped in mourning black, still others in Scottish kilts or Welsh village costume—coursing between banks of umbrella-domed spectators cheering on the sidelines. Divided into more than a hundred marching sections, each was led by Union Jack flag bearers and brass bands. While the hems of their long skirts dragged in the muddy pavement, they carried aloft hundreds of cloth banners bearing the mottoes "We demand war work and service for all," "Mobilize the brains and energy of women," "More munitions wanted—use women's labour," and "Women's battle cry is Work, Work, Work!"[1]

They were rallying to Mrs. Pankhurst's "Call to the Women," and while not all these women agreed with the suffrage cause, they were united in their desire that the government allow them to assume a useful role—to do war work—in the perilous summer of 1915. Their men were serving king and country, and they insisted on the same privilege. The marchers were demanding to be included in a National Register for War Service and to be mobilized for the war effort. They called for government-sponsored training programs to prepare them for this new work, and they wanted equal pay for doing it. They demanded that the "Victorian prejudices" and "Adamite" tendencies of trade unionists, businessmen, and male workers not keep them from entering the munitions factories and other essential war industries where workers were desperately needed.

But what the patriotically indignant women parading through London that afternoon in a great stream of sisterhood did not realize was that this rally had been planned and paid for by the Propaganda Fund of His Majesty's government.[2]

The rally looked like so many other demonstrations Mrs. Pankhurst had led over the past decade—with colorful banners, careful choreography, strident demands—but this one was decidedly different. The war had changed everything. Within days of England's entrance into the conflict against Germany the previous August, Mrs. Pankhurst and her lieutenants in the Women's Political and Social Union entered into a "war truce" with the Liberal government of Prime Minister Herbert Asquith. The women agreed to suspend their militant suffrage activities, which had included smashing the windows of Parliament and firebombing politicians' offices, and to redirect their energies toward the war effort. "What's the use of winning the vote if you don't have a country to vote in," Mrs. Pankhurst famously explained. In return, the stubbornly anti-suffrage Asquith government released from prison dozens of Pankhurst's militant "suffragettes," many of whom were on hunger strikes and were being force-fed with tubes stuffed down their throats.

Making good on her side of the bargain, Mrs. Pankhurst and her daughter Christabel spent this first year of the war using their oratory and organizational skills as war propagandists, encouraging men to enlist to fight and women to "do your bit." By their loyalty and by their service, women would prove themselves, once and for all, without question, entitled to vote. But the war effort came first.

The Right to Serve March appealed to women of all political persuasions and all classes. Militant suffragettes marched together with their more moderate sister "suffragists," ladies of aristocratic title with working-class women, girls in domestic service with girls of leisure, war widows with grieving mothers. "Many women who at ordinary times are quite out of sympathy with the feminist propaganda have declared their intention of taking part," reported the *Times of London* the day before the march.[3]

"Thousands of women from all classes" took part in the demonstration, according to the *Illustrated London News*: "aristocrats, professionals, workers in many forms of art and industry, women who rejoice in demonstrating and women whom nothing but clear conviction and a strong sense of duty would draw from their quiet homes into the glare of publicity."[4]

They set off to the strains of "La Marseillaise," the international anthem of the war. "As section after section swung off in the blowing rain," wrote one march participant, "with pennons twinkling and banners like great kites straining, unexpected women standing to look at us joined in," forming "a great coil of women" that snaked through the streets of central London.[5]

But this spectacular show of women's will had not been Mrs. Pankhurst's idea at all. Earlier in the summer she had been summoned to the Whitehall offices of David Lloyd George, the astute and ambitious minister of munitions. More clearly than most of his cabinet colleagues, he saw the frightening dimensions of a looming labor shortage and the crippling, or even utter collapse, of the war effort without a new source of workers, the women of Great Britain.

In truth, it was a brilliant marriage of convenience. An odder alliance would be hard to imagine—after all, Mrs. Pankhurst's suffragette militants had once bombed Lloyd George's own house. Mrs. Pankhurst herself, prior to the war, had become the most vilified woman in the empire, splitting the suffrage movement with her violent stratagems and losing the public's sympathy for the cause. With this arrangement she might regain her place as the standard-bearer for women's rights. And Lloyd George, with his eye on the prime minister's "despatch box" (the new Asquith coalition government was already tottering), could only benefit from an infusion of women workers eager to take up munitions and other essential war work.

Mrs. Pankhurst and Lloyd George agreed on a little pantomime: she would assemble a small delegation of women, draw up a list of demands regarding women's service, and make a formal request to present these demands to him in person. He would, after a proper show of hemming and hawing, agree to officially receive the deputation of women in his chambers and then respond, mostly positively, to their demands. As icing on the cake, Pankhurst would also call for this massive public show of support to cheer on the delegation through the streets of the capital.

Lloyd George arranged to give Mrs. Pankhurst's Women's Social and Political Union two thousand pounds sterling to cover the expenses of organizing and executing the rally. Mrs. Pankhurst then simply did what she had done so well and often before: she held press conferences, issued proclamations, convened a giant War Service Meeting in the London Pavilion to whip up enthusiasm. In fact, it was easy, because the enthusiasm was already there. The women of Great Britain were eager to help. Already tired of knitting socks, they were frustrated by the government's reluctance to organize and utilize them; they were ready to take on tasks they'd never dreamed of before. The women wanted to serve. Their country needed them. Now it was a question of convincing those who did not think it seemly to have women replacing men in the factories, in the mines, perhaps even in the fields.

Some fifty registration tables were set up along the march's route, and more than eight thousand women signed on for munitions work on the spot that Saturday afternoon. Thousands more volunteered the following week.

As the march made its final loop back to its starting point at Victoria Embankment, Mrs. Pankhurst and four of her lieutenants joined Lloyd George and his war cabinet colleague, Winston Churchill, on a little platform above the embankment's gardens. "It was a strange sight to see Mr. Lloyd George fearlessly fraternizing with Mrs. Pankhurst," a participant in the march wrote in the *Times of London*. "It was as if Daniel had invited the lion to his den."[6]

Lloyd George, a handsome and notorious womanizer (nicknamed the "Welsh Goat"), knew how to play his part as he addressed the throng of women. "If any additional proof were required of the organizing capacity of women"—and he'd been the victim of Mrs. Pankhurst's organizing talents on other occasions, he quipped, to great laughter—"it is amply demonstrated by this procession."[7]

The special advantage of the march was that it would help to educate public opinion on the need to organize both men and women in order to wage the war efficiently, Lloyd George continued. Further, any resistance from men to allowing women to work where they were needed would hurt the national effort.

"The procession was not intended to rouse women," the *Times of London* quoted Mrs. Pankhurst as saying, "that had been done already—but to convince men, some of whom were ready to be convinced, but wished to have pressure brought upon them, that women were ready to serve their country at a time of great national peril, and desired to be organized and trained on a great national scale."[8]

"The demonstration will be historic," predicted *The Illustrated London News*, "and when the story of the World War comes to be written, the patriotic part played by women will be chronicled, and this great demonstration of women craving to work for the war will find honourable place."[9]

At the moment of the Right to Serve March, in mid-summer 1915, Britain was not yet hungry; the pressing need was to supply its soldiers with munitions. "A shell made by a wife might save a husband's life," one Right to Serve banner proclaimed. Both the government and British women initially focused their energies in this direction.

When the fighting began, in August 1914, the British thought the war would be over by Christmas. Then Christmas passed, and the German zeppelin attacks brought death from the air to English children, and tens of thousands of Englishmen did not come home from the trenches at Ypres. The initial rush of patriotic fervor—when men rushed to join their regimental colors and zealous women ran around the streets of London pinning white feathers of cowardice to the lapel of any able-bodied man not yet in uniform—was spent.

By the summer of 1915 almost two million men had volunteered for military service and had been pulled out of the British economy. By the end of the year, that number reached closer to three million men, up to forty years of age, and it was still not enough. By early 1916, conscription had begun. Yet the government of Prime Minister Asquith was astoundingly slow to comprehend the psychological and physical stresses a long war would have on the country.

In 1914 Britain was importing half of the foodstuffs needed to feed its population of thirty-six million people.[10] With improved refrigeration and transport, it was cheaper to buy grain from North America, mutton from Australia, beef from Argentina, and potatoes from Germany than to produce these staples at home. Relying on food imports made economic sense, but now, with the war, Britain became an isolated island surrounded by submarine-infested seas. Its food supply was in jeopardy. With its U-boat blockades, Germany hoped to starve Great Britain into submission.

In May 1915, just as the nation was beginning to grapple with the notion that the war would grind on, William Waldegrave Palmer, Second Earl of Selborne, took up his portfolio as the new president of the Board of Agriculture. An insightful and forward-thinking man who had once served as Lord of the Admiralty, he could see that a food crisis was looming. He fired off memo after urgent memo, imploring Asquith to recognize the danger of the food situation and to construct a governmental plan to avert hunger. He received no response. Most of Asquith's cabinet was convinced that civilian food supplies could easily be sustained without any government involvement. They felt there was no need for a Ministry of Food to coordinate production, no need to regulate food prices, and certainly no need for rationing. Selborne's pleas were brushed aside.

In July 1915 Lord Selborne resorted to writing a personal appeal to the prime minister and begged him to develop a plan to increase the nation's agricultural production. The day before the Right to Serve March, Asquith finally replied to Selborne: the prime minister did not have "the least fear that any probable or conceivable development of German submarine activity can be a serious menace to our food supply."[11]

While 10 Downing Street and the Whitehall bureaucracy dithered, Lord Selborne took matters into his own hands. He initiated a campaign for stimulating British food production. He used propaganda in the place of a real policy and appealed to farmers' patriotism in urging them to plant more acres and raise more food. He also set up local initiatives, called War Agricultural Committees (WACs), in every district and shire to evaluate the local farming needs. Their primary need became immediately apparent—farm labor.

The conscientious Selborne had already done the mathematics of the situation and realized that asking farmers to add acres in production while draining the manpower they needed to tend those fields was pure folly. Like his colleague Lloyd George, he understood that the solution was obvious but not easy: hire women workers. Women were already in the fields of France. The cinema newsreels featured heart-rending photos of brave mothers pulling plows strapped to their shoulders, since all the men and horses were gone to war.

British women eager to volunteer for agricultural work had already put their names on the National Register for War Service in March 1915, but as with their industrially minded sisters, they had not yet been tapped to serve. Because the government was tardy in organizing women for farm labor, Selborne quietly encouraged several private women's clubs with interests in agriculture to take action on their own. Many of these women lived on family estates in rural districts and could see with their own eyes how short-handed farmers were struggling to bring in the crops or were forced to leave them to rot in the fields.

One of the quickest clubs off the mark was a young organization called the Women's International Agricultural and Horticultural Union, founded in 1899.[12] The women who belonged to the union were an assortment of landed gentry, sympathetic upper-class city women, and professionals who had trained at the nation's few agricultural schools open to women. Since one of the union's chief goals was to help women get the training necessary to make a career in farming, gardening, husbandry, or landscape design, the group welcomed the war challenge and embraced it as a rare opportunity. By late 1914 the union had already launched its own effort, called the Women's National Land Service Corps, to recruit and train women for farmwork. In the spring of 1915, Mrs. T. E. L. Chamberlain of the Women's Agricultural and Horticultural Union wrote a letter to her local newspaper, the *Manchester Guardian*:

> May we through your columns make known that we wish to hear from
> farmers wanting services of women on the land. We can supply highly
> trained women of good birth, and those less taught, born on farms, as there
> are some country-bred women working in service or trade who now desire to
> return to the country.[13]

Other voluntary groups, from the Agricultural Section of the Women's Legion and the University Association of Land Workers, also began promoting the idea of women taking the place of men on the land. Local groups of women jumped in as well. In early 1915 a paper in Reading announced "a scheme organized to train young women in Berkshire for light farming . . . a committee of ladies has been formed and a fund of money guaranteed for preliminary expenses."[14]

By the fall of 1915 Selborne recognized the need for better coordination and established special Women's War Agricultural committees in every district to concentrate on recruiting, training, and placing women farm laborers. Usually comprised of three prominent local women, these panels received orders from Selborne to cooperate with the many private groups that were successfully recruiting women for land work. Recruiting women proved to be no problem—the WACs soon had more than forty thousand women on their rolls willing to do agricultural work either full- or part-time—but actually putting them to work turned out to be much more difficult. The farmers, though they desperately needed workers, did not want women.[15]

"[The] task will be to induce the farmers to engage women," explained Miss Broadhurst of the National Political League, which was helping to organize training farms for women workers in 1915. "That is not altogether an easy matter. At present there is some strong opposition and at several meetings of farmers great prejudice has been shown."[16]

British farmers, as most of their countrymen, had been led to believe the war would be a short affair, and even if it dragged on a while, the men in the field, so essential to feeding the nation, would not be asked to go to the front. The farmers hadn't reckoned on the zealotry of the recruitment drive: the women pinning white feathers on those who hadn't signed up yet, the posters urging mothers and wives to get their menfolk into uniform, and the three hundred thousand agricultural workers who'd volunteered in the first eighteen months of the war. Farmers were angry that their skilled farmworkers had not been protected, even though the government was telling them to plow up their pastures to plant more grains. They were especially incensed that women were the only new supply of laborers being offered. Indeed, many of these educated, refined, city women had never before set a dainty toe in a smelly barn. The farmers were not in a mood to be grateful.

"Hundreds of postcards have been sent to farmers, telling them there are women ready to work, and we've had hardly any replies," complained Henry Chapin, a member of Parliament and leader of the Association to Promote the Employment of Women in Agriculture, one of the ad hoc groups that had sprung up around the issue. "Meetings are called and no one comes. Now we're sending missionaries around to the farmers, to make converts."[17]

Lord Selborne himself went out preaching to convert the farmers. Speaking before a large group of farmers in October 1915 he told them that he'd seen women plowing in the west of England. Having seen that, he would ask the farmers "not to sit down and say it was impossible for women to plough."[18]

The farmwife and daughter had historically assumed certain farm tasks, such as milking, butter making, and poultry keeping, and were accepted in those roles. And while farmers' wives and daughters were a common sight at harvesttime in the fields of Scotland and the northern parts of England, in England's southern counties people still considered it undignified for a farmer to have his womenfolk in the fields. It was not only undignified, but also foolhardy, the farmers moaned. Women were not physically strong enough and were not constitutionally suited to the long, strenuous labor, and those coming from cities had no experience, no training, or any idea how to do farmwork. And they had the gall to expect payment for their labor.

Lloyd George watched as his colleague Selborne's efforts to harness women's potential in agriculture hit a wall of government indifference on one side and stubborn farmer resistance on the other. "When in 1915 the Board of Agriculture tried to induce the farming community to employ female labour—the 'lilac sunbonnet brigade' as they were jocularly hailed in some quarters—it met at first with very little success," Lloyd George wrote in his War Memoirs. The aid of the "land girl," Lloyd George recalled, "was at first pressed on the farmers in the teeth of a good deal of sluggish and bantering prejudice and opposition."[19]

The harvest of 1915 was poor. The German submarine menace intensified, with U-boats blasting British cargo vessels out of the water. Casualties at the western front were mounting and enlistment dissipating. With the military needing fresh troops, by early 1916 the Conscription Act drafted every fit man between the ages of eighteen and forty-one. Three million British men were in uniform. Replacing them in the workforce was now urgent. Tens of thousands of women entered into factory and munitions work, into the mines, onto the trolleys, but resistance from the farmers persisted. To counteract the complaint that untrained women on the farm were less than useless—instructing them took up the farmers' time—Selborne's Women WACs established training programs in every district, in addition to six-week programs run by the Women's Farm and Garden Union (WF&GU) to educate the recruits of its National Land Service Corps. By 1916 the WF&GU had established a training fund and trained 870 women, with many more on waiting lists.

In the winter of 1916 the English began to feel hunger. There were long queues to buy potatoes, and sugar and meat were hard to find. Food prices had tripled since the war began. That winter, organizers for Selborne's Board of Agriculture fanned out across the countryside, tacking up recruitment posters, handing out leaflets to farmers, and arranging local meetings to try to convince the farmers to hire women National Land Service volunteers. The board held these meetings in the towns on market day, allowing the farmers, along with their wives, to attend after they sold their produce. The reception was wary. The farm families feared that if they showed an interest in hiring women to replace men, the farmer himself or any able-bodied men still on the farm would be reported to the local conscription board and drafted into the army.

The women volunteers—the Land Girls or "Land Lassies," as they began to be called—were getting frustrated. They had gone through training, but the farmers still would not give them a chance. In Cornwall, in the southwest corner of England, an angry exchange of letters to the editor took place in the pages of the local newspapers concerning women's fitness for farmwork. Rather than just talk about it, the women of Cornwall decided to prove what they could do. In early March 1916 they staged a public demonstration of women's farm abilities in the district of Launceston, showing off their newly acquired skills in plowing, planting, tilling, and handling horses. The farmers took reluctant notice. The Cornish Land Girls put on another demonstration in Truro a few weeks later. According to one local official who attended, "The work was most creditable and astonished a number of farmers."[20]

Lord Selborne was pleased. One hour of these public displays of the Land Girls' farming skills was worth more than any propaganda campaign from his office, so Selborne encouraged all local Women's War Agriculture Committees to coordinate a national Land Girl demonstration week in early June 1916. In towns and hamlets all around Great Britain the Land Girls performed for skeptical farmers while local officials tried to convince them to literally take home a few and try them out. These "Women Workers' Demonstrations" were even held in cities such as Manchester, where Land Girls were put through their paces at the Royal Agricultural Society of England's show. Like prize sheepdogs, they were to prove their worth, showing that women could perform in the field. If the exhibition was a bit circus-like, no matter; it might finally prove that women could, as the organizers emphasized, "take a useful part in the work of the farms, and by their patriotism and self-sacrifice save the situation."[21]

Just as these demonstrations were beginning to force open an entry door for women onto the land, an exhausted Lord Selborne resigned his post as minister of agriculture. Before he left, he established a Food Production Department, a new branch of the

Board of Agriculture, which could coordinate all the government policies on producing and distributing wartime food. Within this new department, Selborne created a Women's Branch, with responsibility for women farmworkers.

By then a reported 57,500 women had registered for agricultural work, and 29,000 were actually working on the land. Everyone acknowledged these official numbers were not accurate, for many more women were actually working on farms and in dairies. Most were women native to the villages and rural districts where they were working, and the farm families accepted them more readily than "foreigners" from the cities or faraway counties. But in many areas the supply of local women could not meet the demand for help, and outsiders were needed.

As winter set in, London faced a general panic as rumors of food shortages spread, shelves emptied, and hoarding was rampant. The U-boat blockade was painfully effective, and food rationing was on the near horizon. In the coal-mining districts of Northumberland, the children of Durham went on strike, with the blessing of their desperate parents, and refused to attend school until the local council provided them with some bread and soup as their families had none.

In December 1916, Asquith was tossed out of the prime minister's chair in a parliamentary coup and replaced by David Lloyd George. Among the many changes Lloyd George made in the way the government conducted the war, he made food production and supply a high priority. He gave new levels of support and responsibility to the War Agricultural Committees, energized the Food Production Department, and elevated the profile of the Women's Branch, encouraging its effort to put the women's labor force on the land.

The "Lilac Sunbonnet Brigade" now had something of a champion at 10 Downing Street, and in February 1917, with an estimated three-week supply of grain left in the United Kingdom, the new minister of agriculture, Lord Rowland Prothero, announced the formation of a mobile force of uniformed women farmworkers, to be called the Women's Land Army. The government would fund this new land army under the auspices of the Women's Branch of the Food Production Department and deployed the women wherever in the nation they were needed. The Women's Land Army recruits would receive training, uniforms, housing, and salaries in return for signing on for the war's duration, or at least a year; and recruits could choose the Agriculture Section, the Forage Section, or the Timber Section of the Land Army. All the private advocacy groups involved in women's farm labor agreed to move under the umbrella of the Women's Branch, and its director, Meriel Talbot, became the leader of the Women's Land Army. This new army's experienced officers were from the Women's National Land Service Corps and took on the training and supervision of the new Land Army's recruits.

At a women's war rally in London, Lord Prothero expressed the government's sense of urgency in recruiting women for the Land Army:

I do not pretend that work on the land is attractive to many women. It is hard work—fatiguing, backaching, monotonous, dirty work in all sorts of weather. It is poorly paid, the accommodation is rough, and those who undertake it have to face physical discomforts. In all respects it is comparable to the work your men-folk are doing in the trenches at the front. It is not a case of "lilac sunbonnets." There is no romance in it: it is prose.[22]

Just a few weeks after the establishment of the Women's Land Army of Great Britain, America entered the war.

2

FEMALE PREPAREDNESS

merican ladies in fashionable hats began preparing for war well before their
country was ready to enter the fray. In the early winter of 1916, while America was still
safely removed from the European conflict, the Manhattan society ladies of the American Woman's League for Self-Defense took up rifles and began marching. With the
modest ambition of enlisting every able bodied woman in the United States and preparing her to defend her country, the Self-Defense League hired a military drill instructor to teach them "everything that men are taught to train them for war." Members
would learn to shoot rifles as well as bows and arrows, ride cavalry horses and drive
automobiles, and of course, learn to march with grace and precision.[1]

"If a war comes we shall be able to defend our homes and the homes of the women
who haven't learned how," explained Mrs. J. Hungerford Millbank, their general. "We
will teach the women who are not too flighty the use of firearms. We are doing this
because of the atrocities suffered by the women at the front in Belgium and Poland."[2]

They aspired to be the distaff standard-bearers of the Preparedness Movement, the
loudest and most organized proponents of America's entry into the war. Led by former
president Theodore Roosevelt and his old Rough Rider pal, former U.S. Army chief of
staff Gen. Leonard Wood, the Preparedness Movement circle advocated a stronger,
modern military and was heartily disdainful of President Woodrow Wilson and other
pacifistic "mollycoddlers." They encouraged red-blooded patriots to prepare themselves
for war regardless of the government's reluctance.

The centerpiece of their efforts was the privately financed military training camps
General Wood established, with the first and most famous being Camp Plattsburgh in
northern New York State. (Financier Bernard Baruch and other sympathetic Wall Street
and industrialist friends helped the movement expand to other cities by funding more
training camps.) Here, well-to-do lawyers, doctors, businessmen, and college students
paid hundreds of dollars for a five-week intensive boot camp experience, during which

they learned to handle guns, operate heavy weaponry, hone navigational skills, and toughen their minds and bodies under the supervision of regular army staff. It became socially attractive for educated, wealthy, or ambitious men to enroll in a Plattsburgh-style camp in their region and return home a reserve officer, albeit an unofficial one. The impact was more political than military when the men returned to their home-towns, firms, and clubs as eager ambassadors for an end to neutrality. By the time America did declare war, some sixteen thousand men had received this kind of private military training.

In March 1916, after two months of practice, the League for Self-Defense women were ready to put on their first public performance, and two hundred "women sol-diers," led by General Mrs. Millbank "in stunning khaki," were put through their drills in the Ninth Regiment Armory in Manhattan. The recruits, "of all classes and kinds of women, of a variety of ages and sizes," included women dentists, lawyers, surgeons, teachers, and private secretaries. "One of my best soldiers is a grandmother," said General Millbank, who was reported to be wearing a khaki uniform of "trim skirt and snug-fitting blouse, a military hat under the brim of which were auburn curls." Another officer sported a saber.[3]

Newspaper reporters assigned to cover the event expended much of their effort de-scribing the ladies' uniforms—or more accurately, costumes—since each woman felt obliged to express her martial spirit in a personal fashion statement. Field Secretary Ida Vera Simonton, one of the founders of the group, wore

> tight-fitting knickerbockers, puttees, and a skirt that came to the knees and rippled out in up-to-date fullness. She wore a white silk shirtwaist [and] the uniform was completed by a short, snug coat and a campaign hat. To show she did not lose her femininity in uniform, she wore small, high-heeled boots and big pearl earrings.[4]

While the stylish League for Self-Defense was playacting, another, more purposeful group of women was making its own early preparations for war. On July 4, 1915, just a few days before the women of Great Britain set off behind Mrs. Pankhurst in the Right to Serve March and eighteen months before America would actually enter the war, a small group of loudly patriotic American women announced they were forming the Women's Section of the Navy League. This new organization would work to spread the ideals of patriotism, "awaken lawmakers to the dangers of insufficient defense," and be "devoted to the duty of insuring the United States against the possibility of being in-vaded." The recent sinking of the liner *Lusitania* by a German submarine, with the loss of 1,200 lives, including 128 Americans, was certainly the catalyst in launching the league.

The league's shrewd organizers didn't simply wait for women to join; they printed up thousands of membership pledge forms and mailed them to women's clubs around the country. By simply signing the pledge card and mailing it back—no membership fee or dues were required—one could enroll as a member of the league. In the first month of the league's life more than eight thousand women signed the pledge cards, invested in a two-penny postage stamp, and joined the roll. By the end of four months more than forty thousand American women were league members, and by the end of 1915 the organization was half a million women strong. When, only a few months after its birth, the league held its first National Defense Conference in November 1915, more than two thousand women attended, along with a large contingent of military brass.[5] The league immediately spoke with a loud voice, advocating for female preparedness.

By January 1916, without any government sanction or direction, the Women's Section of the Navy League had launched its own national service register, or a list of women who pledged to volunteer their services to the nation in case of war or some other national emergency. Within weeks, hundreds of women—many of whom were prominent in their communities, including the daughter of the Speaker of the U.S. House of Representatives and the wife of the governor of New York—placed themselves on the register and pledged their "war aid" in advance, during a time of national peace and prosperity.

Believing that patriotism and eagerness were not enough, the league also established the National Service School (NSS), an innovative concept in training women to serve their country. The essential wartime skill for women was first aid, so the Navy League women consulted with the Red Cross and devised a first aid curriculum that could be taught in a quick, intense course. Another useful skill was telegraphy, which was considered well suited to women, as was the relatively new technology of wireless radio operation; the league recruited the young David Sarnoff of the Marconi Corporation to teach this course. Driving automobiles, another useful skill, also became part of the curriculum. Then the Navy League looked to its martial heritage and came up with a novel vehicle for delivering this practical training: a military-style training camp for women, a Ladies' Camp Plattsburgh.

The moment the first encampment of the National Service School was announced in the early winter of 1916, it became *the* social status event of the Washington season among young women of good society, especially if Daddy was a senator or diplomat and a big brother had done his stint at Plattsburgh the previous summer. The two hundred resident places filled up fast, with a hundred more women signed on for the day school. Groups of debutantes and college girls traveled in "delegations" by train from Boston, New York, Philadelphia, and Richmond. The best families in Chicago reserved fifteen spaces for their daughters; San Francisco league members booked cots for ten eager women. The training course ran for two weeks. Tuition was free, but the recruits faced certain deprivations: each debutante's luggage was limited to one handbag, and no jewelry was allowed in camp. They would have to wear uniforms; live in tents, which they were expected to clean themselves; and submit to a soft form of "military discipline"—no candy was allowed in the tents.

The camp was built on land donated by U.S. senator Francis Newlands of Nevada, in the Chevy Chase section of Washington, and constructed to Marine Corps camp standards. While the *New York Times* wryly described the location of the Women's Preparedness Camp as "midway between the Chevy Chase Club and the Columbia Country Club," the Washington political establishment and President Wilson, who was running for reelection, had to take it seriously. The president officially opened the camp at ceremonies on May 1 and spoke to several thousand legislators and opinion makers with whom he sought common ground.[6]

"God forbid that the United States should be drawn into war," he told the audience, which included his own cabinet members, Secretary of the Navy Josephus Daniels, and Secretary of War Newton Diehl Baker. But if it should, if the test came, Americans would rally together to the defense of national principles, he assured them. The president helped raise the flag and solemnly reviewed the troops, turned out in their long khaki skirts and belted jackets, with high leather boots and wide-brimmed campaign hats.[7]

Standing near the president, in full khaki splendor, was the commandant of the Preparedness Camp, Miss Elizabeth Ellicott Poe. A relative of Edgar Allen Poe, Miss Poe was herself a writer for Washington newspapers, producing mostly light features on the arts and social events. An adherent of the preparedness creed, Poe was one of the founders of the Navy League. She was a tireless organizer and served on the headquarters staff as general secretary and, knowledgeable in the ways of newspapers, as the league's spokeswoman. Poe took delight in expressing utter disdain for those women who advocated pacifism.

Thirty years old and trim in her camp khakis and boots, Poe had supervised every detail of the building of the "tent city" as well as every aspect of the camp's training and fitness regime, and stood ready to take command of her well-bred recruits. They would rise to the sound of a bugle playing "Reveille" and retire by "Taps"; take classes in semaphore signaling, surgical dressings, and hygiene; and be drilled in military calisthenics by Marine officers. The women, most accustomed to dining on white linen, ate simple but ample meals on long wooden tables in the mess tent. Mrs. George Barnett, the wife of the major general commandant of the Marine Corps, volunteered as commissary general of the camp, designed the camp menus, and fed each recruit for just thirty-four cents a day. Marine Corps cooks fixed meals similar to those served to men in Washington's Marine Barracks, but the cooks swore that the women ate twice as much food as the Marines did.[8]

At the end of the two-week course, the women were tested on their proficiency and issued a brass National Service School insignia pin to be worn proudly on their hats. The graduates were entertained at a garden party at the Marine Barracks, serenaded by the Marine Corps Band, and then went home with a new set of skills and a sense of confidence. Following the graduation of her first class, Miss Poe wrote a letter to President Wilson formally offering to the government "in this time of crisis" the services of the thousand women recently trained at the Service School together with the four hundred thousand women members of the Navy League. They "desire most earnestly that peace may continue with all nations, but if war becomes necessary . . . they wish to be on record as willing to do their part in the nation's task."[9]

These hothouse soldiers of the service school received enormous attention—articles in the press, frequent visits from dignitaries and politicians, and even published parodies of the tough life of the female Plattsburgh "rookie." But the idea of getting a dose of vocational training to accomplish something useful was a powerful stimulant to the service school movement. In June another National Service School opened on the grounds of the Presidio military installation in San Francisco, with 250 women encamped there for training in first aid work. Another service school opened in Narragansett, Rhode Island, in the summer of 1916, with many of the wealthy "summer colonists" enrolled.

There were even a few private training camp ventures, most hilariously the Emergency Service Corps camp pitched on an estate in Erskine, New Jersey, where thirty New York debutantes "as plucky as they are pretty" played at being "soldierettes." This camp was a bit more rustic than the one in Chevy Chase—no wooden floors in the tents and no Marines setting up the tents for them—but the training the women received was more useful in becoming a summer camp counselor than a trained war worker: swimming, rowing, riding a man's bicycle, and grooming horses. One innovative touch was the camp policy of "no skirts," an acknowledgment that camp activities were best served by a less-ladylike uniform of khaki breeches and leather gaiters. In respect for modesty, "our coats, however, come to the knees," explained Capt. Candace Hewitt, the leader of the camp.[10]

As the summer of 1916 closed, the Navy League wanted to extend its training mission into a year-round endeavor, so it opened its own school building in Washington, D.C., in a donated home refitted for classrooms and workshops and with the energetic Elizabeth Poe again in charge. She supplemented the original NSS set of courses of Red Cross first aid, telegraphy, wireless, and signal work with classes in care for the injured taught by naval surgeons, food conservation, and lectures on American history. Poe instituted evening classes to accommodate working women and Saturday classes for high school girls. Even as Wilson campaign banners proclaiming "He Kept Us Out of War" swung overhead, Miss Poe trained her women for that war.

Just three days before Election Day 1916, Miss Grace Parker of the Women's Section of the Navy League boarded an ocean liner in New York Harbor and set sail for England. She was on a reconnaissance mission. As an ambassador of the female Preparedness Movement, she went to study how Great Britain was utilizing the resources of its women—how they were organized for war work, how they were trained, how they were employed. Grace Parker moved in the right social circles and had experience in the women's social betterment organizations that flourished at the turn of the century, making her the perfect scout. Her sponsors at the Navy League had made all the necessary contacts and all the proper introductions to the Englishwomen who could make her visit worthwhile.

When Miss Parker landed she was taken in hand by a delegation of women who helped her navigate the complex map of intersecting organizations mobilizing British women for the war. Her hostesses, including the Duchess of Marlborough, the Marchioness of Londonderry, Lady Jekyll, and the wives of cabinet ministers, welcomed her into their homes, escorted her in their automobiles, and gave her entrée to the mobilization effort's leaders.[11] Parker spent two full months traveling, interviewing these leaders, and observing their initiatives in recruiting and training women for industry, relief work, and such nontraditional roles as streetcar conductor and farming. She studied the inner workings and interconnections of their organizations, learning what worked, what failed, and how much the mistakes had cost.

On the voyage home she wrote up a report of her findings, emphasizing the value of disciplined organization and training, and when her ship docked in New York in early January 1917, she carried down the gangplank a detailed program of action for mobilizing American women. Her planning document barely had time to be typed before it was presented, with great fanfare, at the star-spangled Congress of Constructive Patriotism held in Washington the last week of January.

Gathered in the Willard Hotel's grand ballroom were three thousand congress delegates: governors, senators, mayors, generals, businessmen, and nearly five hundred women, all of whom were stalwarts of the National Security League, the political arm of the Preparedness Movement. Since Theodore Roosevelt, General Wood, and former secretary of state Elihu Root founded the Security League in December 1914, it had become the voice of the interventionists, the most vocal critic of Wilson's neutrality policy, and a loud advocate of universal military training. As perhaps the country's premier "patriotic" group, with the wealth of many bankers and industrialists supporting its activities and chapters in every city, it didn't hesitate to flex its political muscle. The National Security League would only gain strength once America actually entered the war, with some degree of "told you so" bravura, and would also veer toward its own narrow, nativist interpretation of "Americanism." But at this congress, the delegates would still have been furious over Wilson's call for a negotiated "peace without victory" just a few days before.

Only one woman was selected to address the Congress: the recently returned Grace Parker. Standing on the speaker's platform, a giant American flag draped above her, Miss Parker spoke to the delegates about the "Woman Power of the Nation" and the way this power might be harnessed. She spoke of what she'd witnessed in England and how its spirit and organizational model should be imported and adapted to America's situation. She outlined eleven vocational spheres where women would be needed if the nation found itself at war—all the types of work already taught at the National Service School plus a few she'd found so impressive in England, including motor driving and agriculture.

She called for the establishment of a national clearinghouse to coordinate the work and training efforts of women's organizations and clubs. She proposed that the federal government undertake a national registry of "woman power" and also appoint a national committee to oversee the deployment of women. The delegates listened attentively and when she finished, burst into applause.[12] Right there in the Willard's ballroom, with the lessons of her English sojourn still so vivid, Parker offered a cogent, fully imagined plan for American women's new role in wartime. It would become the template, if not the actual working model, for the mobilization of American women in the war.

Once the applause for Parker's presentation subsided, a special women's session of the congress was hastily convened to put in motion the practicalities of her plan, which also revamped the role of the Women's Section of the Navy League, sharpening its focus and renaming it the National League for Women's Service. The women delegates to the Congress of Constructive Patriotism left the meeting quite pleased with their efforts, but they barely had time to travel home and unpack before the ground beneath their high-laced shoes shifted: world events shook American neutrality and the national attitude tilted sharply and irrevocably toward war. Preparedness took on a new meaning and new urgency.

On February 1, in a slap to the Wilson administration's policy of neutrality, the German High Command announced the resumption of unrestricted submarine warfare against neutral nations' shipping in the Atlantic. Two days later, on February 3, U-boats sank the USS *Housatonic*. The United States dismissed the German ambassador and severed diplomatic relations with Germany. After training for so long, the women of the newly established National League for Women's Service sprang into action.

On the day of that break in diplomatic relations, the league opened a headquarters office on West Fortieth Street in Manhattan and announced that it intended "to mobilize the women of America after the fashion in which they have been organized in England." The league's D.C. branch opened an office as well. Putting Grace Parker's plan into action, the league proposed to register and classify women "and train them to play the part in America that English women are playing in England—to drive automobiles, till farms if necessary, work as nurses, and in other ways help meet the national emergency."[13] "Women Organized to Aid in Defense" read the headline in the *New York Times* when announcing the league's new plans to "Take Men's Places."[14]

Just a few days later, more than a hundred women, representing all the major women's clubs and organizations, were called to the spacious Fifth Avenue apartment of Anne

Harriman Vanderbilt to discuss coordination in mobilizing women "in case of war with Germany." Eager to foster cooperation and avoid turf disputes, the National League for Women's Service and the Red Cross Society, the organizations with the deepest experience in training women thus far, jointly called this "war union" meeting. The league had already displayed a clever ability to work with existing groups without stepping on their proud toes; it invited these groups to become working league affiliates without sacrificing their own identities.

Grace Parker, who now held the rank of national commandant of the League for Women's Service, presented a more detailed, comprehensive version of her mobilization plan at the meeting. Virginia Gildersleeve, the dean of Barnard College, offered a resolution to accept Parker's plan; it was, unanimously. Joining the new common effort were women's societies of different political stripes, from the National Patriotic Relief Association to the Vacation Association (a benevolent society for working women), from the Daughters of the American Revolution to the Woman Suffrage Party of New York state and city, as well as the Anti-Suffrage League.[15]

The National League for Women's Service moved into high gear as the nation moved toward war. In cities across the country it organized rallies for women featuring speeches on "patriotism for service," presentations by the Red Cross and the league, and patriotic songs.[16] The league also organized a campaign in thirty-two states to convince state governments to include women in their inventories of human and matériel war resources. The league urged that women and their useful skills be counted along with men in the state census and avoid the mistake made in England, which, the league argued, "was much hampered at the beginning of the war because there was no adequate census of her women workers."[17]

The league also began offering training classes in many cities. New York women received league postcards asking them to specify which of six different lines of preparedness they wished to undertake. Every morning at half past eleven o'clock the league office hosted an informational recruiting talk by experts in the various service disciplines: on Mondays, the motor service session brought in representatives of the American Field Ambulance Service, as well as a driving school instructor; on Thursdays, David Sarnoff of the Marconi Company introduced wireless telegraphy; and on Fridays, Professor O. S. Morgan, chairman of the Agricultural Department of Columbia University, and Albert A. Johnson, director of the New York State School of Agriculture at Farmingdale, Long Island, explained agricultural service pursuits. Inspired by the new opportunities presented in these talks, women often registered for work on the spot.

Based on Grace Parker's enthusiastic report of the British Women's Land Service efforts, the league put new emphasis on training women for agricultural work. Mary E. Hamilton of New York City was appointed chair of the league's Agriculture Committee, and while assembling her committee, she sought out women's organizations with some expertise in this rather novel field. She was introduced to Hilda Loines of the Women's National Farm and Garden Association (WNF&GA), the American sibling of the British Women's Farm and Garden Union. The sister organizations were faithful correspondents across the sea, and Hilda Loines had direct knowledge of how the British women of the Farm and Garden Union had summoned all their ingenuity and strength to come to their country's aid, placing women in land service for the war. She was the one who received their letters and reports, marveled at their fortitude, and penned encouraging replies. As the general secretary of the Women's National Farm and Garden Association in America, Hilda Loines was the pen pal of the Land Army movement.

The younger American group (established in 1914) modeled itself on its more experienced British sibling (born in 1899) and pursued similar goals. Neither was simply a garden club; both were more of a professional society. Their primary objective was to make it possible for women to obtain training, find employment, and make a profession, not just a hobby, of horticulture and agriculture. As agricultural employment bureaus would not accept women on their rolls, one of the union's core efforts was to establish an employment exchange and actively help members gain essential practical experience and jobs.

Hilda Loines, a graduate of Bryn Mawr College and the Briarcliff Manor School of Practical Agriculture and Horticulture, came from a wealthy family and could enjoy supervising the small farm at the Loines's summer place on the shores of Lake George. While she did not need to make a living from the soil, she recognized that agriculture could be a viable profession for women. Hilda was not a natural leader—unlike her mother, who was president of the Brooklyn chapter of the National American Woman Suffrage Association (NAWSA)—but she was determined to find her own place, her own cause. Women's right to plow, as well as to vote, became her cause. When the WNF&GA was formed in 1914, she became its secretary and often its spokeswoman. Loines also organized its first annual conference in New York, prompting the *Brooklyn Daily Eagle* to proclaim, "Number of feminine farmers steadily increasing."[18]

Loines conducted a national survey of women's work on the land and gave lectures at New York University about the opportunities the field offered. She didn't gloss over the difficulties. "You will need unfailing patience and a stout heart to overcome the obstacles that beset your way," she told aspiring women farmers. "Yet if your heart cries out for a more normal and healthy life, for the sweet smell of the earth instead of the subway air . . . do not fear, but slip your hand in that of nature, the infinite teacher, and follow on."[19]

So Hilda Loines and the American women of the WNF&GA watched closely, taking careful notes, as their kindred cousins in Britain seized the opportunity presented by the war and assumed the leadership role of recruiting and training women for emergency agricultural work.[20] Suddenly the idea of women in agriculture was no longer a distant, gauzy, goal; instead, it was a sharp national imperative. Hilda Loines, going on forty years old, had been waiting for just this moment. When Mary Hamilton of the National League for Women's Service's Agriculture Committee turned to Loines for help in February 1917, she and the WNF&GA were ready.

Hamilton asked Loines if the WNF&GA would partner with the league to create a "Land Service League," which would oversee the formation of a Land Service Corps, very much on the British model. Hamilton also asked the WNF&GA to rally its membership of now nearly two thousand women in forty states, offer financial support to this new joint venture, and help sponsor a pioneering project, a program right in the heart of the city, to train women New Yorkers to become farmworkers. Loines brought the league's proposal to her fellow WNF&GA officers, and on March 12 the WNF&GA Board approved the creation of the Land Service League, put Mrs. Hamilton at its helm and Hilda Loines on its executive committee, and appropriated a hundred dollars to help launch the Bronx training school.[21]

"At the present time a very serious crisis confronts us," WNF&GA president Louisa Yeomans King, a nationally known horticulturalist, wrote to her members. She went on to explain the importance of this new land service initiative. "If this nation is fortunate enough to escape war with an external power, we must still organize effectively all our agricultural resources to fight the high cost of food." King exhorted her membership to lend financial support to this new Land Service League and to contribute seeds, tools, and expertise to its future training projects. "If we are to meet this situation adequately, we must all put our shoulders to the wheel."[22]

In this strange, frantic interlude between anxious peacetime and full wartime, the second encampment of the National Service School in Washington was also announced. It would open April 16 on twenty-seven acres the federal government donated. Two thousand women applied to attend the two sessions of the training camp, "the largest camp for women ever held in the world."[23] By the time the camp opened in mid-April, those American women were serving a nation at war.

3

AN AGRICULTURAL ARMY

America seemed more worried about bread and beans than bullets. From the moment the nation entered the Great War, food became an anxious issue. While the U.S. government was confident of its ability to produce munitions, the food riots that rocked several cities in the early winter had also shaken the national psyche, challenging America's cherished self-image as a land of plenty.

The riots began in New York City in mid-February, when hundreds of housewives reacted to an overnight jump in the price of vegetables by overturning vendors' push-carts and setting them ablaze. Police had to use their clubs to subdue the mob of moth-ers.[1] The next day the "rioting of housewives" spread to other parts of the city and became more violent as screaming women smashed butcher and greengrocer shops, looted stores, and stormed city hall.[2] They were angry because the price of basic com-modities had already doubled, tripled, and even quadrupled since the European war began. The reasons were obvious: European agriculture was in shambles, and as the desperate belligerent nations bought American grain and vegetables to feed their people, increased demand pushed up prices. War speculators were also at work, manipulating supply to inflate consumer prices.[3]

Food riots also erupted in Philadelphia, where one man was shot dead by police, an old woman was trampled by a mob, and furious mothers declared a school strike.[4] In Cincinnati, community leaders called a boycott of butcher shops, and in Chicago food prices spiked as settlement workers reported acute suffering among the city's poor. Talk of trouble could be heard in other cities as well, as fuel shortages raised the price of keeping warm beyond the reach of the working poor. Rumors of "foreign influence" began swirling—pro-German agents in the United States engaging in an elaborate plot of withholding food and fuel from the market to drive up prices and spark embarrass-ing riots—all with the goal of pressuring Washington to halt food shipments to the Allies.[5] This alleged plot was plausible enough that the Justice Department launched an investigation.[6] Meanwhile, members of Congress denounced the food riots raging in the center of the nation's prosperous cities as a "disgrace" and "the crowning shame of our civilization."[7]

So when, just a few weeks later, America entered the war, the food riots were still fresh and painful in the public mind. The nation's food supply was an urgent concern. "How are we going to feed our Allies across the water and have enough left to feed ourselves?" asked the editorialists of the *New York Times*. "The crops of 1917 will decide whether the world shall be fed or starve in 1918."[8]

While the public debated about the best way to raise an army sufficient for the war's military needs—rely either on patriotism to draw droves of volunteers to the flag quickly or on conscription—there was greater distress about whether the country could muster the manpower farms needed to feed that army, the rest of the nation, and a good chunk of Europe. Even if farmers wanted to cultivate more land and even if they could afford more seed and fertilizer, they could do nothing without workers. As the *Times* warned, "For every man who must shoulder a rifle for military duty we had better furnish inducement for another to take up a hoe for farm work."[9]

A dangerous scarcity of farm labor was nothing new; the crisis had been building for years. Since before the turn of the twentieth century, American farmers had been complaining that finding the hands to bring their crops to market was getting harder and more expensive. The lure of city life with its newly electrified bright lights and the higher wages found there in factory work had already siphoned off many of the most ambitious rural boys. But since the Great War started, bringing a steady flow of lucrative supply contracts to American manufacturers, farm boys, and even their fathers, were dropping their plows and taking up factory floor jobs.

With Connecticut's munitions factories going into production overdrive and sucking in eager workers from New England's fields, farmers there reported that during the summer of 1916 they were forced to pay double the normal wages—up to five dollars a day—to the hired men still available to bring in their hay. Unable to find workers, hundreds of New England dairy farmers announced that they would have to shut down or shrink their milk production in 1917.[10] On New Jersey vegetable farms, manufacturer's recruiting agents circulated through the fields, offering to the farm laborers factory jobs along with a hefty salary boost and free transportation to their new workplace.[11] Early in the spring of 1917 the Canadian government announced it would offer "extraordinary inducements," including 160 acres of homestead land, to American farm laborers who would cross the border and work Canadian fields.[12]

And now that the European war had become America's war, too, it promised to exacerbate the labor situation. After all, April was not only wartime, but also spring planting time. On the day Congress voted to take the nation to war, even before the first American son could run down to his local post office and volunteer to fight, the newspapers reported a plan for raising an "Agricultural Army."

Joseph Hartigan, the New York City commissioner of weights and measures who had helped that city weather the recent food riots, presented a plan to the Council of National Defense (CND) "to remedy the shortage of agricultural labor by the mobilization and training by the Government of an agricultural army." The scheme would enlist those able-bodied men who couldn't pass their military physicals on account of "minor defects," such as poor vision, deafness, or rotten teeth, to proudly serve in this "Army of Farmers." They would be outfitted in uniforms, organized in regiments and companies, supervised by officers, and after brief training be dispatched, according to the crop seasons, to regions in need of labor. The plan envisioned several hundred thousand men in service in the fields, and the government would pay them, just as soldiers were paid. After their service and honorable discharge, they might also be accorded the kind of "war honors" and benefits available to soldiers.[13]

"Under the circumstances, it seems we ought to honor the man behind the plow as well as the man behind the gun," insisted Hartigan. "Each is serving the nation." Of course, Hartigan's agricultural army plan was, with only slight modifications and a gender switch, an exact replica of the Women's Land Army of Great Britain, which had been established only a few weeks before in the late winter of 1917.

Hartigan's was only the first of many schemes for securing adequate farm labor. A few days later the *Washington Post* published a variation on the same idea: let those men who flunked their army physicals become farmers, with a government grant of idle land in the expansive West, together with start-up funds, farm tools, and the practical advice of an experienced farmer.[14] This idea did not fly far.

On the morning after President Wilson's speech to Congress asking for a resolution of war, Charles Bulkley Hubbell, the chairman of the New York Commission on Prisons, wrote a long essay to the *New York Times* introducing his own solution—convict labor. Every state in the union should draft a segment of its prison population to work on farms, or "the 10 to 20 percent of trusty prisoners who can be reasonably relied on for a good day's work in the fields under proper supervision and restraint." Farmers would pay the state for the prisoners' work, Hubbell suggested, and "in order to encourage high-class service," the convicts should be paid an allowance for their toil.[15]

An imaginative citizen came up with another ingenious idea: import those German prisoners of war interned in England and France and have them work on American farms under military guards. Not only would this scheme relieve our Allies of having to feed thousands of POWs, it would help solve the American farm labor shortage with cheap labor (albiet under duress). Moreover, in shipping the prisoners across the Atlantic, the safety of those Allied and American vessels would be assured as German submarines would surely hesitate to kill their own prisoner comrades on board.[16]

The editor of a German-language newspaper floated still another proposal for using German farm labor and caused a minor firestorm. Just days after the American declaration of war, George Sylvester Viereck, publisher of *Viereck's Weekly* in New York, volunteered his offices as an "agricultural bureau" for farmers to find workers among the thousands of unemployed German aliens living in the United States who were unable to return home. Viereck sent his plan to the secretaries of agriculture and labor in Washington, published it in his newspaper, and distributed leaflets in the farm belt of the Midwestern states.[17]

"Traitor!" screamed Estill Myers, a Missouri rural newspaper editor, who wrote to Washington officials and warned them of Viereck's motives. Myers claimed Viereck was a German sympathesizer, apologist, and paid propagandist whose newspaper until recently was titled *The Fatherland* and was notorious for taking the German side in the war debates. His agricultural bureau scheme was nothing more than a blatant attempt to infiltrate the American countryside with carefully selected German propagandists, Myers warned.[18] While anti-German hysteria was building, especially in the Midwestern states with large German-speaking populations, Myers's words of warning were well founded. George Sylvester Viereck was indeed in the German government's employ during America's years of neutrality and was part of what he later admitted was a "propaganda cabinet" to influence American opinion on the war. German government funds even subsidized his newspaper.[19]

But other emerging farm labor ideas had greater credibility, if not utility. Secretary of the Interior Franklin K. Lane suggested a traveling "farm maintenance corps" that could be deployed, like a battalion of military troops, to labor shortage trouble spots.[20] Theodore Roosevelt, long an advocate of universal national service for both men and women, advocated a type of compulsory agricultural service during wartime. "If there should come a shortage of labor in connection with the crops, the Government could mobilize labor and use it in increasing the food production," Roosevelt explained in a speech just two weeks after the nation's entry into the war. "The farmers ought to remember for the next few months that their work in tilling the soil and producing crops is just as important as any army work. If necessary, the authorities should commandeer labor in order to assure our allies and ourselves plenty of food."[21]

The *Wall Street Journal* gave its readers a blunt, front-page assessment in the first week of the war: "No matter how many and urgent are the problems in our war preparations, let it be remembered that victory may depend upon the food supply." The *Journal* also called for the mobilization of "an army for agriculture" and urged the United States not to repeat the European powers' mistakes by ignoring crop production until it was almost too late. "In recruiting a great army, the plow and cultivator are a part of our equipment, as well as artillery and machine guns; the man with a hoe renders service, as well as the one with a rifle."[22]

As Washington began cranking up the gears of war mobilization, the Wilson administration knew it needed to do something about food production, so it moved quickly, but not decisively, to try to deal with the problem. In the war's first few weeks, Secretary of Agriculture David Franklin Houston was bombarded with thousands of telegrams demanding to know what the government was going to do about the food crisis. He had no real answer, so he hurriedly called together a brainstorming conference of seventy-five American agricultural experts to come up with a plan to present to Congress. After two intense days of round-the-clock arguments at the Jefferson Hotel in St. Louis, the deans of the agricultural colleges, presidents of land grant universities, and extension specialists failed to come up with any definite, cohesive strategy.

The White House couldn't wait for the hesitant academics to develop a plan. On April 11 President Wilson summoned the chairman of the House Agriculture Committee, Congressman Asbury Lever of South Carolina, to the Oval Office to hammer out the means of stimulating food production. Lever emerged from the White House meeting carrying two big ideas back to Capitol Hill: the first was the need for vesting complete power for the nation's food supply system in one man, or a "food dictator," and the other was to supply emergency farm labor through "agricultural conscription."[23]

Drafting men for farmwork sounded like a splendid idea—and so patriotic—and immediately won some congressional champions. (At the same time Congress was deeply divided on the need for a military draft and would be paralyzed on that issue for another six weeks.) While Congressman Lever publicly floated the idea,[24] Senator Joseph Frelinghuysen of New Jersey introduced a resolution calling for the appointment of a "commissioner of agricultural defense" to coordinate mobilizing farm labor.[25] Frelinghuysen also asked Congress to take a hard look at the feasibility of exempting all farmers and farm laborers from any military draft that might be imposed. He insisted that enlisting for the "aggie army" was just as noble as—even if less romantic than—volunteering for battle: "Let us give to the farmers the national recognition necessary to show their record of service, in order to protect them against the criticism that in this hour of trial they were slackers, and that this and future generations may know of their faithful service to their country."[26]

Representative Elsworth Bathrick of Ohio also submitted a bill to the House proposing government conscription of an "agricultural army." Any proposals calling for well-paid city men to take up farmwork, or city boys to help with the crops during vacation, were useless, Rep. Bathrick argued. "Nothing but centralized authority, a military authority which has power to send farm help where they are needed most and when, can take care of this situation effectively," he maintained.[27]

The idea of exempting existing farmworkers from military service resonated in many quarters. It made sense: if farmers knew they, their sons, and their hired men would not soon be called away to fight, they might feel confident to plant additional acres of food. "Thousands of men would prefer work on the farms to service in the ranks," said the editorial writers of the *Washington Post,* "and many of them would be far more valuable as farm workers than as soldiers." Some "official assurance" from the administration that farmworkers would be excused from military service if a draft was enacted "would go a long way towards getting more acres planted in the next few crucial weeks," the *Post* said.[28]

President Wilson seemed to offer that official reassurance in his "Do Your Bit" speech to the nation on April 15:

> Thousands—nay, hundreds of thousands—of men otherwise liable to
> military service will of right and of necessity be excused from that service
> and assigned to the fundamental, sustaining work of the fields and factories
> and mines, and they will be as much part of the great patriotic forces of the
> nation as the men under fire.

Wilson then made a special appeal to the nation's farmers, whom he called the "soldiers of the commissary":

> Upon the farmers of this country, therefore, in large measure rests the fate of
> the war and the fate of the nations. The time is short. It is of the most
> imperative importance that everything possible be done, and done immedi-
> ately, to make sure of large harvests. . . . I call upon young men and old alike
> and upon the able-bodied boys of the land to accept and act upon this
> duty—to turn in hosts to the farms and make certain that no pains and no
> labour is lacking in this great matter.[29]

With these stirring words, Wilson set the stage for disappointment and anger when, within a few months, those essential farmworkers were, indeed, drafted.

While Washington vacillated, states, cities, and localities scrambled to formulate their own agricultural plans. Back in March, before war was declared, South Carolina governor Richard Manning had already set up a Commission on Civic Preparedness to convince farmers in the state to grow more food. In Indiana, the day before Congress passed Wilson's war resolution, five hundred people attended a meeting the governor had called to mobilize Indiana agriculture.

Once war was declared, the governor of Michigan appointed a high-profile Agricultural Committee "to tackle the problem of manning the farms." The group immediately announced plans to induce manufacturers to release their factory employees for farmwork.[30] The Michigan superintendent of public instruction offered his own contribution to the agricultural effort: he announced that a hundred thousand schoolchildren in the state could do effective work on farms, and if needed, another hundred thousand younger children, just beyond fifth grade, could be utilized for weeding or picking without causing them undue physical strain.[31]

The Massachusetts Committee on Public Safety also hoped to solve its state's farm labor problem by using schoolboys. The committee made detailed plans for sending groups of twenty-five boys, under a watchful supervisor's eye, to live in camps around the state and work for the local farmers. They would be paid six dollars a week for ten-hour days but would be permitted to skip school from May to October.[32]

New York State also quickly launched a Farm Cadet Program, and the state's education commissioner, John H. Finley, personally oversaw the elaborate mobilization efforts. He summoned all school principals and superintendents in every county to local meetings and dispatched his staff to present the plan for "a farming army of school-boys." Boys entering the farming service would receive full credit for any schooltime they missed, state exams would be waived, and diplomas in absentia granted. School-teachers were expected to encourage their pupils to sign up immediately, in time for planting.[33]

New York governor Charles Whitman, still shaken by the food riots of February, issued a proclamation designating Saturday, April 21, as Agricultural Mobilization Day. He called all the state's farmers to assemble in their communities that day to consider the danger the nation faced from a food shortage, to hear reports on the food situation in their region, and to make definite plans for increasing food production. The gathered farmers were given the results of the "foodstuffs census" taken in the riots' wake and told of the new public and private initiatives aimed at helping them in the present crisis.

One was the Farmers' Patriotic Fund, a loan pool of up to $10 million made available by a group of "public spirited," and worried, New York bankers and merchants to help farmers buy the seed and hire the labor—if they could find the labor—needed for the 1917 growing season. Other private initiatives were launched as well. A group of businessmen and manufacturers met in Binghamton and came up with its own plan of releasing employees to work on farms. Not only did each manufacturer pledge to allow a quota of men to take up farmwork, he also agreed to pay the difference between the usual farm wage and the employee's factory salary. The Delaware, Lackawanna, and Western Railroad Company announced it would release eight hundred to nine hundred of its men for farmwork and would also provide free train transport for all factory employees dispatched to the farms.[34]

New York City was a beehive of farm-relief activity. Barely a week into the war, neighborhood groups around the city began organizing drives for volunteers to sign up for farmwork in surrounding areas. The East Side Protective Association launched a campaign to raise five thousand young male recruits from among the immigrants of Manhattan's Lower East Side. Associations of lawyers and architects got their members to till vacant lots around the city. The Merchants Association, whose members included the merchandising princes of Fifth Avenue, set up a Food Problem Committee. A group calling itself Pilgrims to Plenty organized weekend excursions for city dwellers to do a few days' farm duty upstate and "harden up" for longer tours later in the season.[35]

Mayor John Purroy Mitchel, who'd been a leader in the Preparedness Movement, publicly demanded that each and every employer in the city furnish him with a list of employees—both men and women—who would volunteer to spend their vacations doing farmwork as a patriotic duty. "The food question is paramount to all others at the present," the mayor said. "All individuals who will in this time of great need thus serve their country will be truly soldiers of the soil, rendering a national service."[36]

And there is perhaps no better example of how seriously state governments took the threat of a food shortage than the bill rushed through the Massachusetts legislature, under suspension of rules, hurriedly signed into law by Lieutenant Governor Calvin Coolidge, making it no longer unlawful to till the Bay State's soil on Sunday. "The cultivation of land and the raising and harvesting of agricultural products shall not be unlawful on the Lord's Day while the United States is at war," the new law read.[37]

But within a few weeks, New York's "back-to the-land" effort was being judged a failure. "Volunteers Scarce for Work on Farms" announced the *New York Times* on May 5, when reporting on a "plan B" conference held at city hall. The mayor's attempt to get private employees to take up hoes had been a flop, so an appeal was made to the city's own ninety thousand employees to use their vacation time working for an upstate farmer. As an inducement, the city promised them a dollar a day and free room and board. The Children's Aid Society promised to send some of their wards to work on upstate farms. The Salvation Army also pledged to try to find workers. But though the planting season was well advanced, the schemes attempted so far had "accomplished little worth while in the way of mobilizing labor for farmers," as the *Times* put it.[38]

But the next day, the *Times* carried a large photograph of women driving tractors, with the caption "Women training at Farmingdale Agricultural Camp."[39] The women of New York were preparing their own farm labor solution.

4

SUFFRAGE AGRICULTURE

Just six weeks after the declaration of war, the *Woman's Journal*, the popular sufrage publication, reported: "A suffragist chairman of agriculture has been appointed in every State in the Union, 'Chairmen of Potatoes' being the title in which they rejoice."[1] While the farmers of America fretted and the men crafting agricultural policy hemmed and hawed, women around the country readied themselves to get their hands dirty. In the first weeks of wartime the women of America mobilized with remarkable speed and alacrity in every realm of civilian work and at every level, from neighborhood group to national organization. Existing women's groups took on additional responsibilities while new clubs assembled to accomplish specific tasks.

The earliest, self-propelled agriculture initiatives were products of that civilian mobilization fervor. But the urgency of the food situation and a noticeable lack of male leadership gave women a freedom to thrust themselves into the agricultural arena in a bold way. And like a light, nimble, reconnaissance unit, unencumbered by bureaucracy, they moved quickly.

In Michigan, Rev. Caroline Bartlett Crane, chairman of the Michigan Women's Committee for Patriotic Service, was able to construct an elaborate mechanism for the women of her state to help increase the food supply barely a week after America declared war. A respected clergywoman, civic leader, and champion of reformist social projects, Crane personified the woman who was not willing to be circumscribed by accepted women's roles. She'd already distinguished herself as a journalist and city editor of the *Oshkosh Daily Northwestern* in Wisconsin and as a Unitarian minister, leading a socially progressive congregation in Kalamazoo. When she stepped down from her pulpit, Crane began a new career as full-time civic activist, tackling unsanitary conditions in municipal food and water supplies. States and cities around the country hired her to evaluate their facilities and used her findings to push through corrective legislation.[2]

So when Reverend Crane presented her plan for women to assume a role in state agriculture, taking the place of men in the fields if necessary, few were surprised by her bald assumption that women could assume any job necessary for the war effort. "A patriotic service which we will undertake is to secure immediately the names of women who will undertake to recruit farm laborers, or who will volunteer to go themselves." Crane even offered a practical wardrobe idea: "In order to serve the convenience of women in agriculture and gardening, a uniform costume of overalls or bloomers will be recommended for adoption, and samples or patterns will be furnished on application."[3]

Soon, the Committee for Patriotic Service was codified as the state's official war work coordinating body, the Michigan division of The Woman's Committee of the Council of National Defense, and Reverend Crane was naturally named chair of its Women's Woman's Committee. Similar organizations were being built in every state, city, and town, with such enormously capable women as Caroline Crane in the pilot seats.

And at the pinnacle of this women's mobilization structure, like the all-seeing eye hovering over the pyramid in the nation's Great Seal, President Wilson installed a new panel of women. Responding to pressure for a coordinating body that could set the tone and policy for the American women's war efforts—to keep them engaged but also in line—Wilson created a helpmate for the powerful, all-male Council of National Defense, which directed the nation's civilian war planning. The Women's Committee of the CND was established in the third week of April, and the Rev. Dr. Anna Howard Shaw—a physician, ordained minister, acclaimed orator, and the former president of the National American Woman Suffrage Association—was asked to lead it. She was not so much asked as she was commanded, having received an imperial summons without any polite negotiations as to her powers or terms. The CND also "named" nine other women to serve on the committee. "It seems to us we were conscripted, not even being permitted to enlist," is how Shaw described their appointment to the committee.[4]

But Shaw did not complain that joining her on the Women's Committee panel were other prominent suffrage colleagues, including Carrie Chapman Catt and Katharine Dexter McCormick, the current NAWSA president and vice president, respectively. Several women who were publicly opposed to suffrage, such as Annie Nathan Meyer and the muckraking journalist Ida Tarbell, were also appointed to the committee, but the Women's Committee definitely had a suffragist flavor.

Harriot Stanton Blatch, Elizabeth Cady Stanton's daughter and herself a leader of the cause, said in her letter of congratulations to Dr. Shaw,

> It must be a matter of pride to all suffragists that in building up this committee, the forces of our movement were so largely drawn upon. It is enough to make every "Anti" turn in her grave to think that when our government wished to make an effective committee to mobilize women at this time of world crisis, they had to turn to the woman suffrage movement for material.[5]

But if Dr. Shaw and her fellow members had read the fine print of their committee's mandate carefully, they would have seen that it was meant to be purely an advisory body for the council and not really a coordinator or initiator of women's action. This condition would bedevil this group, the most high profile of all official women's war organizations.

While the prominent women appointed to the national Women's Committee and their equally stellar colleagues whom governors and mayors selected to lead state and city women's committees were settling into their hastily furnished offices, existing women's clubs and local groups were making decisions, raising funds, and putting plans into place. The Red Cross, the Young Women's Christian Association (YWCA), the Women's Trade Union League, the General Federation of Women's Clubs, the Woman's Christian Temperance Union, the Daughters of the American Revolution, and the Association of Collegiate Alumnae all cranked their well-oiled mechanisms into high gear.

The National League for Women's Service and the Women's National Farm and Garden Association marched together in the vanguard of women's mobilization for agricultural production. Hilda Loines and Mary Hamilton announced the fledgling Woman's Land Service League's publicity plan, an elaborate campaign involving lectures, mass meetings, motion pictures, lantern slides, brochures, and organizers dispatched into communities around the country to stir up interest.

The Land Service League's first project, the Woman's Land Service Gardens and Training Camp in New York City, was an ambitious undertaking, a six-week course of agricultural lectures and practice tailored especially for "university women," with special Saturday classes for businesswomen and others for high school girls. Instructors from Cornell and Columbia universities' agricultural departments volunteered to teach on a two hundred–acre plot of land in the still rural borough of the Bronx that was donated to the cause. By the third week of April, seven hundred college and businesswomen had signed up for a stint at the farm, and two thousand New York City high school students enrolled.[6]

The workers were issued uniforms of a blue bloomer overall, white blouse, and "Chinese light straw hat." They were expected to live in tents and temporary bungalows at the site and cook their own meals as part of their home economics class. They would not only learn to use a hoe and plow, but they would also make and repair their farm tools in the camp's machine shop. The farm would have all the most modern equipment, with overhead irrigation, tractors, and a "scientific canning plant" for the farm's produce. The National League for Women's Service pledged $3,500 to sponsor the project while the cost of the camp structures and supplies were the special gift of Miss Grace Parker.

A much smaller League for Women's Service training experiment was unfolding on Mary Lyon Schofield's East Hill Farm in Peterborough, New Hampshire, where ten women were selected to undergo a three-month course in practical food production and conservation. A Wellesley College alumna and wife of a Harvard literature professor, Schofield designed the program for women who already had some college education in home economics or teaching. She likened it to an agrarian version of a Reserve Officer's Training Corps program.[7]

Schofield, who was also the league's New Hampshire chairwoman, set aside thirty acres of her estate for the demonstration farm and loaned a comfortable house on the property as a dormitory and another building for a food conservation laboratory. As she arranged to receive the young women chosen for her training institute—advising them to procure a khaki-colored work costume before their arrival—she also prepared to send her own two sons into military uniform.

The National League for Women's Service, as an umbrella structure spanning scores of affiliated women's groups around the country, encouraged innovative ideas or at least could take credit for the clever ideas local groups invented under its name. League women of New Jersey devised a patriotic propaganda tactic to convince the state's farmers to plant more acres by enlisting their wives and womenfolk. League women drove out to farmhouses, called on the mistresses of the farmsteads, offered a woman-to-woman pep talk on the importance of bigger harvests, and left handbills on the topic to show to their men. How the farmers received this advice is not recorded.

In Tennessee, the state's league chapter hired instructors who made their way into rural communities and began teaching local women the elements of agriculture—"even including plowing," a task traditionally considered off-limits to farm women.[8] The league also stimulated the growth of the community war garden movement, and tens of thousands of acres of vacant lots, railroad sidings, school playgrounds, and backyards were dug up and planted with vegetables that spring. Professional and fraternal societies, neighborhood councils, Girl Scout troops, and church sisterhoods sponsored and maintained community gardens. In many cities, the league ran its own gardens, offering free training to women who volunteered to raise vegetables.

Meanwhile, the chairmen of Suffrage Agriculture were reading from a new, abruptly revised script.[9] American suffragists, so divided by the debate over neutrality and war, consolidated once war arrived, but the bitterness and schisms of the neutrality debate were not completely assuaged. Led by Alice Paul and the Woman's Peace Party, a small but vocal segment of suffragists remained opposed to the war, but the major suffrage organizations changed tack and threw themselves behind the war effort. The American suffrage leaders made the same political calculation as their sisters in England had figured out three years before: the suffragists' war efforts would be an investment in winning the sympathy, confidence, and ultimately the support of lawmakers and the public.

But it had been a wrenching change of heart. Until the beginning of 1917, National American Woman's Suffrage Association leaders Carrie Chapman Catt, Anna Howard Shaw, and Jane Addams were waving the banner of pacifism as founders of the Woman's Peace Party. For their efforts Theodore Roosevelt denounced them as "hysterical pacifists." Germany's resumption of unrestricted submarine warfare and the February 1917 break in diplomatic relations tipped the scales, and almost instantly suffrage leaders publicly pledged their support for the government's war policy and offered to help in any way. Both the New York State and New York City Woman Suffrage parties immediately promised the fealty and services of their half million members. "We offer our service not only as loyal Americans, but also as women thoroughly organized and highly trained in co-operative work," they announced. But at the same time, the New York suffragists began making arrangements for a mass meeting "to protest against allowing twenty million women in this country to remain disenfranchised in a crisis like this."[10]

Carrie Chapman Catt was thrown out of the Woman's Peace Party for her decision to support the war, as was Jane Addams, who reluctantly embraced the need to intervene on Britain and France's side. Now her pacifist comrades accused her of disloyalty to the cause. Meanwhile, Food Administrator Herbert Hoover recognized how powerful a symbol Addams's support for the war cause could be and soon recruited her as a government spokeswoman. She toured the nation, urging women to conserve food so that European women would not starve and peace again might reign. Some viewed her actions as a stunning moral compromise, but her fellow suffrage leaders were relieved to have her on their side.

Harriot Stanton Blatch had no trouble supporting the war. Indeed, she took an approach to it similar to Theodore Roosevelt's, viewing it as a strengthening of the national fabric, a cleansing process for civilization, and a forge for testing men's, and women's, mettle. But Blatch did have intense qualms about supporting President Wilson, whose repeated betrayal of the suffrage cause she could not forgive. Just a few months before, she had campaigned vigorously against Wilson in the 1916 presidential campaign, under the mocking banner "He Kept Us Out of Suffrage"; however, now she supported him in taking America to war. Blatch's erstwhile protégée, Alice Paul, a devout Quaker, would not capitulate to war fever. Leading the single-minded, one-cause wing of the suffrage movement, Paul refused to let Wilson's betrayals be bygones in time of war and continued to picket the White House with signs reading "Democracy Begins at Home."

To complicate matters, several states were entering heated suffrage referendum campaigns in the spring and summer, with women's suffrage on the 1917 Election Day ballot in New York and Michigan, among other places. Trying hard not to alienate the male electorate, suffrage leaders had to strike a careful balance between their "win the war" and their "win the vote" efforts. Mobilizing suffragists for war work helped maintain that equilibrium. While suffragists were certainly eager to help usher women into the new lines of emergency employment that the war opened for them—in mills and factories, on streetcars and in government offices—suffrage women seemed especially attracted to developing women's potential in agricultural war work.

"All over America today suffragists are leading a back-to-the-land movement in response to the nation's call for greater production of foodstuffs," the *Woman's Journal* reported. "They have put their hand to the plow and are not turning back. The woman with a hoe is easily discernible just back of the man with the gun."[11]

The suffragists' promotion of this most primitive occupation might seem odd, but it was attractive to them precisely because it was fresh territory—at least as paid work for women—and was so essential to the war at this time that it glowed with patriotism. Another possible attraction was that the wealthy women who bankrolled the suffrage movement often owned estates, farms, or large gardens, places where women workers could train or be employed and be warmly accepted in that girl-with-a-hoe role. Suffrage promoters of agricultural work had entrée to model agricultural situations while they had little access to or control over industrial facilities.

So the suffrage movement embraced potatoes, as well as other vegetables. "Suffrage schools of agriculture are already in operation. Suffrage war gardens have been planted. Suffrage canning centres are projected," trumpeted the *Woman's Journal*.[12] Demonstrating just how seriously the NAWSA took its part in promoting agriculture as important wartime work for women, the organization's national treasurer, Emma Winner Rogers, was appointed the chairman of its National Committee on Suffrage Agriculture. Wife of the dean of the Yale Law School, Rogers threw her enthusiasm and prestige behind the concept of the National Suffrage Service for Agriculture (NSSA).

The state "Chairmen of Potatoes" took up their new patriotic responsibilities with zest and, according to the *Woman's Journal,* with a sharp eye cast on their appearance. "Just because a woman farms she doesn't have to look like a frump," chided the *Woman's Journal* editors. "Almost at once came the discovery that some sort of 'service uniform' was desirable, aye, inevitable," the editors continued. "You can't plow and you can't hoe in garments that trail, or garments that constrict."[13]

In its fashion spread on the latest in suffrage farming attire, the *Woman's Journal* featured Mrs. Ruth Litt, chairman of the Suffrage Agriculture Committee for New York, who plowed on her own farm on Long Island and "evolved a service uniform that is at once chic and practicable." Other sartorial options included overalls, garden bloomers, and a "khaki farmerette suit with skirt attachment for N.S.S.A."[14]

At the National Service School #6 at Farmingdale, in the potato-growing heart of Long Island and about an hour's train trip from Manhattan, the women were already in uniform—long khaki skirts, blouse, and tie, with a wide-brimmed campaign hat. The teachers, businesswomen, and society ladies were driving tractors and three-horse wagons and learning to plow and to plant. They were "doing their bit on the soil," as the *New York Times* put it, and eager to "prove to other people that they can do it."[15] To extend the hours of instruction and to prepare more acres of soil for a late spring planting, the women even worked into the night, driving the tractors with headlights.

Albert Johnson, the director of the New York State School of Agriculture at Farmingdale who supervised the training, liked to say that one woman with modern farm implements could do the work once done by three men and seven horses. The women enjoyed being called by the traditional nickname for agricultural students— "aggies"—but seemed to prefer the sobriquet "farmerettes." One of them wrote a song about the farmerettes, the first of many celebrating the women's war work on the land. It was published in Farmingdale school's magazine, *The Furrow.*

Planting Song of the Farmerettes
(to the tune of "Tipperary")

Nellie was a pedagogue
And Sue a social light,
But when the Germans sank our boats
They both set out to fight.
Grabbing up a rake and hoe,
They joined the food armee,
Now they're out at Farmingdale,
A-fighting for the free.

(Chorus)
It's a hard job to plant potatoes,
It's a darn sight worse to hoe;
It's a hard job to weed tomatoes,
When the pesky things do grow.
Farewell to all the bright lights,
Good-bye, old Broadway,
We are all out here to serve our country,
And you bet we'll stay.[16]

The Farmingdale National Service School was now the largest, most visible effort to train women for emergency work in agriculture, and by early June almost seventy farmerettes were in residence, with more expected. Needing more housing space, the league, with the assistance from the state of New York financed the construction of a new barracks building on the campus. A long, low structure costing $7,500, the building contained twenty sleeping rooms and a separate bathing pavilion. The barracks' dedication in mid-June was turned into something of a coming-out party for the Land Army movement, with a parade, speeches, reporters, and a contingent of dignitaries from the city in attendance. Under the headline "Girl Farmers Drive in a Muddy Parade," the *New York Times* reported, "Aggies of varying degrees of youth and beauty, all dressed in khaki and muddy boots, appeared in procession" for the opening ceremonies.[17]

The women in the invited guests' section of the audience sat on hard plank benches and, in a sign of the times, did war knitting while they watched the open-air ceremony. Guest speakers delivered their remarks from a hastily built wooden platform. The most stirring words came from Virginia Gildersleeve, the dean of Barnard College of Columbia University and the newly appointed head of the New York City Women's Agriculture Committee.

"I represent the Committee on Agriculture of the Mayor's Committee of Women on National Defense," said Gildersleeve, "and I blush to say it, for I do not know the difference between a carrot and a turnip when they are put before me." The women training at Farmingdale "were solving the problem of work on the farm without frills or foolishness," she told the audience. They were doing what the times demanded, but they were also doing more: "We shall have accomplished a great deal of permanent value, to continue after the war, if we have proved that agriculture, a profession which requires intelligence, science, and muscular work in the open air, can be done by women."[18]

5

SOIL SISTERS

Virginia Gildersleeve was not at all sure how she'd become the doyenne of agriculture for New York City, yet here she was, chair of the Standing Committee on Agriculture of the Mayor's Committee of Women on National Defense. Gildersleeve, regal in bearing and imperious in manner, was quite comfortable in her ivory tower and had no desire to putter in its garden. The daughter of a prominent judge, child of privilege, scholar of Shakespeare, she had never lived anyplace but Manhattan. At forty years of age, she'd already served as the dean of Barnard College, the women's undergraduate school of Columbia University, for six years. She occupied one of the most respected chairs in American academics—at any other college her title would be president—and moved among the city's political and intellectual elite.

By the time America entered World War I she was a seasoned and agile political tactician who could maneuver in both academic and public boardrooms. She'd already sparred with Columbia about admitting her Barnard graduates into the university's professional schools (that battle would go on for decades) and skirmished with her own Board of Trustees over whether to allow Barnard girls to form campus suffrage clubs and participate in suffrage parades. An expert on the interplay between Elizabethan theater and sixteenth-century English politics, Gildersleeve concerned herself with world affairs; regularly contributed essays to journals of political opinion, such as The *New Republic*; and was a star on the intellectual lecture circuit. But she was also deeply engaged in her city's civic life and found it hard to say no to the many leadership positions she was offered. She was also a crackerjack administrator.

She took an early interest in women's preparedness initiatives. Assuming the nation would eventually have to enter the war, she wanted the American college woman to be part of any mobilization plan. When America broke off diplomatic relations with Germany, in the first days of February 1917, she joined with Columbia president Nicholas Murray Butler in pledging the university's resources to the government, and she led

Columbia University's Committee on Women's War Work, investigating the types of services women might undertake. She took a similar role with the Association of Collegiate Alumnae (forerunner of the American Association of University Women), a consortium of female college graduates and professors. She dutifully attended all those prewar strategy sessions of the National League for Women's Service held in Manhattan clubs and living rooms.

Gildersleeve wrote in her memoirs,

> I was young and strong and eager to be active, yet most of my war work
> consisted of just sitting and talking in committee meetings. It was more
> useful than anything else I could have done, but some days I despised myself
> for "fighting an armchair war." However, I did get a few chances for more
> active service of a concrete, human sort. Some of these arose from my rather
> odd Chairmanship of the Standing Committee on Agriculture of the Mayor's
> Committee.[1]

So Virginia Crocheron Gildersleeve, who was only slightly exaggerating when she said that she couldn't distinguish a carrot from a turnip, came to be the city's chief of women's agriculture. "Now, I knew so little about agriculture," she admitted in her memoir, "but I did know something by that time about organizing women."[2]

John Purroy Mitchel already had the idea of convening special citizen advisory panels to deal with political emergencies and develop new policies. Admired by his supporters as a crusading reformer, Mitchel's enemies derided him as the impetuous "Boy Mayor" of New York (he was only thirty-five when he was elected in 1914). Mitchel enlisted prominent citizens, both the powerful and the knowledgeable, to focus on specific municipal problems and build consensus for his administration's controversial reforms of taxation, zoning, and education. He put both the men's and women's divisions of his committees to work during the city's winter food riots, and as soon as war was declared, he anointed them as the official coordinating bodies for civilian mobilization.

Mayor Mitchel appointed an all-star team of politically astute women to the city's Committee of Women on National Defense. Besides Gildersleeve, he named reform leader Belle Moskowitz (who would soon gain enormous influence as a political adviser to the next governor of New York, Alfred E. Smith) and labor rights advocate Frances Perkins (who would become the first woman cabinet officer, serving as President Franklin Roosevelt's secretary of labor). In the first weeks of the war, governors and mayors across the nation appointed similar citizen committees to coordinate their jurisdictions' industrial and civilian mobilization efforts, investing in them varying degrees of autonomy and power.

At the national level, the all-male Committee of National Defense existed, at least on paper, since the summer of 1916, when it was formed in response to Thomas Alva Edison's criticisms of American readiness. In a newspaper interview published in the spring of 1915, Edison said he was alarmed by the nation's haphazard approach to incorporating technological innovations into military weaponry and transport. He said the country needed a national research laboratory to build and test new devices that could give America a technological edge in wartime (as the submarine did for Germany) and also called for an inventory of the nation's manufacturing capability and transport networks.[3]

Edison's critical comments hit a nerve, and the resulting public uproar forced Secretary of the Navy Josephus Daniels to create a civilian Naval Consulting Board. He asked the national engineering, scientific, and medical societies to nominate some of their cleverest members to work on the board, which did undertake a systematic evaluation of the nation's industrial resources. Out of the board's recommendations came legislation creating a new body, the Council of National Defense, which was made up of six members of the Wilson cabinet, chaired by the secretary of war, and assisted by an advisory panel of specialists.

Lethargy and some turf wrangling prevented the CND from doing much until February 1917, when it began to form into subcommittees overseeing readiness plans in medicine, labor, transportation, raw materials, metals, munitions, and supplies. Recruiting leaders from industry, banking, labor, and science—both financier Bernard Baruch and labor leader Samuel Gompers served on the CND—these committees took the lead in fashioning an economic and industrial response once America entered the war. They also formed the nuclei for the powerful entities that would virtually run the economy during the war: the U.S. Railroad, Fuel, and Food administrations and Aircraft Production and War Industries boards.

The Wilson administration created the Women's Committee of the CND reluctantly, under pressure, a few weeks after America entered the war, and the Women's Committee struggled to figure out its function and establish its own identity. The New York City Mayor's Committee of Women, however, did not need to waste time figuring out its mandate. It took stock of what needed to be done and simply divided itself into working groups, with each group responsible for initiating and directing action in a particular sphere. Committees dealing with employment, nursing, social welfare, industry, finance, food, and agriculture issues assembled themselves, recruited women with special knowledge or interest in the field, and set to work.[4]

The concept of a New York City Standing Committee on Agriculture, which seemed at first blush like an oxymoron, grew out of a preliminary gathering of the organizations already involved or interested in using women to help increase food supplies: the National League for Women's Service, the NAWSA, the WNF&GA, the Garden Club of America, the International Child Welfare League, Columbia University Committee on Women's War Work, the New York State Industrial Commission, and the Girl Scouts.[5] There was clearly no shortage of energy or ideas; the real danger was duplication, dilution, or even collision of their efforts. These disparate projects needed to be coordinated and channeled, and out of this need for order emerged the Agriculture Committee.

"At several meetings of the Executive Committee the urgent necessity of doing something to help get women out to work on the land had been mentioned," Gildersleeve recalled. "Something really had to be done about this, and finally I volunteered."[6]

Joining Gildersleeve on the Agriculture Committee were nine other women, including Hilda Loines, representing the WNF&GA; Ruth Litt, chairman of suffrage potatoes for the New York State NAWSA; and Cornelia Bryce Pinchot, wife of the famous conservationist Gifford Pinchot, a suffragist firebrand, and an influential voice in progressive Republican circles. Later in the season, Professor Ida Helen Ogilvie of Barnard College also joined the committee.

The Standing Committee on Agriculture's straightforward mandate was to centralize the agricultural work women's groups in the city were already doing or were contemplating. Its mission naturally forked into two distinct paths: helping create and supervise community gardens to raise more food and "providing some machinery for placing on farms New York City women willing to undertake agricultural work."[7]

Gildersleeve and her committee started constructing that "machinery." She recalled,

> When the committee began its activities in the spring, the newspapers had
> many sensational accounts of so-called "Farmerettes," and it seemed at first
> sight that much was being done by women farm workers. But when the
> committee started to investigate it found that the facts were far different.
> There were, it is true, a few women in New York City desirous of doing
> agricultural work, but there were apparently no farmers willing to hire
> women workers; nor, if they were forced to have them, did they know how
> they could manage to house and care for this sort of helper.[8]

The first mechanism the committee built was a farm employment clearinghouse to provide a way farmers could connect with women workers. Existing agricultural employment bureaus wouldn't accept women on their rolls, so women needed their own. Groups cooperating with the Agriculture Committee, such as the National League for Women's Service and the Women's National Farm and Garden Association, turned over their files with valuable information—the names and addresses of women who'd already registered, trained, or expressed a willingness to do farmwork. The committee then opened its own office to place women on farms. The women of the mayor's Standing Committee on Agriculture were not afraid to ask questions or seek advice. They went to the New York State Industrial Commission's Employment Bureau for help in setting up the structures for their women's work clearinghouse, and they went to the county Farm Bureau agents to determine what sort of help the farmers needed. They discovered that what the farmer needed was not necessarily what he wanted.

"Many farmers were seeking women, but all wanted them to do housework, not outside work," Gildersleeve wrote in her first committee report. "On the other hand, of all the women who came to the committee's office to register, not a single one could be persuaded to do housework in a farmer's family. This seemed to be a hopeless deadlock."[9]

To break this deadlock the committee would have to encourage a change of heart or twist a few arms. Gildersleeve, a great champion of women smashing through barriers and entering academe and the professions, was not about to try and convince patriotic women eager to work the land to volunteer instead for farmhouse kitchen toil. So she turned to persuading the farmers that women could be more helpful in the fields. "Farmers must be made to see the value of women's service on the farm," she told her colleagues on the Mayor's Committee.[10] They launched a publicity drive in the state's rural districts, distributing leaflets and dispatching emissaries to the Grange and Farm Bureau meetings to talk to the farmers.

Women had always worked in the fields, of course, but they were farmers' or sharecroppers' kinfolk—their wives and daughters, mothers and sisters, or they were "Negro" women in the cotton and sugar cane fields of the south, or "peasant" immigrant women. Farmers did not work with American-born white women. Further, women on farms were not, as a rule, paid for their labor, because it was part of their familial responsibilities. Although they were expert in their tasks—farmwomen often ran the poultry, dairy, or bee-keeping aspects of the farm—they did what they were told. The committee was offering a different kind of worker—strange women, city women, women who wanted to be paid. The farmwives weren't thrilled about it either.

The farmer feared domestic friction. "Do you expect me to take a bunch of girls into my house and have them knock off at 4 o'clock while my wife cooks their supper and washes the dishes?" asked one incredulous New York farmer when the committee approached him.[11]

An additional point of contention with the farmers was the committee's insistence that women land laborers work only an eight-hour day, just as their sisters entering industrial work did. The hard-fought and ongoing battle for the eight-hour day was a shared ambition of the labor, women's rights, and reform movements. Most important, the eight-hour day was a shield for protecting the woman farm laborer from exhaustion and exploitation. It was not negotiable.

The committee searched for a compromise, a way to finesse the difficulties. They looked to the Women's Land Army of Great Britain, which was now an official government service, but their workers usually lodged with the farm family or boarded in village hostels. They looked to Canada, which as part of the British Empire had been at war for almost three years with more than half a million of its men fighting in Europe. Canada suffered from acute farm labor shortages, but its provincial governments were only beginning to send out women on a large scale to help with fruit crops. The thorny logistics of the women's living and work conditions had been thrown into the lap of the YWCA of Canada, which was planning to open a dozen or more farmerette colonies to house the women that summer. But neither of these Land Army "big sisters" offered a perfect role model.

The Mayor's Committee received an answer from an Austrian countess transplanted to Westchester, New York. Camilla Hoyos Short, daughter of an Austrian nobleman, studied horticulture in England. She came to America in 1912 when she married architect Charles Wilkins Short Jr. With such close ties to England, Camilla Short watched intently as her friends there assumed important roles in the war effort. As a woman trained in horticulture, she had a keen interest in promoting women's work in that field, and as a woman with a Germanic accent, she was also anxious to display her loyalty to her new country. Mrs. Short ventured down to Manhattan and presented a new idea to Virginia Gildersleeve.

Her idea was an ingenious solution to the farm labor problem, one that might assuage both the farmers and the women volunteers. Known as the "unit plan," it provided the logistical, and even philosophical, underpinning for an American land army of women. Her simple concept meant women farmworkers would not be a burden to the farmwife at all, for they wouldn't need room or board or pose any bother. Instead, they could live together on their own, self-sufficiently, as a "unit;" that is, they would house themselves, cook for themselves, and hire themselves out in squads to farmers who needed them in the field on a daily basis.

The advantages were obvious: the farm family wouldn't have to accommodate strange women entering or disrupting their households (this situation had already proved to be a source of tension in Britain), and at the same time the women could feel more secure and comfortable, protected from any possible abuse in their communal living situation. The farmwife would have neither extra mouths to feed nor nubile young women living under her roof. Also, living in a community, or a sort of pastoral sorority house, would ease the notorious isolation and boredom of rural existence and give recruits the promise of a pleasant social life together. Equally important, the sponsors and supervisors of such a venture—in this case, the Mayor's Committee—could be in control. It would be able to screen applicants, hire staff, set the rules, negotiate the wages and hours of farm employment, and retain the flexibility of independent contractors. All in all, it made farmwork for women seem more respectable.

As an experiment, in the summer of 1917 the Mayor's Committee supervised and supported eleven separate units of farming women working in different parts of the state. The committee's recruitment efforts—leaflets, speakers, even paid advertisements in newspapers—paid off, both in attracting women to work and in convincing individual farmers to gamble on a unit of women farmhands. The Agriculture Committee dipped into its treasury to lend money to the units for start-up supplies and groceries.

One small unit was comprised of six teachers and art students who spent five weeks of their summer vacation picking berries on a fruit farm near Milton, New York. They were paid on a piecework basis, so more speedily filling the berry boxes made for fatter pay envelopes. Living in a farm outbuilding, the women paid a housekeeper to cook and tidy up their quarters (each woman's share for this was 50 cents a week) and paid another $2.59 a week out of their earnings for food. Counting the $1.50 they paid in travel expenses, each of the women cleared an average of $14.12 for the five weeks of work. Hardly riches, but the women enjoyed the outdoor tasks and felt they'd performed a patriotic duty. "The farmer was evidently satisfied with the women as workers," according to the Agriculture Committee's fall report, "for he plans to have two units next season and has already re-engaged this one."[12]

Another farm unit was formed of "trade union girls" from such seasonal trades as millinery and seamstress work. Laid off from their factories in the slack summer months, the prospect of working in the fresh air for Uncle Sam attracted them. They organized themselves into a "self-governing" unit, one without a chaperone or assigned leader; found their own lodging. They negotiated their hours and pay with the farmer themselves. Their trade union background may have given them a certain bargaining confidence.

Elizabeth Allen, the owner of Endaian Farm in Newburgh, hired eleven "girls" from Columbia University's Committee on Women's War Work to pick berries on her farm. She furnished a large sleeping tent and cooking shack while the girls brought their own supplies and took turns cooking and keeping the camp. They dressed in bloomers or overalls and were paid "at the community rates" by the pint or quart of berries. "It took about three of these inexperienced girls to do as much as one experienced man picker would do," Miss Allen reported, but still "they seemed to find their compensation in their enjoyment of camping life, the unusual freedom from convention, and the sense of being useful in a time of national emergency."[13]

In addition to these early attempts, Gildersleeve's Agriculture Committee kept close tabs on several other wartime farming ventures developing on the leafy campuses of eastern women's colleges. One of these was at Vassar, where patriotic zeal met economic necessity to create a prime opportunity. Vassar's fifteen hundred students and staff depended on a 740-acre farm to provide the vegetables, grain, and milk consumed in the dining halls, but in the spring of 1917 it could not find the needed field laborers to operate. So Vassar, a school that prided itself on nourishing literary minds—poet Edna St. Vincent Millay was in that spring's graduating class—now looked to its own students to help feed the college.

Vassar president Henry Noble MacCracken, a strong advocate of women assuming new roles in the war effort, pushed the plan and appealed to his skeptical board of trustees' fiduciary duty: if the college had to buy, rather than grow, the produce needed for the dining halls, the exorbitant cost would drill a deep hole in the college's finances. The trustees reluctantly agreed to MacCracken's plan. "Partly to make the college independent of outside markets, partly as a patriotic service to test out untried women and see whether they could do farm work efficiently and without danger to their health" was the rationale the trustees settled on.[14] But the trustees authorized the scheme with a proviso: the farm was a business proposition and the Vassar farmerettes must prove their worth in dollars and cents, not just in "a feat which would bring Vassar sensationally before the public."[15] It could not be a publicity stunt.

An appeal went out to the Vassar students. Of the thirty-three volunteers, the twelve women who scored best on the physical exam were chosen. All but one were "town-bred girls" without any farming experience. Alice Campbell, the editor of the college newspaper who had just graduated with the Vassar class of 1917, traded her mortarboard for a pair of "rompers" and became the student manager of the farm unit. "For the first week blisters, sunburns and lame backs were in order," Campbell wrote in a memoir of her experience. "Before long these settled into calluses, coats of tan, and hard muscles."[16]

The women toiled eight hours a day, beginning at forty-thirty in the morning, and worked for two hours before breakfast. They lived in the comfort of the main dormitory, where they took their meals, paying $5.50 for their weekly room and board. They were given a half day off on Saturday from their six-day week and kept up the pace for eight weeks. The Vassar women were not paid equally to men laborers, however; the women received 17.5 cents an hour while those few male farmworkers still remaining in the neighborhood could command 20 cents. This disparity was a capitulation on the equal-pay-for-equal-work standard the Mayor's Committee insisted on in the units it supervised, but Vassar felt it was necessary to blunt local resistance to the women entering the workforce.[17]

As Alice Campbell reported,

> There were drawbacks, of course, but they only helped along the fun.
> Getting up early was made easier by instituting races to see who could work
> the greatest number of hours in a day. Hot weather was a real trial, but the
> object was to prove it could be endured by girls as well as men. Skepticism
> on the part of outsiders was no source of worry; rather an obstacle to be
> overcome in as short a time as possible.[18]

They hoed and harrowed, scythed and shocked, cultivated and harvested acres of corn, grains, and vegetables for the dining tables, as well as the feed for the college's 180 Holstein cows, 350 chickens, 130 pigs, and 17 horses. "By the end of the summer each girl could milk four cows at a milking," boasted Campbell. "And these tasks they performed so satisfactorily that at the end of the season the men said that the girls should have received the same wage that they had," according to the Mayor's Committee report on the Vassar venture, bolstering the case for the insistence on equal pay for women farmhands. "They did the work just as well as the average man," reported Louis Gillespie, the farm's superintendent, "and made good far beyond the most sanguine expectations."[19]

Just as Vassar students took over their college farm, four hundred Mount Holyoke College women took up hoes to coax food from their college land in central Massachusetts. "All that was necessary to set the crops growing was faith in young college women, and this was very essential, for objections to the plan were numerous, and faith in women as farm laborers was weak," a Holyoke alumna reported to her schoolmates that summer.[20]

Mary Woolley, Mount Holyoke's president, was a great booster of the notion that her highly cultured and highly pampered students could set their dainty hands toward increasing the food supply, but she faced incredulous shaking of heads among her trustees and faculty. "Can anyone possibly visualize," asked one college official, "young women accustomed to stroll in white gowns and shoes, cutting potatoes or going to the fields with hoes over their shoulders?"

"Will they be willing to wear potato sacks over their heads and work on when it rains?" asked another gloomy male professor.[21] Would they even be willing to try? The answer came swiftly, when more than 600 of the college's 800 students volunteered to do spring planting work, along with 17 faculty members. The college physician and physical training director scanned the list of recruits and weeded out 200 of them as admirably willing but not physically fit enough for the labor. A second call went out for students willing to work for a month over the summer. Out of 150 students who volunteered, 100 of these were accepted.

Funding wasn't a problem, either: the students contributed $150 of their own money, the Dramatic Club kicked in the proceeds from their latest production, and President Woolley cajoled a friend of the college to write a $500 check. But unlike the Vassar trustees, who insisted that the farmerettes prove to be a good "business proposition," the purpose of the Mount Holyoke experiment "was simply to do our bit . . . not to make money, but to produce food as a small but material contribution to the resources of our allies in arms."[22]

In May, the four hundred spring workers were organized into squads of thirty or forty women and then broken into divisions of ten, with an upperclasswoman as leader. The director of the college's botanical garden provided instruction in technique. Local farmers were hired to do the initial plowing of the grasslands, for the college did not have a farm; but students did all the other work. They learned to cut potatoes for seed and to fertilize the fields, and here the cultural sensibility of the educated woman more familiar with art history than agriculture was revealed: "Millet would have rejoiced in the picture of forty young women in short skirts and middy blouses moving lightly against a background of greening fields and blue hills and flinging out dusty puffs of odorous fertilizer," as one student observed.[23]

Bryn Mawr College, outside Philadelphia, also jumped into farming in the summer of 1917. President M. Carey Thomas arranged for a tract of land a few miles from campus to be converted into a practice farm. A few dozen students and several faculty members—including the newly appointed dean of the college, Helen Taft, daughter of the former vice president—took up residence at the farm, produced foodstuffs for the college tables, and helped the local farmers bring in their crops. Goucher College in Baltimore also established a war farm, tended by the "city students" who did not leave town for the summer, and the women of Grinnell College in Iowa produced six tons of vegetables on their college plot.[24]

The women land workers were beginning to be called "farmerettes" in the press, a sassy diminutive that was also a contraction of "farmer" and "suffragette," which the workers themselves seemed to enjoy. It made some veteran suffragists wince, as they remembered the sarcastic origins of the sobriquet. It first surfaced in 1911 when Alva Vanderbilt Belmont, one of the movement's most flamboyant benefactors, tried to create a "suffrage farm colony" composed entirely of young society women on her Long Island estate. Belmont's venture failed spectacularly when the feckless women deserted the farm before the harvest, and the newspapers had great fun with the colony's stunning collapse. It was an embarrassment, and any women taking up land service for the war would have to live down that reputation for frivolity and prove the new farmerette's sincere intent.

As they toiled in the fields, these first wartime farmerettes recited poems and sang songs, and as the shock of strangeness wore off, they began to earn the respect of the local citizenry. During a July hot spell, solicitous neighbors offered the Mount Holyoke students ginger tea to help prevent heat prostration, and the women worked right through the scorching weather. Watching them, one South Hadley, Massachusetts, villager was heard to exclaim, "What them women can't do!"[25]

6

A Feminine Invasion of the Land: The Bedford Camp

While Dean Gildersleeve's Agriculture Committee kept an eye on these early and idiosyncratic forays into women's land service, the committee launched its own bold experiment with the opening of the Women's Agricultural Camp in Bedford, New York. The camp was the second phase of Camilla Short's development strategy: a full agricultural training camp that would not only give city women some practical knowledge of farming, but also serve as a controlled experiment in how to structure and manage the unit plan concept and how to deploy women in the fields on a large scale. The Bedford Camp was to serve as the working model for a full national movement.

Camilla Short did not intend to be an aloof patroness of this test camp. She promised Dean Gildersleeve that she would drum up adequate financial and logistical support among her friends in Westchester, and she would put the camp together. She'd already secured the loan of an estate and had a prospective band of financial angels. All the camp needed was the imprimatur of the Mayor's Agriculture Committee and an able staff to operate it. Dean Gildersleeve supplied the committee's stamp of approval and, quite serendipitously, provided for the camp's long-term leadership and success when she introduced Delia West Marble to a member of her Barnard faculty, Ida Ogilvie.

Miss Marble had initially approached Dean Gildersleeve to offer the Garden Club of America's assistance to the mayor's Committee on Agriculture. Marble was a name with which Gildersleeve was well acquainted. Delia's father, Manton Marble, had been a famous newspaper editor and publisher; the former owner of the *New York World*, mouthpiece of the Democratic Party; and a confidante of presidents and politicians. Miss Marble, now almost fifty years old, had devoted her life to good deeds in Westchester County, where her family owned a farm near the town of Bedford. Besides volunteering on various educational boards, she indulged her passion for flowers by serving on Gardem Club committees.

Like most women's organizations at the time, the Garden Club was looking for an appropriate patriotic expression for its members and some way they could be useful. This new idea of land service for women sounded like a possibility. Miss Marble was deputized to offer the GCA's resources to the diva of agriculture, Dean Gildersleeve. "After conferring with her," Gildersleeve recounted, "I put her in touch with Professor Ida H. Ogilvie of our Department of Geology, because I knew she was a wonderful field worker in geology and thought she might take to this outdoor type of war service."[1]

Ida Ogilvie was indeed an outdoor type of woman. As a child she'd frolicked in the grass near the easel of her artist father, Clinton Ogilvie, a member of the Hudson River School of painters, and inherited from him a love of the landscape and an appreciation for natural forms. The wealthy Ogilvies had artistic and social ambitions for their only child and sent her to Europe to polish her rough edges. Ida managed to escape her fate as a debutante by enrolling at Bryn Mawr College, where she abandoned art to study the sciences and took geology classes with Florence Bascom, the first American woman to become a professional geologist. Young Ida was fascinated by the colorful Bascom, who conducted her fieldwork on horseback, and settled on geology as her career. When she received her doctoral degree from Columbia in 1903, Ogilvie was hired as Barnard College's first lecturer in geology. She established and led its Geology Department, which for decades she maintained as a woman-only preserve, hiring only women faculty and staff to serve as role models for the Barnard students.[2]

Professor Ogilvie, at the dean's suggestion, invited Delia West Marble to her office to discuss this idea of agricultural war work for women. With that meeting they began a lifelong partnership—a romance and working collaboration. They would remain a couple for the rest of their long lives. Between them, they also managed to assemble the missing pieces of Mrs. Short's plan: Delia Marble offered her family's farm in Bedford as additional acreage for the training camp, and Ida Ogilvie offered to spend her summer serving as the camp's director.

Mrs. Short assembled an advisory panel of Westchester neighbors, coaxing them to pledge $5,000 to equip and run the camp. One supporter offered a farmhouse for the women to live in while others provided cots, chairs, and tableware to furnish it. Even more important, the local organizers acted as goodwill ambassadors to the neighborhood and urged local farmers to hire the women. Dean Gildersleeve authorized several Barnard College chauffeurs to work at the camp for the summer and lent a college bookkeeper to the enterprise. Columbia's Teachers College sent three of its students to serve as the camp's dietitians, designing and cooking a nutritionally sound diet for the women workers, and a Columbia agricultural expert came to coach the workers.

Recruitment proved to be no problem. Between the various war placement bureaus and word of mouth, 142 women worked at Bedford in the four months of its maiden 1917 season. At the height of the season, 73 workers lived in camp. They were housed in the old farmhouse as well as in the carriage house and the barn or slept on cots in the corncrib and in tents outside. Ranging in age from sixteen to forty-five years, 6 were married women, and 60 of them were either college students or college graduates, many from Barnard. The Manhattan Trade School sent a contingent of women who'd attended the school and now worked in factories as seamstresses. There were 38 "working girls" in camp that season along with 18 school teachers, 4 college professors, 5 secretaries or stenographers, 7 licensed chauffeurs, 2 concert singers, 2 florists, 2 designers, 2 governesses, and a news reporter.[3]

The Women's Agricultural Camp opened on June 4 with 24 "farmhands," and the first order of business was to give each worker a physical exam to see if she was up to doing strenuous labor. "The aim [was] . . . to get workers who were 'absolutely sound,' though not necessarily stronger than the average woman," as Ida Ogilvie explained.[4] Then they worked in the camp garden, under a woman agriculturalist's instruction, to learn techniques and get their muscles in shape.

"We were all city girls, enthusiastic but sublimely ignorant of farming," recalled Helen Kennedy Stevens, a Barnard student who signed up for duty at Bedford. "We had to be taught several things, among them the difference between a nice little tomato plant and a weed. We learned that cows had to be milked at rather regular intervals and that only hens would lay eggs."[5]

After a week or two of this practice, they ventured out in squads of six or eight to work an eight-hour day for farmers who agreed to pay the camp the going rate for male laborers—that is, twenty-five cents an hour, or two dollars a day. The camp paid the women fifteen dollars a month for their toil and provided their room and board. In the evening the camp truck retrieved the workers from the fields and brought them home to a communal dinner and jolly camp life.

That routine was the general outline. Filling in the details and figuring out the nettlesome particulars—everything from camp chores to efficient car routes, thrifty meal menus to farmer relations—was the mission of the Bedford Camp. Ogilvie approached these tasks with an air of scientific inquiry, as a specimen to be analyzed, an opportunity for experiment. She was comfortable with trial and error. She called herself the camp's "dean," and she would come to describe the Bedford experiment as "the most comprehensive and scientific of all the feminine invasions of the land."[6]

Ida Ogilvie was the camp's rock and soul, but she was hardly the Earth Mother type. "When Dr. Ogilvie swung by," remembered Harriet Geithmann, a recruit from Seattle, "I thought of Gibraltar Rock on Mt. Rainier."[7] But Professor Ogilvie understood the camp experiment had one essential, immutable element: the farmers had to be persuaded to hire the women workers. And initially, they would not do so. "As we opened in haste with no previous publicity, the demand for farm workers was slight at first," Ogilvie reported, "and as farmers are notably conservative and by nature disinclined for change or for feminine labor, it took time for us to become established."[8] "Disinclined" was putting it mildly.

Gildersleeve, in her report of the Mayor's Committee, put it more bluntly: "At first the farmers in the neighborhood looked with extreme scepticism upon the women's enterprise."[9] Helen Kennedy Stevens offered a worker's wry perspective: "We were there for business, though the farmers did not seem to realize it. They did not hurt themselves in a mad rush to secure our services."[10]

Bedford's farmers were not mentally prepared for the concept of women farmworkers, much less the sight of them dressed in men's overalls. In one of Ogilvie's first bold moves, skirts were abandoned. "Men's blue overalls and blue work shirt were adopted as the camp uniform. The long trousers and stout material are essential where work in rough places is to be done; and where there is kneeling, as in weeding, any form of skirt or tunic is too much in the way," she reported. Cotton gloves, shade hats, and stout shoes accessorized the camp outfit. The sight of women in overalls raised many an eyebrow, but the unflappable Professor Ogilvie explained, "Although somewhat startling to a conservative neighborhood at first, this costume was accepted remarkably soon as a matter of course."[11]

Also startling to the farmers were the Bedford Camp administrators' demands regarding their workers' wages and hours. Agriculture had never been a nine-to-five sort of occupation, and long days in the field were an accepted, time-honored part of farming life. Here came these women, however, treating farmwork as a whistle-blowing, clock-punching factory job and demanding all the protections that trade unionists screamed for in the city.

And when it came to wages, the women expected to be paid the same as men. In this new wartime labor market, Professor Ogilvie and the camp's advisers had to make some basic decisions: should they ask the farmers to pay the women the prevailing wage for male farm laborers in the region or to pay less because the women were inexperienced or more because of wartime labor scarcity? The strong influence of the women's trade union movement is evident in their policies. "It is felt to be most important in every way that women should not in any sense undersell men in the agricultural labor market," Ogilvie explained, "and that the principal of equal pay for equal work be maintained."[12] Ogilvie was also sensitive to the farmers' needs. She realized that even though wartime labor scarcity was driving up wages in the neighborhood—Italian immigrant laborers in Bedford were demanding, and getting, three dollars a day—she decided her women would hold to the normal peacetime rate for men.

The farmers doubted they were worth it, but by mid-June they were desperate for help. Some camp advisory committee members went out to talk to the farmers, as did George Powell, a sympathetic local farmer and president of a state agricultural professionals' organization. He could speak the farmers' language; they might listen to him. Slowly, one by one, farmers began to inquire about getting a gang of "those girls" over to their place, just to try them out. The farmer was pleased with their work and reported that while they were not as strong as men were, they were diligent and eager to learn with a good attitude. He engaged them for another day and asked for a larger gang. He then told his friends the girls "made good." By mid-July, the camp could not keep up with the farmers' demands. Sixty women were dispatched each day, and "we could have employed at least fifty more girls," said Ogilvie. As the season wore on, a waiting list developed. Ninety-nine employers in the vicinity put the women to work.

They had surmounted the major obstacle to the camp's success, but Ogilvie still faced logistical problems. Transportation was one. Getting the women to their assigned fields, often fifteen miles from the central camp, turned out to be cumbersome and expensive, even with three donated Fords at their disposal and chauffeurs at the ready. The camp trucks, which the women had named "Henry," "Henrietta," and "Lizzie," were dispatched on daily shuttle routes covering a hundred miles. By the season's end, their odometers logged fifteen thousand miles. The gasoline was costly, the tires always blew, and the exhausted girls were left waiting for their rides home. Based on this experience Ogilvie came up with two suggestions for the future: satellite encampments of workers could be established closer to employers on outlying farms, cutting down commuting distances, and future camps should keep a supply of yarn so the farmhands could knit mufflers for soldiers while waiting for their ride from the fields. These patriots of the soil would have no idle moments.

Efficiency was also the order of the day in the camp kitchen. A modern canning kitchen kept the workers busy conserving fruits and vegetables when rainy weather prevented fieldwork. With the help of the student dieticians, two farm cows, twenty-six hens, and a vegetable garden, the camp managed to feed its hungry women for just forty-eight cents a day. "The four dieticians are a marvel," Geithmann wrote in her diary. "They feed each of us on fifty cents and less a day. Most scientifically do they dole out calories warranted to produce energy for farm laborers. The food is plain and good and sufficient."[13]

Ogilvie and her bookkeeper kept scrupulous accounts of every expenditure ($12.02 for paint and whitewash, $138.81 for blankets, $1.08 for farm hats). Even though the workers brought in just less than $5,000 in wages from the farmers and the camp had $10,500 in expenses, it broke even—but only because of the cushion Mrs. Short's advisory sponsors provided.[14] The camp was not a "paying enterprise," but it served a larger purpose.

Dispassionate scientific observer that she was, Ogilvie admitted that some basic assumptions she and the Mayor's Committee had made about the nature of the women and the nature of the work had been faulty. They had assumed that the college recruits—students, faculty, and alumnae—would provide the brains, and the factory and shop girls the brawn, for the teams in the field. It didn't work out that way.

As Ogilvie reported,

> The original plan had been to have college women as squad captains, and
> girls from the various trades as workers, but this plan was soon abandoned,

all workers being put to an equal basis and those best qualified made captains. The qualities necessary for squad leadership were found to have little or no connection with previous training or occupation, and the college girls proved on the whole stronger and better able to do the heaviest work than the trade girls.[15]

The *Barnard Bulletin* put it most vividly:

Be it said to the credit of both, that the college girls were found to be most husky young animals fit for the hardest of labor, and that the trade school girls displayed splendid executive power. For once in the world, ability was the sole standard; she who hoed best hoed, she who directed best shouldered the responsibility . . . and blue shirts and overalls made distinctions impossible.[16]

Bringing women of different ages, backgrounds, and social classes to live and work together, with class distinctions rendered meaningless, was also part of the Women's Agricultural Camp experiment. As with their brothers donning military uniforms, this wartime service could be a great social leveler. In the camp mess hall, in the fields, in the barn, and in the bunkhouse, both the college woman and the factory woman, and the working girl and the lady of leisure, were just doing their bit for Uncle Sam. "In the democratic atmosphere of our camp there is a camaraderie of all types and classes of individuals," wrote Harriet Geithmann in her journal. "The stolid Russian peasant, lover of the soil and Tolstoi, toils by the sweat of her brow side by side with daughters of New York's eminent pastors."[17]

The camp "proved beyond shadow of doubt that women of the most diverse types and antecedents could be held together in a group without internal friction and with enthusiasm and pleasure in the life and work," Ogilvie said proudly. Still, Professor Ogilvie revealed some lingering class prejudice when she analyzed the camp's social dynamic. "While it might be argued that agricultural labor was the province of the trade, rather than the college woman," she said, "nevertheless an admixture of college women is necessary for creating the right atmosphere. The majority of trade girls think of a job as a necessary evil whose units of success are more pay and shorter hours. An admixture of college women is needed in order to infuse a finer spirit into the group."[18]

The camp's spirit and the women's hard work won over the Bedford farmers. The president of the Bedford Farmers' Club, James Wood of Braewold Farm, reported that his members were very pleased with the work of the "farm girls." The club members "gave emphatic testimony as to the efficiency of their labor, their marked intelligence, their eagerness to learn the 'reason why' of agricultural operations, their zest and steadfastness, and their pleasant and unexceptional demeanor."[19]

The Westchester Farm Bureau received not one complaint from farmers employing the women, "although at the beginning of the season farmers were reluctant to employ them," the local farm agent reported. "The unanimous verdict of the farmers," reported George Powell, was "that while less strong than men, they more than made up for this by superior conscientiousness and quickness."[20]

The Mayor's Committee was enormously pleased with the results of the experiment. "They can cut fire wood, dig holes for fence posts, wield a scythe, milk cows, hoe weeds, pitch hay, do any of the jobs that used to be considered the exclusive property of the male sex," exclaimed Helen Shaw Rider, an agricultural expert serving on the Mayor's Committee, after visiting the Bedford Camp. "And when they come back from a day's chores, they are always ready for a dance to the strains of the farm's Victrola."[21]

Dean Gildersleeve agreed. In her report to the Mayor's Committee, she stated the camp "demonstrated most successfully what its founders set out to prove, that women with little or no technical training could perform satisfactorily most kinds of farm labor and help remedy the shortage caused by the withdrawal of men for agricultural work."[22]

Ida Ogilvie saw even deeper meaning in the success of the Bedford experiment. As Harriet Geithmann wrote in her diary,

> Dr. O—lectured us tonight on the significance of our Camp, its example to other States in the Union. We were, as she says, making history that will count in three great economic issues, namely, the problem of the twentieth century woman, the labor problem and the agricultural problem. We felt our backbones stiffen as she fired out cannon balls straight from her broad shoulders.[23]

"Old values that hinge on sex, social prominence and the like fade into insignificance," Ida Ogilvie said, Delia Marble by her side, proclaiming the Bedford Camp experiment a success.

7

FARMERETTES AND HOOVER HELPERS:
FALL 1917

Carl Schurz Vrooman, an assistant secretary of agriculture, came up from Washington to see the experiment for himself. Word had reached him about these New York women working in the fields, living in camps, wearing overalls. His colleagues at the Agriculture Department were dismissive—they felt boys, not women, should be organized to help the farmer—but Vrooman was curious.

Making a connect-the-dots arc across New York State in mid-September, Vrooman toured all eleven units of the women land workers the Mayor's Committee supervised. Wherever he went—and as an old soybean farmer he did not hesitate to stomp into the field and see the farmerettes close up—a posse of his staff, Mayor's Committeewomen, and news photographers trooped after him. His last stop was the Bedford Camp, and he asked to speak to the farmerettes there. Ida Ogilvie and Delia Marble gathered all the workers who could be spared from the harvest rush, and they sat cross-legged below the porch of the old Woodcock farmhouse, eager to hear what the man from Washington thought of them.

He stood on the farmhouse steps and struck a neighborly tone, saying he wanted to "talk shop" with the farmerettes, with those who wore "the wedding garment" of the movement, the camp uniform. "You have won my admiration for the spirit with which you go to work; you have won my respect by the solid results that you have achieved," he told them. "I have been agreeably surprised and amazed by this good performance, this perfectly startling performance."

Secretary Vrooman continued:

> Nor am I throwing any undeserved bouquets. This little company in the
> army of food producers of America corresponds to the Battalion of Death in
> Russia. Probably the work you have started is bigger than any one realizes.
> Numbers do not count. We need the effort, the spirit and the demonstration.

And I find these here. This small beginning should start a movement which should continue. If you are able to put in the zest and the energy as well as the determination, the charm of the idea will be caught up and carried over the land, until we find not fifty or sixty, but a hundred, a thousand, a hundred thousand girls next year doing the same thing that you have started.

I do not know what part official Washington is going to take in this enterprise, but I will talk about it at my office and the Committee of National Defense will then discuss this as a part of the great programme of national preparedness. You are part of the army of progress which is beating back the spectre of famine now hovering over the skyline of every European country, and which only America can prevent.

I am more than glad to have been here. I am more than glad to take back to Washington the report of my inspection. It is something tremendously big that you have started, with promising results. You are a credit to yourself, to your sex, and to your country.[11]

The farmerettes sitting on the grass must have been pleasantly stunned by Carl Vrooman's speech. They might have expected him to be polite, complimentary perhaps, or patronizing maybe, with a pat on the head sort of thing, but they did not anticipate this praise, not "this perfectly startling performance." Of course, he might have gone a bit far in likening the farmerettes to the Battalion of Death, those fierce (even crazy) women warriors of Russia who had gotten special permission to organize themselves into a fighting force. At that moment, according to the latest newsreels, they were gleefully throwing themselves into the battle's front lines with the Hun. But Vrooman was clearly impressed with the farmerettes' little rows of well-tended beans, with their predawn muster, and with their muscular patriotism. Now he would tell everyone in Washington how impressive the farmerettes really were. And how they could save the day.

Secretary Vrooman did go back to Washington and tell those who would listen that the women had done remarkably well, and the farmers were undeniably pleased with their efforts. Vrooman knew that most American farmers were struggling to bring in their harvest. The labor situation on America's farms had deteriorated over the summer, even as the newly established Food Administration under "Food Dictator" Herbert Hoover was given war powers to guarantee a high price for essential commodities—wheat was set at $2.20 a bushel, for instance—to lure farmers into greater production. Without assurance of adequate labor, though, the high prices were just a tease to the farmers, and Vrooman's Agriculture Department had done little to help them. Earlier in the summer, after weeks of hemming and hawing, the department had unveiled its version of a master "system" to meet the labor shortage. It consisted of a balky scheme that threw responsibility to the states but gave them few resources, and it assumed only a vague federal role in relieving shortages by redistributing labor from state to state and attempting to recruit retired farmers. When the Labor Department sent the obstreperous kids of the Boys' Working Reserve to help, the farmers could only laugh, bitterly.

Then, at the end of August, the peak of the harvest season, President Wilson announced that farmers would not be exempt from the military draft after all. "The matter of leaving the farmers on the farms has been given the most careful and sympathetic attention by the War Department," Wilson explained. "I feel that a class exemption would lead to many difficulties and heartburnings, much as I should personally like to see all the genuine farmers left at their indispensable labor."[2] The farmers felt betrayed.

Vrooman sent members of his staff back to the Bedford Camp to do a more thorough investigation of how the camp worked and what it had managed to accomplish. They filed a glowing report, saying that the camp's "experiment of this kind of labor and mode of living" had been surprisingly successful, and it was "the universal testimony from those who employed the women that the presence of the camp gave much relief to the labor situation. Such a camp is evidently feasible."[3] Nationwide duplication of the Bedford Camp model might not be a full solution to the labor problem, Vrooman understood, but it could definitely help.

The newspapers were now running headlines to bolster this assertion. "Results Show That Women Have Made Good as Farmers" trumpeted the New York *Evening Sun*.[4] A wider public then began hearing about the farmerettes. Alice Campbell and her fellow Vassar farmworkers were invited to demonstrate their agricultural acumen at the Eastern States Dairy Exposition in Massachusetts in October. Their show-and-tell trip, sponsored by the Women's University Club of New York, was a huge success and helped convince some skeptical farmers to try the farmerettes the next season. Campbell also vividly chronicled her experience in an article, "Eight Hours a Day on a Vassar Farm," that was published in many newspapers and widely distributed as a brochure. Virginia Gildersleeve wrote her own article for the *New Republic* extolling the advantages of women farm laborers, lending the concept of women's land service the kind of intellectual imprimatur it needed to become an accepted topic of dinner party conversation.[5]

While Secretary Vrooman was making his grand tour of the farmerette camps, the National League for Women's Service members of the Agricultural Committee were also driving through the back roads of central New York State, urging farmers to plant more winter wheat. As part of their campaign to boost grain production, the league women of Oneida County plastered slogans on their automobiles and drove through the countryside, stopping at farmhouses to talk to the farmers. They could tell them that the farmerettes had proved they could help bring in that extra grain.[6]

Vrooman's entourage must have also bumped into the motorcades of suffrage campaign workers who took to the New York roads that early autumn, drumming up support for the woman's right to vote referendum that would be on the state ballot in November. Their autos were festooned with banners and sported the campaign's official "suffrage radiator cap." Huge billboards were erected near the state's military induction camps to persuade the new soldiers to grant their sisters, wives, and mothers the right to vote before the men left for the front. In their stump speeches, suffrage campaigners pointed to the New York farmerettes' accomplishments and saluted their war service.

A pictorial spread in the early September edition of the *Woman's Journal,* the National American Woman's Suffrage Association's magazine, celebrated "cheerful women workers" with on-the-job photos of female railroad workers, longshorewomen, and farmerettes doing their part for the war effort. Beyond the sheer novelty of the women's labors, newsworthy in itself, the article made a political point: suffragists were loyal to the nation and committed to patriotic service.

By now suffrage leaders understood, rather painfully, that their loyalty was not taken for granted and had to be loudly reaffirmed. Their own Carrie Chapman Catt, president of NAWSA and member of the Women's Committee of the Council of National Defense, found herself waging an ugly war of words in the press. She was forced to publicly defend her own patriotism, which anti-suffrage forces called into question. While her movement's pacifist arm still excoriated her for caving in to war hysteria and supporting America's participation, Mrs. Catt also had to parry accusations made by an officer of the Anti-Suffrage Association concerning her role in the failed Woman's Peace Party. Adding to the Antis' insults, Catt had to fend off their "malicious" implications that she sympathized with the radical labor activities of the Industrial Workers of the World, the Wobblies. (That's ridiculous, Catt shot back, for the IWW doesn't support suffrage.)

Moderate suffragists were working furiously to distance themselves from their movement's militant wing—particularly, Alice Paul and her National Woman's Party adherents, who were still picketing the White House, getting themselves arrested, and capturing headlines. Paul's tactics were tainting the whole cause, the moderates wailed, jeopardizing the fall's suffrage referendum campaigns and exposing suffragists to vicious allegations of disloyalty.[7]

In a bit of comical patriotic zealotry, but still a sign of the times, Food Administrator Herbert Hoover even accused Emma Winner Rogers—the venerable chairman of NAWSA's National Committee on Suffrage Agriculture, the group's treasurer, and wife of the Yale University Law School's dean—of "promoting the interests of the Kaiser" by "discouraging economy." In a newspaper interview, Mrs. Rogers had mentioned that "there were other avenues of waste besides the one through the garbage pail, and that the sins of the housewife must not be blamed to the exclusion of the sins of the food manipulator." To criticize or question government policy was toying with disloyalty, in Mr. Hoover's view, and he took offense. Then he took aim at Mrs. Rogers, but she stood her ground.[8]

So it was no coincidence that the *Woman's Journal* editors pointedly included in their "Cheerful Women Workers" article a portrait of Mrs. Ogden Reid, treasurer of the New York State Woman's Suffrage Party (and later an officer of the New York Woman's Land Army), standing in her kitchen while dressed in the full "Hoover costume" of long, belted smock and stiff nurse-like hat. "All of the Hoover regulations are rigidly observed in her household," read the caption.[9]

To be a "Hoover helper," to "Hooverize" one's household, or to take the "Hoover pledge" was the epitome of the patriotic American woman's duty during the war. Motion pictures with such titles as *Practical Hooverism* featured film stars exhorting housewives to avoid the sins of waste and to practice the virtues of self-sacrifice. "Hoover helpers" pledged their families to Meatless Mondays, Wheatless Wednesdays, and Porkless Saturdays and promised to "preach the gospel of the clean plate" and the empty garbage pail. For the most part, suffragists gladly jumped on the Hoover bandwagon.

The National American Woman Suffrage Association mailed "Be a Hoover Helper" cards to all its members, with instructions to "hang these rules on your Kitchen Hook."[10] As the second Hoover pledge drive got under way in mid-October, tens of thousands of women, including many NAWSA members, went door-to-door and signed up twelve million more housewives to eliminate waste and conserve food, adding to the millions of women who had already signed up during the first pledge drive in July.

Besides its agriculture committees, the NAWSA also sponsored an active Suffrage Thrift Committee, which ran local produce markets and canning centers in many cities. Thousands of American women helped preserve the summer's harvest, donating their time to canning centers in school gymnasiums, in church basements, on flatbed trucks, and even in traveling railroad cars. Canning was fine, for food conservation and waste elimination were vitally important, but this effort hardly blazed new paths in women's work or roles in society. Instead, it was an organized extension of the traditional kitchen. This work was not what some women had in mind when they enrolled in the great civilian army to win the war.

The July Hoover pledge drive was the first major campaign handed to the Women's Committee of the CND to execute. The Hoover pledge became an iconic element of the home-front war, a testament to American women's self-sacrifice and resourcefulness, their voluntary efforts to forestall food rationing. But the pledge drive, while modestly successful, also demonstrated the tight girdle that bound the movements of the Women's Committee.

The committee was a fountain of bubbling ideas, with a constant spray of announcements aimed at American women—bulletins, campaigns, press releases, and publications. The talented journalist Ida Tarbell, who'd earned the honorable sobriquet "muckraker" with her exposé of John D. Rockefeller's Standard Oil Corporation for *McClure's* magazine, coordinated all of the committee's missives. With sixty women's organizations cooperating under the committee's umbrella, it saw itself as both a clearinghouse and a directing agency for American women's war activities. This self-image was not an accurate reflection, however. While the committee was busy, with its members always speaking and writing, what it was actually able to do, initiate, and accomplish off the printed page was not so evident.

The CND's men treated the Women's Committee with chivalrous disdain, as companions whose opinions could be solicited and then safely ignored. The Women's Committee could "consider" policies and plans but could not approve anything without the men's consent, and the women had no budget or power to enact any programs on its own. The problem was that the men understood that their distaff counterparts had been convened in Washington to serve as political window dressing and were empowered only as advisers, not actors. The women were not enfranchised. The Women's Committee pretended otherwise or simply refused to acknowledge this situation, however. It took the Women's Committee members some time to recognize what historians would later see so clearly: "After a while, it became evident that the government viewed the Women's Committee as a device for occupying women in harmless activities while men got on with the business of war."[11]

The Rev. Dr. Anna Howard Shaw, the proud suffrage stateswoman and eloquent standard-bearer for moderation (her critics would say "stultification") within the movement, may have recognized her predicament by then but would not admit it. Shaw had been Susan B. Anthony's protégée and had served as the NAWSA president for more than a decade. Now seventy-one years old, Shaw was a safe choice to serve as the Women's Committee chairperson: she was publicly admired, even if she was not known for her administrative skills, and though a powerful speaker, she was certainly not the rabble-rouser sort of suffragette.

Soon after her appointment as chairwoman, Shaw squirmed within the strictures placed upon her and railed against the pretty wrought iron fence placed around the Women's Committee, marking its small, decorative territory. She was embarrassed by the role the CND men allowed her, or proscribed to her—as a figurehead but not the leader of the great civilian army of women. All the immensely talented and strong-willed women on her committee who were greatly accomplished leaders of national organizations were placed in the humiliating but familiar role of the wife: they had to ask for money, they had to beg for permission, and they could be in control only over those parts of the domestic landscape deemed appropriate. Theirs were the traditional domains of women—the kitchen, the nursery, the sewing room, the sickroom—as they began canning food, raising garden tomatoes, rolling Red Cross bandages, knitting socks, weighing babies, arranging dances for soldiers, and distributing Meatless Monday menus. The surge of women entering industry—into the factories, into the railroads, into elevators and offices—was the result of market forces, not government policies or initiatives. The Women's Committee could do little but watch.

Harriot Stanton Blatch understood the subservient role of the Women's Committee and was determined to denounce it in public. Blatch went about things differently than her compatriot Anna Shaw did; she always had. Blatch was, quite literally, born into the suffrage movement. As Elizabeth Cady Stanton's daughter, she had spent her life trying to come to terms with the mantle she'd inherited and to forge her own role in the movement. An energetic, passionate, and prickly woman, she never hesitated to speak her mind or use her birthright.

A young Harriot is credited with helping to mend the rift between her mother's National Woman Suffrage Association and rival Lucy Stone's American Woman's Suffrage Association. Harriot had written a chapter on Stone's accomplishments and convinced her mother and Susan B. Anthony to include it in their landmark book *History of Woman Suffrage,* paving the way for the two groups to merge in 1890. While this joining of forces unified the suffrage movement in America, Harriot's marriage to an English businessman carried her away to live in England for twenty years. She took up the suffrage torch there, becoming an acolyte of Emmeline Pankhurst and then the leader of several suffrage societies.

Returning to America in 1902, Blatch brought a new energy and urgency, as well as Mrs. Pankhurst's confrontational tactics, to the suffrage fight. As she saw it, the American movement "bored its adherents and repelled its opponents" and needed a jolt.[12] Bankrolled by wealthy patrons like Alva Belmont, Blatch attempted to bring the raw energy of working-class women into the suffragettes' ranks, establishing the Equality League of Self-Supporting Women (later called the Women's Political Union). Blatch became as famous for her provocative street tactics and publicity ploys as for her cunning political maneuvers. In the process, she made a host of enemies, quite a few within the suffrage movement, including her longtime rival, Carrie Chapman Catt, and Anna Howard Shaw, both of whom disdained Blatch's manipulative tactics. For her part, Blatch had grown impatient with these women's old guard–style leadership and openly supported Alice Paul's militant strategies.

Though Blatch campaigned hard to defeat Woodrow Wilson in 1916, incensed after he reneged on a promise to support the national suffrage amendment, she was an early and vocal supporter of his entering the war. Unlike Catt and Jane Addams, who abhorred war and feared its retrograde effects on society, Blatch was enthralled by the war and gave it her full-throated endorsement. She allowed herself to be swept up in the romantic notion of war as an ennobling, purifying, and transformative cleansing agent for sluggish societies. Women would benefit from war too, she thought, not just in terms of eventual suffrage but in the dignity of their service. War made women more important, she contended, and more active. "When men go to a-warring, women go to work."[13]

But Blatch was not impressed with the kind of war work the Women's Committee was promoting, spreading the gospel of Hooverism. In the fall of 1917 Blatch was finishing her book *Mobilizing Woman-Power,* a passionate manifesto on the importance of women's work for the war effort that used the European experience as a template for what could be accomplished here. Theodore Roosevelt agreed to write an enthusiastic foreword for the book. "Mrs. Blatch's aim is to stir the women of this country to the knowledge that this is their war, and also to make all our people feel that we, and especially our government, should welcome the service of women, and make use of it to the utmost," TR wrote. "Mrs. Blatch has herself rendered a very real service by this appeal that women should serve, and that men should let them serve."[14]

In *Mobilizing Woman-Power*, Blatch slices to shreds Hoover's "Adamistic" food policies and propaganda. She derides them as "accusing Eve of introducing sin into the world, and calls upon her to mend her wasteful ways" while government war work policies waste the potential of women's brains and energies. "Instead of just conserving, women should be producing, becoming soldiers of the soil, not just the garbage pail," she contended.

While gathering the material for her book, Blatch found ample proof of her suspicions that the Women's Committee, while well intentioned, was simply a singing puppet delivering the government's unenlightened message, without the ability to think or act on its own. Never a woman to mince words or whisper when a bullhorn could be had, Blatch began to shout this observation aloud. In a startling "emperor has no clothes" public dispute, she broke ranks with her fellow suffragists—something she felt no qualms about doing, indeed she had done many times in her career—and blasted the committee's passivity.

"Dr. Shaw's committee has no funds at its disposal. It is told by the government to be good, raise your own funds and do as the government tells you to do," Blatch told a Boston audience in the fall. "We cannot afford to have women making bandages and knitting things for our men to wear," Blatch declared. "We must not waste women's labor in that way. They ask us to conserve, but I don't believe in peeling peaches thin when hundreds and thousands of bushels are going to waste because labor is lacking to gather them."[15] Put women in the fields, organize a land army, and produce, Blatch insisted, and don't just have women sitting by the hearth, knitting, or peeling.

The Boston Women's Committee mailed a clipping of Mrs. Blatch's incendiary comments to Dr. Shaw in Washington, and Shaw was forced to refute the accusations to her own troops. "It is true that the Women's Committee . . . is not at liberty to carry on any distinct lines of work, or to issue any form of propaganda, which does not come directly under Government control," she wrote to the Massachusetts Women's Committee branch, but all civilian committees worked under that restriction, Shaw explained. Further, while the Women's Committee had no budget of its own, it could ask for money anytime, she maintained, trying hard to dispel the image of the group going to Daddy for their allowance.

"I greatly regret that Mrs. Blatch should have been so misinformed in regard to the treatment of the Women's Committee by the government," Dr. Shaw wrote. She was not being completely honest, however; in private correspondence, Shaw had already voiced the same complaints.[16] And she voiced them to, of all people, Harriot Blatch.

"As you probably know, we are not allowed to do anything without the consent of the Council of National Defense," Dr. Shaw wrote to Blatch back in June 1917, in response to Blatch's suggestion that the newly hatched Women's Committee sponsor a speaking tour by Helen Fraser. Blatch thought Fraser, a British suffragist and organizer who was deeply knowledgeable about how Englishwomen had been mobilized, could help get the same ball rolling in the States. "Perhaps you may have guessed, even if you have no direct information on the subject, there is no appropriation for the Women's Committee," Shaw confided. When the women asked for money to invite Fraser, the men on the council said no.[17]

"The great trouble with us is that now as always men want women to do the work while they do the overseeing, even if they don't do anything about the work except the overseeing," Dr. Shaw wrote to Blatch, already frustrated after just six weeks on the job.[18] It would only get worse. But Shaw, just as a dutiful wife trapped in a bad marriage, kept up appearances and publicly defended her committee's mandate.

Ida Clyde Clarke was a veteran journalist who, in the fall of 1917, compiled a meticulously detailed account of American women's creative efforts to organize themselves for war work. Her monumental reporting effort became her book *American Women and the World War*. She immediately recognized the predicament of the Women's Committee. In assembling her homage to women's ingenuity and industry in every state, on every level, and in every line of endeavor, Clarke could, with her reporter's clear eye, see the structural weaknesses and congenital defects that would hobble the Women's Committee for all its short life:

> When the Government created its war body, at least, it followed the precedent set by the Creator of the universe, in that it created its man body first and made woman a side issue, extracting or subtracting nothing whatever from the man body in the process not even a rib or a piece of governmental backbone. That is why the Women's Committee for all the intelligence and experience and executive ability that comprise it cannot stand alone; that is why it is so frequently reminded by its superior body that it is not expected to *initiate* but should only *advise*. It was a consummation devoutly to be wished that the Government, having created the woman body of its war machine, should have breathed into it the breath of life.[19]

The nation's private women's organizations were not restricted to the role of Eve. Indeed, they had the freedom and the financial wherewithal to take action. As reports of the first farmerette experiments circulated in the fall of 1917, a wider sphere of these women's groups took notice and took steps to enter agricultural work in their own way.

The YWCA was so effective in supporting women's civilian efforts through its War Work Council that it began to explore what role, if any, the Y should take in putting women on farms. The YWCA dispatched Anna Clark, its regional field secretary, to survey the situation. She met with labor and agricultural experts who predicted an increasing demand for women's labor on farms, but they admitted the government did not have a plan for meeting this need. The dean of the Cornell School of Agriculture told her, "There was going to be a definite need for women in the more intensive farming sections. This problem should be faced." But at both the state and federal levels, Clark found, the government was not yet willing to face this problem squarely.[20]

The Land Council of the WNF&GA, buoyed by its summer successes, invited Sophia Carey of England's National Land Council to report on the work of their British "soil sisters." Carey convinced the Land Council to sponsor an American tour of a British government propaganda film starring the work of the Woman's Land Army. Land Girls on the silver screen sounded like a fine idea, and the group agreed to import and distribute the film "with the view to promoting similar work in the U.S."[21]

The WNF&GA's Midwest chapter convened a special war work conference in Chicago, with the theme of "The Need of the Hour: Young Women on the Land." The three-day program at the Morrison Hotel included reports on the land armies of Great Britain and Canada and the unit plan experiments in New York, especially the Bedford Camp. It concluded with members planning to put women on the land near Chicago in the 1918 season.[22]

The Women's University Club also decided to jump into land service. Besides sponsoring the Vassar farmerettes' public relations tour, it announced plans to enroll college women for farmwork in the spring and appointed a special Agricultural Service Committee. The club invited Vassar president MacCracken and officials from the other women's colleges who'd experimented with farmerettes to talk about their experience. MacCracken emphasized that women must take the initiative in organizing the Land Army on a national level. "Women must demonstrate their ability to do this piece of service and not depend on the Government to move first," urged MacCracken.[23]

The season of experimentation was over; the women were through waiting for a plan from Washington. If women hoped to be organized in a more comprehensive fashion for land service the following year, some central authority needed to direct the effort. If the Department of Agriculture was still resistant, if the Department of Labor was slow, and if the national Women's Committee was sympathetic but feeble, then the more intrepid women's groups and the nimbler state women's committees would have to move ahead on their own steam.

"Refusing to be in the least crushed by government neglect, far-seeing women are determined to organize widely and carefully their solution of the farm-labor problem," Harriot Blatch reported. "The mobilization of woman-power on the farm is the need of the hour."[24]

Isabella Selmes Ferguson led her New Mexico WLA farmerettes into the field. Later in her career she served in the U.S. Congress. *Palace of the Governors, New Mexico History Museum*

The WLA's Wellesley College Training Camp and Experiment Station, the West Point of the Land Army. *Wellesley College Archives*

New Mexico farmerettes cool off in a horse trough, supervised by the state WLA chair-woman, Isabella Ferguson. *Palace of the Governors, New Mexico History Museum*

Edith Diehl was already a reknowned book binder when she donned the uniform of the WLA as director of the Wellesley Camp and then national director of training. *Schlesinger Library, Radcliffe Institute, Harvard University*

Zelda Knowlton of Connecticut, an officer-in-training at the Wellesley Camp, poses in the uniform designed by Edith Diehl. *Wellesley College Archives*

The Wellesley Camp measured the physical capabilities of women to undertake hard manual labor. Here they do push-ups to get in shape. *Schlesinger Library*

A U.S. Marine leads the Wellesley Camp cadets in marching drills. Edith Diehl employed military standards to achieve discipline and efficiency. *Schlesinger Library*

Wellesley Camp WLA officers-in-training outside the tents they built themselves. Edith Diehl is seated on chair, third from right. *Wellesley College Archives*

The New York State WLA used this poster in its campaign to recruite a million "members" of the Land Army who could provide financial and moral support. *Library of Congress*

The New York State WLA campaign in September 1918 featured parades of farmerettes collecting money for the cause; this parade marched in Manhattan. *Library of Congress*

A farmerette places a membership pin on the lapel of a young Woman's Land Army supporter as part of the N.Y. state WLA membership campaign. *Library of Congress*

Farmerettes march in the Fourth Liberty Loan parade in NYC in October 1918. The Woman's Land Army had earned its place in the iconography of the war. *Library of Congress*

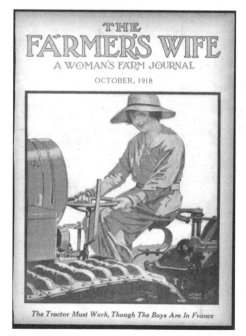

This October 1918 cover of Farmer's Wife magazine expresses the lingering ambivalence of the farming community toward the WLA: is the smiling woman driving the tractor a farmerette in a skirted uniform, or a farm wife who doesn't need city women to do heavy chores? *University of Minnesota Library*

The Farmerette was the WLA's official periodical, serving as both a source of news and a way to connect farmerette alumnae. *Barnard College Archives*

The Street Uniform

The Field Uniform

WOMAN'S
LAND ARMY
OF AMERICA

The Design

Has been adopted officially by the Woman's Land Army for spring and summer wear.

It has excellent lines—a plain box coat and straight skirt with two box plaits in the back.

The insignia, which gives the distinctive touch to the uniform, was designed by Paul Manship and executed by Gorham. It consists of bronze belt-buckle, buttons and decoration for hat and coat lapels.

The Material

Is Rookie Serge, 60% wool, with dark brown broadcloth collar. It has been shrunk and sponged against inclement weather.

The Cost

This uniform, like the field uniform, will be furnished at cost—purchaser paying express or postage.

The costume complete —suit, insignia, brown straw sailor and tie —$21.50.

A Natty Costume

for Spring and Summer Wear— Suit, Hat, Insignia, Tie $21.50

Place Order With the Chairman of the Woman's Land Army in Your State

The Design

Has been adopted officially by the Woman's Land Army.

It was developed by the Uniform Committee assisted by a practical field worker.

Clever designing and ingenious devices have made it a successful "2-in-1" costume for wear during and after working hours.

The Material

Is olive drab Khaki Kenworth cloth with green linen collar.

It is light weight and cool, but durable and is guaranteed fast color.

The Cost

The uniforms will be furnished at cost.

By ordering from the manufacturer in quantity, this cost has been cut down to the lowest figures:

Overalls—$1.80.
Coat—$2.30.
Hat—20 cents.
Total—$4.30.

Purchasers must pay express or postage.

Place Order With the Chairman of the Woman's Land Army in Your State

Official
Uniforms
for
Field and Street

National Office
19 West Forty-fourth Street
New York City

YOU will want the New Convertible Field Uniform BECAUSE—

It Is Practical   It "Standardizes" You and Your Work   It Is Attractive

Overalls $1.80   Hat 20 cents

For the Field—
You have overalls
COMFORTABLE
SERVICEABLE
CHEAP

Pull Up the Trousers —

and

Don the Coat, and You Will Have—

Turn Down the Bib—

Coat $2.30   Complete $4.30

For the Village—
A costume which is
APPROPRIATE
DISTINCTIVE
NEAT

A brochure introducing the new national WLA uniform, a "convertible" model suitable for both field and town wear: "Pull up the trousers, turn down the bib, and you will have a natty costume." *Barnard College Archives*

Dorothy Nicoll Hubert took over the presidency of the WLA just as it was negotiating to merge into the U.S. Department of Labor. *Chautauqua Institution Archives*

A WWI farmerette (right) poses with her daughter, who is dressed in the uniform of the WLA of WWII. *Library of Congress*

8

WOMEN ON THE LAND

A few days before Christmas 1917, Hilda Loines greeted the delegates walking into the Hotel Astor for what she believed would be the "Continental Congress" of the women's land service movement. At this conference, in an elegant hotel ballroom in the middle of bustling Times Square, the Woman's Land Army of America was born.

As the delegates walked into the Hotel Astor on a sunny, unseasonably mild Friday morning, the dozens of women and a few men stomped the slushy snow from their shoes. Some in the hotel ballroom were already veterans of the land service movement, including Virginia Gildersleeve of the Mayor's Committee, Delia West Marble for the Garden Club, and various members of the National League for Women's Service and the Women's National Farm and Garden Association. Representatives of the General Federation of Women's Clubs, the Intercollegiate Bureau of Occupations, and the YWCA were already involved in a wide array of women's war work initiatives. Still other women's organizations—the Association of Collegiate Alumnae, the National American Woman Suffrage Association, the New York State Suffrage Party, the Women's University Club, and the Cosmopolitan Club—saw the land service movement as a natural complement to their own goals and wanted to become more involved.

Suffragists were still giddy from their big victory in the November elections—New York State women had won the vote, the first eastern state to grant full suffrage—and they were convinced that the women's patriotic war work over the summer helped secure the win. More spectacular and visible war work by suffrage-affiliated women could be valuable in pressuring Congress to finally pass a Constitutional amendment, and this land service movement was just the ticket.

Some delegates carried the portfolios of their government bureaus born of the war: the federal Food Administration, the Labor Department's Committee of Women in Industry, and an assortment of state women's committees of defense. Members of the Farm Bureau, New York State Grange, and Cornell College of Agriculture represented the agricultural community, and state Employment Bureau officials provided expertise in labor issues.[1]

The WNF&GA organized the meeting—Hilda Loines mailed out all the invitations—in cooperation with the Garden Club of America. They had the blessing of the Women's Committee in Washington, which did not have permission to authorize this sort of war work on its own and could offer only moral, but not substantive, support.

The delegates listened to Cornell and Farmingdale agriculturalists talk about the need for women workers and heard a pep talk on the accomplishments of the Mayor's Committee units and the Bedford Camp. The Employment Bureau also gave them a sense of employment patterns. By the time the final speaker, the celebrated Helen Fraser from Great Britain, took the podium and delivered a rousing, inspirational sermon on the heroic efforts of the English Women's Land Army, the delegates needed no further convincing.[2] They agreed America needed its own army of women on the land to meet its own wartime crisis. The hour was now. In honor of their brave sisters across the ocean, they would call it the Woman's Land Army (WLA) of America.[3]

The delegates created a working committee, representing all the cooperating organizations, to figure out the details and launch the enterprise. Calling itself the Advisory Council of the Woman's Land Army of America, the group stayed at the hotel another night and spent Saturday building the framework for a nationwide program of placing women on the land. Going beyond simple patriotic fervor, these women summoned the organizational skills they'd learned in their own volunteer groups and lost no time in frivolous motion.

They formed an Executive Committee to streamline decision making. They chose Delia West Marble as chairman of the Advisory Council, Anna Gilman Hill of the Garden Club of America as vice chairman, and Louise Edgar Peters of the Woman's University Club as executive secretary. The devoted Hilda Loines again took on her customary role of recording secretary. Mary Louise Potter Bush, wife of a Columbia University philosopher, accepted the treasurer's position for an organization with no funds, while Ethel Puffer Howes, a professor and delegate from the Association of Collegiate Alumnae, became chairman of the Committee on Organization. Emma Winner Rogers, treasurer of the National American Woman Suffrage Association (and target of Herbert Hoover's ire), also joined the Advisory Council, as did WNF&GA president Louisa Yeomans King, Ida Ogilvie, and Harriot Stanton Blatch.[4] Virginia Gildersleeve also agreed to serve on the council, even though she had resigned from the Mayor's Committee following John Purroy Mitchel's defeat on Election Day. Of the two dozen or so members of the Advisory Council, only two were men: George Powell, the farmerette's staunch advocate and friend, and John G. Curtis, a Westchester County Farm Bureau agent who had witnessed the women's land work capabilities the previous summer.

The Advisory Council sketched out a mechanism for task-specific working groups and for building state and local divisions of the Land Army, but it left most details for another day. After all, the members had just three days to hurry home and wrap the modest, thrifty gifts appropriate for this first Christmas of the war in America. They had accomplished what they came to do.

This Woman's Land Army existed on paper now, however crudely, but it still needed to be built: its shape, structure, and systems designed; its working parts fabricated. The Advisory Council had to put together an army—quickly.

The council could not wait for the printed stationery to arrive, so the first Woman's Land Army communiqués simply bore a plain typescript letterhead with a borrowed office address and a telephone switchboard number. By the first days of the New Year, letters announcing the debut of the Woman's Land Army, its raison d'être, and its plan of action arrived on desks of people whose help and cooperation the WLA needed around the country. "The seriousness of the approaching crisis in the agricultural situation calls for immediate and concerted action," Delia West Marble wrote. "Let us know what you will be able to do in this great movement to place women on the land."[5]

The first weeks of January were a blur for the Advisory Council members, who attended a long chain of meetings and strategy sessions and heard proposals. These experienced club and organization women knew how to get things done. They got their message out in long, detailed policy letters; in handwritten personal notes; and in snappy public relations ploys.

Copying the model that seemed to work so well for the National League for Women's Service, the Advisory Council decided to tap the structural resources of existing women's groups and avoid reinventing the wheel just to get rolling. The WLA also decided to try and work through the agricultural and Employment Bureau machineries already in place in the states—that is, if they were willing to include women in their plans and willing to accept the WLA's rules on wages and hours.

As to financing, they did not kid themselves. The government was not going to write them a check anytime soon, so the money had to come from cooperating groups' coffers and sympathetic supporters' purses. Patriotic pleas were dispatched to a wide variety of women's organizations, from garden clubs to suffrage and even anti-suffrage societies, college alumnae groups to labor and working women's welfare organizations, with very specific instructions on how they could help recruit and sponsor units of women farmworkers in the spring.

The WLA asked agricultural colleges to provide short training courses for unit leaders and speakers to convince the farmers. Alumnae groups and the YWCA could help find older women who would be suitable for leadership and chaperone duties. Trade schools and college departments of "home economics"—a new field—could offer trained dieticians to cook for the workers. A special request also went out to women's colleges to substitute gardening classes for gymnasium requirements and to give academic credit for women's spring Land Army service. The council assigned the Garden Club of America to gather information on local farming conditions and labor needs and to begin raising money to support units in their communities. It also asked trade unionists to start "a propaganda among the women employed in the seasonal trades" to join the Land Army and women's social club members to recruit "among the women of leisure living in their towns and villages, with the object of persuading them to do their part in this work in a spirit of wholehearted patriotism."[6]

To stimulate the growth of state branches, the WLA decided to piggyback on the shoulders of its faithful benefactor, the WNF&GA. Its representatives in every state were instructed to confer with their state's Council of Defense Women's Committee and draw together all other interested regional parties to plan for the Land Army's deployment. Within a few weeks WLA chairwomen were appointed in fifteen states, and state organizations began to take shape. It was at the state and local levels that the nitty-gritty work of putting units on the ground had to be done.[7]

Instructions were also issued to the state chairs on how to elicit cooperation from their state labor and farm bureaus, how to develop county working groups, and how to launch recruitment drives. Arrangements were also made for Helen Fraser, the famous British woman's war work propagandist, to tour the states and whip up enthusiasm.

George Powell, the Land Army's devoted friend, provided an essential bridge to the agricultural community: he used his influential position as president of the Agricultural Experts Association to promote the fledgling WLA. He personally attended Grange meetings in many rural communities during the winter of 1918, securing a spot on the agenda to give a firsthand testimonial to the farmerettes' work and women's potential for solving the labor shortage.

On Powell's visits to the Grange halls, sometimes Vassar or Barnard farmerettes accompanied him and often women from the Advisory Council joined him to answer questions. Occasionally the women struck out on their own, sponsored by a grant from the Women's University Club. Their tour of Grange halls was sponsored by a grant from the Women's University Club. Agricultural school staff, Farm Bureau, and extension agents also gave lectures advertising the WLA. The WLA's emissaries carried with them lantern slides of the farmerettes at work, and sometimes, if there was a moving picture projector available, the British Land Army film to illustrate their talks. As one WLA organizer explained, persuading the farmers is "best done by eye."[8]

At the Grange halls they also distributed the new, hot-off-the-press WLA brochure "Help for the Farmer," one of a series of quickly penned pamphlets the Advisory Council issued in January and February.[9] The first publication was an eight-page call to plows entitled "Women on the Land," which, adorned with gorgeous art nouveau pen-and-ink motifs, set out the philosophical and practical case for forming a Land Army in America. Beginning with a sketch of the British experience in organizing women farmworkers, it continued with a report on the Mayor's Committee experiments, the

Bedford Camp, and Vassar farmerettes, and included highly complimentary letters from farmers. It emphasized the WLA's role as a patriotic endeavor.[10]

Another publication the WLA headquarters' volunteers churned out in the first few weeks was a step-by-step manual on "The Organization of Agricultural Units" for state and county WLA affiliates to use. Every WLA chairwoman kept this slim guidebook on her writing table or in her purse, its pages creased, dog-eared, and underlined. The manual detailed everything from financing and staffing different types of units to negotiating with farmers; from the best size sleeping tents to the most durable automobile tire tubes; from the advisability of keeping a pig to the use of paper plates. It made important distinctions between unequivocal standards—the eight-hour day, equal pay, no undercutting of male wages, and social equality within the units ("all workers shall be on the same social plane")—and those rules that could be bent when necessary, such as household duties and disciplinary measures.

The organization manual is an impressive work of synthesis, analysis, and fearless induction. Drawing from the scanty data of the previous summer's few field experiments, the WLA's architects contrived an elaborate blueprint of how to build, feed, and manage a Land Army unit anywhere in the country. With only slight modifications for regional conditions or special situations, the tabletop model they glued together in their minds held up remarkably well in the dust of the field.[11]

The Woman's Land Army introduced itself to the public in a little pamphlet handed out at recruitment meetings, mailed out to organizers, and distributed to the press. The brochure presented the rationale for the Land Army, opening with "The Problem" the agricultural sector faced and the "Facts Which Have Been Proved" about women's ability on the land and concluding with "The Solution" that the Land Army promised to provide. With the voice of calm reason dismissing absurdity and cool logic trumping silliness, the WLA founders assert, "Prejudices against women as farm laborers will not hold against the desperate sense of need of the farmer and the proved fact of women's efficiency. It is idle to say that women can not do farm work when it is known that they actually have done it." The proof was in the women-plowed fields of 1917, the pamphlet maintained, and the nation could not afford to waste time debating the matter. "The question of questions for the farmer and for the world is not what women can do but what they will do."[12]

After launching the first publications, after several weeks of frenetic activity, it became obvious that a different, more direct structure of responsibilities was needed for the WLA to function efficiently. The Advisory Council was too large and unwieldy, it could not respond quickly, and tasks were too broadly defined. So the council went through a process of natural differentiation, dividing itself into working organs—namely, a General Executive Committee and four standing committees: finance, organization, publicity, and training. As in all formative organizations, there was some jockeying for power and some bruised egos. Delia West Marble was gently removed from administrative power, though she still stood as the head of a reduced Advisory Council, while Emma Winner Rogers was asked to lead the Executive Committee. The headquarters also moved from its borrowed rooms within the WNF&GA office in the YWCA building on Lexington Avenue and settled downtown on lower Fifth Avenue near Tenth Street.

While the WLA was busy inventing itself, financial matters took a backseat to structural concerns, but as spring approached, funding became an urgent issue. "In April it appeared obvious we must have money," recalled Ethel Puffer Howes, who was then serving as the WLA's vice chairman. "And we couldn't have money by popular subscription. We had to have people of influence to get it."[13]

Realistically, the WLA could not sponsor a Land Army fund-raising drive of pennies from schoolchildren or pay-envelope deductions like those used for war bonds. The WLA was a patriotic employment service, a self-sustaining operation and not a charity. To begin operations and to prime the pump, it would have to rely on the largesse of sympathetic and wealthy supporters; the WLA needed to attract influential people who knew how and whom to ask for money. The WLA consulted lawyers, who advised forming a legal corporation as a vital first step toward being able to solicit donations, sign contracts, and execute loans. The proper papers were drawn, and in late April the Woman's Land Army of America was incorporated under the laws of New York State. The members of the corporation included Harriot Stanton Blatch, Juliet Morgan Hamilton, Mary L. Bush, Martha Brooks Hutchinson, and Marion C. Davison of New York; Edith Macy of Washington, D.C.; and Mary Belle King Sherman, president of the Federation of Women's Clubs of Chicago.[14] So the WLA restructured again, dissolving the Advisory Council and Executive Committee and replacing them with a twenty-one-member Board of Directors, which wrote a constitution and set of bylaws, to meet the stipulations of a proper corporation.

While the list of names on the official WLA letterhead kept getting longer, and the titles under those names kept changing as the corporate structure shifted, the fledgling organization's basic mission remained constant—to put women on the land in the 1918 season. This effort required several simultaneous feats of persuasion: coaxing experienced women to assume WLA leadership roles, cajoling clubs and individuals to put up the money to sponsor units, convincing government and agricultural agencies of the efficacy of women laborers, and converting the farmers of America to the idea that women could really help them.

> Women of America, you can save the world in this crisis.
> Women of America, will you do it?
> Farmers of America, give the women a chance![15]

9

A HYSTERICAL APPEAL

On a Monday morning in early February, Delia West Marble and Anna Gilman Hill took the train from New York's Pennsylvania Station to Union Station in Washington. They planned to lobby on behalf of the Woman's Land Army. When they arrived at the offices of the U.S. Department of Agriculture (USDA), they were treated to the royal runaround.

"On February 4 Miss Marble and Mrs. Hill of New York City called here to discuss the question of woman farm labor," Assistant Secretary of Agriculture R. Pearson wrote to another secretary. "They came to my office, and I think they were referred from your office.

"I pointed out to them some of the difficulties as well as advantages of women workers on the farm, and I emphasized that many women could serve best toward increasing food production by helping in the farm homes, or by taking the place of certain men in factories and stores who in turn might go to farms." He observed that Miss Marble and Mrs. Hill took his advice politely but were nonetheless persistent. "They are going forward with their plans to get women into farm work," Pearson reported wearily.[1]

The WLA lobbyists were bounced from one bureaucrat's office to another, and their encounter was only the beginning of a strange and strained relationship with Washington. It was a most awkward dance, and the federal government was a reluctant partner, doing its best to pretend that the Woman's Land Army did not exist and ignoring the hand the WLA proffered. The official Washington attitude was that these women in khaki overalls and bloomers had not been asked to help in the fields, it was not their place; they were not needed; and they were a nuisance.

The Agriculture Department's policy makers seemed genuinely hostile toward the concept of women farmworkers. The positive report that Assistant Secretary Carl Vrooman's staff had written the previous fall after visiting the Bedford Camp was deep-sixed. Though Vrooman circulated it to his departmental superiors, it went unacknowledged and was buried in a file cabinet.[2]

A USDA chief inspector in New York also had his knuckles rapped. Harry Shaw attended a February meeting the WLA Advisory Council convened to bring together WLA organizers with labor and agricultural experts. Shaw was impressed with the sincerity and practicality of the WLA's plans and wrote a note to his boss in Washington: "As you well know, the President has urged the farmers of this country largely to increase farm production, but the labor situation has become acute. The women realize this and are nobly and patriotically offering their services. They seek the recognition of the Administration."[3]

This request did not sit well, especially with Assistant Agriculture Secretary Clarence Ousley. The man in charge of public and press relations, Ousley was adamantly, almost apoplectically, opposed to using women labor on farms.

> Please say to Mr. Shaw that the Department does not care to take any
> leadership in the matter of urging women to do farm labor because we
> believe that if the able-bodied men of farm experience in towns and cities
> can be released for agricultural labor, it would be better for women to supply
> their places in the towns than for any general movement to be undertaken at
> this time to use women for farm labor.[4]

Of course, Ousley's policy was predicated on a rather large "if"—that in the cities there would be enough able-bodied men unfit for the draft and willing to take on low-paying farmwork when they could earn much more in factories or that sallow male office workers would be eager or able to abandon their desks for plows. But no matter; that was the official USDA line, and no one could deviate from it. "We do not deem it discreet or in the least necessary for the Department to make any special utterance on the subject," he insisted.

Ousley was not an old hand at the department. A newspaperman from Texas who had been in his Washington job less than a year, he wasn't really the public servant sort. Agriculture Secretary David Houston had brought Ousley aboard after the 1917 food riots to help fend off critics and craft a coherent, calming message. Ousley was blunt, opinionated, and accustomed to expressing his thoughts colorfully in his publications. Some of his editorial opinions were outrageously racist and inflammatory, some just conservative, and some just ill tempered. He had a hard time biting his tongue but no trouble biting off heads. Ousley was not a booster of suffrage-type women clamoring for their chance to put on pants and to plow.

Another USDA staffer upset Ousley when he wrote a memo with the clear assumption women laborers would be needed and should be used on farms that coming season. It was just a matter of building the best apparatus for placing them there, the staffer told Ousley. He suggested an official government program to recruit, train, and place women farmworkers, including "one or more 'Plattsburgh Schools'" for training their leaders.[5] Ousley made his displeasure known.

A similar fate awaited a policy statement USDA agriculturalist E. V. Wilcox wrote. He asserted it was time to acknowledge the summer experiments' positive results. "The experience has shown that women can do any kind of manual labor which does not require physical exertion beyond the limits of their strength," he wrote. Then he set forth an approach for evaluating whether women were needed in a particular farming community and how they could be adequately trained and housed. It was exactly the sort of thoughtful response the Woman's Land Army and its supporters were so eager to receive, but Wilcox's policy statement never saw the light of day.[6]

While Clarence Ousley struggled to keep the USDA staff in line, he also tried to protect his department from the noisy attack of outside agitators—advocates of this Land Army nonsense—banging on his department's door. Miss Marble and Mrs. Hill's unwelcome visit was only the first of a parade of Woman's Land Army ambassadors assaulting USDA's offices in person, by mail, by petition, and by pressure. There were a "great number of organizations . . . making a hysterical appeal for the use of women on farms," Ouslcy complained.[7]

Perhaps no episode better illustrates the Department of Agriculture's equivocation than the campaign to have President Wilson give his blessing to the Woman's Land Army of America. The WLA leaders believed his endorsement would give the organization a stamp of legitimacy, provide a boost for recruitment and fund-raising, and help convince reluctant farmers, making it almost unpatriotic to refuse the women's help. Ethel Puffer Howes of the WLA's Executive Committee tackled the task of shepherding a statement of endorsement through the bureaucratic maze and getting the president's signature, but she didn't realize just what a frustrating quest it would be. Dr. Howes, a Harvard-trained psychologist, started the assignment with brisk enthusiasm. At age forty-six she was on leave from her academic career to care for her two children, who were younger than three years of age, in her Scarsdale house.[8] Dr. Howes was eager to harness some of her formidable mental energy to the cause of war work, and this innovative Land Army appealed to her.

With professorial care she prepared the documents to make the WLA's case to Secretary Houston, including a description of the group's lofty goals, its organizational chart (which was changing every day), a list of its prominent officers and supporters, and letters of recommendation. Recognizing the pressing demands on President Wilson and his staff and wanting to frame the tone of the message herself, Howes also included a draft of the kind of letter of endorsement the WLA sought:

> I am gratified to hear of the plan of the Woman's Land Army of America to
> help increase the food supply of our country and our allies by calling on our
> active and patriotic young womanhood to form self-sustaining groups or
> units to aid in cultivating crops where the farmers have need of them. I trust

that like the farmers of Great Britain and Canada, they will avail themselves
of this aid to the full extent of its offering, and that the response of our loyal
young women will be as generous and complete.

It was brief and to the point. "We trust this letter would not be in contradiction to your
views," she wrote soothingly to Houston.[9]

Mrs. Howes received no reply. Two weeks later she wrote to Houston again. Her
tone remained pleasant, with just a hint of annoyance at the lack of response. She cast
this letter as an update of the first; things at the Woman's Land Army were moving so
quickly that they had accomplished so much more in the intervening weeks. "The
organization is a thoroughly responsible one and is becoming increasingly well backed
financially," Howes wrote. She emphasized the well-known women serving on the board,
aware that their names would ring a bell in Washington: Emma Winner Rogers, Virginia
Gildersleeve, Mrs. August Belmont, and Mrs. Willard Straight. In case Secretary Houston
didn't get the point, Howes also dropped the names of men who "are warmly in favor of the
movement," such as the friendly agriculturalists George Powell and Lou Sweet of Colorado. She included Westchester area gentleman farmers who had employed farmerettes
the previous summer on their estates, men with such recognizable names as Felix Warburg
and Adolph Lewisohn—names not usually associated with feminist fringe elements.

"The farmers want it," Howes emphasized, citing the farmer's letters that were "pouring in in great numbers, not only at our headquarters but at the [federal and state
employment] bureaus," asking for women to help. "A letter of encouragement and approval
from President Wilson would be of the greatest service," Howes repeated. "May we not
now count on your concurrence with the idea of such a letter of endorsement?"[10]

Still she received no reply.

Mrs. Howes and the WLA Board of Directors were losing patience. They decided to
ask their friends to intervene and badger the administration on their behalf. "The officers of the Woman's Land Army have asked me to intercede for them with you," wrote
James E. Russell, the dean of Teachers College of Columbia University, to Secretary
Houston. "There is a tremendous shortage in farm labor, and I do know personally of
the success which the camp at Mt. Kisco met with last summer. The women actually
saved the crops when men were not available."[11]

"A Mrs. Howes has been after me for weeks," complained George Creel, the
director of the Committee of Public Information, the government's powerful and
highly effective war propaganda machine, in a memo to Secretary Houston. Obviously Ethel Howes was waging a two-pronged advance and going straight to the
White House by way of Creel's office, which would actually issue such a presidential letter. This Howes woman was "asking a letter from the President endorsing her
scheme for 'The Women's Land Army,'" Creel bellowed. "I told her frankly that I
would not move a hand in the matter without your specific endorsement. Will you

be kind enough to let me know your feeling in the matter?"[12]

Responding to Creel, Secretary Houston ducked the issue. "I turned [Mrs. Howes's] letter over to [Labor] Secretary William Wilson, in as much as the proposal involves the question of mobilizing women in urban communities and therefore comes within his jurisdiction," he explained. The departments had divided responsibilities: USDA would handle rural recruitment of workers while the Labor Department would take on mobilization of urban dwellers for agriculture and industry. "I do not know to what extent Secretary Wilson has been in touch with this movement or to what extent he might care to take action in this direction. . . . I prefer that he indicate whether or not he wishes any endorsement given to the movement."[13]

The Department of Labor's stance was as conflicted as the USDA's but perhaps less dogmatic. The Labor Department's job was to get working bodies where they were needed, and those bodies' precise anatomy seemed less important as the war and the military draft progressed. And unlike the Agriculture Department, the Labor Department had already acclimated to the shock of women working in new places. In late January 1918, the Labor Department announced plans to register women for farmwork, hoping to avert severe shortages forecast for the eastern states. "Women will be needed for light labor, not called upon for heavy work as long as men are available," a departmental bulletin explained. But six weeks later another bulletin insisted that any labor shortfall could be met without using women workers. "The sources of farm labor lie this year in the local unemployed farm laborer, single and married men in cities, and boys."[14] But a week later, the official U.S. Employment Service publication reported that county farm agents in numerous states would be experimenting with paid women labor on farms.[15] There was a disconnect between what was happening in the field and what Washington was willing to condone.

Neither Secretary Houston nor Assistant Secretary of Labor Louis Post wanted to sign off on an endorsement of the Woman's Land Army, yet George Creel seemed to think that the Land Army was a good idea—both a new and picturesque type of war work and a novel expression of women's patriotism. Creel knew the British got a great deal of mileage out of their Land Army, such as terrific newsreel footage, and he liked the idea of giving the venture a presidential endorsement. So by April 10 the WLA could release to the press an official letter of endorsement, on White House stationery, signed by the president: "I am gratified to hear of the plan of the Woman's Land Army. . . ."

Ethel Puffer Howes was very pleased that the text of the president's letter was exactly the statement she had written for him. It was "signed by Woodrow Wilson without the change of a comma," she noted with pride.[16]

Still, just as the president's endorsement of the WLA was being published in newspapers around the country, Assistant Secretary Ousley wrote on USDA letterhead, "The Department has not given its endorsement to any particular organization directing the work of women on farms."[17]

10

A FINE PROPAGANDA: THE FAIR
FARMERETTE AND HER PUBLICITY MACHINE

For a newspaper or magazine editor the Woman's Land Army had it all: war duty, novelty, controversy, pretty girls in exotic costume, crusty old farmers, and picturesque poses. It was something new—wholesome but also outlandish, bucolic but patriotic. It made for great copy and terrific photos.

It even provided fodder for biting satire. The WLA was barely a month old when it was first lampooned in the political cartoon magazine *Puck* with illustrations by the up-and-coming artist Rockwell Kent, using a pseudonym, no less. With a wide wink Kent took the nom de plume "William Hogarth, Jr.," when penning illustrations for magazines ranging from the socialist standard *The Masses* to the cocktail set's *Vanity Fair*. Since its founding in 1877 *Puck* had delighted in skewering the politicians and social movements of the Gilded Age and often put suffragists within its bull's-eye. Now *Puck* paired Kent's illustrations with the humorist George S. Chappell's sly verses to create "The Fair Farmerettes and Their Shameless Chauffeurs" in its January 20, 1918, issue.

> *When lovely ladies cease to loaf*
> *Their chauffeurs do not have to chauf*

Accompanying Kent's stunning modernistic drawings of lithesome young ladies in frilly-bottomed overalls and pointy shoes tending the soil and handsome drivers sleeping or snacking by their idle limousines were Chappell's cutting couplets.

> *Dora, for her country's sake*
> *Labors till her muscles ache.*
> *Joseph, always wide-awake*
> *Wishes he might be a rake.*
> *Rhoda, loyal to the nation,*
> *Does her bit for conservation.*

Adolph, though of lowly station,
Quite approves her cultivation.[1]

And so on.

While the WLA Advisory Council may not have appreciated seeing their young movement parodied in verse, they could take some pleasure in knowing they'd arrived on the national scene in sophisticated style. And as many were veterans of the long and often-spoofed suffrage campaign, they'd been the target of Puck's slings before and knew how to take them.

Further, the Woman's Land Army was also able to present its own calling card to the press, one of more agreeable design. Announcing that its members were eager to talk, the WLA made them available for interviews and offered the press story ideas. Just as George Creel was selling the government's war aims to the public by feeding the press a tasty diet of stories, the WLA would sell its whole-grain farmerette story to the nation.

The press ate it up. "Call for Women for a 'Land Army'" was the headline in the *New York Herald* in January, "Fifty Thousand Farmerettes to Be Recruited for Farm Work as a Patriotic War Service." The long article continued on a second page—"Fair Farmers Working to Win War; Sex Makes Good at This Hard Labor"—and featured pictures of women in overalls harrowing and hoeing and Professor Ida Ogilvie in a cameo portrait. "Women farm hands have proved a success wherever they have been tried out," Dr. Ogilvie assured the Herald's readers.

"We shall probably meet a great deal of opposition from the farmers and have a difficult time persuading them to give the girls a chance," she cautioned, with the air of a general assessing battlefield dangers. "We did last year up at our Mount Kisco centre, but after the farmers once tried the farmerettes their objections were promptly overcome.

"The success of our plan depends upon the women of America, who can save the world in this food crisis," said Ogilvie.[2]

From the outset the WLA did its utmost to dispel the impression—so hilariously conveyed in the *Puck* parody—of farmerettes as frivolous dilettantes who joined the movement as a lark and treated it as a costume party. Over and over the leaders spoke of the diversity and the mixed-class (though never mixed-race) nature of the ideal WLA camp. The WLA welcomed to its ranks young women office workers, teachers, and factory workers, along with those of the leisure class. "The army is a body of women who have enlisted to serve in the fields just as their brothers are serving in the trenches," emphasized Mrs. A. Gordon Norrie, a WLA Executive Committee member, in a newspaper interview. Trying to distance the new movement from the earlier female Preparedness Movement "show camps," she continued, "They are to work for the farmers and under their direction as regular paid farm hands. They are not to be tea party gardeners nor vacant lot experimenters. They will not have fancy camps to show off their uniforms. These women farmers will go out into regular barracks, like soldiers."[3]

The WLA's cultivation of the press through the first weeks of its organizational life paid off handsomely in February, when the *New York Times* ushered the farmerettes into the national spotlight. On February 3 the *New Times Magazine* featured a guided tour of the Land Army's ambitions—"Girl Laborers on Small Farms at $2 a Day"—conducted by the vice chairman of the WLA Advisory Council, Anna Gilman Hill.[4]

The article let Mrs. Hill paint a portrait of the WLA as it wanted to be seen—as a serious war work agency that was also healthy and fun for the women. Mrs. Hill's own portrait graced the center of the article; in a carefully posed tableau, she is seated on a bench in her East Hampton garden, surrounded by trellises of roses, blooming potted plants, and gardening tools tucked against the garden wall. She wears a stylish striped dress with lace at the collar, visually reassuring the *Times*'s readers that the WLA was not some radical suffragist conspiracy to undermine the nations' agrarian morals.

But what Mrs. Hill actually said to the *Times* reporter was not typical lady gardener fare. She wrestled to the ground the rumors and misconceptions still stalking the farmerette movement, most especially the fears about women's health and safety. "We hear an outcry that it is cruel to make women work in the fields, that it is un-American and all wrong generally. Well, we shall not allow it to be any of those things," she told the *Times* reporter. "The reason women's work on farms has not generally been successful is because of the housing problem. You cannot expect girls to live as day laborers can—in tin boxes or corrugated iron shacks. You make provision for them to live in a healthy fashion. That is the great need behind our unit plan."

The decorous but straight-talking Mrs. Hill was blunt in her assessment of the frosty reception WLA volunteers could expect to receive when they first entered into service:

> At first the farmer is prejudiced against the idea, and does not want the "farmerettes". One farmer after another says, "I won't have girls fussing around on my farm." Then there comes a day when something must be done at once, and there aren't enough men. He decides to try a pair of these despised "city girls". They work out well. After that he is a steady customer. The Bedford County farmers declared with one voice after the last summer that they could not get along without the "farmerettes".

The *Times* published an accompanying editorial on the same day. In "Women on the Farms," the newspaper approached the WLA with a wide-angle lens, putting it into the context of women replacing men in industry during the war. While women entering factories encountered hostility, especially from labor unions, "one phase of the female labor development is exceptional in that it meets no opposition from unionized male labor," the *Times* noted. "This is the effort, now expanding, to supply girls as unskilled farm laborers." The reason for the contrast, the *Times* reasoned, was that farmworkers did not pose a threat to organized labor.

> The unionized workman is a city dweller, disliking the country, caring not at all who does the farm work. It is no affair of his if the woman chooses to toil on a farm for $2 a day. He will fight back if she takes his place in a factory or store, or on a street car; but she can till every farm and plantation in the universe without arousing his ire.
>
> So the Land Army of America faces no handicap of male objections, so long as it can enlist girls sturdy enough to satisfy the farmers that they are worthy of their hire.[5]

The *Times* made it sound so simple.

As part of its public relations campaign, the WLA's organizers ingeniously kept the Land Army in the public eye with a barrage of letters to the editor and news articles written by or about the Land Army. WLA Advisory Council member Louisa Yeomans King, who was also president of the WNF&GA, engineered more mileage out of the *New York Times's* editorial by writing a long letter of thanks to the editors. "The subject grows more insistent with each day of melting snows," she wrote from her gardens in Alma, Michigan. "People are now fairly well alive to the need of food saving; to the more important one of food production many are still dead. If we do not produce, how can we save?"

Besides questioning the priorities of Hoover's Food Administration, Mrs. King— known as the "Queen of American Gardens" for her popular books on the subject— took a jab at the stubborn resistance of the Labor and Agriculture departments:

> In the Eastern States today men are scarcely to be had for farming. The value of the high school boy on the farm is one concerning which there is a wide difference of opinion. Women in England have shown most nobly what they can do for the crops. Women in this country are showing their will and ability in the same direction. Those who undertake it will learn new lessons which will serve them well throughout their lives. They will have established for themselves a new connection between brains and agriculture.[6]

Brains and agriculture were the topics of another spread the *Times* devoted to the WLA just a few days later. This strategic placement was clearly timed to the kickoff of the WLA's recruitment campaign. Helen Kennedy Stevens, a Barnard College senior who'd served at the Bedford Camp, wrote a firsthand account. The model of an ideal farmerette—articulate, pretty, athletic, and funny—she would serve as the farmerettes' public face, embarking on a campus recruitment tour for the WLA and then coordinating publicity in its headquarters. The *New York Times Sunday Magazine* of February 24 featured her vivid report of farmerette living and of the dual existence of the sophisticated but dedicated Land Army girl.

"City Girl as Farm Worker—Her Own Story" opened with a diptych set of portraits of Stevens: on the left side, looking coyly at the camera she is in a flowing, blousy dress, with her hair coiffed and her hand poised on a parlor wall; and on the right, looking forthrightly at her readers, she stands squarely in overalls, boots, and a middy blouse, with a hoe hoisted over her shoulder. "In two roles," the caption explains, "New Yorker in winter, farmerette in summer."

In her rollicking memoir Stevens described:

> apple picking in an old orchard, where we had to use forty-foot ladders. Coming down a forty-foot ladder with a full basket of apples is a circus stunt, I can tell you. Then there was cutting and loading corn for the silo, and potato digging was also a husky harvesting job. The corn cutting was picturesque, but the corn rash we got was not. Preparation for a day in corn was chiefly putting old stockings on our arms.[7]

Like Stevens, Harriet Geithmann was a literary-minded young farmerette from Washington State who had also served in the Bedford Camp in 1917. She had written about her own experiences in "Chronicles of Woodcock Farm: A Glimpse of Woman's Labor on the Farms of 1917," published in *Overland Monthly.* "Morning came, the gong rang at five and I tumbled out of my blankets, washed, jumped into overalls, grabbed a milk pail and dashed for Susie, a big-eyed Jersey," Geithmann quoted from her diary. "Tilting merrily on a three-legged stool with the pail pinched between my knees, I soon persuaded the rich yellow streams of milk to dance into the pail."[8]

The patriot woman could have it all. Stevens's and Geithmann's narratives afforded the kind of endorsement the Land Army movement needed most. They told the dear readers that it was perfectly acceptable to have their daughters, sisters, and perhaps even wives enter into land service. Becoming a farmerette was respectable.

Besides using the nickname of "farmerette," the press began to call the woman volunteering for land service "Maud Muller," a reference to the heroine of a popular John Greenleaf Whittier poem by that title, one that every schoolchild learned by heart. It was an easy but not an apt allusion. Whittier's Maud Muller is a simple, uneducated, but luscious-looking farmer's daughter who regrets not riding off with a handsome stranger and spends the rest of her life, trapped and resentful, on the land. Not exactly

fitting the image of the smiling and eager Land Army woman captured by press photographers, American newspapers still found "Maud Muller" a convenient shorthand
for any woman who engaged in farmwork, who "on a summer's day, raked the meadow
sweet with hay." The farmerettes just had to accept their literary fate.

As spring planting season approached and food supply tensions mounted, the WLA's
publicity efforts intensified. Hoping to make service in the Land Army the equivalent
of other, perhaps more romantic war work options available to women—Red Cross
nurse, Western Union "Hello Girl," and Motor Corps driver—WLA organizers didn't
wait for editors to notice them and good press to come their way. Instead, they sharpened their pens and wrote their own tributes to the movement.

WLA leader Emma Winner Rogers made her pitch in "Wanted—The Woman's
Land Army!" published in the May 1918 issue of *Forum* magazine.[9] Louisine (Mrs.
Harry O.) Havemeyer turned her attention from suffrage activities to campaigning for
the Land Army. She supported it in the flesh, embarking on a grueling recruitment tour
and serving on the WLA Advisory Board; with cash, making generous financial contributions; and in print, writing most notably for *Touchstone* magazine "The Woman's
Land Army of America: What It Can Do for the Farmer." Here Mrs. Havemeyer, widow
of the Sugar King, mixed standard Land Army rationale (borrowed whole cloth from
WLA publications) with riffs written in her own wondrously florid style:

> Women have been advised to keep well in the background during this
> war and not to disturb anything or anyone! But, Mother Earth says:
> "Come and disturb me; the more you dig me up the more I will yield;
> plow me deep, score my wide and broad surface with furrows and great
> will be your harvest. While you till the earth by the sweat of your brow, I
> will paint your cheeks with the color of the rose; I will increase your
> stature, your health, your knowledge and your happiness. I will teach
> you, daughters, the beauty of dawn, your ears shall learn the music of the
> rain and of the birds. Sleeping under God's beautiful service flag, the
> sky, you will find a new meaning in life."[10]

Land service also called the daughters of presidents. In mid-March the *Washington
Post* reported that "Abraham Lincoln's great-granddaughter announces she will plow
her family farm fields in Vermont on a tractor this summer." It quoted Mary Lincoln
Beckwith as saying, "I could not sit on a veranda . . . and knit when there was a man's
place to be filled here." Further, she "has purchased a tractor which she will attach to an
automobile and thus do her plowing without discomfort."[11]

And Helen Taft, the twenty-six-year-old daughter of former President William

Howard Taft, gave a great boost to the Land Army's cause when the *Ladies' Home Journal* published her memoir of serving as a farmerette the previous summer. Taft, who had served as her father's official White House hostess during her mother's illness in 1909 and was the dean of Bryn Mawr College, made it seem a perfectly natural thing for her to choose to become a farmerette:

> The first impulse was to learn nursing and go to France; but for a good
> many of us that was impossible. Then we began to hear of the shortage of
> laborers on the farms and of the great need of increasing the supply of
> food. . . . I don't think that I deserve much credit for choosing farming as
> my form of patriotic service; but one has the satisfaction of knowing that
> there is no form of work which is more needed.

Taft recounted how she took time out from her summer dissertation research to serve her country with a hoe, first on her brother's farm in Ohio and then with the Bryn Mawr farmerettes on their war farm in West Chester, Pennsylvania. The most formidable challenge she faced "was in making the farmer take my labor seriously," she explained.

> This is bound to be everyone's difficulty in the beginning. American farmers
> being a conservative race, as are farmers everywhere, and never having seen
> women working in the fields, are hard to convince that a woman has any
> business being there. She can manage a little weeding or hoeing perhaps, but
> when it comes to plowing or cultivating or haying the farmer insists on
> regarding female assistance as absolutely out of the question. If left to
> himself, therefore, the farmer gets very little good out of women helpers, and
> we have to face the difficulty of proving to the farmers that women can be
> taught to do pretty nearly anything that men can do, and that the heavier
> tasks in farming they really enjoy."[12]

Attending women's war work conferences around the country, Taft also helped the WLA muster support and recruits with a lecture series on "farmeretting."

Local newspapers began carrying news of the Land Army, first in carrying gee-whiz features based on the East Coast experiences and then covering the detailed organizational efforts in their own state or community. The articles about the WLA usually appeared on the "woman's page" adjacent the Hoover-approved recipes and waste elimination tips distributed by the Food Administration; newspapers were expected to publish them as part of their war obligations. In every local paper, no matter how small, space was devoted to women's war work news. The papers highlighted the national and state activities of the Women's Committee of the Council of National Defense

(supplied by Ida Tarbell and her busy press writers) along with local initiatives, including weekly inventories of the number of socks and hats knitted and of bandages rolled
by every church basement affiliate of the Red Cross in town.

In the spring more Woman's Land Army features appeared in America's most popular magazines, from *House Beautiful* to *St. Nicholas* (an article for children entitled
"Farmerette's Battalion"), *Touchstone* to *Scientific American*, and of course, the modern
homemaker's bible, *Ladies' Home Journal.* As one of the most widely read women's
publications, the *Ladies' Home Journal* assumed a special role in educating the American
woman in her wartime responsibilities as both commander of the household and citizen of the world. *Ladies' Home Journal* editor Edward William Bok brought the war
directly into his middle- and upper-middle-class subscribers' parlors, but he carefully
placed it on a lacy doily. In its pages readers could find recipes for War Cake, Liberty
Ices, Victory Crust, Victory Bread, and Wheatless-Wednesday menus Herbert Hoover
personally endorsed. Hoover's byline appeared on *Journal* articles exhorting voluntary
rather than compulsory food and fuel conservation, for he argued, it was a test of
American character. He even fielded readers' questions in the regular feature "Questions to Mr. Hoover."

While the *Journal's* advertisements promised products to help the patriotic woman
maintain her complexion as she kept her proper Hoover household—all while wearing
her Hoover Helper costume, so easy to sew—its editorial pages gave glimpses of a
wider war-torn world, with articles about the extraordinary work American women
accomplished. In March 1918 the *Home Journal* ran a pictorial spread on "War
Winning Women: What They Did Throughout the Country Last Spring and What
You Can Do This Spring," which featured the work of female farmworkers and photos
and glowing descriptions of the Bedford and Farmingdale camps. Smiling farmerettes
plowing, driving horses, and milking cows were accompanied by such captions as "The
girls effectually demonstrated that general farm work is not too hard for even 'city'
girls."

So when an editor for the *Journal* approached the Agriculture Department and requested information for an article on women's farm labor in the war, the agency could
not just brush him off; the *Journal* was too influential. Staff editor Dudley Harmon
simply wanted to know how the Agriculture Department planned to utilize women's
labor on farms that coming spring. Clarence Ousley told his staff that his agency would
only cooperate "provided [Mr. Harmon] does not make it appear that the Department
of Agriculture is engaged in an effort primarily to put women on the farms, but that
discussion of woman labor on the farm is merely incidental. . . . There must be nothing
to go out authoritatively that will indicate any other view by the Department of Agriculture."[13] Dudley Harmon took the Ousley-approved material and did not sugarcoat
it in his May 1918 article "Is the Woman Needed on the Farm? What the United States
Government Has to Say About Farm Work for Women This Summer."

Woman's eagerness to serve in this war has frequently outrun the Government's ability to place her in the fields of service of her own choosing. Washington has nipped in the bud many a prospective romantic career by its chilling consideration of the facts in a given situation. It has told many an enthusiastic aspirant: "No, not yet. Later perhaps, but not now; the needs of the situation do not warrant our sanctioning the service you propose to render in the way you propose to render it."

And so it is that proposals that the women of America leap overnight almost into the places of the farmers and the hired men of America find the government somewhat cold. Washington sees a great many ways in which women can help in the production of our food, but the suggestion that women from our cities seek jobs on our farms is not the first among them.[14]

Harmon's article was an earnest attempt to synthesize the wildly conflicting evidence he encountered: the farmerettes' record of accomplishment in 1917, the women's eagerness to resume the work on a larger scale, and the national organization already in place and dedicated to putting them there posited against Washington's intractable "not-till-hell-freezes-over" policy. "The Government would prefer to see the return to the land of some of the thousands of available men in our cities before undertaking to place untrained, unaccustomed women on our farms," he reported.

Harmon's article tried to find balance while poised in a precarious position during wartime. The national press, and specifically the *Ladies' Home Journal*, was expected to perform as a mouthpiece for the government, obliged to preach to its readers the Hoover food sermons and to teach them the virtues of self-sacrifice. This effort was nationwide, after all, and the *Ladies' Home Journal* was just a stylishly shod foot soldier in the greater battle. So if the government frowned upon Land Army volunteers, that message must be duly reported. "That women can successfully do farm work cannot be disputed," Harmon wrote, "that the nation may later have need of an army of women organized for farm work is recognized in Washington. But Washington is convinced that there are tens of thousands of women already on our farms who can do vastly more this year to help food production than the possible hundreds who could be recruited from the cities and trained for farm work."

But the editors of the *Ladies' Home Journal* obviously recognized just how untethered from reality the federal government's positions really were. As this May issue went to press, thousands of women were already enrolling in the Woman's Land Army or its local affiliates and desperate farmers around the country were agreeing (whether with enthusiasm, resignation, or trepidation) to employ them. Events had already overtaken government policy and dogma. So the editors inserted a box in center of the article's page, alerting its readers:

The formation of farm groups, or units, of women workers, which may become necessary, is outlined on page 113 of this issue of *The Home Journal* and should be read in connection with this article. It explains very clearly how such units can be recruited, trained and operated, and has an important bearing upon a subject that vitally interests every person in America.

On page 113 of the *Ladies' Home Journal* appeared "How to Form a Farm Group of Women Workers," which was simply a reprint of the WLA's instructional manual on organizing units. At the end of the piece interested readers were advised to contact the Woman's Land Army of America.

Perhaps frustrated by its failure to control this outbreak of farmerette-friendly coverage in the mainstream press, Ousley's USDA press office took a new tack. As the May issue of the *Ladies' Home Journal* hit the newsstands, the USDA published a ten-page pamphlet, which reprinted a weepy short story entitled "A Woman Who Needs You," meant for distribution to women's clubs. This piece of dime novel fiction, reprinted from *The Designer* fashion magazine, tells the tale of a rich city woman who forsakes all other war work to clean the house of a pathetic, over-whelmed farmwife. The teary farmwife cannot find any household help. "No girl will touch farmwork with a ten-foot pole," she moans. She also has to cook for all the hired hands: "I've four men to feed. The three hired hands my husband's got don't do any more than one ought to—they drink and lay off—but they are awful eaters."

If this story appears to be a perfect advertisement for sending farmerettes to the rescue—they're not lazy and don't need to be fed—that's not what the Agriculture Department had in mind. Following the preposterous climax of the story in which the rich woman moves in with the farmer's family to clean and cook for the war's duration and prompts the farmwife to cry with joy, Ousley's office "comments" on the story in an afterword called "Hands That Can Help." The USDA says of farmhouse service,

> It is a service which must be performed without the thrill of martial music,
> the excitement of adventure, or even the inspiration of working shoulder
> to shoulder with a regiment of others enlisted in a common cause. Yet so
> sincere are our American women in their patriotic devotion that some will
> surely welcome this suggestion of a way to help, however humbly and
> indirectly, in the task of the feeding of the nations.

In an ungloved swipe at the Land Army, the commentary continues that if college girls, teachers, and women in the trades would volunteer in the farm house, "they would contribute to the world's food supply as surely as if they ran tractors or hoed vegetables." In this USDA fantasy, patriotic women in cities and towns could do country women's laundry and bake pies and cookies to be taken to farms. It asked, "If a town woman can not scrub and cook all summer for a country friend, could she not go regularly to do the mending?"[15]

So imagine Clarence Ousley's frustration when he found on his desk, at this very same time of early May 1918, the script for a newsreel the Committee on Public Information had prepared on "Women's Work on the Land." The staff writer for the CPI Division on Women's War Work seemed blissfully unaware of USDA's posture on the issue and opened his scenario with these words for the film's first frame: "Farmers are being converted to hiring women farm hands."

"No, no, no," Ousley fumed as he penciled in his corrections on the script. It was no use trying to stop the newsreel from production—George Creel's CPI wielded more power than the USDA's press office—Ousley could only edit it. With his pencil Ousley softened this first sentence: "Farmers in many places are hiring women for the lighter tasks of the farm." Ousley then tackled the next sentence that would appear in the film as the narrative caption (white letters on a black card) for the silent newsreel: "The local branch of the Women's Land Army of America has been asked to send a unit of women to Silecia [Silesia], Maryland." Even though President Wilson had officially endorsed it, Ousley crossed out the WLA's mention and substituted, "The local branch of a women's organization. . . ."

Then Ousley seemed to weary of the fight. He gave up trying to deny that women were, at this moment, entering the fields and jumping on tractors instead of baking pies or doing laundry in the farmhouse. He let stand most of the rest of the script. "They will cause the farmer's wife no inconvenience, for with them they will have a chaperone who will be their housekeeper and cook," the script continued, without correction.

Still, the clashing approaches of the Committee on Public Information and the Department of Agriculture were remarkable. While the CPI found the farmerettes and the Land Army worthy of praise and good press as a great example of American wartime initiative and spunk, the USDA found them threatening. So the vexed Clarence Ousley would not be one to cheer at the end of the movie reel, when the narration cards announced, "Last year in Idaho 90 percent of the fruit in six counties was most satisfactorily picked and graded by women. This year women will be used for this work all over the country. . . . When girls are physically able and not temperamentally unfit, they should be able to answer the call for help."[16]

Ousley's counterparts at the Department of Labor displayed an equally clumsy approach to handling the WLA issue. While department field agents reported unprecedented farm labor shortages and near panic in the countryside, Assistant Secretary of Labor Post announced to the press in early April, "The American farmer is the victim of publicity. So many people have been crying that there is a great shortage of labor that the farmer is beginning to believe it himself. Two thirds of the farm labor shortage is imaginary and the other third can be remedied." Post continued, "What we need now is less agitation about putting women on the farms, less talk about the importation of Chinese thousands of miles away, and more teamwork and mutual confidence."[17] Meanwhile, department field offices were registering women for farmwork.

A month later, in early May, the Philadelphia *Evening Star* reported the comments of another Labor Department official under the headline "Women Should Not Engage in Farm Work." The chief of the Farm Service Division of the Labor Department, M. A. Coykendall, publicly announced that "women can show more patriotism by signing up in active government work [as clerks and stenographers] than in farming this year. The chief reason women in the city should not leave to work on farms is that they are not physically fit to do real farm work." Coykendall continued, "There is enough man power in the U.S. to handle the 1918 crop if the men will work six days a week."[18]

The next day, the *Evening Star* gave Coykendall and his agency a stinging slap:

> A Department of Labor official is quoted as declaring that women are not fitted [*sic*] for service on the farms. It is strange if the American women are not as capable of agricultural labor as those of England and France. Those women have given service of the highest value on the farms of their countries. Have our own women grown incompetent that they cannot do what their sisters of England and France have done in this great emergency? It is not desirable to discourage women from going upon the farms. To tell them, officially, that they are not wanted is to close one of the channels of labor supply upon which we may have to draw heavily before the war is concluded.[19]

Even while Washington war bureaucrats tried so furiously to stuff the farmerette genie back inside her bottle, she made her appearance on Broadway. *Starting Something: A Farmerette Comedy* opened at the French Theatre on May 23 for a special one-week run. The playwright, producer, and star was the popular actress Elizabeth (Bessie) Tyree, a Broadway darling acclaimed for her versatility in playing complex comic characters in George Bernard Shaw's works as well as for delighting audiences in lighter fare. When war was declared the previous spring, she threw herself into organizing her fellow actresses to aid the war effort, helping form the Stage Women's War Relief group within a week of America's entry into the fray. The Stage Women used their talents to raise funds for the Red Cross and other relief causes by singing at rallies, performing skits, reciting patriotic poems, and lending star power to fund-raising events.

Starting Something was Tyree's latest contribution. Cast as a benefit for the Red Cross, its starring role was one for which Tyree was particularly well suited. She and her husband, the drama critic James Stetson Metcalfe, owned a small farm in Bedford, New

York, where they employed Bedford Camp farmerettes. Bessie herself was said to have donned overalls and joined them in the field. So in penning and performing this three-act comedy Tyree could write from some experience, however well exaggerated. As a *New York Times* reviewer put it, the play "shows how our city girls go back to the land in North Westchester, sending their boys to the front and incidentally inspiring adjacent parts with patriotic fervor."[20]

Tyree's play was not the first opening night for the farmerette character, however. Six months before, she had made her debut in a Flo Ziegfeld review called *Miss 1917*. In a sketch written by satirist P. G. Wodehouse, she sang a song called "The Society Farmerettes" with lyrics by Wodehouse and music by composer Victor Herbert.

> *Girls have found a way, Today,*
> *To do their bit:*
> *They do not sit,*
> *At home any more,*
> *And shirk, Hard work,*
> *For ev'rybody's doing it:*
> *Uncle Sam they adore*
> *Working for.*
>
> *Ev'ry girl, says Mister Hoover,*
> *Finds that farm work will improve her;*
> *From the city he'd remove her,*
> *To become a farmerette.*
>
> *Mabel, Mamie, Maud and Lizzie—*
> *Watch the dear things getting busy!*
> *Working never makes them dizzy,*
> *Now that they are farmerettes.*
>
> *Ev'ry day there's something doing:*
> *From the corn the hens they're shooing,*
> *Or the pig requires shampooing,*
> *Now that they are farmerettes.*
>
> *Ever since they introduced her,*
> *For the farm each girl's a booster:*
> *And her closest friend's the rooster,*
> *Now that she's a farmerette.[21]*

In February 1918 the farmerette had another stage presence, this time in a flop called *A Cure for Curables*, featuring a cast of "potatriots." In the fall of 1918 she would take another bow in the comedy *Crops and Croppers.* Tyree's play was the most sympathetic. Among her farmerette heroines were "a girl from a paper-box factory, a cabaret dancer, a hello girl, an unmarried mother, and a fat girl training down for the matrimonial handicap," the reviewer explained.

> With perhaps a single exception, [the playwright's] facts and her local color are authentic. The single unveracious detail is the costume of the farmerettes. Instead of the blue jeans and suspenders which prevail in North Westchester, Mrs. Metcalfe has arrayed her heroines in the trimmest of knickerbockers with skirted coats. What the play loses in grim, bucolic realism it gains in decorative quality. The farmerette colony in Bedford Village will please take note.[22]

The performance was a boffo hit during its one-week run, generating "much pelf" (as the *Times's* critic put it) for the Red Cross and healthy exposure for the Woman's Land Army. The farmerette was now a genuine American character.

11

ENLIST NOW!

Helen Fraser, auburn-haired crusader with a Scottish accent, went forth to rally the women of America. Imported from across the sea, Fraser brought her war mission to American towns and cities in late 1917 and early 1918, thrilling audiences and inspiring women to help win the war by the sweat of their brow.

Joan of Arc was the patron saint of the Allied women during the war. The embodiment of all things noble and just and the ideal of sacrifice, her image was everywhere. She appeared in magazines, she graced the frontispiece of Harriot Stanton Blatch's *Mobilizing Woman-Power*, and she rode on horseback and in costume in nearly every war parade on both continents. Beautiful and charismatic, Helen Fraser could not lay claim to being the Maid of Orleans's modern British incarnation, for Fraser was too sensible and too worldly, without any pretensions to visions or martyrdom. Instead, Fraser was a magnetic presence roaming the countryside, summoning women to meet their destiny and to fulfill their role in vanquishing tyranny. Fraser was, after all, a professional crusader.

Daughter of a Glasgow politician, Helen Fraser grew up with pungent political banter as a dinnertime staple, so her family was not shocked when she abandoned her art studies and devoted herself to the suffrage cause. She apprenticed herself to the masters, Mrs. Emmeline Pankhurst and her daughters, Sylvia, Christabel, and Adele. They had broken away from the moderate suffragists of National Union of Women's Suffrage Societies (NUWSS) to form the less patient, more provocative Women's Social and Political Union (WSPU), nicknamed the "suffragettes." As one of Mrs. Pankhurst's young protégées, Fraser was initiated into organizational work in England and then established a Scottish base for the WSPU in 1906. Fraser became a familiar figure at auditorium lecterns and on curbside soap boxes, exhorting women and convincing men that the time had come to stop asking for and start demanding the right to vote.

Soon Fraser began to chafe under the Pankhursts' notoriously autocratic style of leadership, and she argued with them over their tactics. Fraser disagreed with the WSPU's escalating use of violence—throwing rocks, bombing mailboxes, smashing windows, and setting fires—which she felt was hurting the cause. In mid-1908 Fraser split with the Pankhursts, quit the WSPU, and joined the moderate NUWSS. It is deeply ironic that Fraser was replaced as the Scottish WSPU organizer by a pair of American Pankhurst acolytes, Alice Paul and Lucy Burns, who would later bring the Pankhurst-WSPU style of militancy back to the States. Helen Fraser's skill and experience made her a valuable lieutenant to Millicent Garrett Fawcett and the NUWSS. Fraser also became a trusted adviser to Liberal members of Parliament, who kept her in their confidence even as their party repeatedly betrayed the suffragists and abandoned the promised universal franchise bill again and again.[1]

Like all her suffrage sisters, Fraser redirected her energies into war work in 1914, transferring her organizational and persuasive skills to this new national cause. Once again she proved herself a popular and effective stump speaker. The Treasury Ministry asked her to join the staff of the National War Savings Committee, which sold the British equivalent of Liberty Bonds, and she crisscrossed the isles while organizing local War Savings Associations. While Britons were putting their pence into these war certificates, Fraser also campaigned for the government Labour Exchange, giving pep talks that encouraged women to enter the new occupations crucial to the war economy. Pouring her heart into this war work recruitment, which seemed a natural extension of her suffrage vocation, Fraser took a special interest in the efforts of the "land lassies" to replace men on the farms. "We are looking forward to having you for the week," wrote a Labour Exchange official in Cardiff, Wales, in May 1916, where Fraser was to help recruit for the local Land Army. "Would it be possible for you to extend your stay?"[2] While she traveled from town to town, Fraser took extensive notes and conducted interviews with the women organizing war efforts in each community she visited. In scores of hotel rooms, she wrote her book *Women and War Work*, an exhaustive study of the British experience. She completed it in late 1917. By then she was packing her bags for an evangelical tour of America.

Harriot Stanton Blatch was well acquainted with Helen Fraser from her own years of suffrage work in England, and she greatly admired Fraser's zeal and political savvy. She also heard glowing reports of Fraser's war work drives. Soon after America entered the war, in her first note to Anna Howard Shaw at the newly appointed Women's Committee of the Council of National Defense, Blatch urged the committee to bring Fraser over for an American tour.[3] Lacking an independent budget and freedom, Shaw couldn't act on the suggestion just then, but by the fall of 1917, the Women's Committee was able to join with the National American Woman Suffrage Association, a consortium of women's colleges, and several state Women's Committees and invited Fraser to bring her war work crusade to America.

Henry Noble MacCracken, president of Vassar, was also familiar with Fraser's reputation as a brilliant speaker and was eager to employ her persuasive talents in awakening the nation's college women. MacCracken agreed to write the foreword to the American edition of Fraser's book and engaged her for a week of lectures and seminars at Vassar. He arranged with his fellow women's college presidents to do the same.

Helen Fraser arrived in New York at the end of November 1917 and was met at the dock by her American publisher, G. Arnold Shaw, who had also arranged her ambitious American tour. Shaw operated a small, highbrow publishing and lecture tour operation, specializing in ethereal poets and opinionated intellectuals. The war had slowed business terribly, and he was looking to the vivacious Miss Fraser as his meal ticket. Shaw went all out publicizing Fraser's visit: he bought advertisements for her book and speaking tour in all the political magazines and major newspapers, sent copies of the book to notable women and President Wilson, and plastered posters with her portrait all over the cities on her tour calendar. Shaw was also most careful to play down Fraser's prominence as a British suffragist, promoting her talks as purely patriotic and war-related. "She is speaking in America solely on what she considers the most vital subject before women today, namely 'Women's Part in Winning the War,'" Shaw told prospective lecture sponsors. "Her addresses do not touch upon the Suffrage question."[4] Shaw had originally scheduled Fraser for a six-week tour, but by the time she arrived in New York, he had more invitations than could fit into that time frame, so he asked her to extend her visit to fourteen weeks. She happily agreed, not realizing that her success would snowball and demand she stay even longer.

Fraser's first stop was Vassar, where she gave nine lectures, based on her book, on the lessons (learned from the British women's experience while organizing themselves for the war). The Vassar farmerette experience of the previous summer fit nicely into her talks, and the students "followed her around, and packed every room in which she spoke, out to the doors and sometimes up to the ceiling," the student newspaper reported.[5]

Her next destination was Washington, where President Wilson warmly received her at the White House. She also met with Secretary of the Treasury William McAdoo, Secretary of War Newton Baker, and labor leader Samuel Gompers (who was totally unsympathetic to women entering the workforce in America and used his CND position to make life difficult for women workers). The next day she was in friendly territory, among her suffrage sisters, and received a heroine's welcome as the featured speaker at the NAWSA annual convention. She sat on the podium with Anna Howard Shaw, Carrie Chapman Catt, Katharine Dexter McCormick, Emma Winner Rogers, and other NAWSA officers. Quite a few of the convention delegates, moved by her talk, asked her to visit their home cities. Mr. Shaw gladly signed them up, and Helen Fraser's visit was extended again into the summer.[6]

Fresh from the suffrage convention, Fraser attended the founding meeting of the Woman's Land Army at the Hotel Astor in New York, where she gave a rousing sermon on the British Land Army's importance. She included a whole chapter about it in her book. She told the attendees how the Land Army had progressed since it was made an official government service in the spring of 1917: it now claimed about sixteen thousand women in official uniform, pledged to full-time agricultural work for the war's duration, and almost two hundred thousand more women had organized for part-time land service. While the Land Army still struggled with housing and training problems and still battled against farmers' resistance, it had finally won most Britons' acceptance and even affection. She could report a scene she had witnessed just days before her departure for the States, a moment that symbolized the role the Land Army had come to assume in the war effort:

> In the Lord Mayor's Procession in London, on November 9, 1917, with the
> men-in-arms of all our great Commonwealth of Nations, with the captured
> German aeroplanes and guns, the munitions girls and the Land girls
> marched. No group in all that great array had a warmer welcome from our
> vast crowds than our sensibly clothed, healthy, happy and supremely useful
> Land girls.[7]

The new Woman's Land Army of America could aspire to a similar role. Fraser's address to the WLA convention afforded an inspirational boost to the delegates, and they too wanted her to visit their home districts and preach the gospel of women's work, specifically the value of land service. She was the apostle of a new creed, and she was in high demand.

Helen Fraser set off, employing every type of transport—save, perhaps, riding horseback—to carry her message to American women. She presented 232 lectures within her 228-day stay, sometimes giving four talks in a single day and sometimes twenty-two in a single week. She spoke in twenty-two states and two Canadian provinces. She addressed national organizations, such as the War Work Council of the YWCA and the Federal Food Administration, and small civic forums in Peoria, Illinois, and Ashtabula, Ohio. She talked to businessmen at Chamber of Commerce gatherings in Missouri, Illinois, and Virginia; met with union organizers in Kansas; and gave sixty-two lectures to women's clubs, from the Women's Civics Club of Madison, Wisconsin, to the Saturday Morning Club of New Haven, Connecticut. She was also invited to several state houses, including those in Rhode Island and Iowa, where she addressed a joint session of the legislature.[8]

Fraser gave fifty-two talks to women's colleges and coeducational universities, from the Massachusetts Institute of Technology to Ward-Belmont College in Nashville. Enthusiastic crowds of eager students welcomed her and quickly exhausted the supplies of war work registration cards distributed at her lectures. Ada Comstock, the dean of Smith College, wrote in her note of thanks to Fraser,

You gave us the very best and broadest presentation we have had this year of the part which women can play in a country at war, and you gave us at the same time a thing which America especially needs—an illustration of what it is to be terribly in earnest without being in the least hysterical. I cannot say how glad I am that you are in this country.[9]

The WLA made special use of Fraser's talents, engaging her to speak to its newly formed state organizations, and it was no coincidence that Woman's Land Army units subsequently sprung up where Fraser visited. She was the featured speaker at Caroline Bartlett Crane's "Food Will Win the War" conference in Michigan, where she delivered her war work sermon in the House of Delegates' chamber, and at a Woman's Land Army inaugural meeting in Chicago.[10] Harriot Stanton Blatch invited Fraser to her New York City apartment to dine with WLA Executive Committee members.[11] Many more state WLA divisions formed during the seven months of Fraser's tour. By the summer of 1918, there were twenty-three state organizations, and many of the women organizing those state Land Army programs had heard Helen Fraser speak at their club, alma mater, civic group, or local Women's Committee meeting. Henry MacCracken described Fraser's tour as "educating American women to a sense of what the mobilization of the entire citizen army of a democracy must mean."[12]

By mid-winter WLA state organizations were thriving in Massachusetts, Connecticut, New York, Pennsylvania, Illinois, New Jersey, California, and Maryland, with county chairwomen and committees in place and their plans for sponsoring units developing nicely. The New York State WLA chairwoman, Laura Crane Burgess, took the initiative of writing to the forty Farm Bureau agents in her state and urged them to encourage the farmers in their districts to use women workers. To sell the agents on the concept, she enclosed the Bedford Camp report as proof that farmerette units were practical and economical. Burgess reached out to the agents, asked for their opinions, and prepared them for a personal visit from a Land Army coordinator sometime soon.[13] Her approach was so pleasant and direct that the national WLA office mailed out her letter as a template for other state and local WLA divisions to use.

In Connecticut, the WLA mailed five hundred letters to farmers asking if they would agree to employ women in the coming season. In California, prominent civic women assumed the helms of both the northern and southern state WLA divisions, and while plans for several large farmerette camps were moving apace, still they hit pockets of resistance. "The western spirit has objected to having women as farmworkers," a California Women's Committee publication lamented in the early spring. "This chivalric conservatism must be judiciously overcome."[14]

In other states, conservatism, chivalric or not, was proving problematic. Helen Fraser

gave three lectures in Nebraska (centered at the university in Lincoln), and ingenious
Nebraska Women's Committee planners used telephone central switchboard operators
to call every woman, especially farmwives on isolated rural homesteads, to alert them to
upcoming meetings and war work opportunities. Many Nebraskan women, however,
were not sympathetic to the WLA. The Nebraska Women's Committee adopted a resolution against forming a WLA division in the state, calling the concept of employing
women on Nebraska farms "unspeakably ridiculous and wrong."[15] The women even
went so far as to employ the clever new propaganda tool invented by Mr. Creel in
Washington, the Four-Minute Man (or woman), to deliver a 240-second speech on the
topic of why townswomen were not fit for farmwork. In theaters and public venues
around the state, Nebraskans were treated to short soliloquies on why women workers
were a hindrance to the farm, it was better to use boys as workers, and farmers should
only allow townswomen to relieve the farmwife of housework.[16] Nevertheless, later in
the summer a Woman's Land Army representative was installed in Nebraska.

In January, a group of Kansan women wrote to the Kansas War Council and offered
to help harvest the wheat crop later that season. The Kansas War Council declined the
offer, saying women would not be needed; however, the council would come to regret
that statement.[17] Beyond the social conservatism of the midwestern farm states, the
greater size and diverse crops of western farms gave farmers practical reasons to balk at
hiring women workers. These places were more expansive and complex organisms than
the typical eastern family farm was, and adequately supervising untrained women, the
farmers claimed, was simply impossible.

The sentiment in Minnesota was revealed in an article the director of the Minnesota
Women's Committee wrote for St. Paul's *The Farmer's Wife* magazine. Under the heading "What Minnesota Is Doing for the Woman on the Farm," Mrs. T. G. Winter asks,
"Have women got to work in the fields? Both our Federal Bureau of Employment and
the Public Employment Office of our state answer emphatically 'NO'—not this year, at
any rate."[18] While the Women's Committee urged Minnesota city women to volunteer
in farm kitchens—"the good old woman's job of cooking and washing dishes and scrub-
bing takes on the glory of a great patriotic service, and the women must rise to the
occasion"—the article also reports the efforts of Annie Shelland, the state supervisor of
rural schools, to register teachers and other women who could help with farmwork.
Miss Shelland mailed a questionnaire asking women about their farming experience,
including fieldwork and work with horses; their physical strength; and their "willingness of spirit."

In Missouri women workers were organized in time for the early strawberry crop,
with units forming in St. Joseph, Jefferson City, St. Louis, and Carthage and supplied
with cooks and chaperones.[19] A Missouri chapter of the WLA had not yet been formally established, but as in other states, it operated under the rubric of the state Women's
Committee, often directed by a chairwoman of Food Production. The Missouri

chairwoman, Mrs. Massey Holmes, managed to quickly establish good relations with the state's farmers. "A call has been issued for one thousand berry pickers, girls and women, to save the berry crop of 1918," the Women's Committee reported. "Arrangements have been made with the Berry Grower's Association to comfortably house the women who will be sent to them for this purpose, and Mrs. Holmes asks for at least ten women from every county."[20]

In Illinois, Margaret Day Blake and her Woman's Land Army committee used Helen Fraser's swing through Chicago as the springboard for organizing a comprehensive training camp for women agricultural workers. And in Maryland, the Women's Committee Food Production chairwoman brought in Laura Burgess from New York to consult on forming a Maryland Land Army and sent a questionnaire to the state's farmers asking their sentiments toward women laborers on farms.[21]

While all this activity was bubbling in the states, the national Women's Committee was slow to officially sanction the WLA, but it finally did, in April, and wholeheartedly. Katharine Dexter McCormick, the committee's Food Production chairwoman, wrote to all state Women's Committee chairs announcing the endorsement. She emphasized that the committee "wishes to do all it can to further this movement for supplying women farm laborers where ever they are needed." She urged county leaders to form their own local Land Army, win the cooperation of their agricultural extension agents, and adapt the "unit plan" to their local needs. This official recognition was important in helping persuade the state committees that the WLA was a legitimate war work service, even if the national Women's Committee could not offer financial or structural support—not even money for postage. Still, McCormick cautioned that the farmers and their families would have to be delicately persuaded of the Land Army plan's advantages. "In some sections there is undoubtedly a prejudice against the employment of women on the land," McCormick wrote to her state chairwomen, "and unless this is tactfully and cautiously met the movement will not be successful."[22]

While Helen Fraser toured around the country and witnessed American women rising to the war's challenges, her agent forwarded her mail, which caught up with her in far-flung places with odd-sounding Native American names and severe winter weather. The intrepid Miss Fraser was undoubtedly warmed by the news that reached her in late January: the franchise bill that she had worked so hard to craft and patiently shepherd through Parliament—the Representation of the People Act—had finally won passage and gained royal assent on February 6, 1918. Somewhere in the American prairies Helen Fraser learned that her countrywomen (at least those older than thirty years of age and property owners) had won the vote. "Let me congratulate you upon the successful ending of your struggle for the franchise in Great Britain," Anna Howard Shaw wrote to her. "I hope you may have the opportunity to rejoice with us soon upon our own success in the U.S. Senate."[23]

American suffrage campaign veterans, no strangers to the rigors of long, exhausting speaking tours, worried aloud about Helen Fraser's health and well-being. "We cannot send you back to England broken down from your task of telling America about the war," Carrie Catt chided her. "Do, I beg of you, for the sake of us all, take a little more care as to your program."[24] In truth, Helen Fraser thrived on the tour's rigors and excitement. She loved the applause, the adoration, and the sense of sacred mission. If she could spark the women of America to perform their duty, rise to new heights, and thrill them with her message delivered in her lilting brogue, she was glad. And there was no doubting she was effective.

While Helen Fraser was barnstorming through the country in the winter and spring of 1918, the Woman's Land Army of America took its own show on the road. It introduced the public to the patriotic farmerette with lushly romantic poster paintings, grainy film footage, magnified lantern slides, and personal appearances of khaki-clad farmerette veterans just bursting with enthusiasm for the cause.

In addition to Helen Fraser's long and looping national tour, WLA organizers embarked on recruitment drives and traced smaller trajectories. Springing out from major cities and county seats, these road tours brought a sprightly girl-and-hoe show to factories, high school auditoriums, college lecture halls, church basements, and Grange barns. In addition to recruiting workers, the tours were also meant to persuade farmers and rural communities of the WLA's value.

State and county WLA divisions flooded the national headquarters in New York with requests for speakers to visit their districts. The WLA built a speakers bureau and dispatched some of the more loquacious veterans of the Bedford Camp and the Vassar farmerettes, decked out in their working uniforms, to recount their agricultural adventures for audiences in thirteen states. They were accompanied by a WLA official (sometimes also dressed in uniform) and in rural districts by a sympathetic Farm Bureau or extension agent. It was not unusual for the Land Army performance to conclude, as did so many public gatherings these days, with the singing of patriotic songs.

If the public speaking classes the college student farmerettes had taken stood them in good stead on this lecture tour, then the extensive campaign experience of the suffrage movement veterans now involved in the WLA was also immensely valuable. That fierce and seasoned suffrage campaigner Harriot Stanton Blatch took charge of the WLA speakers' bureau. From her command base at WLA headquarters, like a general directing troop movements, Blatch plotted many of the propaganda and recruitment tours launched that spring.

It was through Mrs. Blatch's machinations that one of the richest women in America and a plucky college girl found themselves riding together in a convertible automobile and careering through rural New York's curvy roads. Louisine Havemeyer and Barnard farmerette Helen Kennedy Stevens traveled in this Land Army publicity and recruitment tour through the farming heart of central New York State. Mrs. Havemeyer was sixty-three years old that spring and was more than happy to lend her landaulet auto and her driver to make the ten-day journey more comfortable. Helen Stevens, tall, strapping, and barely twenty-one years old, might have packed her weeding hoe (the one with which she appeared in that portrait in the *New York Times Magazine* a few months before) to use as a prop during her speeches.

Harriot Stanton Blatch and Louisine Havemeyer were friends and suffrage compatriots. Now they both dedicated much of their time and talents—and in Havemeyer's case, her considerable fortune—to women's war work and, just as other suffragists, were especially drawn to the Land Army. Blatch was already deeply involved in the WLA, serving on the national and New York State boards. She cajoled her pal Havemeyer to go on this publicity jaunt, a nostalgic reprisal of the many suffrage tours and publicity stunts they'd cooked up together over the years. They were the creators, after all, of some of the great attention-grabbing gimmicks of the suffrage campaign trail, including the popular Suffrage Torch and the electrified Ship of State mascot. They were masters at drawing a crowd.

Louisine Welder Havemeyer was the wife of Henry (Harry) Osborne Havemeyer, whose family owned the American Sugar Refining Company, which controlled virtually all the nation's sugar supplies. The Havemeyers enjoyed collecting art, and with the advice of her closest friend, the American painter Mary Cassatt, Louisine bought the works of the French Impressionists and assembled one of the world's great collections. When Harry died in 1907, Louisine had kept busy by plunging into suffrage activities—even Harry had been a suffrage supporter—displaying a taste for the movement's more radical strain. She joined and helped bankroll Blatch's Women's Political Union and later threw her allegiance, and checkbook, to Alice Paul's Congressional Union for Woman Suffrage. She didn't flinch and absolutely enjoyed being called a "militant suffragist."

Louisine Havemeyer found her voice, quite literally, in the suffrage movement, and it was thanks to Harriot Blatch. "Mrs. Harriot Stanton Blatch . . . was the head of my first political party and my guide and friend for many years," Havemeyer recalled in a series of articles for *Scribner's Magazine* entitled "Memories of a Militant." "It was Mrs. Blatch who insisted that I could speak; that I must speak; and then saw to it that I did speak. I think I spoke just to please her."[25]

Havemeyer became Blatch's sidekick and coconspirator during the losing 1915 campaign for the suffrage ratification referendum in New York State. Not only did she raise money for the campaign by exhibiting her art collection for the cause, but Havemeyer also made scores of impassioned speeches, often from the back of her touring car. In the middle of that summer campaign frenzy, after Blatch's husband was electrocuted when he touched a live wire on his lawn, Blatch took a leave of absence to mourn him, and Havemeyer was forced to campaign on her own. During her lectures, Havemeyer held aloft the electric "Ship of State," the Mayflower-like model she'd designed and outlined with tiny light bulbs, which she would flick on dramatically at a pivotal moment in her speech. (Men and boys were particularly fascinated by this electric wonder, and since men were the ones voting to ratify the woman's suffrage amendment, they were an important audience to hold.) And it was Havemeyer who appeared in nighttime suffrage parades wearing light bulbs strung on her body and a battery strapped onto her back, the walking embodiment of the Ship of State.

Now she and Mrs. Blatch were reunited in the Land Army, and Blatch urged her to speak up again. Havemeyer said, "I always appreciated Mrs. Blatch's encouragement and discipline, for, when we entered the World War, I was able to serve my country in a small and humble way, and I spoke continuously, while the war lasted, on Liberty Loans, land army, food conservation, economy and relief."[26] Havemeyer also praised the Land Army in print; her article extolling the WLA would appear in the coming issue of *Touchstone*. When Mrs. Blatch suggested she use her oratory skills before a live audience, she could hardly refuse.

In late April, while working out the shape of Havemeyer's tour, Harriot Blatch wrote to Virginia Gildersleeve:

> My dear Dean Gildersleeve, is it possible for you to allow Miss Stevens to
> take a week off? We need Miss Stevens or some one like her very much. The
> situation is this, the Land Army has not been able to strike very deep roots
> up State and now at last an opportunity has opened for us to do something
> fundamental. We have gotten in touch with important people in Elmira,
> Syracuse, Rochester and Buffalo who are arranging three or four meetings in
> each place for Mrs. Havemeyer and some representative of the college farm
> units. . . . If you cannot possibly allow Miss Stevens to make this little tour
> (of course it will be at our expense) can you give us the services of any girl
> equally clever in holding an audience?[27]

Dean Gildersleeve did give Helen Stevens permission to miss classes that week in May, just before her Barnard commencement exercises, and Helen did not disappoint Mrs. Blatch's trust in her ability to hold audiences. She was a very experienced speaker by that time. She told one Baltimore audience, "You have to get over your fear of snakes. You have to let a snake follow you, if it feels so disposed, down the row of potatoes you are cultivating, because snakes and birds are the farmer's best allies." Her "remark caused a polite shiver to pass through her audience, but it did not prevent a half dozen or more young women from signing registration cards for the Women's Land Army of Maryland last night," according to a Baltimore newspaper account.[28]

"One hundred and seven girls, inspired by Miss Gregg and by Miss Stevens, pledged themselves to do at least two months farming this summer," reported one college newspaper after Stevens's recruitment presentation. "It was probably due to these speakers that farm work, in connection with the Land Army, was by far the most popular occupation."[29]

Campus recruiting was a top priority that spring, and the WLA tapped its friends and affiliations to spread the word quickly and widely. The Association of Collegiate Alumnae, with a membership of nearly a hundred thousand college-educated women, used its chapters around the country to help recruit college women into the Land Army's ranks and asked alumnae groups to sponsor units in their districts. The ACA even asked the deans of women's colleges to grant leaves to their students who signed up for Land Army duty in the early spring, before the end of the spring term, and requested they be given full academic credit. Barnard College offered a special "Farmer's Preparedness" course to all women registered with the WLA for work that summer. The free class met two evenings a week in the college gymnasium for exercises "to train the large, unused group muscles to be used in hoeing, haying, etc."[30]

Ida Ogilvie and Delia West Marble were already preparing the Bedford Camp for a much larger population that summer—150 Barnard students had enlisted—and Professor Ogilvie requested a year's leave from her Barnard teaching duties in order to devote herself to her WLA responsibilities. Dean Virginia Gildersleeve granted the leave. Mount Holyoke president Mary Woolley made her own recruitment appeal to her students: "The college farm is a training camp for young women just as military camps are training camps for young men. Consider your work on the farm this Summer as a step similar to that of the enlistment of your brothers. It is work not for the college, but for the country."[31]

College women were under intense peer pressure to perform some sort of war work during the summer, and those not temperamentally suited to nursing or ready for overseas ambulance driving, telegraphy, or canteen hostess assignments often looked to the Land Army as a respectable alternative means of service. War work recruitment fairs were a staple of college life that spring, and many impressionable young women, having already heard the tales of agricultural adventure from recruiters like Helen Stevens or Helen Fraser, were further charmed by whimsical Woman's Land Army recruitment booths. The one at the Goucher College war work fair in early April was festooned with crepe paper vegetables and a Kewpie farmerette doll in blue and gold overalls.[32]

Sometimes recruitment enthusiasm overtook realistic demand, as when University of Michigan women got all fired up to volunteer as farmerettes and then found they had nowhere to go. Twenty Michigan women "are anxious to work this summer," Dean of Women Agnes Wells wrote to Virginia Gildersleeve at the end of March, but she lamented, "At present we have more applicants than positions to be filled. Michigan does not seem to have the confidence in college women's ability to work on the land. We hope to prove to them this year that they can be of definite use."[33]

The gung-ho WLA campus recruiters and Mount Holyoke's farmerettes probably had some choice words for the *New York Times*'s editorial writers when they read the highly patronizing "The College Girl With the Hoe" essay in late March. The *Times*, like a sarcastic younger brother, teased,

> Considering that a college girl, if she is a normal young woman, never forgets her complexion, there is something heroic about the act of the fifty-four Mt. Holyoke students who have volunteered to work on farms this Summer, all through the caloric intensities of July and the wilting dog days of August. If their war patriotism takes the form of helping on the farm, instead of knitting socks for soldiers, they will "carry on" heroically. The hand of encouragement should be held out to them. But for the less substantial and resolute sister, light farming must be recommended. The orthodox and realistic toil of the field she is not fitted for, and she must forever banish the dream of marrying a farmer.[34]

WLA recruitment activities also moved into women's trade union meeting halls, especially those in the needle trades, millinery, and others where production stopped during the summer months and workers were temporarily unemployed. Recruiters in New York City began a vigorous drive to reach those factories where women who made candy and artificial flowers would be out of work in the warm months. In Pennsylvania and New York, women's unions and working girl societies formed their own WLA units.

To illustrate their talks, Stevens, Havemeyer, and the other WLA recruiters used lantern slides, or photographic images on glass slides that were slipped into a "magic lantern" projector (grandfather of the slide projector), showing farmerettes hard at work, giddy at play, healthy, and happy. If a moving picture projector was available, they might be able to show the British Land Army films Sophia Carey had imported or some newsreel footage of last summer's exotic women workers.

They were also able to tack up some colorful new recruitment posters the WLA headquarters distributed. These advertisements were fine specimens of the powerful propaganda tools that had become this war's new type of ammunition. Borrowing the popular style of the commercial advertising poster, the European Allies used the color lithographed poster as a potent communications tool, for it could evoke emotions and stimulate actions in a way words alone simply could not. Employing their nation's best artists and coupling the paintings or drawings with pithy orders and memorable slogans, governments used posters to give instructions and warnings to their citizens.

The most popular American illustrator of the day, creator of the "Gibson Girl," and president of the Society of Illustrators, Charles Dana Gibson understood the psychic power of pictures and thought the U.S. government's early graphic publicity efforts were pretty lame. "The unimaginative manner in which the Government was using pictures greatly distressed him," recalled one member of the wartime administration in Washington. "The various branches . . . failed to realize as he did what momentum could be imparted to the popular mind by dramatic, well-drawn pictures."[35] Gibson summoned the members of his society to volunteer their talents, then went to Washington, and offered their ready pens and brushes. He met with profound indifference. "When he first broached his conception of mobilizing the talent of our artists in the cause for which we were fighting, he met with rebuffs on every hand," recalled Edward Hurley, who served as chairman of the U.S. Shipping Board. "A less ardent spirit would have accepted defeat in the face of indifference and opposition. Instead of retiring into his shell . . . he persisted in his efforts. Finally Mr. George Creel was infected by Gibson's enthusiasm."[36]

In his Committee of Public Information, Creel created a Division of Pictorial Publicity and made Gibson its head. Gibson mobilized every commercial and fine artist not serving in the military—every painter, sculptor, cartoonist, and calligrapher, more than three hundred artists in all—to lend their talents without compensation. Among them were artists whose work was already famous or was about to be: Joseph Pennell, Cass Gilbert, Herbert Paus, Wallace Morgan, Haskell Coffin, Charles Livingston Bull, James Montgomery Flagg, Henry Reuterdahl, J. C. Leyendecker, Howard Chandler Christy, and a young Norman Rockwell. Each week the Pictorial Division's Cartoon Bureau created sheaves of war theme-approved editorial cartoons that were published in hundreds of American newspapers. With a clear sense of mission Gibson "built up an organization on almost military lines" and gave his artistic troops instruction as well as inspiration, urging them to depict the war's deeper significance and to "draw 'til it hurts," as he liked to say. Gibson would gather his principal artists every Friday evening at Keens Chop House in Manhattan to brainstorm and to hear firsthand accounts of soldiers in the field, the better to vividly portray the war. Collaborating with the creative writing minds in the CPI advertising section, Gibson's artists created thousands of designs with slogans for military and war work recruitment, Liberty Bonds, the Red Cross, all the war-related government agencies, and especially the Food Administration. The artworks were published in the nation's magazines and newspapers, with publishing companies donating space, and were mass-produced as posters, even appearing in the native language of the ethnic immigrant neighborhoods where they were hung. Gibson's artists were aware of the pictorial concepts used in other nations' posters, too. Probably the most famous American war poster of all time, James Montgomery Flagg's "Uncle Sam Wants You," was simply a Yankee borrowing of a successful British recruitment poster that featured John Bull in the pointing role. Though America was officially in the war for only eighteen months, its poster output far surpassed the combined poster production of all the European fighting nations.

Herbert Paus was assigned to draw the first Woman's Land Army recruitment poster: a muscular yet highly romantic depiction of patriotism in the fields, drenched in red, white, and blue and suffused with a sense of nature's bounty and solemn duty. Paus was already a successful magazine illustrator for *Collier's*, *Ladies' Home Journal*, and *Life* as well as a sought-after commercial artist who created advertising images for many products and corporations. Primarily a water colorist, Paus took up oils when the project demanded more intense colors, and he was known for his superb color sense. Though he certainly drew many strong-jawed, muscled men—he also did war poster work for the U.S. Navy, Liberty Bonds, and War Savings Stamps—Paus was especially talented in drawing elegant but strong women. He used his skill to capture the essence of the Land Army.

Three women stride toward the viewer. Two are dressed in blue bloomers and smocks, wearing puttees on their legs and broad-brimmed straw hats on their heads. A hoe is tilted over one woman's shoulder, a milk pail in the hand of the other, and between them they share the load of a large basket overflowing with vegetables. Behind them on horseback is a third woman wearing a khaki-colored version of the same uniform, with her sleeves rolled up and one arm holding the staff of a huge American flag, which waves majestically behind her. The walking women are smiling but purposeful while the rider has an intent gaze, looking beyond the viewer and ahead to some future vision of glory. The stars and stripes of the flag push up beyond the frame of the pictured scene and into the graphic space, where "The Woman's Land Army of America" is lettered. The flag even obscures a bit of the writing in an evocation of urgency, of pride, of duty. At the bottom, the poster bears the message: "WOMEN enlist now and help the FARMER FIGHT THE FOOD FAMINE."[37]

Other artistic interpretations of the Woman's Land Army would appear soon. Edward Penfield drew his take on the farmerette for the YWCA's Land Service Committee, with a close-cropped view of four attractive young women in belted khaki uniforms, armed with hoes, rakes, and the ubiquitous produce basket leading a team of horses through a field. The women seem more glamorous but less heroic than their comrades in the Paus painting; their hair is bobbed short, their uniforms are more fashionable, and the colors more muted, in a palette of tans, brown, and green. The caption reads, "The girl on the land serves the nation's need," and gives instructions to apply to the YWCA Land Service Committee. Maintaining a prickly, arm's-length relationship to the WLA, this committee ran its own recruitment drive.[38]

Charles Dana Gibson himself took a simple, direct approach to visualizing Land Army service in a drawing that appeared in the May 23 issue of *Life* magazine and was subsequently used as a WLA recruitment poster. In it, a virile Uncle Sam in red striped pants, his muscles bulging from his rolled shirtsleeves, tips his hat and gives a hearty handshake to a blue bloomer-uniformed farmerette (holding her iconic hoe, of course). In the background is a sketchy penciled image of American soldiers parading by, waving a flag and tipping their own campaign hats in tribute to the deal being struck between Sam and the Land Army girl. The poster's slogan is equally forthright; in big red letters it exclaims, "HELP! The Woman's

Land Army of America." Below, written between the figures of Uncle Sam and the farmerette, is a slogan that tries to capture the Land Army's purpose and promise while also emphasizing its temporary, emergency nature and reassuring those who still viewed women's farm labor as unseemly: "Until the Boys Come Back."[39]

Later in the season the New York State WLA commissioned its own membership and fund-raising poster. Featuring a young woman tending a garden with a sketch of a soldier in the background, its banner read, "Get Behind the Girl He Left Behind Him—Join the Land Army."[40]

In the summer and fall of 1918 the Woman's Land Army of America organized and supervised more than fifteen thousand volunteers who undertook farm labor as their patriotic contribution to the war effort. This number is considered a conservative estimate of the women who entered land service that year, as it does not count either those who were working as farmerettes in "unofficial" units (not directly supervised or sanctioned by the WLA) or the many "emergency" squads of women mustered at the local level for specific crop-saving duties. This estimate also does not include the many college and university units that worked on their own campus farms. Most important, it does not account for the thousands of eager women who registered for Land Army work but could not be placed in units because of community resistance, a lack of available start-up funds, or a shortage of qualified unit chaperones.

The Woman's Land Army of America was organized, on paper, in forty of the forty-eight states of the union and the District of Columbia, twenty-three of its state divisions were considered active in the 1918 season. The state division was the functional heart of the WLA movement: creating its own leadership structure, raising its own funds to operate camps, recruiting its own supervisors and workers, and imparting its own regional flavor to the operation.

Following the farmerette into the fields of California, Maryland, Connecticut, Illinois, Vermont and the New England states, New Jersey, Georgia, and New York—with forays into New Mexico, Michigan, Oregon, Ohio, Missouri, and Kansas—captures the movement's color, breadth, and texture. In these states the WLA made the greatest impact, or caused the greatest sensation, and its record has been preserved, however deeply buried. Examining these state divisions reveals common themes and shared patterns and illuminates the distinctive political and social cultures that had to be considered, confronted, and even ingeniously circumvented for the WLA to grow in the native terrain.

As the Woman's Land Army marched into America's fields in the summer of 1918, the farmerettes overcame resistance, earned respect, and inspired many lyrical tributes, including this song for the girl with a hoe:

Working Song of the Farmerette

(to the tune of "Over There")[41]

Brother's got his gun, gone to France, for the fray.
Sister's gone away, first of May, for to stay.
Planting crops to win the war.
Things she's never done before.
Kaiser Bill's afraid, Hindenburgh is dismayed,
Watch that Yankee maid learn a trade, use a spade,
Soon a farmer she will be
Planting crops for liberty.

(Chorus)
Plow away, plow away,
Gidd'ap horse, turn the ground under there,
Big crops we're sowing, the plants are growing,
The girls are farming everywhere.
Kaiser Bill, write your will,
Food we'll send without end to a friend.
We are working, there'll be no shirking,
And we won't stop farming
Until food has won the war.

Part Two

The Patriot Farmerette

12

IN BIFURCATED GARB OF TOIL: CALIFORNIA

A brass band welcomed the first unit of the California Woman's Land Army when it arrived in the town of Elsinore on the first of May. The whole community turned out to greet the fifteen women dressed in their stiff new uniforms. The Chamber of Commerce big shots gave speeches of welcome, the Farm Bureau president thanked the farmerettes for coming, and the mayor gave them the keys to the city.[1]

California did not fear the farmerette. Then as now, California prided itself on the imaginative impulse and progressive nature of its citizens—women had won the vote there seven years before—so a platoon of patriotic girls in "bifurcated" work costumes did not rattle or provoke as it might have in the East. Tradition did not weigh so heavily on the far coast of the continent, and the Wild West's spicy spirit was still nurtured. The *Los Angeles Times* even poked fun at the difference in attitude between the coasts:

> With even the conservative New England country-sides admitting as much
> [that the farmer needs the farmerettes] with very good grace, considering the
> utter lack of correct precedent in their traditions bearing on the subject, it is
> not surprising that California communities fairly march to meet the fair
> invaders with a "Welcome to Our City" banner and a band.[2]

The Golden State also suffered from an insatiable hunger for farm laborers and had long displayed a willingness to import workers from afar and exploit them if possible. For the California growers, ranchers, and packers, blessed with a long growing season for a great variety of crops, employing squads of women was simply a logical, practical business decision. Although the Food Administration had urged Californians to "produce and then produce more," Washington had quashed the farmers' petitions to import "coolie labor" from China, the war had shut off the flow of European immigrant laborers, and while Mexican workers were available, they were scorned as unreliable.

California could not be so foolish as to turn its back on any farm help available now, especially respectable, American women.

The leaders of the Woman's Land Army in California were politically powerful women of the progressive wing who recognized the strength of their bargaining position and the complexity of their task. They divided the state into northern and southern WLA divisions; established dual headquarters, in San Francisco and Los Angeles; and put in the key regional positions experienced women who knew how to talk to the growers, to finesse arguments, and to negotiate deals. Because California women already had the vote and some real political clout, these WLA leaders knew how to handle the knobs of the state bureaucratic machinery and which levers to pull and valves to turn to get things moving.

Katherine Philips Edson certainly did. She had championed the drive for the California suffrage referendum in 1911, pushed through landmark pure milk laws in the legislature, and spearheaded eight-hour-day and minimum-wage statutes for women. Edson was not only a trusted adviser to reformist Hiram Johnson—the former California governor, now U.S. senator, and Theodore Roosevelt's vice president on the Progressive ticket of 1912—she was also an expert on labor conditions and chairwoman of the state's Industrial Welfare Commission.

In these war years Edson wore two other hats, which made her a powerful friend of the Land Army movement: she was state chairwoman of the National League for Women's Service and served as the head of the Women in Industry Committee of the California Women's Committee of the Council of National Defense. After a careful survey of agricultural labor needs, conducted in the winter of 1918 and with the advice of the dean of the state's College of Agriculture, Edson and her Women in Industry colleagues decided to throw their energies and devote their considerable organizational resources toward a California Woman's Land Army. "We believed the recruiting attraction of the WLA was great," Edson recalled, "so all work of the Women's Committee in the farm labor needs was transferred to it."[3] Edson added to her hat collection by joining the Advisory Board of the California WLA.

Because the state's growers held lucrative government contracts to supply the U.S. Army and U.S. Navy with dried and canned fruits, they experienced high anxiety about their ability to plant and harvest enough to meet these commitments. Edson and her WLA comrades were able to demand extraordinary cooperation and protections for their Land Army workers. The state's Employment Bureau and agricultural agencies were put at their disposal. The WLA was able to get written labor contracts and enforce wage, hour, and working condition requirements for the farmerettes that were far ahead of the time; in fact, agricultural laborers in California would rarely enjoy these benefits again.

The grateful citizens of Elsinore gave the farmerettes three loud cheers as they welcomed them that May Day morning. The women, whom the *Los Angeles Times* labeled the "Intrepid First Fifteen," drove the fifty miles from the WLA headquarters in downtown Los Angeles to Elsinore in style: the mayor had dispatched a truck to chauffeur them. At the gala welcoming ceremonies, Mayor Burnham apologized for the lack of an official municipal key ring and offered instead a rake, hoe, and shovel to the farmerettes, "emblematic of their toil for patriotic defense." It was the thought that counted.[4]

The southern California WLA administrators, Myrtle Shepherd Francis in Los Angeles and Orpha Eastman in Elsinore, had prepared the ground carefully. They held letters of support and employment commitments from the town's major farmers. The promise of an assured pool of labor allowed the WLA to extract extraordinary concessions: a guaranteed term of employment; equal pay to what local male farm laborers could command, with a minimum wage of twenty-five cents an hour for an eight-hour day and overtime pay for any work beyond eight hours; and a limit of ten hours worked in a day. The employers also had to provide healthful, comfortable living quarters, subject to both WLA and state inspection; designated rest periods; lifting limits; and workers' compensation insurance.

In special negotiations with the Elsinore Development Corporation, the local growers' cooperative, the WLA also demanded that 2 percent of all profits resulting from their women's work be donated to the Red Cross. "If women help us plant and harvest a crop we otherwise would not have had," the Elsinore farmers happily conceded, "we can easily afford to give a patriotic bonus to the country's cause in this direct way."[5]

In preparation for the Land Army workers, an additional four thousand new acres outside town were planted in tomatoes, and a new cannery was built in Elsinore to handle the extra fruit. The WLA sent out an initial call to fill fifteen hundred positions in southern California. In the first week more than three hundred women visited the Los Angeles headquarters to apply, and in the next few weeks a coordinated recruitment campaign was put in motion. The superintendent of the Los Angeles school system sent letters to his principals and teachers, urging them to join the WLA during their summer vacation and enclosing a registration form in the envelope.[6] The California Federation of Women's Clubs got its membership behind the Land Army effort. And with the state WLA's encouragement, the California Civic League, an African-American civic organization, launched a recruitment drive for enlisting units of "colored girls." With several prominent African-American community leaders endorsing the plan and helping to sponsor it, the two Los Angeles "Negro weeklies" touted the Land Army service opportunity in their newspaper columns, and enlistment pitches were made at Sunday meetings in Odd Fellows' halls in the African-American neighborhoods of the city.[7]

The *Los Angeles Times*, notorious for its antipathy toward organized labor, trumpeted the arrival of the "Great Land Army" in Elsinore as an "epochal experiment" and proclaimed the farmerettes were "To Turn New Earth in History of the American Woman."[8] Looking "very businesslike" in their official uniforms, a one-piece outfit designed especially for the California WLA, this first brigade of "conquering heroines" at Elsinore included a trained nurse, several teachers, the wife of a famous New York City artist, and, of course, a girl with a sweetheart at the front "who says that his sacrifice will seem more worth while to him knowing that she is also giving active personal service."[9]

Supervised by a housemother, the farmerettes lived in a spacious twenty-room house. Photographs of their first day at work, handling horse-drawn cultivators and gangplows or driving giant tractors, were spread across the pages of the state's newspapers. Asked if the strenuous labor might prove too hard and whether some farmerettes might give up after a short stint, the recruits denied that was even possible. "Would we quit?" one farmerette told a reporter. "No, soldiers don't."[10]

Idella Purnell was an underage recruit when she volunteered for the WLA's northern California division, which opened its San Francisco headquarters just a week later. The daughter of American parents, Idella had been reared in Mexico but came north in preparation for entering the university at Berkeley that fall. As a patriotic gesture, she wanted to serve in the WLA in the summer months, but she was only seventeen years old, or a year short of the official entrance age. She passed her physical at headquarters, "and as I am 'husky' they decided to let my youth go unnoticed and simply make me 18!" Purnell confided, after the fact.[11]

The San Francisco recruiting officers were probably willing to bend the rules as they faced the prospect of trying to fill their quotas. The northern division WLA secretary predicted the group would need twelve thousand farmerettes, which turned out to be a wild overstatement, but farmers' requests were pouring in daily. An "advanced guard" of women, mostly Berkeley students, was sent to the University of California's agricultural farm at Davis for training and soon proved themselves "extremely efficient and as capable as men workers." Another WLA unit, based in Stanford's dormitories, worked the Santa Clara Valley's crops.[12]

"This is the recruiting slogan of the Women's Land Army of America," reported one San Francisco area newspaper: "Joan of Arc Left the Soil to Save France, We're Going Back to the Soil to Save America."[13] The slogan certainly worked. When Sacramento set up a district WLA office, more than 175 women enlisted for service in the first month, with two units placed in the field during the first week of June. The newspapers reported the units were "winning praise" from the farmers, who were "more than enthusiastic" and even "jubilant" about the work of the women. "Up in Sacramento they are nearly as proud of the WLA as of the new aviation field," reported the *San Francisco Examiner*. "In both cases justification lies in actual achievement . . . the WLA shows that the women and girls are serious . . . and mean to do their bits."[14]

In mid-June on the eve of their deployment, twenty-four fresh recruits gathered in the San Francisco WLA headquarters, located in the Underwood Building on Market Street. They were the first group assigned to the brand new farmerette camp at Vacaville, one built especially for them, and they were summoned together for a predeparture pep talk.

The Vacaville Camp represented the power and promise of the Woman's Land Army, and for the sake of the movement, the women must not fail. A consortium of local fruit growers constructed and furnished the camp and paid for it out of their own pockets. Unlike the typical WLA unit or camp situation, in which sponsoring women's clubs had to scrounge for suitable housing accommodations and then cobble together donated dollars and supplies, this camp arose shiny and whole from the dusty Vaca Valley floor. Even better, it had all been the growers' idea.

Early in 1918 the Vaca Valley growers had analyzed their labor options for the next five years—that is, for the duration of the war and beyond. Their options for a stable male labor pool looked dim, but they were convinced the prospect for obtaining women farmworkers was far rosier. To these farsighted, if self-interested, Vacaville growers, the WLA women's camp was the beginning of a long-term solution to their labor problems, even if it was launched as a patriotic lifeboat.

On high ground near the Vacaville train station, they built the camp with a six-foot-high pine stockade surrounding it, to lend what was called "a delightful sense of privacy to the whole establishment." It would at least keep out any Peeping Toms. Inside the stockade were canvas sleeping tents with wood floors, a screened kitchen and dining room, showers, a dressing room, and a hospital tent. The camp cost about $4,500 to build, and the growers agreed to share the investment: each grower pledged to pay a quarter-of-a-cent tax on every package of fruit shipped out of Vacaville, and the dried-fruit entrepreneurs agreed to donate fifty cents on each ton of fruit they sold. Only those who contributed toward the camp could then enjoy the farmerettes' assistance. The camp was ready on June 15, and the growers sent a request for "workers in fruit" to the WLA office in San Francisco.

These workers now assembled in that WLA office, listening as their supervisor, Alice Graydon Phillips, explained what their life and work would be like in the Vacaville Camp. She warned them that the summer heat would be brutal and that picking fruit atop ladders would make their backs, arms, and fingers sore. She read them the Woman's Land Army pledge and then asked aloud if they willingly would arise to the sound of a bugle at five thirty in the morning. "Yes!" they shouted. Would they consent to the WLA military-style structure? "Yes," they agreed in unison. Would they agree to muster for inspection, line up for exercise drills, take kitchen police duty, and eat the rations they were served without complaint? "Yes!" Would they submit to strict rules of discipline—including the provision that five offenses for lateness constituted one breach of discipline and an honorable discharge? Here the "Yes" chorus was punctuated by some sighs, but they assented. They signed the pledge forms. Then they elected two "majors" from their ranks to lead them—one, a girl who had four brothers fighting at the front; the other, an older woman from Santa Barbara with girl club experience. Led by a college girl from Berkeley, they all joined in a rousing cheer:

> Don't be a slacker!
> Be a picker or a packer!
> WLA, rah, rah, rah![15]

They took the early train to Vacaville, just beyond Napa, a journey of about sixty miles. "It was hot in the orchard at Napa," Idella Purnell recalled.

> The sun rose higher and higher, and the long ladders grew heavier and heavier. Perspiration started on our foreheads and beaded our lips. The golden peaches were so high—so hard to reach! The peach fuzz and dust on our throats and arms began to irritate the skin, but we did not dare scratch—we knew that would only aggravate the trouble. One who has never had "peach fuzz rash" cannot appreciate the misery of those toiling, dusty, hot-faced girls.[16]

Purnell, who would make her career as a writer and editor of an influential poetry journal, was getting a crash course in the less romantic aspects of farmerette life. "You will notice that I do not glorify the work—nobody could," Purnell wrote in one of the blunter assessments of Land Army service. "When we started we had nice new blue uniforms, and we called a rotten peach an 'over-ripe' or a 'spoiled peach'. When we had been there a few days we called them 'little green marbles' or 'rotten peaches'. No, it was not pleasant."[17]

The federal farm labor agent assigned to the territory watched the Vacaville experiment "as a chemist his crucible," reporting to the *Pacific Rural Press* that the women surpassed his expectations, and in many instances, they could pick just as much fruit as men could.[18] The women also tended to be more careful with delicate fruit than the average male worker and displayed a better eye for judging just the right blush of color signaling a perfectly ripe apricot or peach. As word of the farmerettes' good work spread throughout the region, more farmers asked for units to be based near their orchards and fruit ranches. The newspapers charted the farmerettes' summons into the golden groves: "Hundreds Go Into Fields at Once," "'Nother LA Unit—20 Occidental Girls in Khaki," "Women to Till Thousands of Southern California's Acres," and "Women Enlist for Month of Farm Work—Bifurcated Garb? Sure! And Charming!"

Just as those in the southern part of the state, the Vaca and Napa Valley employers were well pleased with the farmerettes. Their only complaint was that the constant parade of newspaper reporters, photographers, and motion-picture cameramen chronicling the women were a disruptive nuisance. The press certainly did not ignore the farmerettes. *Sunset* magazine, a regional publication, carried an editorial in its July issue titled "The Woman's Land Army Is Winning" and illustrated it with a photo of farmerettes in uniform posing with hoes slung over their shoulders like rifles.

The *Los Angeles Times* sent one of its star reporters, Alma Whitaker, to spend a day working with a Land Army unit, and she came away rather dazzled. She described one farmerette as "tall and husky and wields a spade like a young Amazon her sword" and another as possessing "a pair of shoulders and muscular arms like a bantam lightweight." Whitaker was also taken with the farmerettes' serious attitude:

> This woman's land army, composed of able-bodied young women,
> selected just as the men are selected by the army, for their physical
> capacity, their good characters, their general deportment, and trained
> and disciplined even rather more strictly than the men, that no petty
> frivolities or paltry scandals may mar the success of these first pioneers
> who must break down the prejudices of tradition, are acquitting themselves
> with amazing efficiency.[19]

A few days later the editorial board of the *Los Angeles Times* decided to weigh in on the Woman's Land Army. "It seems to be time that American men should reconsider any prejudices on this subject," the editorial maintained, seeing how the farmers at Elsinore and elsewhere had given "unstinted praise of the capacity and endurance of the attractive young women" now in the fields, who display "a zeal and dependability that have astonished the farmer." Overall, the farmerettes were proving to be smarter and more dependable than the average male farm laborer, the *Times* said, and they could handle farm machinery quite nicely.

> *The Times* believes the Woman's Land Army should be given a fair trial and
> every encouragement: that old prejudices should be held in abeyance. . . .
> But when it comes to solving the vast impressive food problem confronting
> America and her allies . . . *The Times* ventures to timidly suggest that ONE
> HUNDRED THOUSAND IMPORTED CHINAMEN in jumpers,
> working twelve hours a day, can raise more grub than twenty-two or thirty-
> four fair and clever women in vaudeville clothes.[20]

Those "vaudeville clothes"—the Land Army uniform—became quite the fashion topic in California that summer. "The women of the Land Army wear a uniform," explained the *San Francisco Examiner*.

> It is a nifty garment, this "regulation" prescribed by the organization. It is
> called the "freedomall" and is designed to give the greatest amount of bodily

freedom and to combine grace with utility. It is bifurcated, of course. Else how could the farmerettes climb trees and fences or stride through hedges of raspberries and other bushes?

> The whole is built of a blue cotton stuff much like gingham, called "Lad and Lassie" cloth. The upper part is a jumper blouse sewed to the bloomers. It looks like a two-piece suit, but is not. It is all in one garment and so cut that the farmerette may be slender as a rail or given to excessive *embonpoint* [plumpness] without the contour of her figure being given undue emphasis.[21]

Another reporter gave this description of the California farmerette's uniform:

> A one piece garment that was apparently born in the mind of some conservative who wished a middle ground between the lawless overall and the Victorian skirt. The overall cut is there—and with it the freedom of the ladder—but there is also a coat effect that might almost be called a skirt. It is a sort of survival skirt like the supplementary claw of the cat—a tribute to tradition.[22]

The one-piece uniform that the California WLA adopted also featured a red silk armband and broad-rimmed hat. The farmerette was expected to purchase her uniform; the overall cost $4.25 and the hat 25 cents. "The official uniform has called forth criticism," reported Alma Whitaker. "Farm laborers don't wear uniforms. But those uniforms are proven to be an essential and desirable asset," Whitaker explained, "for not only are they intensely practical, but they have exactly the same effect on girls as they do on the men—one lives up to a uniform."[23] The *Los Angeles Times* later admitted that some Californians considered the WLA uniform "ostentatious," but the editors defended it, saying, "The young women declare that that uniform affects their whole attitude towards the work—they must live up to it; they must do it credit."[24]

As in the military services, the Land Army uniform also served as a great social equalizer and provided a powerful sense of social cohesion. "The cotton uniform," wrote one California farmerette, "soon muddy and fruit stained, in which some girls looked picturesque, but no one overwhelmingly beautiful, leveled all distinction except those of personality, manners and speech."[25]

No matter how they looked, the picturesque farmerettes were definitely in demand by California fruit and hop ranchers. The southern WLA established thirty-three units in the field while in the northern part of the state the Vacaville "ideal camp" idea took root and seven more camps blossomed, dotting the San Joaquin, Sacramento, and Santa

Clara valleys. A call went out for two hundred women for the Coffin Ranch Camp in Florin, where deluxe accommodations were advertised to lure the more pampered patriots. These units featured electric lights, hot and cold showers, a piano in the mess hall for dancing, and even an ice cream freezer for cold treats.

The typical northern California farmerette was paid three dollars a day and charged a dollar a day to cover her food. An additional ten cents a week was subtracted from her pay to support a "Health Benefit Fund," which supported a well-stocked medical tent. California farmerettes earned significantly more than their sisters in other parts of the country, where fifteen dollars a month was the norm; the lowest gross wage for an eight-hour day was twelve dollars a week in California and the highest was twenty-one dollars for a week of eight-hour days. For all that, the northern WLA region could boast that not only were all eight of their camps completely solvent at the end of the 1918 season, but the larger camps actually reported a surplus of several hundred dollars.[26]

The rapid replication of the Vacaville Camp throughout northern California was not the result of a headlong rush of enthusiasm but of a careful, empirical process. That's the way the growers of Lodi went about it. Lodi is situated in the heart of grape country, a late-season crop, and the grape growers could take full advantage of the lessons learned by their stone-fruit colleagues. The Lodi growers appointed a scouting committee to visit Vacaville, see it for themselves, and determine whether it would meet their labor needs. The three appointed Lodi fruit ranchers returned, eager to convince their fellow growers to support a Woman's Land Army camp. The growers approved the plan and then went to city hall to get political support. Realizing the imperative of securing adequate labor for the town's primary industry, the city trustees gave their permission to use a piece of prime real estate, Hale Municipal Park, as the site for the WLA camp. The growers agreed to pick up the tab for constructing the camp, with the expenses to be apportioned among all those farmers who would benefit from the farmerettes' work.

The Lodi Camp was constructed in the town's park, in a plot about two hundred feet on each side. Surrounded by a privacy fence, its seventy-five wooden huts with canvas tent tops were tucked under the park's eucalyptus trees. Each hut housed two narrow cots, accommodating about 150 women in the camp. There was also an airy, screened dining hall and a kitchen fitted with every modern appliance. Banks of new toilets, showers, and dressing rooms completed the comfortable accommodations, and the whole camp was strung with electric lights. The camp cost close to $7,500 to build and equip.[27]

The Lodi Camp's farmerettes were experienced farmworkers by then. Most had already served in other California camps and units, picking early season fruit. One of those veterans, Susan Minor, reported that the long season had not dampened their enthusiasm. "I found there the same eagerness to put the venture through; the same buoyancy of spirit," she reported. She also experienced the sense of freedom, of fresh start, and new identity that the WLA camp offered.

> As in the old Western frontier days our past had no direct bearing on our
> life in camp. The camp life was an isolated experience and we were taken
> for what we were worth at the moment. The nature of the work was also
> a democratizer, work requiring speed in judging the color of fruit, speed
> of motion, and grit to maintain that speed. The possession of these
> qualities made two or three girls accustomed to piece-work in factories,
> two or three college students, a waitress, and an office clerk, the fastest
> workers.[28]

Idella Purnell was also assigned to Lodi after her stint in the Napa peach orchards and was promoted to the captaincy of her own small squad of workers. But amid the grapevines of Lodi, Captain Purnell encountered what every American feared in this time of war and what countless government posters warned citizens of the snake in the garden, the saboteur. At first Purnell assumed the woman was simply that lesser form of wartime menace, a slacker not willing to do her share, but Purnell's suspicions hardened when her lazy farmerette resorted to shoddy picking. "She took to sabotage," Purnell explained. "Green grapes, rotten grapes—anything and everything went into her boxes, tossed there by a hand careless of the precious bloom—and they all were only half full." At first, Purnell tried handle the situation herself:

> I remonstrated—mildly at first. I showed her again. . . . At noon I made a
> special talk to the girls for her benefit, in which I pointed out that we were
> soldiers just as much as the ones "over there," that we too had a chance to
> make good—or to be classified as slackers and cowards. I made it clear that a
> slacker was a person who tried to palm off poor boxes of grapes for good
> ones. One bad bunch ruins a whole box, and that is the same as helping
> shoot cannonballs at our boys.

But the slacker farmerette did not improve. "In fact, she seemed to take a malicious delight in doing her worst, and trying to get away with it," said Purnell. "I argued, pleaded, threatened and scolded by turns. Commanding did no good. That night I made a report to the camp supervisor, and learned that mine was not the first complaint against her. Mine was the last straw, and she was dishonorably discharged."[29]

This instance was also not the first time that the California WLA was confronted with a traitor in the ranks. Within the first week of the initial Land Army unit entering the fields at Elsinore, one of those "Intrepid First Fifteen" was accused of "pro-Germanism and insubordination" and subjected to a "court-martial" and a federal investigation. "It is charged that she identified herself with the initial campaign here with the deliberate purpose of disrupting it in its inception, and, by making the first expedition appear to be a failure, to cast discredit upon the whole national movement," the *Los Angeles Times* reported.[30]

Just days after the Elsinore brass band welcomed the farmerettes, the accused woman began her "traitorous" activities, according to her fellow land girls and Orpha Eastman, the WLA organizer who helped chaperone the Elsinore unit. After a barrage of early complaints about the woman's comments and actions, Eastman convened a unit tribunal. It turned into a "dramatic trial of her case at Elsinore, where she was faced with witnesses among the girls of the unit and given an opportunity before the entire membership to disprove the charges," according to the newspaper.[31]

Her denials were not convincing, and the explosive matter was quickly brought before the southern California WLA board in Los Angeles. It held a second hearing and alerted the Department of Justice, which opened its own investigation. The woman admitted to some of the charges against her conduct but excused herself on the grounds of "temper and temperament," the *Times* reported. She even "admitted having been charged with pro-Germanism on previous occasions, though she denied the justice of such accusations" and "asserted her innocence of all disloyal design."[32]

The WLA tribunal in Los Angeles did not believe her and announced that as a result of evidence presented at the court-martial, she was dismissed with a dishonorable discharge from the WLA. "A successful effort to disrupt this first field unit would have been serious," Mrs. Eastman admitted to the *Times*. "No precaution is too small, no safeguarding too complete to devote to the protection of our organization against any traitorous attempts." She continued,

> Too much importance cannot be placed upon the value of public confidence
> in this nation-wide movement. From the first we have realized that upon the
> proven worth of this initial effort depends the fate of the tremendous
> patriotic work that lies before us. To shake that confidence might mean utter
> disaster. The whole nation is looking to California to set a successful
> example in the task undertaken when the first unit of the Woman's Land
> Army of America marched out to take up the burden of food production on
> the land. We must not fail.[33]

Special Agent Keep of the Justice Department assured the WLA leaders that his office would undertake a speedy but thorough investigation of the woman's actions and

possible affiliations and determine whether she was part of a larger plot to torpedo the
Woman's Land Army. (The results of this investigation were never published.) For her
part, the dismissed farmerette said she welcomed the federal investigation. Perhaps more
significant, she also "stated her willingness to begin work again in whatever unit the
officers of the army might wish to assign her, declaring that, if she is not reinstated
in the Land Army, she will do independent productive work since she has chosen
this field of usefulness."[34]

Whether she reenlisted in the northern branch of the WLA, where the local recruiting office had no knowledge of her troubled history, and popped up again a few months
later in Lodi's grape arbors in an attempt to sabotage Idella Purnell's squad and undermine the Woman's Land Army is only delicious speculation.

The California Woman's Land Army ran a tight, centralized, and highly efficient
organization, recruiting more than two thousand women and probably becoming the
largest in the movement. All was not peaches and roses, though. Power plays and turf
wars occurred, several of which spilled into public view. In the northern California
WLA, the Executive Committee of the Sacramento office resigned en masse and shut
down the office in a dispute with the San Francisco headquarters staff over money and
supplies. The office closure and the prospect of interrupting the farmerette units' placement frightened the local fruit growers so profoundly that they called a meeting, decided the WLA was too valuable to lose, and pledged substantial financial backing to
the Sacramento office.[35]

The southern WLA region experienced its own leadership meltdown. Los Angeles
chairwoman Myrtle Shepherd Francis swooped down and forced Orpha Eastman to
resign from the WLA board, charging her with the equivalent of insubordination. "Had
to eliminate Mrs. Eastman," the *Los Angeles Times* quoted Francis as saying, a bit cold-
bloodedly, in one of many articles covering the unseemly coup. Francis maintained that
Eastman, who as Management Committee chairwoman was in charge of organization
for the southern district, "wished too much publicity and personal advancement" and
"stirred up dissatisfaction."[36]

The rift went beyond personalities and into real policy disagreements and manage-
rial disputes. Mrs. Eastman's "elimination" did not sit well with either the farmerettes or
the Elsinore growers, who had negotiated their labor deals with her. Mrs. Eastman did
not go quietly, either. The Elsinore farmerettes rallied to her defense and bombarded
the newspapers with outraged letters while the Elsinore Growers Association appealed
to the WLA national headquarters in New York to intervene and set things right. "Crisis Near in Affairs of Woman's Land Army," the *Los Angeles Times* warned. Then *Times*
staffer Alma Whitaker jumped into the fray, decidedly on Eastman's side, and called for
new leadership in Los Angeles:

> The Woman's Land Army, with 500 strapping wenches gladdening the
> hearts of Southern California farmers, has passed the stage of criticism and
> ridicule. It's one of those established war revolutions that has happened
> with bloodless efficiency and nobody is sorry. The thing is so good, so
> successful, so buoyantly efficient, has grown to such immense propor-
> tions, that it is certainly deserving of a smooth-working and capable
> headquarters staff.[37]

Whatever bickering went on in the WLA headquarters, the farmerettes won praise
and respect in the fields. They handled every machine, harvested every one of the state's
great range of crops, mowed hay, milked cows, and managed horses. The Walnut Growers Association requested their quick, careful hands to help bring in that valuable nut
crop, as did the almond growers. The agricultural community predicted that the following year Woman's Land Army "cantonments" would multiply all over the state, with
the Lodi and Vacaville "ideal camps" used as models.

In fact, the Lodi Camp became a real model at the California State War Fair, a huge
exhibition in Sacramento of the state's war industry capacity, including seventy-five
types of tractors and other machines used to fight the food battle. There, on the main
exhibition hall's balcony, was the contribution of the California Commission of Immi-
gration and Housing, the state agency overseeing agricultural workers' living conditions: a wooden scale model of the Lodi Camp, the "ideal" facility growers had built for
their farmerettes.[38]

Just a few days later, in early September, one of the last WLA camps of the season
was erected on Santa Monica Boulevard in Hollywood. Capt. Louis Derocher, a Spanish-
American War veteran who donated his sixty-four-acre farm tract to the WLA,
designed the "California School for Farmerettes" as a training facility. Derocher also
cajoled the brass at nearby Fort MacArthur to send a brigade of artillerymen to help
build the farmerette school's barracks in Hacienda Park. Thirty-five Coast Artillery
Corps privates from the fort paid their own bus fare and worked all day, elbow to elbow
with the farmerettes, hammering and sawing the building materials local businessmen
and WLA patrons had donated. It made for a great photo, and the gunmen must have
enjoyed their work for they promised to return every Sunday until the barracks were completed and the long list of applicants for the school's sixty-day training course could finally
be properly housed.[39]

And when those brave farmerettes moved into the new twenty-seven-cot barracks, by all rights they should have had above their cots a proper "pinup," a photo
of a handsome movie star to inspire them, just as their brothers in the army
and navy had their starlets. That provocative *Los Angeles Times* reporter and
columnist, Alma Whitaker, proposed the pinup idea and archly exhorted the
nascent movie industry's matinee idols to do their bit by becoming "godfathers" to
land girls and the other patriotic women war workers.

Now, while our masculine regiments are well supplied with fair godmothers, not a single godfather has arisen for the benefit of the land army girls or the war efficiency motor maids or the Red Cross chapter girls. . . . It isn't fair. What are the stylish picture heroes thinking about? Why isn't Charlie Chaplin or Douglas Fairbanks offering themselves in this guise? Is masculinity trying to assert, in this day and age, that women's patriotism is not as important and self-sacrificing as men's patriotism? Pshaw!

Think of the land army girls, exuding honest sweat on California farms, day in and day out, in uniforms quite as becoming as any at Camp Kearny . . . all without a godfather. I don't know how they keep their courage up under such wanton neglect.

And in a suggestion that perhaps only the star reporter for the newspaper of record in Hollywood could make, Whitaker proposes, "It would be such a nice compliment if, say, Charlie Chaplin should adopt the first unit of the woman's land army and go down to see them decked in a land army uniform, just as Mary Pickford wore khaki when she went to San Diego."[40]

The farmerette was truly accepted in California. She had powerful friends and an astute organization behind her, she elicited unprecedented cooperation from growers, and she tickled the public fancy. So it's no surprise that when San Francisco launched the Fourth Liberty Loan campaign in October, the city asked farmerettes to help sell bonds and promote the cause. A contingent of nine uniformed farmerettes drove into the City by the Bay in a fruit-festooned truck. Within the first three hours of their arrival they had collected $1,500, and they spent four days singing, giving four-minute speeches, and "harvesting" bond dollars.[41] Besides their uniforms, the farmerettes also donned face masks as a precaution; the influenza epidemic had reached California.

There is perhaps no better tribute to the image the California farmerette groomed for herself and to the respect she earned than her participation in the Sacramento women's work parade on October 9, a Liberty Loan extravaganza featuring six marching bands, a drum corps, and more than twenty-five hundred marchers. Farmerettes wearing their "bifurcated garments of toil," as the *Sacramento Bee* put it, joined with Red Cross, YWCA, Salvation Army, and other women workers in the spectacular nighttime parade through the streets of the capital, "carrying Japanese lanterns extended above their heads on slender wands . . . forming long lines of moving light." At the end of the long parade arrived "one of the prettiest features of the evening," the *Bee* reported—a contingent of farmerettes from the California hop fields, dressed in their official blue overalls, marching under an archway of hop vines.[42]

Land Army Song
by Myrtle Shepherd Francis
(to the tune of "Battle Hymn of the Republic")[43]

Our Mother Earth has called us, for the Nations we must feed.
We have rallied to her standard to produce our greatest need.
We will labor on her bosom and achieve that worthy deed,
As we go working on.
Glory, glory, hallelujah, etc.
We are told by Herbert Hoover that the war by food is won,
So we're laboring at production from the dawn till set of sun.
We have donned the khaki uniform to fight the mighty Hun,
And we go working on.
Glory, glory, hallelujah, etc.
We are going to whip the Kaiser and our hearts are unafraid,
We will help to win this wicked war with hoe and rake and spade.
Though our tasks be of the hardest we will never be dismayed,
But still go working on.
Glory, glory, hallelujah, etc.
We have joined our hands for service with our sisters 'cross the sea,
We have forged a mighty weapon in our fight for liberty,
By the spirit of our labor in the Woman's Land Army,
As we go working on.
Glory, glory, hallelujah, etc.

13

HORTENSE POWDERMAKER IN MARYLAND

Hortense Powdermaker's awkward status—as a brilliant student but social outsider at Goucher College, as a child of wealth with rebellious inclinations—made her the perfect soldier for the Woman's Land Army. Being smart and rich wasn't quite enough to secure her ease in the porcelain teacup world of a southern women's college. She was the daughter of a well-to-do Baltimore businessman, she earned honors in her history studies at Goucher, and she took a keen interest in politics and loved to dance; still, she felt like an outsider. Her religion, she was shocked to learn, placed her apart. When refused entry into a sorority, Powdermaker was startled about the reason why: the college sororities were simply not open to Jews. "I was not sure that I wished to join one, but I wanted to be invited," Powdermaker confessed, years later, in her memoir. "A relatively unimportant snub by college sororities was thus my first awareness of social restrictions on Jews."[1]

In a desire to rebel against her own family's smug materialism, Powdermaker "developed socialistic interests" at college, became fascinated by the Baltimore slums (a part of town she'd never before seen), and took a serious interest in the trade union movement. To understand the plight of workers, during a vacation, she even took a factory job running the sewing machine and making men's shirts, which she found mind numbing and body bending.[2]

So in the spring of 1918, when recruiters for the Woman's Land Army came to Goucher and sang of the nobility of patriotic toil on the land, Hortense Powdermaker was their ideal candidate. The "food problem" was the war issue that caught her fancy. Hortense's older sister Florence was already taking time from her doctoral studies at Johns Hopkins and was helping write a college textbook, *Food and the War*, that was sponsored by the Food Administration.[3] Hortense had already done her bit toward making her classmates aware of the dire situation when she presented to the Goucher History Club the report "College Women and the Food Situation," cribbing a few statistics from Florence's research sources. She'd also heard Helen Fraser's stirring testimony of the work of English women in the field; she'd sat in the college chapel as Helen Kennedy Stevens recounted the Bedford girls' escapades; and she took to heart the notices in the student newspaper headlined "To Farms! To Farms! Ye Maids." She wanted to be a farmerette.

This new Land Army would be beyond the social strictures that made her so uneasy and outside the power of gentile girls to exclude her. It would take her to a place where her religion might not matter. And what better way to gently rebel against her proud, cerebral, and sophisticated family than to take up the manual labor of the peasant class.

Marylanders did not hide their nervousness about the farm labor situation. They did not put on a brave front and declare there was no problem or that it could be solved easily. This honesty allowed for an early spirit of cooperation and a greater willingness to consider a range of unorthodox solutions.

During the winter and early spring the state extension service convened biweekly farmers' meetings in each county and district to discuss problems and anticipate the stresses that the new season would bring. The military draft and the high-paying shipbuilding and munitions industries in the port of Baltimore had already drawn away at least nine thousand of the state's farm laborers, and more were expected to be called up in a second round of conscriptions. The Maryland farmers were anxious and losing patience with Washington's approach of denial coupled with halfhearted measures.

The state's leading newspaper, the *Baltimore Sun*, voiced the state's exasperation with federal policy. It mocked Washington's "all will be well" assurances by printing an article headlined "Alarming Facts About the Farm Labor Situation." Summarizing a national canvass of state agricultural commissioners and Grange masters, it pointed out the "wide differences" between the optimistic reports issued by government labor bureaus and the reality on the ground expressed by farming professionals.[4]

A few weeks later, on the eve of the planting season, the *Sun* wrote a scathing editorial that castigated the government's lack of a workable farm labor policy:

> Outside of official Washington, we are no longer in a state of complacency,
> no longer satisfied that everything will come out all right in the end. But,
> unfortunately, the people of the country cannot help themselves effectually.
> They must depend on Washington to help them, to mobilize them, to
> direct them. Washington must give the word of command and must plan the
> thing that is to be done. Now, the question is, has anything of any value
> been done. Is anything comprehensive being planned?[5]

The paper challenged Secretary of Agriculture Houston and President Wilson's paltry plan—calling on inexperienced city men and boys to help out on the farms—as completely inadequate. In addition, it called the newest federal solution, which involved offering furloughs to farm men in the army so they could return home for planting or harvesting, "totally unworkable." The paper pointed out each man would have to personally petition for the furlough, and most would already be shipped to France by the time any such leave could be approved.

By now the women of Maryland, as in the rest of America, had learned not to wait for Washington to plan or direct their efforts; so they got busy mobilizing their own response to the farm crisis. "The principal industry of Prince George's County is agriculture and as there will undoubtedly be a shortage of farm labor during the coming season, our women must consider going into agricultural work as a patriotic service," wrote the chairwoman of that county's Women in Industry Committee back in December 1917.[6] By January the Women's Committee of the Maryland Council of Defense had invited Laura Crane Burgess, chairwoman of the New York State Woman's Land Army, to visit and advise it on how to start a state WLA organization, and by February a WLA structure was in place. Reports of the farmerettes' successful work in the summer 1917 were presented at many of the farmers' county meetings, just to get them used to the novel idea. It was, as always, a slow process, and in a racially segregated state like Maryland, there were special problems.

When the Maryland Women's Committee Food Production task force circulated a questionnaire to gauge the farmers' sentiment toward women laborers on farms, they initially received a disheartening response. They discovered the farmers fully expected to face a serious labor shortage but were not eager to employ untrained women workers. One county, however, reported that "colored woman labor would be acceptable" while white women's would not be.

"Because of the number of colored farm laborers in some sections of Maryland, efforts to secure employment for a woman's land army (composed of white women) may meet with opposition here," the committee reported.[7] Allowing white women into the same fields as black male farm laborers, especially in the southern Maryland counties, would not be tolerated. Of course, black women working in southern fields was commonplace, but white women were rarely, if ever, seen there, making the WLA's plans for white college women doing fieldwork all the more outlandish.

But the plans went ahead, with the understanding that those northern counties that were closer to the Mason-Dixon Line and the regions around the principal urban areas might be more hospitable hosts to WLA units. In late winter, Mrs. Janon Fisher of Baltimore was appointed chairman of the Maryland WLA organizing effort, and she brought Helen Kennedy Stevens down for a series of recruitment rallies.

Of course, while the Maryland state authorities were not overtly hostile to the WLA's formation plans, it was not the sort of labor solution they had in mind. Instead, their plans revolved around city men and boys volunteering to go to the fields. In Frederick

County a "Farm Vacation Club" was proposed, in which city men, bookkeepers, and shop clerks would be asked to spend their summer vacations working on a farm. When the farmers pointed out that these indoor men's untrained and flaccid muscles would not be up to strenuous farmwork, they were reminded that gentler duties, like poultry raising, might be suitable for soft city men. (That poultry raising was often women's work on the farm was not mentioned.) Factories and companies in the state, especially those holding government contracts, were encouraged—or strong-armed—to give their male employees leave to work on local farms during the harvest.

Maryland, like many other states, eagerly hoped its teenage boys would come to the crops' rescue. Unlike the young women who so enthusiastically signed up for Land Army duty, the young men of peach fuzz age often had to be convinced and cajoled into joining the U.S. Boys' Working Reserve. For those too young or frail to don a soldier's uniform and painfully envious of those who could, the call to the farm simply could not match the romance of the call to the front. When Working Reserve recruiters entered Baltimore's large public high schools and addressed the biggest pool of boys available, they discovered the young patriots had other plans for the summer, such as signing up for well-paying factory jobs. "The enrollment of the boys could only be secured by persuasion and appeals to their patriotism," admitted the Maryland Council of Defense. Even then, "enrollment of a large number of boys [was] exceedingly difficult."[8]

Even if the boys did enroll, however, the farmers weren't sure they wanted them. "Many farmers had a deep-seated prejudice against the city boy," the Maryland Council acknowledged. "This mental attitude was reflected by the statement made at a public county meeting by a well-known farmer that he would rather have a mule blind in one eye and a half-witted negro than a dozen city school boys."[9] But the Boys' Working Reserve was the only organized farm labor supplement plan Washington had up its sleeve to offer to the frightened states, so in Maryland, as elsewhere, "it therefore became necessary to conduct a campaign of education among the farmers of the State to eradicate this prejudice" against boy workers.[10]

The women of the WLA, meanwhile, were left to eradicate prejudices against them on their own. They conducted persuasion campaigns at farmers' meetings, bringing in Ethel Puffer Howes and other WLA speakers to explain the practicalities of the unit plan. They emphasized that unlike the Boys' Working Reserve teenagers, who boarded with the farm families, the farmerettes wouldn't require any room, food, or behavioral supervision. The farmers weren't thrilled with their Hobson's choice, the prospect of using untrained city boys or similarly green city girls on their farms. "The farmers have been discussing the problem," the *Washington Post* reported in late March, "and about 30 reported at the meeting [that they were] interested, if not wholly committed, to the plan" of using women.[11]

The Maryland WLA's appeal to the state's farmers was certainly helped by the publicity that greeted the opening of the National Service School's third encampment, which, as the *Baltimore Sun* put it, "will be devoted to the training of an army of farmerettes."[12] Nearly two-thirds of the 250 women enrolled were pursuing agricultural training in a six-week course of intensive instruction that included tractor operations. Miss Elizabeth Poe was back as the camp commandant, looking as spiffy as ever in her crisp uniform, and to her credit, she had designed this third encampment to meet the nation's urgent needs of the moment. Besides the usual Red Cross training and the new farming curriculum, the camp had developed a business training course for women moving into commercial and government desk work.[13]

"When the staccato notes of reveille sound over the historic Potomac River . . . hundreds of khaki-clad women will spring to arms, and, shouldering their rakes, march in military formation 'back to the soil,'" the *Sun* reported. "Each woman will apply herself for six weeks to the serious business of raising food to furnish 'ammunition' to our men and our allies' men who are fighting the war in her name 'over there'."[14]

Further, it certainly boosted the Land Army's cause when the newspapers also reported Secretary of the Navy Josephus Daniels's words at the camp's opening ceremonies in April, as he greeted the female trainees as "Comrades!" Daniels went on to explain, "Time was when we addressed young women on public occasions as ladies, but now they are our comrades in the work of the war."[15] Daniels paid special tribute to the agricultural work the women would do in the coming season: "We eat corn bread to conserve wheat, but unless you and other women all over the country raise the corn, where is our conservation?"[16] Daniels's emphasis on the women's role in production, rather than just conservation, was a marked departure from the governments' official stance. Being an old newspaperman himself, Daniels did not clear his comments with the Agriculture Department's Clarence Ousley.

Women from every state were enrolled in the third encampment. The Daughters of the American Revolution sponsored a "Company of the States," assembling a woman from each of the forty-eight states of the union. The press emphasized the camp's social melting pot ideal:

> The wife of the general fighting in France, the wife of the millionaire aviator will work side by side with the small-town woman whose club has given an entertainment to raise the money to send their representative to this school. The business girl will ply her hoe in company with the debutante of the season who has scorned the festivities of springtime pleasure resorts to devote six weeks to preparing herself for national service.[17]

When Hortense Powdermaker became a farmerette in the Maryland Woman's Land

Army, her fellow Goucher recruits were sent to one of three units: Catonsville, Maryland; Fallston, Maryland; or Long Island, New York. Before shipping out to the fields and while still in spring term classes, Powdermaker and the other Goucher farmerettes had the opportunity to learn how to run tractors on the grounds of a nearby farm.

The Goucher girls' real toughening up would take place once they reported to their assignments, though their accommodations were anything but spartan. At Catonsville, about fifteen miles southwest of Baltimore, the Land Army occupied the baronial estate of shipping magnate Bernard Baker, who donated his manor house and three hundred acres of farmland as a patriotic gesture. Along with a chaperone, who managed the unit and negotiated with the neighborhood farmers, the farmerettes moved into the elegantly furnished fieldstone mansion with its red Italian tile roof and hand-carved fireplace. "It is not expected that the farmers will be induced to adopt woman labor on their farms without some convincing," the local Catonsville paper explained in April, "but the organizers of the units are convinced that a demonstration will prove the practicability and efficiency of the women workers, and they do not anticipate any serious difficulty in securing employment for their squads."[18]

To ease their way into the labor marketplace, the local WLA organizers agreed to a significantly lower wage scale than other Land Army units demanded, charging the farmers only $1.20 a day for each woman's work rather than the going rate of $2.00 a day in the northeastern states. As usual, the farmers' initial response was hesitant, but some Catonsville farmers were quickly convinced of the value. "The farmerettes have been doing excellent work on the farms, and all who have employed them speak in the highest terms of their efforts," the Catonsville paper reported.[19] When the farmers obviously still needed some prodding, the *Catonsville Argus* scolded them in early July:

> The harvest is ripe, masculine laborers are few, and still many farmers in
> Baltimore County are not availing themselves of the industrial assistance
> offered by the patriotic Women's [*sic*] Land Army. The farmerettes are
> available and anxious to assist in this important patriotic work. They
> can, and will, work in the harvest fields and those desiring their aid can
> secure it.[20]

Thinking perhaps a pep talk from the governor might help, Emerson Columbus Harrington agreed to lend the authority of his office to bolster the farmerettes' mission in Maryland. On a balmy Saturday afternoon in July, Governor Harrington stood on the porch of the Ingleside mansion and spoke to a gathering of neighborhood farmers, explaining the common sense of employing farmerettes, extolling their accomplishments, and urging more farmers to hire them.[21] Harrington was definitely a Land Army booster, and he'd already publicly called for Maryland women to join the WLA corps.[22] He also knew that at this point in the season the attempt to recruit city men for farmwork was a resounding failure while the Boys' Working Reserve kids were earning a reputation as unreliable and mopey.[23] (The state director of the Boys' Working Reserve had made a public appeal to farmers to "be patient" with the boys sent to them.[24])

The women, meanwhile, were getting rave reviews, and one Catonsville farmer decided the women working for him deserved more than he had agreed to pay. He unilaterally raised their wages to two dollars a day. "And he feels that at that price the farmerettes are so extremely worth while that he has engaged two of them for the rest of the summer," the *Argus* reported.[25] The Ingleside farmerettes charmed the neighbors, too, who vied for the privilege of entertaining them. The townsfolk recognized that they were, after all, refined young ladies under their overalls. One neighborhood matron gave the hot and tired workers permission to enjoy her swimming pool and even supplied them with bathing suits; others invited them to lunch or tea in their sun parlors. "So the competition goes on, with everybody trying to see who can be nicest to the farmerettes," reported the local paper. "Oh, for the life of the farmerette! Oh, to be a soil-soldier at Catonsville!"[26]

Hortense Powdermaker was a soil soldier in the Fallston unit, where the majority of the Goucher farmerettes, thirty-eight in all, were stationed. Her voice comes through in the account of the unit's summer experiences published in the school paper. Later in her life Powdermaker would win acclaim for her anthropological fieldwork in the South Pacific islands, in Africa, and in the American South, where she meticulously observed and analyzed the details of native life. In the Woman's Land Army Powdermaker encountered a tiny new society forming, one with its own structures, mores, taboos, and rewards.[27]

Those who "went farmeretting" at Fallston lived in a big stone house, slept on straw mattresses, and propped their washbasins on packing crates. As in so many other hastily assembled WLA camps, friends and neighbors of the local WLA organizers donated the furnishings—rocking chairs, stools, crockery, and most important, Victrolas for musical evening entertainment. Farmerettes were not a somber bunch.

"We felt so patriotic and so satisfied with what we were accomplishing for Mr. Hoover and Uncle Sam," wrote the Fallston unit memoirist, probably Powdermaker herself. And as college women, they approached their stoop labor with an intellectual bent. "We sang, we talked on such subjects as 'the Immortality of the Soul, Justice upon Earth, etc.,'" and "we took to naming the weeds. There was the Hun which sent its thorns through the strongest kid glove, and there was German Propaganda that spread all over three or four rows, but which could be all traced back to one little root."[28]

They also took immense pride in their toughening and in their growing ability to do heavy work. As in any society, primitive or not, the strong were given privileges and envied. "The work that proved us and showed just how capable we could be came with the harvest time," said the Fallston farmerette. "Of course only the huskies were sent out for hay and wheat and oats, but the rest of us envied them." And even the locals took notice of the farmerettes' striking physique, but not in the usual terms of praise for feminine loveliness. "Having served their apprenticeship in thinning and hoeing corn, these husky, sunburned maidens with muscles that are becoming more steely than they could ever hope to become in the best gymnasium are now doing the heaviest kind of farm work," said the Catonsville newspaper, with clear admiration, "and doing it with a vim that would put the average sluggish masculine farm-hand to shame."[29]

The farmerettes usually emerged the winners when they were compared to the male farmhands left in the fields, those dispirited laborers not fit for military duty nor ambitious enough to find industrial work. These men were often resentful of the peppy young women sent into their midst, women who didn't feel doomed to manual labor for the rest of their lives and could afford to display such high spirits through the drudgery. "The man with the hoe is being out-distanced by the woman with the hoe and she is far from a stolid and forlorn looking object," said the *Catonsville Argus* in what the farmerettes could consider the highest of compliments. "She is instinct with energy and ability and in her garden hat is something fair to look upon."[30]

The Fallston farmerettes could even joke that the male laborers they worked with took the cushier, less strenuous tasks. While threshing wheat, "of course the men ran the engine, filled the bags with wheat and did the other easy things while we did the pitching," reported a Fallston woman. "We had a little song that we sang, a part of which might express our sentiments on this subject:

> *We work through rain, and we work through heat,*
> *While the men drive the horse from a comfortable seat.*[31]

The contingent of Goucher farmerettes dispatched to the WLA unit at St. James, a farming community on the north shore of Long Island, New York, were forced to prove themselves on two fronts; initially, even the Land Army organizers didn't want them. "The local committee of the Woman's Land Army at St. James had decided that they did not want college girls in their unit," wrote a Goucher woman stationed there, "but wanted working girls who were accustomed to good hard work, girls who could do something besides having a good time. We were taken as a last resort and that was the reputation we had to live down."[32]

That tension between the proven work ethic of the factory or shop girl and the untested resolve of the college girl or woman of leisure was still very much present in this second season of the Land Army. But a tenet of WLA policy was that the mixture of both classes of women into a unit created a positive energy: the working woman brought her sensible patriotism, coupled with a practical need to make a little extra

money during her off-season, and the college-educated woman brought her refinement, her book-learned sense of higher purpose, and her dormitory sense of fun to the
Land Army community.

Such class distinctions, hidden by the WLA uniform, were invisible to residents of
the communities where the farmerettes worked. To these neighbors, all the farmerettes
looked strange. "It certainly did amuse the people who lived in the towns where we
worked," recalled a Dorothy Von Houten, a Baltimore student who worked as a Maryland WLA farmerette around Takoma Park and Kensington that summer and submitted an essay about it to the *Washington Post*.

> They would all run to the tracks and stare at us as if we were live trained
> monkeys performing for the children at a circus. People along the road
> started yelling "there go the crazy farmerettes" for they made all kinds of fun
> of us for wearing overalls and doing men's work, except the farmers, who
> said they didn't know how they would have gotten along without the girls to
> help them this summer.[33]

The citizens of Fallston were also prone to stare at the farmerettes. "The people
stared at us, as tho we were a circus," Stella Rothschild wrote in a letter, describing the
locals' reaction when two jitneys filled with uniformed farmerettes drove into town for
an outing to the movies.[34] But the local gentry welcomed the patriot farmhands. "The
main citizens of the village invited us to the Soldier's and Sailor's Club where we danced
on a splintery floor to the tune of a creaky victrola," Rothschild, also a Goucher student, wrote to her cousin serving in the Army.[35]

Other WLA camps at work in Maryland that summer were located on the Eastern
Shore at Claiborne, in the fields around Frederick and Hagerstown, in Prince George's
County at Silesia, in the Baltimore outreaches at Pikesville, and in the District of
Columbia's suburbs near Rockville. By harvest time the *Catonsville Argus* could say of
the farmerettes, "Even the most skeptical farmers in this vicinity have accorded them
unstinted praise. Many of the crops have been saved for the country."[36]

And even the *Maryland Farmer*, the major agricultural publication in the state, which
assiduously ignored the WLA in the early part of the season, began publishing occasional photos of the farmerettes at work. It even carried an article by William McC.
Hillegeist, a USDA farm help specialist, whose experience gave him clout in the farming community. Any Maryland farmer who still scoffed at farmerettes had to slump in
his chair and take a long puff on his pipe when he read Hillegeist's unabashed valentine
to them:

> Is it out of place at this time to confess that the writer has been converted to
> the employment on the farm of seriously-minded women who are physically

fit for this work? Having visited the camps of the Woman's Land Army at Catonsville and Fallston and learned of their activities, I am assured that the farmer cannot say any longer that "wimmin ain't no good". In another year—may I venture to predict?—women will be employed in much larger numbers on the farm.[37]

Hortense Powdermaker was convinced of that, too. She returned from the fields for her senior year at Goucher, assumed the chairmanship of the college's Farm Committee, and became the school's liaison to the WLA organization. She wrote articles, made speeches, propagandized, and organized on the Land Army's behalf, telling the romantic tale of those who "went farmeretting" for Uncle Sam. She spent the next winter and spring recruiting a new troop of volunteers for the 1919 Goucher units.

With the Woman's Land Army Hortense Powdermaker found a campus role that suited her, one where her religion did not restrict her. In the fields, her intense intellectual mind found release, and she gained respect for those who must live by the sweat of their brow. (Her first job after college would be as a labor organizer for the Women's Trade Union League, and she would write about workers in many of her celebrated anthropological studies.) While Powdermaker had no interest in becoming a farmer, she could happily observe the folkways of rural life and marvel at the peculiar rituals and bonds that evolved in the evanescent society of the farmerette unit camp. She experienced the freedom of entering into a totally strange society, living in it for a while, and then leaving it. She would make a distinguished career of doing just that, all over the world.

New York suffragists used their patriotic land service as an argument for granting women the vote in the 1917 state referendum. *Library of Congress*

Ruth Litt, chair of the Suffrage Agriculture Committee of New York, plowing on her Long Island farm, wears the "chic and practicable" uniform she designed. *National Archives*

Recruitment poster for the British Women's Land Army, the model for American land service. *Library of Congress*

National and state Councils of Defense formed women's committees to coordinate volunteer recruitment and. war work efforts. *Library of Congress*

The National League for Women's Service featured a farmerette in this recruitment poster. The League's National Service Schools trained women for war work, including agricultural service. *National Museum of American History, Smithsonian Institution*

The Bedford Camp worked out the practical details of women's land service and the "unit" system. *Barnard College Archives*

The Women's Agricutural Camp at Bedford, New York opened in spring 1917 and continued through summer 1920. *Barnard College Archives*

Suffrage activists reporting for agricultural duty in 1917. The suffrage movement embraced land service as a pioneering new role for women. *Library of Congress*

Bedford Camp farmerettes were driven by car or truck to work on neighboring farms. Their overalls were shocking. *Barnard College Archives*

The accomplishments of the Bedford Camp laid the groundwork for establishing the Woman's Land Army later in 1917. *Barnard College Archives*

Ida Helen Ogilvie, professor of Geology at Barnard College, served as dean of the Bedford Camp and director of recruiting for the WLA. *Barnard College Archives*

City women trained to handle farm tasks and appreciate the rhythms of rural life at the Bedford Camp. *Barnard College Archives*

Vassar College students in Poughkeepsie, N.Y. took over the work of the 740 acre College Farm in 1917 and demonstrated that women could handle farm work. *Vassar College Special Collections*

Herbert Hoover's Food Administration urged food conservation and voluntary rationing with this image of French women farming in dire wartime circumstances. *Library of Congress*

The ability to operate a tractor allowed women to do the kind of heavy farm work once reserved only for men. *National Archives and Records Administration*

Vassar College women chopping wood. Students at Mount Holyoke, Bryn Mawr, Goucher, and other colleges were also farm volunteers in the summer of 1917. *Vassar College Special Collections*

14

CULTIVATING THE SOOTHING WEED: CONNECTICUT

The perfect specimens of Progressive-era womanhood who ran the Connecticut division of the Woman's Land Army found themselves in a quandary. The farmers of New Milford, in the hilly western side of the state, were willing, even eager, to employ women laborers to help with their crops. In New Milford the WLA encountered none of the usual resistance, and the farmers wanted at least twenty women to start right away. Their crop, however, was tobacco— Housatonic Valley tobacco, the broadleaf variety that grew so well in the river bottomlands, that most surprising of Yankee cash crops. Wartime demand for tobacco was great, and the farmers stood to make a great deal of money. Food might win the war, but tobacco kept the troops happy. While canned veggies were all fine and good, what the troops really wanted was smokes.

This situation bordered on a moral dilemma. Should the WLA's patriotic efforts be expended on growing essential foodstuffs needed to nourish troops at the front and stave off European famine, or on the soothing weed needed to calm the nervous cravings of the American Expeditionary Force? This policy issue was thrown into the lap of the Connecticut WLA Executive Committee at its pivotal April planning meeting in Hartford.[1] Around the conference table on the Capitol Building's second floor sat some of the most politically savvy women in the Nutmeg State, all of whom were veterans of the suffrage and various reform movements and used to the rough and tumble of political affairs. A leader in women's education and the founder and headmistress of the Rosemary Hall girls' school, Caroline Ruutz-Rees brought her strong suffrage sentiments and canny political skills to both the state Council of National Defense (she was chair of the Women's Committee) and the Democratic National Committee. Corinne Robinson Alsop, niece of Theodore Roosevelt, followed her mother (TR's sister, Corinne Roosevelt Robinson) into the highest echelons of the Republican Party, where she used her formidable connections to advance a variety of social causes. She also served on the Women's Committee of Connecticut.

Joining Ruutz-Rees and Alsop was Grace Knight Schenck, the state WLA chair-woman. She had enjoyed a career as the chief surgical nurse at a major New York City hospital before moving with her young family to the Connecticut countryside in 1911. Within three months of her arrival in Wilton she had organized the first women's suf-frage meeting at the town hall, and within her first year in town she had launched the Women's Civic League and an Equal Franchise League branch.[2]

Leo Korper, the director of the U.S. Department of Labor office in Connecticut; his staff assistant; and the U.S. Employment Service field director were also at the table. They worked closely and amicably with the WLA, and unlike their bosses in Washing-ton, these federal bureaucrats on the ground had no illusions about the state's looming farm labor shortage. Connecticut was a throbbing hub of the nation's munitions indus-try, and those factories and the wages they could pay lured any farmhand still not in uniform. These federal officials showed no hesitation in putting women on the land.

Perhaps those around the table should have foreseen the tobacco dilemma. After all, tobacco was a significant state crop, with nearly thirty thousand acres in tobacco culti-vation, and 1918 promised a bumper crop. The WLA pledged to help the farmer, and working this crop was what the New Milford farmers needed. The War Department had already signed deals with tobacco manufacturers to provide the soldiers at home and abroad with cigarettes and loose tobacco, or what was called the "tobacco ration." It afforded a simple pleasure for men at war. If American troop morale was at stake, who could argue?

The Executive Committee decided that Land Army work in the tobacco fields was justifiable and approved the New Milford Unit, which turned out to be the largest and most successful of all ten of Connecticut's WLA units. This ability to combine patrio-tism and pragmatism, service and shrewdness, became the Connecticut WLA's hall-mark. Before the season was out the Connecticut WLA would need that skill to handle a basketful of nettlesome problems—local varieties of the thorniest issues facing the movement—and invent some ingenious solutions.

"One feels sort of like a stage manager trying to manage the appearance at the right time of the hero, the villain, and all the other vital characters," Grace Schenck would write to her WLA colleague Alsop as the season progressed.[3]

The Connecticut WLA enjoyed the good fortune of a lucky child brought up in a comfortable home: it was not considered a freakish step-daughter of the state's war work efforts, it was not treated with contempt by the men's state Council of Defense, and unlike its sister organizations in other states, it was not willfully ignored. Indeed, just a few weeks after the WLA's official establishment in December 1917, the chair-man of the Connecticut State Council of Defense Publicity Committee, George B. Chandler, wrote a long, enthusiastic memo to Caroline Ruutz-Rees about the exciting potential of a Land Army of women in their state. "The publicity value of something like this of a rather spectacular nature would be of great value in developing morale," he wrote to her in January 1918. "It would supplement the work of my Committee. It would have a splendid moral effect upon the slackers. It would be an object lesson to workmen in factories."[4]

Chandler especially liked the idea of an official romper-style uniform for the workers; not only would it "render the women more efficient in their work by enabling them to move more freely, it would appeal to their pride, and give them a consciousness of solidarity for their country." As for any resistance of the farmers toward women workers, Chandler was a great believer in the power of positive spin. "If farmers were indifferent or hostile last year, it was because the matter was not properly played up and handled," he said. "Some striking posters and first-class publicity matter, spread all over the State, would get them into the proper spirit."

To get a better sense of the Connecticut farmers' spirit, five hundred personally addressed letters from Mrs. Alsop's "Committee to Investigate the Possibilities of Women in Agriculture" appeared in their mailboxes in the early spring of 1918. The letter took the form of a questionnaire, asking if the farmers would consider employing women on their farms in this season's expected labor emergency. Fifty percent of the farmers replied that they would use women "if necessary," 25 percent said they would not use women, and another 25 percent did not respond to the inquiry.[5] The spirit seemed willing enough.

Still, the Connecticut WLA organizers were cautious and took pains to build rapport with the state's agricultural community. That both Corinne Alsop and Grace Schenck served on their local farm bureaus was a distinct advantage. Alsop lived on a farm in Avon, where her husband raised dairy cattle and various crops, including tobacco, as a sideline to the two Hartford insurance companies he headed. Schenck had created a small farm and extensive gardens on her Wilton property. They had both earned their agricultural stripes. They also had a good feel for how to drum up support. Early in the season, in conjunction with the Farm Bureau, they launched an educational campaign aimed at farmers and sent speakers to meetings of the Pomological Society, the state Vegetable and Fruit Growers Association, and various dairy groups to spark interest in employing women on the farms.[6] The women also took good advantage of the enthusiasm of a prominent gentleman farmer, Samuel Russell, Jr., for the Land Army's cause. He not only sponsored a large unit on his Middletown farm, but also stumped through the countryside to convince his fellow farmers of the value of women workers.

In just a few weeks, Schenck was happily "overwhelmed" by inquiries from both women eager to join the Land Army and farmers willing to employ them. Yet recruiting chaperone-housekeepers to supervise the workers was going to be a tougher sell; Schenck understood all the states had this problem. The housemother role was a dull, mostly thankless job, with none of the glory or romance of working as a farmerette in the field.

It also required an older, more mature woman. Schenck came up with a brilliant recruitment plan: she wrote to every clergyman in Connecticut and asked all of them to read an appeal for Land Army chaperones in their churches. "If we could get the Clergymen to make an appeal to the women of their church, women of refinement who would go as their share of war work, we might get some of the right sort," Schenck said.[7]

"Many splendid young women are giving their strength and inspiration" to the Land Army movement, Schenck wrote in her sermon, which was read from the pulpits of many Connecticut churches in May and June. "The urgent need at present time is for women of mature age to go as Chaperone-Housekeepers with these girls. They must have such women to be truly house-mothers to them and here is an opportunity for the older woman to do real war work.

"They must be sensible practical women who will cook for the girls, who will advise and be their confident [sic], who will mother them when they are tired and make a cheerful atmosphere in the home. The position is almost the most important factor in the success of the work and there must be plenty of women in New England who would be glad to help. If we cannot get such women," Schenck warned in the sermon's fire-and-brimstone section, "the amount of help we can offer to the world through food production in our own State will be limited."[8]

The pulpit appeal worked well enough. Chaperones were found for all ten units established around the state: Greenwich, Litchfield, Middletown, New Canaan, New Milford (it was so large it got two), Stonington, Washington, Wilton, Old Mystic, and Pomfret. An additional two units in Redding and Ridgefield were at work but not under the official WLA banner. Connecticut College, in New London, mustered its own small army of farmerettes, dispatching about thirty students to three WLA units on Long Island in New York, so Mrs. Schenck didn't have to worry about their chaperones. With the chaperones she did recruit, all 270 women in the Connecticut units were properly fed, supervised, and if need be, mothered.[9]

Daisy Day was the type of Connecticut farmerette who did not need to be mothered. A graduate of Smith (class of 1901) and a high school mathematics teacher already in her late thirties, she signed up to "do her bit" in the Connecticut Land Army. On a Saturday morning in late June, as soon as classes ended at Hartford High, she took the train to join the New Milford unit, paying the fare out of her own pocket, and joined several other women from her hometown to make up what she called in her diary the "Hartford Bunch." There were four other Hartford schoolteachers in the unit and two clerks and a stenographer from the Travelers Insurance Company, all ranging in age from twenty to forty-eight years old.[10]

When Daisy Day arrived at New Milford, a picture-postcard New England town, her unit captain met her at the station and drove her to the unit headquarters to meet Mrs. Adeline Buck Strong, wife of a prominent tobacco farmer. Mrs. Strong was the driving force behind the New Milford unit and convinced the farmers to hire women. She also personally handled all the organizational logistics and housed the farmerettes in the comfortable quarters of the Ingleside School for Girls, a once posh but now abandoned boarding school near the center of town.

Day unpacked her bags, removing the items the WLA had told her to bring: stout, low-heeled shoes; overalls; middy blouses or men's soft shirts; rain gear; bedding; towels; and a lunch box.[11] Told not to bring any jewelry or good clothes, this daughter of a Congregational minister brought only a simple but appropriate dress for church on Sundays.

On her first day of work, Daisy arose at 5:45 a.m., donned her "working togs," went to a farm, and learned how to hoe tobacco. While the state organizers had planned to initiate every recruit in a two-week training program before she began work, that ideal gave way to the pressing need for women to get on the land as soon as possible. Some women were able to take advantage of the special five-day crash course offered to the Land Army at the state's Agricultural College at Storrs, but most, like Daisy Day, started cold.

"Some job to get the swing and not cover the leaves with dirt," she wrote in her diary that night, the soft leather-bound volume she reserved for special adventures in her life. Here she recorded her life in the Land Army, which by her second day was more painful. "For two hours we pulled tobacco plants from the hot bed, then we set them until about 3 o'clock. Walked about five miles through the plowed ground. The rest of the day we went back to our hoeing. At night my back was as stiff as a ramrod and I was some lame."[12]

While Daisy Day confronted the physical strains of a novice, middle-aged farmerette, her contemporary, Grace Schenck, was wrestling with the policy and practical issues of the young organization. Grace Schenck was not the fretting type; she was a robust woman with a sunny disposition and a can-do mentality. She loved her Land Army work and believed in it fiercely, proudly donning her khaki officer's uniform whenever she stepped out on WLA duties.[13] But during her tenure as WLA chairman, she suffered more than her share of policy headaches. "Being a stepmother to ten must be a simple task as compared to the trials offered by [this] unit," she would write in mock desperation to her WLA collaborator Alsop at one point.[14]

Schenck and Alsop worked closely and well together, and the two women were able to share the burdens and the occasional absurd moments of leading the Land Army. Schenck could be honest with Alsop about the strain their war work might be imposing on their families. "I know it means a sacrifice, as it takes you away from home and children so much," Schenck wrote to her. "I only hope with both of us that our example will do as much for them as our daily companionship."[15]

Schenck had three young children at home, and Alsop had four children. Fortunately, both women were wealthy enough to afford adequate staff to look after their children while they ran the Connecticut Land Army. Alsop's boys would grow up taking to heart their maternal inheritance of civic and political engagement. John would follow the family's footsteps into the Republican Party, working at the state and national levels, while Stewart and Joseph would become perhaps the most influential political journalists of the second half of the twentieth century.

Besides the usual mix of logistical foul-ups that every state chairman endured, Schenck encountered a veritable sampler box of the most delicate social and political issues facing the Land Army movement and the nation. Using her combined gifts of witty imagination and earthy common sense, she became adept at finding novel solutions or at least a gentlewomanly way out of jams.

First there was labor unrest. "At present the Italians are striking for higher wages" in the area of one proposed unit, Schenck reported in April, "but it is hoped that this will be over by the time the unit arrives."[16] Even though farm labor was not unionized, and the WLA was spared wrangling with the unions so opposed to women entering industrial shops, the Land Army needed to stay clear of this dangerous situation. "The Committee urges that the unit not be hurried there, as it may cause the feeling that the girls have been brought in to break the strike."[17] Eventually, this situation eased, but the labor atmosphere in the area remained so tense that the WLA shied away from establishing a unit in that region.

Then there were tensions that mirrored the ethnic frictions of melting-pot America. In the early part of the season, Connecticut had trouble recruiting enough women to meet the farmers' demands, as most of their native recruits were teachers and students whose terms did not end until mid-June. To fill the gap the WLA turned to New York City, which had a surplus of college student volunteers available in mid-May. An entire squad from Hunter College, the well-respected public women's college, volunteered to go to New Milford. The Hunter girls were smart, spunky, patriotic, but all of them were Jewish.

"To our dismay we discovered that they had picked out all the Jewesses for that unit and New Milford refuses to have a solid unit of them," Schenck complained to Alsop.

> We have been so careful to avoid making a distinct race line in selecting
> workers. It seems that in New Milford there is a very Bitter feeling about
> some of the Jews who are Farmers and also some store keepers, and the
> Christian Farmers will not employ Jews. We have no trouble about it where
> we make no discrimination but the entire group being made up of them has
> raised a very disagreeable situation and I dread having to go to town
> tomorrow and feeling that I must find some tactful solution for an impos-
> sible state of affairs.

Schenck had come smack up against the common strain of anti-Semitism that permeated American society at the time, especially in rural areas, and while she found it distasteful, it did not shock her. "It is dreadful to have everyone dislike you just because the Stork dropped you down a Hebraic chimney or you have skin of a yellow or black shade. I don't believe it is right but it is a very real fact. I hope I can avoid hurting their feelings."[18] Though she displayed admirable disdain for the intolerance shown by the New Milford farmers, Schenck put the WLA's role as a service to agriculture first and deemed it prudent to give in to the farmers' demands. The group of "Jewesses" was dispersed and offered positions in other state units.[19]

Such problems did not affect Daisy Day's service in the New Milford unit, and she relished the hard work. "Hoed in same tobacco all day, eight hours. It is not easy work," she recorded in her diary. "Tobacco is about a foot high, and a little easier to hoe except that it takes more muscle for the extra amount of dirt needed," she wrote a few days later, describing herself as "wet with perspiration and dirty all over."[20]

The New Milford farmerettes learned to use the normal farm implements along with some pieces of specialized equipment, such as the tobacco hatchet and the two-person, horse-drawn plant setter. And like all other farmerettes, while they worked, they sang. "The singing of the 'tobacco queens' reminded one of the plantation melodies of the cotton pickers over the Mason-Dixon," wrote a *Hartford Courant* reporter after observing a unit in East Windsor. "It was a sort of crooning, a blending of close harmony pleasing to the ear. The little army took up song after song and soon it swelled up like an immense rondo."[21]

When Daisy Day and her comrades were carried back to the Ingleside camp via automobile, hay wagon, or horse-drawn surrey after a long day in the fields, they still had household chores to do on a rotating basis. "My household duty this week is to help put up the luncheons," she noted in her diary. The New Milford farmerettes had decided to adopt a "self-governing" model of running their unit, and everyone was expected to pitch in. The unit swelled to forty-six women at the height of the season. They all received their pay directly from the farmers, by way of the unit captain, instead of the set salary of $15 a month used at other WLA camps. "Got our envelope of pay on the way home," Daisy wrote, "and we had earned it. After deducting $4.50 for board, received $4.50." Receiving a weekly paycheck was something Daisy Day, the other teachers, and working women enlisted in the Connecticut WLA were accustomed to, but it was a distinctly new experience for many farmerettes, including a twenty-two-year-old woman from New York who enrolled under an assumed name, Eleanor May. Her real name was Eleanor May Guggenheim, but as the eldest daughter of mining magnate Solomon R. Guggenheim, she dropped her surname during her Land Army service, believing it was too "conspicuous." "I wanted to be accepted for myself," she explained, and like other wealthy farmerettes, she probably donated her earnings to a war charity.[22]

The sight of farmerettes in the New Milford fields was a novelty, but the local attitude was one more of curiosity than hostility. "The [farmer's] children were quite interested in us," Daisy Day jotted in her diary. "One was afraid of us and did not believe we were girls, so I took off my hat to show her my hair."[23] The WLA leaders also made an effort not to shock the sensibilities of the more rural districts where farmerettes were dispatched to work. While working they wore the official Connecticut working uniform of blue overalls embossed with the Connecticut WLA logo, but Daisy Day reports that while traveling on public transport—a local train line—the farmerettes were instructed to dress in a more acceptable ladylike manner: "We had skirts over our overalls and mine came below like panteletts." One WLA field organizer even teased Daisy and her fellow farmerettes: "Mrs. Mac thinks it would be very picturesque if we wore 'chintz overalls.'"[24]

While the Connecticut farmerettes did not wear chintz, they did work hard and steadily and began to impress the Connecticut farmers. The farmers of New Milford were uniformly pleased by the work Daisy Day and her comrades did, and the local paper noted a certain change of heart. "Some were inclined to think a few months ago that the farmerette was a joke," the *New Milford Gazette* reported in August, ". . . and that girls as farmhands would be an utter failure. But all the farmers who have employed them this summer have found out that the farmerette has been very much of a success."[25]

"New Milford Farmers Laud Women Who Come to Help Them" was the headline in a *Hartford Courant* dispatch, noting that the area farmers "will testify that the dainty but determined young women are making good . . . and find them as capable as men and much more earnest."[26] That sentiment was echoed all over the state. "Veteran Tillers of Soil Take Their Hats Off to Women Who Have Helped Solve Labor Problem," trumpeted the *Courant's* headline later in the season.[27]

True to predictions, Connecticut enjoyed a bumper crop of tobacco that year, and the farmerettes patiently attended to the soothing weed's every need, from "topping" the buds off the growing stalks to "suckering" any secondary shoots and "worming" the tobacco—that is, picking off the plump green tobacco horn worms from the plants and killing the worms by squeezing them between their fingers. "She was a real sport and took the worms like a soldier," Daisy Day said in true admiration of a fellow farmerette's fortitude for worming.[28]

Besides tobacco work, the farmerettes in Connecticut cultivated and harvested corn and potatoes; tended rows of vegetables and picked tree fruit; herded livestock; gathered wheat, barley, and rye; and rescued the huckleberry crop. "The girls operate tractors and do all the work that men can do on a farm" was the caption for a photo spread in the *Courant*.[29] "The girls have ploughed with a tractor—a particularly Amazonian member of the unit accomplishing a feminine ploughing feat of seven acres in eight hours," another reporter exclaimed.[30]

The farmers were especially impressed with the women's work ethic and their endurance during the August 1918 heat wave that gripped New England. "Very hot day, lunch under trees but too hot to sleep," Daisy Day noted in her diary entry for August 6. "Hotter yet, mercury 100 in shade," was her entry the next day. "We stopped work for 20 minutes, as the captain wanted to . . . but we did not mind the heat, though the perspiration ran in streams."[31]

The *New Milford Gazette* noted that the male farmhands working in the heat along-side the farmerettes in New Milford often retreated to the shade of an old apple tree while the girls kept going. "All of the girls seemed possessed of a grim determination to make good and they did."[32] A reporter asked one farmer "how the girls endured the heat. Do many of them faint? The scorn of the farmer was immeasurable. 'Faint', he exclaimed. 'Farmerettes? Not on your life! They are not the fainting kind.'"[33]

Especially gratifying to Grace Schenck and the WLA leaders was the conversion of the Litchfield County Farm Bureau agent to the Land Army's cause. "Mr. Manchester had been a doubting man," Schenck boasted to Alsop. "This he admitted publicly and said he must take it all back, and acknowledged that owing to the work of the girls a large number of acres of food had been saved." Manchester made this dramatic recanta-tion at a farmers' meeting and announced he wanted to begin planning for a larger WLA presence in Litchfield the next year. "He had no faith in their ability earlier in the season, but has quite changed his mind," Schenck reported with enormous satisfaction.[34]

The farmers of Kent also had a public change of heart about the value of women workers. Earlier in the season they had refused to accept Land Army workers, but when their crop of huckleberries was about to rot, they swallowed their pride and put out a desperate distress signal to the WLA. Schenck ordered the New Milford unit to dis-patch five of its workers to Kent every day to save the crop, "which is extravagant in transportation, but is probably worth while in experience," she reasoned. The lesson to the Kent farmers was worth the gasoline money.[35]

Relations between Connecticut's farm families and the farmerettes were, for the most part, exceptionally cordial. "There has been a feeling of good fellowship among the farmers and the farmerette," explained the *Courant.* "A grateful sense of service faithfully rendered has resulted in many kindly acts."[36] The farmer's wife often expressed her gratitude with food, as Daisy Day chronicles: "Were treated to lemonade and cook-ies. At noon they brought us apple dumplings on the front porch. Fine place to work, they are so considerate."[37] And New Milford enjoyed a favorite soda fountain treat that summer when a shop owner mixed vanilla ice cream with chocolate and pineapple syrups and named it the "Farmerette Parfey" after the town's new heroines.

The community also held dances in the high school gym for the Land Army women and treated them to picnics at Candlewood Lake. When they took the farmerettes on a hayride, it merited a mention in the *Gazette:* "Last Friday evening all went on an old-fashioned straw ride. There were more than twenty comfortably decorating a hay wagon as it passed through Main Street, and all were singing extremely well."[38]

The Land Army did bring a new element of spice to Connecticut farm communities that summer, and one highly appreciative group was the farmers' sons. Walter Orr was the teenage son of a New Milford farmer who employed farmerettes, and "he really enjoyed having the farmerettes around," according to his friend Robin Stacks. "They were nice girls, college girls, highly bred girls. Quite outgoing girls. You can imagine these farm boys didn't get the chance to meet girls like this."[39]

That element of spice could cause problems, however. Almost inevitably, Grace Schenck had to handle a few instances where the behavior of the city-bred farmerette, the dreaded "modern woman" of loose morals, shocked the local farming community. Sometimes it amounted to nothing more than old-fashioned coquettish flirting. Schenck had to dismiss one farmerette who had "abandoned the typewriter to till the soil but was evidently overwhelmed by the beauties of nature and the male of her species," as Schenck so colorfully reported to Alsop. "For she did nothing but gaze at the former and charm the latter—and especially did the smart looking chauffeur of Mrs. Fisher entrance her."[40]

When the *Hartford Courant* reported that farmerettes in Simsbury were seen "to be going about their work in rather scanty bathing costumes, to hail every automobile that goes by for a ride, and the manager doesn't know half the time whether they are on the job or are climbing trees," Schenck and other members of the Connecticut WLA hierarchy were furious.[41] First of all, the women working at Simsbury were not official Land Army farmerettes. Instead, they had been recruited privately, did not live in an authorized unit, and were not under the supervision of the WLA, so the Land Army bore no responsibility for their outrageous behavior. But, knowing full well that in the public eye an "official" farmerette was hard to distinguish from an "unofficial" one, the Connecticut WLA was forced to uphold its honor. It deputized Adeline Strong to write a firm letter to the *Courant,* pointing to the plus-perfect behavior of her New Milford farmerettes, their admirable record of achievement in the fields, and their acceptance by her local community.

But the Simsbury incident exposed a raw reality: occasionally there was a genuine clash of cultures that even wartime exigencies could not smooth over. The Simsbury farmers simply did not like the city women's attitude. "Many of the farmerettes who came here in a large group to work on a tobacco plantation were brimful of patriotism and rather expected to have extra consideration shown them because of the patriotism," the *Courant* reported. "In fact they were so conscious of their patriotism that it rather overshadowed their work and caused so much trouble that the employer has been obliged to let them go."[42]

The Simsbury episode also brought into the open an internal struggle that Schenck and other WLA field officials had been grappling with all season—how to deal with such "unofficial" units, ones whose organizers or patrons did not wish to submit to the rigors of WLA regulations and structure or simply chose not to bother with all the inspections and paperwork. Schenck recognized early on that these private units posed a danger to cohesion and control and put the farmerettes involved in a vulnerable nether land, beyond the WLA's protective rules.

A line must be drawn: "Mrs. Riddle has obtained a unit for her place in Avon, but owing to the fact that they do not wish to comply with our regulations, we cannot recognize them as part of the Land Army and give them official recognition of their services," the Connecticut WLA reported, rather testily.[43]

Schenck displayed rare flashes of anger when discussing the unofficial units in Ridgefield, which were organized by the local Garden Club, and in Redding, run by the Women's University Club of New York City. "You see we do not include Ridgefield and Redding [in our list of units] as they still fail so utterly to conform to our system of working," she explained.[44] In the end, this prodigal Redding unit was dropped on Schenck's doorstep. "The Women's University Club established a unit at Redding which they have asked to have recognized as an official Connecticut unit," Schenck reported to WLA national headquarters. "We have had no jurisdiction over or supervision of this unit and we feel in many ways it has not been desirable, but it seems unfair to the individual worker who signed up in good faith, not to have any official recognition."[45] A farmerette was, after all, a farmerette.

Although Schenck insisted that a farmerette needed to live within the protection of the unit system, she was under constant pressure to make exceptions. For instance, she was asked to dispatch workers singly or in pairs, where a full unit was infeasible, to meet the emergency demands of a distant farmer. Time and again Schenck warned against this sort of ad hoc placement, which went against the grain of the accepted WLA unit plan, put the farmerette into unsupervised jeopardy in the farmer's home, and eroded the state organization's authority. "We are getting a flood of requests for one or two workers for all sorts of positions," Schenck reported. "The Land Army is sending only through the unit plan, so we are safe till the whole broad question of women joining out as laborers on unsupervised farms is a problem."[46]

It did indeed become a problem. At first Schenck and Alsop held firm. "Mrs. Alsop says that it would be entirely impossible for us to supply girls except in the 'Unit Plan' where they are housed for agricultural work," Alsop's secretary wrote to John Luddy of the Connecticut Leaf Tobacco Association in June.[47] "We feel very strongly that the women should not be placed in individual farm houses to live," Schenck reiterated in July. "From the experience of this and other states, we feel that they should be under the general supervision in their own camps. That fact I wish to strongly accentuate."[48]

The enormous demand for these smaller details of workers and the occasional pleading farmer could sway even the steadfast Mrs. Schenck. "In response to an urgent call from the Litchfield Farm Bureau I have rather suspended one of our rules," she admitted to Alsop in early August. She had dispatched a small squad of women to rescue a berry crop while boarding with the farmer's family. She justified her turnabout by saying that she and the local WLA organizers knew the farm family and could vouch for the women's safety. "I decided it was best to send them rather than to stick to the rules and regulations." Everyone involved "are delighted, so I think it was justified," she rationalized.[49]

Still, this instance had to be the exception rather than a new rule, Schenck emphasized:

> There are a great many things to be considered in the placing of girls in
> individual homes on a large scale. I think it is going to be difficult to get the
> right type of girls. . . . A large number of them will go out where there is a
> camp spirit and camp life, and many parents will consider this where they
> will not let the girls go out singly or in groups of two or three to the farmer's
> houses.[50]

It might have been simpler to put workers directly into the farmhouse rather than operate a unit camp, but the WLA could not abandon its commitment to the poor farmwife, too. "Then again with the girls going into the homes of farmers, the question of all the extra work for the farmer's wife, which is a serious problem, comes up," Schenck insisted. "And they have all commented many times this summer upon the relief of being able to get outside help without increased indoor labor."[51] The Woman's Land Army had an obligation to protect and support the interests of all the women touched by its work.

The governor himself should award the farmerettes their official Connecticut Woman's Land Army brassards for faithful and patriotic service. A gentleman on the Connecticut Committee of Defense made this suggestion, proving once again how unusually well the men's and women's sections of the state war mechanism worked together. Schenck needed to make a formal request on behalf of the Land Army, but she was nervous. "I am not perfectly sure how I should address a formal communication to the Governor," she fretted to Alsop, "and if it is wrong, do correct it. If it is all right, won't you give it to him personally and add your gentle plea, which I am sure will carry great weight?"[52]

The ceremony took place in Governor Marcus Holcomb's office in the Capitol Building. Select dignitaries were in attendance, including former U.S. senator Morgan Bulkeley, whose daughter-in-law Margaret served as captain of the Greenwich unit while her husband was off fighting in France. Though thirty-three of Connecticut's farmerettes qualified for the brassard by dint of their three months' service, only twenty-four could actually attend the ceremony; the others were too busy with their farm duties and could not be spared during the harvest. More than 250 WLA women who'd served on Connecticut's farms were not considered eligible for the brassard, presumably because they hadn't worked the full three-month stint. This group included Daisy Day, who had returned to her classroom at Hartford High and regaled her algebra students with tales of farmerette life. The women at the ceremony received the official Connecticut

WLA brassard, a dark blue armband emblazoned with the state shield, and not the national WLA version, which was green with a stylized sheaf of wheat.[53]

Governor Holcomb graced the occasion with a rather rambling talk, and when he finally got around to commending the young women being honored, he was forthright if not exactly effusive in his praise. "The women have done a man's work, and they deserve recognition for the manner in which they helped men," he said. "It was necessary that young women take the place of men, or agriculture would have suffered. There is nothing romantic about hoeing potatoes or corn, but by means of such a humble task the character is bettered."[54]

Then Governor Holcomb, who was never subtle in his opposition to suffrage for women, could not resist a little jab. "Nothing can be accomplished without women," he said, "and it was not necessary that they should have the suffrage to accomplish it." The ardent suffragists in the chamber could not have been too pleased with the governor's remarks, but they knew not to expect much of him. (In 1920 Governor Holcomb would simply ignore a petition signed by 103,000 Connecticut women and refuse to call a special session of the legislature to consider ratifying the Nineteenth Amendment.) For now, it was best to ignore the governor's jibes while he was according the Connecticut farmerettes the recognition they so richly deserved. The ceremonies in the governor's office were brought to a rousing conclusion when a chorus of ten members of the Middletown Unit sang "The March of the Land Army," whose words and music were written by their captain, Miss Cornelia Brandreth.

With the season winding down, Grace Schenck turned her attention to the future. Training was the element still missing from the Connecticut WLA organization, but Schenck hoped to remedy that. "A big training camp is essential," she told Alsop, inspired by reports of the Libertyville training farm in Illinois and the Bedford farm in New York.[55] By September Schenck had found a possible place for a Connecticut WLA training facility. "My heart is quite set on getting the Gilbert Farm School for a training camp," she reported to Alsop, "patterned more or less after the very successful one in Illinois."[56] Grace Schenck had big plans for the next season of the Connecticut Woman's Land Army.

15

Libertyville: Illinois

When Mrs. Tiffany Blake succeeded in making a gentleman eat his hat, she did so in such a charming, effortless manner that he might well ask her to kindly pass the gravy. So when some of the most powerful men in Illinois—the leading dairy and livestock barons, the farm organization heads, the agricultural journal editors, and the industrial titans of Chicago—laughed at her idea of training women to become skilled farmers, she just smiled. She maintained her composure, calmly asking for their advice and indulgence. And when, barely six months later, they saw with their own eyes what women had accomplished at her Illinois Training Farm for Women at Libertyville, they graciously and publicly dined on their summer straw boaters.

"I was skeptical as any of you when Mrs. Tiffany Blake came over to see me one day last winter and told me about her plan for making farmers out of city girls," admitted the editor of the influential *Prairie Farmer*. "I told her that the girls might do well picking strawberries or apples, or chasing butterflies or cheering up the hired man. But as for pitching hay . . . Mrs. Blake had her revenge a week ago Saturday, when I went up to Libertyville to see her 240-acre farm. That visit opened my eyes to the great possibilities of women as farmers."[1]

Mrs. Blake could only smile.

Margaret Day Blake understood that the variety of Land Army that was growing so quickly in the eastern states could not just be plopped down into the loamy soil of Illinois and expected to thrive. Conditions—the types of farms, the work, the attitudes—were different in the Midwest. She would need to develop a hybrid, one suited to the chemistry of the middle states. A Land Army here would have to shed some of its eastern dilettante ways and be both more ambitious and more practical, less dreamy and maybe less intellectual. To put it bluntly, the Land Army movement in Illinois needed to be more than simply a war work effort tailored to city girls. It needed to be earnest, long term, and useful, featuring a hardy grain rather than a pretty flower.

To be honest, Margaret Day Blake didn't know much about farming, but she did know about working within her city's power structure to get things done. She had the social connections of a well-bred Chicago lady and the social conscience of a Chicago city reformer who'd spent her formative years working at Jane Addams's Hull House settlement. She helped establish the Women's Trade Union League in the city, advocating for better working and living conditions, and was also a leader of the Immigrants' Protective League. She'd helped the women of Illinois win the vote back in 1913; unlike their eastern sisters, they were already able to vote in municipal and state elections. Blake's father had been president of the Chicago Stock Exchange, and her husband, Tiffany Blake, was a respected newspaper editor who shared her progressive political ideas (they had met at Hull House). She knew how to move in those circles, and she enjoyed playing the role of a charming woman with a cause.[2]

In the Woman's Land Army movement Blake saw a new vehicle for expanding opportunities for women and for improving the lot of working women. It fit nicely into her progressive worldview. She was a professional reformer, and if need be, she would even undertake to reform the Woman's Land Army itself, reshaping it to fit her region's needs.

The Land Army idea arrived in Chicago in the early winter of 1918, carried in the travel cases of Virginia Gildersleeve and Helen Taft, who met with local leaders of women's war work efforts. After Gildersleeve emphasized the practical potential of a Land Army in the Midwest and Taft gave a vivid account of her own service as a farmerette, Blake was tapped to chair the group formulating plans for a WLA division in Illinois.[3]

Helen Fraser's visit to Chicago in early March heightened enthusiasm for the project. Margaret Blake used the visit to launch her WLA recruitment drive, giving it some pizzazz. She announced a contest to design the Illinois farmerette's uniform, rejecting a New York apparel design firm's offers in favor of a more homegrown Chicago style. "There is to be a contest for the most suitable and practicable farmer girl costume for the army and leading modistes are wracking their brains to concoct something neat but not gaudy, absolutely without ruffles, and inexpensive enough for the slenderest purse," said the *Chicago Tribune*. Ushers at Helen Fraser's lecture at the Art Institute modeled the best uniform candidates, and Fraser herself was asked to serve as a uniform judge.[4]

As soon as Margaret Blake took the helm of the planning group for a Land Army in Illinois, she utilized her political skills to build consensus and support for the task. She and her committee went out to talk with experts who understood agriculture and appreciated what the Illinois farmer needed immediately and what he might need in the future. She listened, took notes, endured many a skeptical glance and mildly condescending statement, and in so doing, implicitly secured some essential people's attention and further cooperation. They were, even if reluctantly, on board; they could be convinced later.

What emerged from Blake's consultations probably shocked the WLA national organization. First, she recognized that farmerettes were probably not going to be needed in the Illinois fields immediately. "In considering the problem as applying particularly to Illinois, it seemed to the Committee that there was no labor shortage that could not be taken care of by the Boys' Working Reserve, and the men of the towns," Blake explained, regarding the 1918 season.

The Boys' Working Reserve, that favorite and overindulged son of the Labor Department and the state councils of defense, turned in a better performance record in Illinois than some other places, though it was still an unproven solution in the winter of 1918 when Blake made this decision. Blake's bowing to the assumed superiority of teenage boys' labor to women's labor galled many in the Land Army movement. Perhaps accepting the prevailing Boys' Working Reserve cure-all attitude was a way for Blake's committee to mollify male skeptics, but in truth it also nicely served the committee's purposes. Without the pressure of hastily mustering Illinois farmerettes into the fields to catch up with the crops, as the other states were forced to do, the Illinois WLA could pursue a more deliberate route. It had time to devise its comprehensive training farm and allow for a full season, or even a full year, of practical vocational training. If the war dragged on, women would definitely be needed in the Illinois fields the next year. "If women were to be used," Blake maintained, "we would have first to train them. . . . The unskilled woman would not be useful."[5]

Blake had received an earful from her agricultural advisers, who were adamant that the Illinois farmer did not need a group of well-meaning but totally clueless city girls who would require his constant supervision. Eastern farms were smaller and usually more specialized, and supervising a novice farmerette there was feasible. It was not so on the Midwest's much larger, highly diversified farms, where the farmer raised grains, vegetables, and livestock on hundreds or thousands of acres. The Illinois farmer needed a skilled and knowledgeable worker, competent in many different tasks. He might accept a woman in that role but only if she could prove capable of doing the job.

Furthermore, Margaret Blake saw a broader opportunity in the Land Army movement, with a more substantial role than simply supplying wartime labor. She would mix into the established formula of the Woman's Land Army a pinch of sensible salt. She saw the principal goal of an Illinois WLA was not simply to serve Uncle Sam or Herbert Hoover, not to meet the Illinois farmer's immediate wartime labor needs, and not to give city girls an outlet for their pent-up patriotism. Instead, its intent was to prepare and support the woman on the farm, particularly the woman who wanted to make her life in the country and not just pitch in or visit. That ideal farm woman might be a properly trained farmerette who could hire herself out as a competent worker, or an independent woman owner of a farm, or—and this element was the strange spice in the recipe—the farmwife.

This emphasis on the farmwife sent shudders down the spines of the WLA's eastern leaders because it smacked of the proper-place excuses the more conservative states' Women's Committees used to keep the Land Army out of their regions: These groups maintained that the only proper place for women on the farm was in the house or chicken coop, and the only proper place for city girls on the farm was indoors, helping the farmwife keep house. It also smelled unpleasantly of the "traditional women's roles" attitude that the entire war work movement was fighting to overcome. The WLA's early organizers had been careful to structure the unit system so as not to burden the farmer's wife with more cooking or caring for laborers, but they saw no real kinship between the farmerettes and the farmer's womenfolk. Avoiding friction between the two groups of women was prudent; anything beyond was nice but not essential.

Blake and her colleagues, meanwhile, saw the role of the farmwife as central to the health of rural life in America, and they knew the farmwife was hurting. While there was definitely a chronic problem with farm labor shortages, deeper, more dangerous maladies afflicted the farm and threatened the whole rural way of life in America. Dissatisfied, overworked, and bored, the farm woman was angry as well about her husband's expenditures on new labor-saving devices for his fieldwork—gasoline tractors, mechanical corn shredders, and other such technological innovations—while she went without indoor water, electricity, washing machines, or oil-powered cook stoves.[6]

Blake's view reflected the popular Country Life Movement of the time, which advocated reform and modernization to protect America's rural foundation. Just a decade before, in 1908, the rapid population shift away from farms to the cities alarmed President Theodore Roosevelt, who appointed a blue-ribbon panel to investigate rural America's economic and social conditions. After surveying almost half a million rural citizens in hearings around the country, the commission's conclusions were shocking: rural America suffered from inadequate schools, substandard medical care, social isolation, and primitive living conditions. The commission made a series of suggestions for improvement: instituting free rural postal service, establishing a farm credit loan system and an agricultural extension service, and bringing electricity and mechanization to the farm. Some ideas were implemented—Roosevelt's Bull Moose Party inserted a Country Life plank into its platform in the 1912 election—but when Roosevelt lost his bid for the White House, the issue died on the federal level. Some states and localities established their own Country Life panels to improve conditions in their areas, and the idea remained alive in the imagination of reformers like Margaret Blake. Meanwhile, life had not really improved for the farmwife and her family.

"If we are to have a healthy democracy, we must develop and advance conditions in the country as conditions are developed and advanced in the city," Blake explained. "If we are to build up our rural population, women must have their share of education for country life."[7] Blake wanted to bring the settlement movement—a rural Hull House—to the countryside.

While Blake did accept that in the war effort "the immediate need, as presented to us, was to help the farmer's wife," she rejected the plan of simply sending city women to assist in the farmer's household. This idea had already "proven itself a failure," Blake argued.

Farmerettes in the kitchen were not the answer. "It seemed out of the question to aid the farmer's wife in this way. The problem of the farmer's wife would have to be considered from a new angle." And this new angle was not just to help her with the dishes but to educate her. "Is the country best off where the farmer knows his business and his wife does not know hers, is incompetent and restless?" Blake asked. "As the wife of a farmer, her status on the farm is more authoritative if she is trained in diversified farming, speaks the language of her husband and understands the problems of his work."[8]

The beauty of Blake's approach to the Land Army movement was that it bundled together in the same package traditional and progressive elements, combining aspects of both the Country Life and Back-to-the-Land movements. Yes, she wanted to educate the farmwife to be a true partner on the land with her husband, but she also wanted to bring college educated city women to find their place on the land and to provide the highest levels of agricultural training for them. For the farmwife or daughter, she wanted to turn the farmhouse into a laboratory where "scientific domestic methods" could be explored. "We see the light for the farmer's wife approaching the question from the fresh angle of training her for her work," Blake explained, "giving her the protection of intelligence in her work and something of the attitude of an investigator or experimenter towards food, housekeeping and homemaking."[9]

The plan for the training farm took shape speedily, and by early spring Blake and her farm committee of nearly thirty women began approaching their friends and working their connections. Charmed by Helen Fraser's land work presentation in Chicago, the husband of one of Blake's committee members stood up after the speech and offered the rent-free loan of his two hundred–acre dairy farm at Libertyville, sixty miles outside of Chicago, for three years. The farm was run down, but it included a ten-room house, a barn, 18 cows, and 187 chickens and could bear enough crops to sustain the stock and the workers. His gift was also a gesture that demonstrated a certain amount of male confidence in the concept.

Blake knocked on the doors of other sponsors in a campaign to lend both legitimacy and expensive equipment to the farm. Chicago-based International Harvester Corporation was eager to promote its new Titan farm tractors and lent several to the farm, along with an instructor to teach the women how to operate them. It was perfect public relations for Harvester. What could be a better advertisement for these new labor-saving contraptions than to demonstrate that even a city woman could quickly learn to run one.[10]

Blake and her committee launched into what she called "a three-ring circus," procuring money, girls, and equipment from a small office on West Adams Street that the Women's National Farm and Garden Association lent to them.[11] These ladies were never chary about asking for donations. They got the king of the Chicago meat producers, Armour & Co., to donate livestock; John Deere & Co. gave a farm wagon; and Sears, Roebuck and Co. offered an engine. American Can Company supplied the farm with packing tins, Standard Oil pitched in with a stove and oil, Oliver Typewriter Company gave one of its typewriters, and A. B. Dick one of its patented mimeograph machines.[12]

In a tribute to the skill with which the training farm's organizers managed to coax public donations, no fewer than sixty-five companies are credited with helping to sponsor the enterprise. Some of the most famous American companies supplied the Libertyville Farm family's domestic needs: Ball Brothers Glass Manufacturers provided preserving jars, H. J. Heinz gave food production machinery, Carson Pirie Scott donated blankets for the farmerettes, Marshall Field's outfitted the farmhouse with kitchen utensils, Montgomery Ward gave the cider press, Thomas Lipton offered tea, and Oscar Mayer & Bros. provided hams.[13] They did pretty well in the money arena, too. During April and May, they brought in $4,100 in cash contributions, enabling the farm to buy an automobile truck. The final cash gift tally would rise to $7,600, with another $6,000 worth of donated goods.[14]

As to the third essential ring, recruiting the farm's students, Blake and her board orchestrated a word-of-mouth campaign, fanning out to speak to women's clubs, labor organizations, girl's schools, the YWCA, and local universities. They estimated that their pitch probably reached a total of forty thousand women and girls.[15] Blake pressed her contacts at the University of Chicago and Northwestern University for permission to make direct appeals to their women students, and she gave several recruitment speeches in the campus chapels as well as at student war work conferences. She even managed to persuade the Chicago faculty to accept a plan that would allow seniors to work at the farm during May and June and still receive their diplomas. University of Chicago women accounted for more than a quarter of the students offered admission to Libertyville.

As word of the farm spread, the response was overwhelming. Four hundred applications flooded the Illinois training farm's little office, swelling to thirteen hundred as the 1918 season progressed. After careful vetting and interviewing, seventy-six women were accepted for training during the first year. They received free training and board in exchange for a commitment to remain in farmwork for the war's duration. Ranging in age from eighteen to fifty-three years old, 75 percent of the training farm students were college-educated women, 15 percent were professional women, and 10 percent were women of leisure or homemakers.[16] Some recruits were moved to apply as a war service, stirred by the example of brothers or lovers at the front, and some women owned land and wanted to learn how to operate a farm. Other applicants were city women, "growing tired of pegging at the typewriter and wishing to fit themselves for self-support in some open air employment," as Blake described it, and some were country girls who'd gone off to the city, found themselves discontented, and wished to return to rural life. Still others were married women who thought their husbands might become farmers when they returned from the war and wanted to be able to be true partners in the enterprise.[17]

They all went through a two-week probationary period on the farm to test their physical and mental fitness for the work, and fifteen of them washed out. "A few were not in earnest," Blake recalled, "a few disliked the work, several wept on dismissal."[18]

The farm itself was a mess. Barrels of glass and rubbish had to be cleaned from the front yard. The buildings needed fixing, water pipes repairing, and ditches filling. Years of accumulated manure had to be shoveled out of the cowshed, a feat five girls accomplished by working steadily for two days. The farmhouse was too small to accommodate all the students, so a horse stable was transformed into a dormitory, with one woman in each stall. "We slept in the [horse] barn, and this was fixt so that it looked very attractive," one farmerette explained, "with cretonne curtains and with rugs on the floor and some easy chairs and books and shaded lamps and the furniture different people had given us." The girls used the stalls' feed boxes to hold their toiletries and trinkets.[19]

From the rising bell at five thirty in the morning till lights-out at nine o'clock at night, the students were given a comprehensive survey course in all aspects of "diversified" farming: the care of livestock (a full month spent on horses, two weeks each on sheep and pigs), plant pathology, poultry, beekeeping, dairying and cheese making, farm management, and accounting. This training would begin to approximate the education found in state agricultural colleges, but it was in a shorter, more intense time frame and coupled more directly with practical experience. The training farm mixed class work with fieldwork, and the students' lecture notebooks were graded. They learned to plow with both horses and gasoline-powered tractors, to cultivate grains and corn, to raise fruits and vegetables, and then to can and preserve them. It was a liberal arts farming approach. Schemes for successfully marketing these farm products were also emphasized. Libertyville developed a thriving market for its eggs and chickens among the fine houses of Lake Michigan's North Shore, sold its butter and cheese in the city's stores, and its green tomato mincemeat was a big hit.

The basic books of a small agricultural library were donated to the farm, and "after dinner you might see girls lying on the grass or in hammocks or on the porch reading and studying and writing up their lecture notes," a Libertyville Farm recruit explained. Sometimes they took their newfound book knowledge to comical lengths, as when one recruit, a botany teacher, read that cows could be milked more easily if it were done to music.

> I said I meant to try it, take our Victrola out to the dairy and turn on a waltz
> tune, before I began to milk the cow I was struggling with. She was very

hard to milk. I began singing to her—and it worked. The milk really came much more easily and quickly. After that when I went into the dairy at milking-time, I used to nearly die laughing. Every girl would be humming a different tune, milking away, with her head leaned up against her cow. There was a perfect pandemonium of tunes inside that dairy.[20]

Margaret Blake, being the wife of a newspaperman, proved to be a brilliant public relations strategist and used her editorial access to splendid effect. She sent the Chicago and suburban newspapers story ideas or prepared items twice every week. She prodded her board members to write columns glorifying the farm and got them placed in major papers and magazines around the country. Her board vice chairman, Anne Spicer, was a published poet (one of her sappier poems, "The Last Crusade," became a popular hit when the march king John Philip Sousa set it to music) and helped recruit professional women by penning a Women in Wartime column about the farm for the *Chicago Tribune*. Blake wrote a few articles under her own byline and got several farmerettes to put down their thoughts on paper, resulting in numerous published first-person accounts of life on the farm.

Blake invited the editors of important agricultural magazines to visit the farm and escorted them through the barns and fields herself. They inevitably came away surprised and impressed. "I expected to see Maud Muller in overettes or bloomerettes and a starched sunbonnet raking hay," admitted the editor of the *Prairie Farmer*. "What I saw was Mrs. Tate, a wiry little woman whose husband is fighting in France, out in the field, in a pair of blue overalls and a ten-cent straw hat, her face streaked with dirt from an afternoon of honest toil."[21]

"They have learned to do real honest-to-goodness work," wrote the editor of the *Orange Judd Farmer*, "spread manure, operate tractors, and the average hired man would have to jump lively to work as quickly and efficiently as they do."[22]

Blake also knew just how to milk a publicity opportunity, perfecting a do-well-by-doing-good approach. When Chicago was preparing to host a giant war exposition in Grant Park on the shore of Lake Michigan, the exposition's organizers couldn't find laborers who knew how to run tractors to smooth the show grounds. Libertyville farmerettes to the rescue! Blake drove four of her women to Chicago to tackle the job. On the lakefront, in their uniforms, they cranked up and climbed atop the tractors and worked for three full days, leveling and scraping the grounds. They even helped pull loaded wagons out of the mud. They provided a public spectacle of farmerette prowess, and newspaper photographers, whom Mrs. Blake had so kindly alerted to the photo opportunity, recorded their every move. "Farmerettes run tractors in Grant Park" photos ran on the front pages of the Chicago newspapers the next day.[23]

In certain respects the Illinois Training Farm for Women was more self-contained than other WLA ventures were. It was more isolated from the daily pressures of wartime agriculture and from the logistical struggles of the Land Army movement at large. The Libertyville farmerettes were not shipped out each day to a neighboring farm, there were no balky Ford trucks to strand the workers, and they did not face wage negotiations or acceptance problems.

They did gain some practical working experience when, in the press of haying season, the farmerettes helped out on neighboring farms. "We found we could keep up with the men," one Libertyville farmerette said proudly, and when the girls were sent out to work on a farm, they made special efforts to fit in with the rest of the crew. "At noon the men threshers all went up to one solitary basin with just one towel and washed and wiped their faces and hands," the farmerette recounted. "We didn't know quite what to do. Then we thought it best to follow, each in turn with the same basin and towel."[24]

In true neighborly fashion, the farmers also came over and helped fill the silos at the women's training farm. When the girls put on a dance to benefit the Red Cross, more than 120 farmers, with their wives and children, turned out to mingle with the farmerettes in the flag-bedecked and lantern-lit hayloft.

The great event at the Libertyville farm—the culmination of the farmerettes' hard work, the sponsors' faith, and Mrs. Blake's indefatigable publicity pump—was graduation day, when the governor of Illinois agreed to give a valedictory address and award the students their WLA service brassards. Invitations went out to more than a thousand people: local farmers and their wives, county and state agricultural agents, Illinois Farmers' Institute representatives, state Dairy Council folk, state politicians, notable industrialists, all the corporate sponsors, the state Council of Defense, and of course, journalists.

The Chicago press wasn't at all sure how to handle the training farm graduation story. Some papers made it into a fashion piece. Lucy Calhoun, the distaff side of a *Chicago Tribune* team of reporters assigned to cover the ceremony, began,

> There was no organdy and lace, no pink ribbons and rosebuds about the graduation dresses of the girl farmers who met in the leafy grove on the farm of the Woman's Land Army yesterday. The graduates wore overalls instead, garments which had obviously seen hard service. A bright kerchief worn about the neck or on the head, a feather placed Indian fashion in the hair— these were the only signs of "dressing up." They realized they were there as pioneers in a new work for women.[25]

The male *Tribune* reporter, Henry Hyde, took the hardware slant:

> Miss Jane Brown, late stenographer in a Loop law office, took her hands out of her trousers pockets, cranked the tractor, sprang up on the seat, and

started away down the forty acre field. The crowd of 800 farmers, headed by
Gov. Lowden, watched how straight and even was the triple furrow cut by
the gang plow and applauded the plow maid as she turned her machine.[26]

Along with the other spectators, reporters were no doubt surprised by the rather
emotional speech one of the invited speakers, Professor Perry Holden of International
Harvester, gave. He offered a heartfelt tribute to the farmerettes of Libertyville:

> These young women have not been content to simply talk about what they
> were going to do to help win the war, they have come here and demon-
> strated determination to accomplish; have shown by their own hands what
> women can do. They have turned their hands to tasks that were new and
> strange to them—to tasks that were hard and strenuous and wearying. They
> have not consulted their pleasure or comfort; they have followed fearlessly
> and courageously where they felt that duty called them. And they have set
> an example to the women of America of real patriotic service. They have
> started a movement of greater importance than even they themselves may
> realize—that may have a greater influence upon the outcome of the war
> than they even dream of. It is a movement that deserves to grow and
> extend, as I believe it will.[27]

The Land Army movement could claim another high-profile booster when the governor of Illinois climbed onto the makeshift stage. Governor Frank Orren Lowden was
a farm boy himself who then became a teacher and then a lawyer and served a decade in
Congress. He still owned a big farm in the Rock River Valley, so his presence and his
words at the farm that day were accorded a level of respect from the farmers that an
ordinary politician could not command. "I've seen enough of what has been accomplished here to be able to tell you that you have rivals in the field," he told the hundreds
of farmers, farm families, and agricultural professionals attending the festivities. And
they applauded.[28] Then he gently chided them:

> My old friend the Conservative Farmer: I know that many of you think that
> these girls will not do on the farm. I welcome these young women into our
> ranks. . . . These young women who shall help us to raise the food to feed
> their brothers on the battle front . . . And by helping us to raise the food
> we need, will become comrades of these heroic boys in the trenches on
> the battle fronts of Europe.

The newspaper reporters scribbled in their pads as the governor continued:

> I hope that this movement begun here in a simple, modest but very effective
> manner, may communicate itself to other portions of this State and other
> States, so that if need be we will match the irresistible army of our heroic
> men on the battlefront with an equally strong and equally patriotic army of
> women in the field and in the dairies of our land.

Just to prove that he knew what he was talking about, Lowden sat down on a three-legged stool and, in his fine suit and fedora hat, milked the farm's cow named Evangeline. That picture was in all the Chicago papers the next day with the headline "Gov. Lowden Milks Cow for Girls."

Perhaps the greatest tribute to the accomplishments of the Illinois Training Farm women came from a Lake County farmer in the crowd that day. Watching the farmerettes perform their new skills, he commented, "Well, I can say right here and now that those girls are all right."[29]

Margaret Blake saw the graduation ceremonies not as a finale but as a springboard for the Illinoise Training Farm for Women's continuing mission. Seven graduates won scholarships to further their agricultural education and went on to winter courses at the University of Wisconsin at Madison and University of Illinois at Urbana. Three grads took jobs in dairy farming and another in general farming. International Harvester hired one Libertyville alumna to go to Russia and teach the peasant women how to use tractors and other farm machinery. Other graduates planned to become Woman's Land Army unit directors the next spring. And one Libertyville alumna was given a singular honor, as reported by a Chicago newspaper:

> There was a thrill in the big audience at the International Livestock Show in
> Chicago last week when the parade of draft horses entered the ring. The
> leading horse, a magnificent Belgian, was in [the] charge of a young girl in
> khaki, who wore the brassard of the Woman's Land Army of America, and
> who managed the great animal as easily as if she were leading a kitten. She
> walked at the head of a long line of prancing horses—all the rest of them
> held by men. Miss Helen Hecketsweiler was the Land Army Girl. She is a
> product of the State of Illinois—and of the Training Farm of the Illinois
> Land Army at Libertyville, where she spent the summer, and evidently
> learned, among other things, how to manage horses. Not a man at the show
> could have done better than she did—and they said so.[30]

Margaret Blake had succeeded in creating a quintessentially midwestern institution that was well suited to her region's needs. But the goals of her Illinois women-on-the-land venture were not congruent with those of the national WLA movement, and as the Land Army changed shape to meet emerging national realities, the fit became more strained. By the first days of 1919 the Illinois division, led by the charming and politically astute Margaret Day Blake—the woman who could so deftly turn skeptics into believers—would secede from the Woman's Land Army of America.

16

GIRLS WHO THOUGHT POTATOES
GREW ON TREES: NEW ENGLAND

Alice Holway had never been away from home before she boarded a train to Vermont to join the Land Army. Carrying a small, worn travel case she stepped onto the train at the Worcester, Massachusetts, station; waved good-bye to her family; and terrified but excited, set off to meet her unit in Brattleboro. Mildred Buller Smith heard a Land Army recruitment talk in the University of Chicago chapel, and entranced by the opportunity to try something new, she left her classes to enter the Illinois Training Farm for Women at Libertyville. Abandoning her premedical studies and Chicago socialite life for a gritty course in practical farming, Mildred discovered she liked the rhythm of farm life more than the jazzy tempo of the city. She eventually took a Land Army assignment at an orchard in Vermont, north of where Alice was assigned. A graduate of Smith College (class of 1916), the scholarly Elizabeth Clarke stunned her friends by signing up for the WLA officers' training course at Wellesley, donning the Land Army brassard, and accepting an assignment at the same Vermont farm where Mildred Smith was working. And on that farm in East Corinth, Julian Dimock and his wife, Annette, embarked on their own headstrong experiment on the land, trying out new methods and new ideas and taking a chance on newly hatched farmerettes in a bold bid to create the modern, scientific American farm.

Alice stepped off the train at the Brattleboro depot, in the southeast corner of the state, and traveled to the nearby village of Dummerston. Her unit was assigned to work at a small farm and orchard called "Naulahka," the former residence of the British author Rudyard Kipling and his American wife. While living there in the 1890s, he wrote *Jungle Books* and *Captains Courageous* and started *Just So Stories* and *Kim*. Kipling fled Vermont after a fistfight with his wife's brother, and the owner of Naulahka at this time was Grace Holbrook, an officer of the Vermont WLA.

Just seventeen years old, Alice was eager to join the Land Army, though she had to fudge her birth date to meet the minimum age requirement. She joined her fellow farmerettes, ten University of Vermont students, to form the Naulahka unit. They all wore a uniform of khaki knickers with a strap at the knees, a belted tunic with a sailor collar, work boots, and a soft-brimmed, round hat. Alice was assigned to a numbered cot in the coachman's cottage. "It was all supposed to be very military and regulated," she recalled many years later. "We were all supposed to look the same; even our shoe-laces were the same."[1]

Mildred Smith's father was a wealthy commodities trader with the Chicago Board of Trade, and she had lived in a whirl of salon parties and debutante balls. A serious student, she had entered the University of Chicago with the "grand plan" of earning a medical degree, but in the spring of 1918, as the campus was abuzz with war activity, Mildred heard Margaret Day Blake deliver a recruitment pitch for the Illinois Training Farm for Women. Mildred took an enrollment form-, and as soon as her spring semes-ter classes ended, she entered Libertyville as a farmerette in training. When the summer regimen at Libertyville was over, she did not return to college; instead, she had won a WLA scholarship to take agricultural courses at the University of Wisconsin over the winter. This decision alarmed her family, but Mildred was thrilled with her new voca-tion. She accepted her first WLA assignment at a farm in Warren, Virginia, where she learned to drive a mule team and drill buckwheat into hard ground.[2]

Elizabeth (Beth) Lawrence Clarke inherited a fine academic pedigree: her father was a professor of biology at Williams College, and her mother was also a scholar. Beth distinguished herself at Smith, intending to pursue a career as a landscape architect. In the summer of 1918 she joined the Smith College Hilltop Unit of the WLA and won nomination to the WLA officers' training camp at Wellesley later in the summer.[3]

Julian Anthony Dimock was not born a farmer, which ultimately proved of great advantage to him. The son of a New Jersey businessman, Dimock was given a seat on the New York Stock Exchange as a young man, but he soon switched to a career as a magazine writer and photographer. When he went to Vermont on an assignment about maple sugaring, he was smitten by its beauty and vowed to return. In 1912 he gave up his city job, purchased an old apple orchard in Topsham, and joined the Back-to-the-Land Movement popular at the time. Dimock knew nothing about farming, so he enrolled in a short summer course at the Massachusetts Agricultural College at Amherst. At "Mass Aggie" he met a young home economics instructor, Annette Chase, who returned to Vermont with him as his wife.

The orchard at Topsham grew the fine old New England varieties—Bethels, Hamp-shire Sweets, and Lincoln Greenings—and Dimock studied the latest reports from the agricultural colleges and experimental stations. Dimock had no "old ways" of farming to rely on, no traditions of his fathers stubbornly to uphold; instead, he was keen on the latest methods and wanted to be a "scientific" modern farmer. With the advent of war,

Dimock encountered two new farming realities: male farmhands were impossible to find, and good potatoes, especially seed potatoes, were suddenly valuable. Dimock parlayed the two situations into a profitable combination by applying for Woman's Land Army workers and establishing a seed potato business.

The New England states' hills and river valleys were sprinkled with farmerettes in 1918. As the proximity to high-paying munitions and military fabrication factories siphoned away any able-bodied man who was not already in the army, the region's small family farms were almost totally drained of workers. Although the farmerettes were eager and almost begging to work, breaking down the sturdy stone walls of Yankee farmers' resistance was difficult.

While the Land Service Committee of the WNF&GA's New England branch signed up more than 1,200 Massachussetts women keen to do farmwork in 1918, the committee could find places for only 250 of them on Bay State farms. More New England women might have signed up for Land Army service, but as the Land Service chairwoman for Massachusetts reported, "We were requested very early in the season by manufacturers in essential industry to refuse to place their employees." So women working in munitions factories who might have preferred the Land Army's more pleasant work environment were not encouraged to apply.[4]

Thirteen Woman's Land Army units were active in Massachusetts during the 1918 season. Several more "unofficial" units of organized women who were not residing in a WLA camp but living at home and driving daily to neighboring farms, plus about a dozen college farm units, brought the Massachusetts farmerette total closer to five hundred on duty. The Land Service Committee of the WNF&GA's New England chapter sponsored and operated two "demonstration units." In the town of Westwood, thirty farmerettes worked from May to October, furnishing labor for fifty area farmers and running a community produce market and a canning operation. When the Westwood unit threw a Farmerette Festival in September, five hundred local people showed up to watch the farmerettes strut their skills. The unit at Lancaster began with asparagus cutting in the spring and worked through the harvest season. Most remarkably, a third of this unit's thirty farmerettes decided to remain on the land through the winter.

WLA units also thrived in Pittsfield, Barre, Ipswich, Alford, South Natick, Hamilton, Hubbardston, and Marshfield, Massachusetts. Thirty-five high school girls, too young to join the Land Army, lived in tents and worked on a farm in Upton. Nonresidential units of wealthy girls on summer vacation at their family's beach retreats were formed in Osterville, on Cape Cod, and in Beverly, where farmerettes raised and canned vegetables for the local hospital. The Beverly unit "was very successful, not only in the amount of food raised, but also in developing the spirit of service in the girls," reported the Land Service Committee, "and as an example to the village girls, who had looked upon this form of labor as fit only for peasant women."[5]

The Land Army was stronger in some New England states and much weaker in others. Connecticut an extraordinarily well-organized WLA state, managed its own three hundred farmerettes while New Hampshire organized just five Land Army units, employing about seventy women in 1918. Rhode Island hosted only a few workers, Maine had no WLA units in the field, and Vermont had only three, putting fifty women into Land Army uniforms.

Alice Holway was one of those Vermont farmerettes, and like all WLA recruits, she was required to furnish at least two character references (preferably one of these from a clergyman) and a physician's certificate before getting her farm assignment. If a prospective farmerette did not have her certificate, she could submit to an exam by a local doctor, usually a woman physician who volunteered to perform physicals for the Land Army gratis. The doctor checked the recruit's heart, lungs, feet, skin, and back curvature and noted her nervous system and menstrual history. The physician certified that the recruit would be "able to do eight hours daily of farm labor without injury to her health" and graded her abilities. An *A* meant she was "unusually strong, absolutely sound, able to do the heaviest work," and a girl with average strength was rated *B*. If the candidate earned a *C* ranking, which noted some physical "defect which must be guarded against," or a poor physique grade of *D*, the physician was asked to note in which ways the recruit "should be spared or safeguarded."[6] WLA guidelines also advised that "fussy, complaining, or quarrelsome" personalities should not be accepted into the farmerette corps. Once accepted, the New England farmerette signed a pledge to serve for an agreed length of time and to obey the unit's rules.[7]

Hale, husky, and cheerful Alice Holway gained acceptance into the Land Army, but she was destined for some percussive culture shocks. Growing up in a strict Methodist household that prohibited dancing or playing cards, she was bashful in the uproarious company of the college girls, who sang slightly naughty songs and wrote love letters to their soldier boyfriends in France. Alice was also too shy to jump into the bathtub with the other girls who, while washing off the day's farming dirt, invoked Kipling's spirit by singing parodies of his verses at the top of their lungs.

But these spirited girls did not take kindly to the strict regimentation and discipline the Naulahka unit supervisor, the humorless Miss Susan Swanton, doled out. Alice recalled,

> She was the strangest old maid you ever did know. She was in charge of us, and she ordered us around. She was our chaperone and thought we ought to be under her wings. The girls in the regiment with me were very independent Vermont girls, they were college girls, and they weren't used to reporting on their comings and goings and keeping tabs on their bedtimes. Susan Swanton was very irritated about these independent women.[8]

Mildred Smith's first Land Army assignment after she graduated from the Illinois Training Farm for Women was no bed of roses, either. At the Virginia farm where she was posted, the supervisor was sour and often mean spirited, the housekeeper was prone to wild fits of temper, and the farmerettes were miserable.

"What an Easter! I never spent one like it and don't want to again. Mrs. Gaynes [the housekeeper] had her Irish temper up and started to cut loose and swear around until we were all disgusted," Mildred wrote in the leather-bound journal she kept in her bunk. "So I stayed at the clubhouse all day and read Nietzsche, Science and Health, Common Prayer, and the Bible. We're all a little peeved." Mildred and her fellow farmerettes were determined to stick it out, for the sake of the Land Army's reputation. "This pioneer work is tough, when the whole movement looks to us to succeed, and we run into this kind of a job."[9]

Despite the discomfiting surroundings, Mildred was thrilled with the farm skills she was learning—most especially, driving a team of mules. "I hauled gravel all day with the mules," she wrote in her journal, "and tonight my throat is raw from hawing at the brutes, my neck hurts from driving, and I'm sore where I sat on the hard board that I had for a seat." And dorm life at the University of Chicago could hardly compare to this: "We had a little revolver practice in the evening. I knocked the block of wood off the stake five times out of eight, which isn't bad for a beginner." But Mildred yearned for a more convivial Land Army environment, one without constant frictions with the supervisors, and applied to WLA headquarters for a transfer.

Elizabeth Clarke, meanwhile, distinguished herself in the Smith College unit and also excelled at the Wellesley Training Camp. The camp's mixture of academic and aesthetic lectures with practical instruction and outdoor living suited her perfectly and played to her strengths. She came to the attention of Miss Edith Diehl, who recommended her for the plumb position of assistant manager for the farm owned by Mary Lyons Schofield of the New Hampshire WLA. Late in the 1918 season, Elizabeth packed her bags for East Hill Farm in Peterborough.

Julian Dimock found farmerettes to be the answer to both his labor needs and his scientific farming aspirations. They were quick, conscientious, eager to learn, and spirited. Dimock concentrated on building his potato seed business during the war years, providing certified, disease-free stock to commercial growers and dealers for a premium price. This enterprise involved careful, almost obsessive inspection of his potato crop; an ability to spot and diagnose any disease; and painstaking application of potent compounds to protect the spuds. This work demanded keen observational skills, delicate care, patience, and persistence. Women are better than men at this type of work, Dimock told anyone who would listen, and he boasted of his farmerettes' work in articles he wrote and in stories he encouraged to be written about his farm. An article about

Dimock's seed potato enterprise in the *New England Homestead* magazine explained,

> His use of girls has been simply because he has found them better qualified
> for this special job. No man on earth has the persistence to do the sort of
> work these girls do for him. It requires the enthusiasms of the girl fresh from
> the Agricultural College. Any man would go crazy at the very thought of this
> contract, but the girls keep plugging along, day after day, and as persistently
> as if they were clicking the keys of a typewriter or manipulating knitting
> needles.[10]

The farmerettes spent nine hours a day "roguing"—that is, moving in pairs, on
either side of a potato row, checking the plants to detect any sign of mosaic, leaf roll,
yellow dwarf, blacking, or an assortment of other maladies. It took eye-popping con-
centration and attention to detail. "Only girls can ever accomplish what is being done,"
Dimock explained. "It is too much of a nervous strain for men."[11]

Dimock trained the women to spot diseased plants quickly. "They could tell them
in their sleep and usually did dream about them," he said proudly.[12] Precise records on
note cards were kept of disease incidence and location, and affected plants were immediately culled to prevent sick plants being used for seed. The farmerettes protected the
rest of the crop by roaming the rows and spraying a dry mixture of copper sulphate,
lime, and arsenate from long-nosed cans called "hand dusters."

Answering Dimock's request for more farmerettes, Mildred Smith and Elizabeth
Clarke both eventually found their way to his farm and quickly took to this new type of
scientific seed-breeding work. Life at the Dimock Orchard was just grand. "I really
don't believe I deserve such happiness and peace of mind as I have here," Mildred wrote
in her journal soon after arriving at the Dimock Orchard. "Mr. D. is so jolly. He often
defers to me on little questions to do with the farm and evidently appreciates my mea-
ger knowledge of scientific farming. What a pleasure it is to work for such a man!"[13]

Annette Dimock made a comfortable home away from home for Mildred, Elizabeth, and the other farmerettes at the orchard farmhouse. She read choice excerpts from
The Atlantic Monthly and *Overlook* magazines to the women at the breakfast table;
arranged musical evenings in the parlor, with one talented farmerette playing violin and
another cello; and gave them encouragement and motherly advice.[14] When Julian asked
Mildred and Elizabeth to stay beyond the fall apple picking and packing season and
through the winter to develop the potato seed enterprise, they gladly accepted. Elizabeth spent a decade at the Dimock farm while Mildred lived and worked there for
eleven years.

In the southern tier of Vermont, Alice Holway and her Naulahka unit did not fare as well. Though they worked hard shifts, sometimes nine or ten hours at haying, hoeing, and spading sod in an orchard of a thousand trees, their employer treated them like cute curiosities. "For recreation the girls were several times called directly from their work to attend teas at the Manor House," Mrs. Holbrook explained, with no trace of irony, "to show their picturesque costumes to the guests."[15]

Miss Swanton was the type of unit supervisor who gave WLA field organizers headaches. So poorly suited to the job of leading a group of high-spirited young women, she simply couldn't handle the college girls' high jinks. She complained to the owner, as Alice remembered:

> Miss Swanton asked Mrs. Holbrook to give us a disciplinary talk. Mrs. Holbrook had us all come together in the big house where she lived, we all had to be in the dining room and ready to listen. Mrs. Holbrook came in, very dignified, high-piled white hair, duchess type, and she had a cane. On the wall of the dining room there was a set of camel bells, mementoes of Kipling's travels. Mrs. Holbrook came in and gave us a lecture on behavior and obedience—and when she was finished with that she took her cane and pointed to the camel bells and said to us, quoting from Kipling:
>
> > *These are the laws of the jungle,*
> > *And many and mighty are they,*
> > *But the head and the hoof of the law,*
> > *And the haunch and hump is OBEY!*
>
> And she hit the camel bells with her cane and she left. It was not very long after that we decided we'd had enough. The girls got me to tell Miss Swanton we were leaving.[16]

New England college women had an easier time serving in their own school units. Besides serving as base camp for Edith Diehl's training and experiment station, Wellesley College had its own War Farm unit, where about thirty-nine students took month long stints in working a twenty-acre plot. A faculty member took charge of the Wellesley farmerettes; Shakespeare House was turned into a drying room, with electric fans drying corn and vegetables; and sorority kitchens were commandeered to make ketchup and conserves from the farm's tomatoes. Farmerettes who could drive the college's Ford truck carried freshly dug potatoes into town to sell.[17]

Other Massachusetts women's colleges—Smith, Radcliffe, and Wheaton—maintained war farms and sent many of their students, faculty, and alumnae out to join other WLA units. A hundred and fifty Mount Holyoke women worked on the college farm as well as on neighboring farms that summer, but a Mount Holyoke farmerettes' duties did not simply begin with the five o'clock wake-up bell and end after a full day in the fields. As farmerette Charlotte Wilder explained,

> There may be on hand a patriotic meeting in Belchertown or Holyoke and in that case the farmerettes are always called on to come in their working regalia, sing popular and college songs, and perhaps give a "stunt" or so. We like nothing better, so whether it is a Fourth of July parade or a Sunday-school picnic, we go in a bunch to convert the country-side to the shocking idea of girls, in men's clothes, farming.[18]

The college librarian directed the War Land Service of Smith College and deployed students to three farm units in Hockanum, Chesterfield (where Beth Clarke served), and Conway, Massachusetts. Smith's farmerettes won accolades from the farmers for whom they toiled. "The farmers who have employed them have reported that they were amazed at first to find that the girls were capable of doing almost every kind of work that their regular farm hands did," a local newspaper reported.[19]

Besides the eager farmerettes, other types of first-time agricultural laborers tended the Massachusetts soil that summer. In addition to the adolescents of the Boys' Working Reserve, men who registered as conscientious objectors to the war were assigned to do farmwork as an alternative to military service, and Massachusetts farmers could apply to have them work in their fields.[20] And then in the Camp Devens's cantonment in central Massachusetts were the hundred German POWs sentenced to hard agricultural labor who worked sullenly under the watch of military guards holding bayoneted rifles. The "farmer Fritzies" as the *Boston Globe* called them, were growing cabbages, beans, and potatoes for the New England boiled suppers and baked beans served to Camp Devens soldiers. "The Germans work well," said the U.S. lieutenant supervising the POWs. "They have to."[21]

The Naulahka farmerettes felt they did not have to put up with the glowering Miss Swanton, however. In late July, fed up with Naulahka, Alice and the rest of the unit moved about ten miles north to the hill town of Putney, Vermont. They went to work in the raspberry fields of George Aiken (Vermont's future governor and senator) and found the less regimented situation much more to their liking. Aiken gave the workers canvas tents, which they pitched by a brook on the property. They cooked their own meals in a shack, negotiated their own pay, and when raspberries slowed, helped in Aiken's plant nursery or hired themselves out to pick on other farms. They ran their own Land Army unit.

Alice Holway liked working for George Aiken, and she seemed to have an affinity for the plant work. Aiken invited her to work for him in the spring and help build his nursery business. Alice returned to Putney in the spring of 1919, along with a few other of the farmerettes, and never left Vermont again. She made her life there as a plants expert and landscape designer for the next seventy years. "The Land Army brought me to Vermont," she always said, "and I just stayed."[22]

Mildred Smith hadn't expected to stay on the land; she had fully intended to return to the University of Chicago. "And look what I've done," she wrote in her journal soon after arriving at the Dimock farm. "I wouldn't trade it for anything." But after the armistice, she had some qualms. "I wonder if the farmerette fad is all over. Will I get a job or have to start in along a new line?" The "farmerette fad" was not over for Mildred Smith, however; she lived and worked at the Dimock Farm for another decade, as a teamster, as manager of the 2,500-tree apple orchard, and as supervisor of the other farmerette workers, who made up the bulk of the Dimock farm employees. She eventually did finish her degree at the University of Chicago and then earned graduate degrees from Radcliffe and the London School of Economics. She became an economics professor at the University of Connecticut and a consumer affairs expert with her own radio show.

All through the 1920s Mildred roomed at the Dimock Farm with Elizabeth Clarke, who moved up to become chief inspector for the Dimock Potato Seed Company and became an acknowledged national expert in the burgeoning field. Beth Clarke's Smith College friends were still aghast that she was working on a farm. "Well, of all the things in the world. Who would ever dream that Elizabeth Lawrence Clarke would go in for a thing like that," one classmate was quoted as saying in the *Boston Globe*.[23]

Julian and Annette Dimock built a prosperous apple and potato business while using women workers, and Julian's marketing ingenuity made the Dimock Orchard brand a favorite at city grocery stores. Annette's experience nurturing and advising her resident farmerettes became the basis for a newspaper column she began writing for the *Burlington Free Press* in the early 1920s, and continued for more than twenty-five years. Her "Aunt Serena" column, with commentaries on topics ranging from farm life to state politics, from recipes to book reviews, was immensely popular. Annette's fame as a columnist also launched her political career, and she won election to the Vermont legislature.

17

THE FARMERETTE IN WANAMAKER'S WINDOW: SELLING THE LAND ARMY IN NEW JERSEY

Like any self-respecting working girl, the WLA had to support itself. The farmerette earned her twenty-five cents an hour by toiling in the field, but the leaders of the Land Army at the national, state, and local levels had to work tirelessly to keep her there. To help feed the world, the Woman's Land Army had no choice but to provide its own nourishment.

There was no free lunch for the WLA. It did not have any federal funding, postal privilege, state support such as the Boys' Working Reserve enjoyed, or a national charity to provide for its needs. The Woman's Land Army relied on the generosity of individuals, the largesse of women's clubs, and the ingenuity of WLA administrators. Fielding a Land Army was an expensive enterprise. While individual camps and units often managed to break even or even turn a small profit, the larger expenses—the rent for WLA offices, the recruitment campaigns, all the publications and posters,had to be met by private donations. Whereas the farmerettes' duty was to raise crops, the WLA board officer's job was to raise funds.

New Jersey offers a vivid example. The organizers of the New Jersey Woman's Land Army were not squeamish about financial matters and certainly not shy about asking for money; their finance committee chairwoman, after all, was Mrs. Junius Spencer Morgan. But even a member of the House of Morgan couldn't relieve the New Jersey WLA's incessant financial headaches. The New Jersey WLA took a straightforward, supremely businesslike approach toward funding and promoting the organization; while not fundamentally different in method from the WLA's efforts in other states, its tone was more direct.

"I am writing to ask if you will become a member of my Finance Committee, representing [your] county," Josephine Perry Morgan wrote from Constitution Hill, her manor house in Princeton, when the state WLA was getting organized in March 1918. After explaining that the Finance Committee's role was to raise money for the headquarters' operating expenses a secretary, travel and speakers' expenses, printing, and postage, Mrs. Morgan laid out the economics of the deal she was presenting:

> We have roughly estimated that we shall require from $400 to $500 a month for this part of the work. I am dividing the amount among the twenty-one counties of the State and find that $25 a month from each county will furnish the necessary funds. Will you serve on this Committee and be responsible from your county for $25 a month or $300 a year?[1]

The recipients of Josephine Morgan's letter were the right sort of people, with the right connections and funds, who had been identified through her wide circle of social and club acquaintances. "My Dear Mrs. Morgan—The two people best suited to your committee from Short Hills are . . . ," was the advice offered by Mrs. Hack, the mistress of Oakridge Place, whom Mrs. Morgan asked for recommendations. "These women are from New Jersey families, and besides having financial independence, they should know more or less about Essex County."[2] This sort of networking was the mainspring of the great engine of voluntary enterprise built by American women during the war. The WLA women of New Jersey, many of them married to wealthy businessmen, perfected this technique. As seasoned veterans of many a charity ball and good works fundraising drive, they didn't bat an eye when asking friends of friends to whip out their checkbooks.

Mrs. Morgan devised a multitiered fund-raising system, one that spread responsibility and broadened the sense of involvement in the movement. She put in place an Executive Board Membership Fee Fund, obligating the state WLA officers to cough up a sizable contribution, which was a standard feature of philanthropic board membership. The suggested donation was $500, and Mrs. Morgan kept careful track of her fellow board members' pledges in a penciled list. Next there was the County Fee Fund, the $300 in dues expected from each of New Jersey's twenty-one counties, intended to finance the state WLA organization; this money was usually raised in small pledges of perhaps $10 from a few dozen people in each area.[3]

The foundation level of Mrs. Morgan's funding structure was the County Chairman's Fund, a targeted campaign to support the individual Land Army units established in each county. This fund provided start-up loans to the units, helped buy supplies and pay supervisors' salaries, and also bailed out any needy units. The WLA County Committee also pleaded with neighbors and cajoled local businesses to give donations of furniture, food, and automobiles to the units. To reach a broader set of pocketbooks, the New Jersey WLA relied on its version of the trusty bake sale, selling jams and pies made from the fruit of farmerettes' labors. Benefit vaudeville shows, concerts, dances, and farmerette movie nights were also popular fund-raising vehicles.

Although the New Jersey WLA was fundamentally a woman-powered and woman-funded enterprise, it welcomed the help of men, especially if they could bolster the cause. The WLA organizers sent their husbands out to have man-to-man chats with the state's political and agricultural leaders and in this way secured some valuable additions to the WLA Advisory Council. The names of U.S. Senator Joseph S. Frelinghuysen, Princeton University president John Grier Hibben, and state Secretary of Agriculture Alva Agee graced the New Jersey WLA stationery's masthead. The governor even offered the WLA a rent-free headquarters office in the State House at Trenton.

The New Jersey WLA also came up with a truly novel fund-raising idea—a public appeal issued through the state's largest-circulation newspaper, the *Newark Evening News*. The *News* covered both the military and domestic aspects of the war with a vivid hometown slant, so it had a natural journalistic interest in the new state branch of the Woman's Land Army. It also didn't hurt that two members of the Scudder family, owners of the *News,* served as New Jersey WLA officials: a niece, Anne MacIlvaine, was the state WLA chairwoman and a Scudder's wife was on the state WLA Advisory Council. The *News*'s editors arranged for a full month of glowing publicity, feature articles, and large photos, topped off by an appeal for public donations to the cause. The *Newark News* Fund for the New Jersey division of the Woman's Land Army made the WLA into a bona fide wartime charity, but it was still only one of many worthy organizations whose emergency supplications were competing for the American public's spare dollars.

New Jersey put thirty-two units in the field in the 1918 season, including some interesting variations and adaptations of the standard unit model. Some units were run according to the Bedford Camp's system, which Ida Ogilvie worked out the previous summer: the farmer paid the unit supervisor two dollars a day for each farmerette assigned to his fields, but the farmerette received only fifteen dollars a month, the rest of her wages went toward her board and the camp's upkeep. Other New Jersey units chose a cooperative plan in which the farmers paid the farmerettes directly and then all shared the camp's expenses, including the salaries of a supervisor and cook and the food supplies.[4] Unforeseen emergencies—a broken water pump, an expensive truck repair, or long stretches of rainy weather leading to unemployment—could easily plunge even the best-managed unit into financial disarray. It fell to Mrs. Morgan and her colleagues to mop up that red ink.

Mrs. Morgan and her Finance Committee cohorts were spared worry about one unit, at least, thanks to an unusual arrangement established with Seabrook Farms in southern Cumberland County. Charles Franklin Seabrook requested a large unit of women for his sprawling farm and, in what was closer to the California model of employer-financed WLA camps, offered to house and feed the workers. This arrangement freed the WLA from the tasks of finding a sponsor for the unit, designing a system for the unit's self-support, or, if need be, coming up with a financial rescue plan.

Charles Seabrook, who would come to be called the "Henry Ford of Farming" for bringing the lessons of the modern factory to the farm, was already known as an ambitious farmer who was open to new ideas. In a few years he would become the agricultural pioneer who put Clarence Birdseye's quick-frozen food patents to work, building a freezing plant at Seabrook Farms to package the vegetables grown there, but during the war he held government contracts to supply the military with tons of vegetables. Seabrook desperately needed labor for his fields. If those laborers were women, that was fine with him.

Seabrook asked Cumberland County WLA organizers for thirty farmerettes. He rented a large house for them, hired a cook, and paid each worker fifteen dollars a month, plus free board and transportation, with the stipulation that they work exclusively for his farm. He later requested thirty more women. Seabrook was willing to employ any worker who earned her, or his, keep, and in the next half century he built a huge farming empire by bringing displaced people from around the world to his company town. From Italians fleeing conscription to White Russian soldiers escaping the Bolshevik revolution, from miners leaving Appalachia in the Depression to Japanese Americans granted permission to work at Seabrook instead of languishing in West Coast internment camps during World War II, Seabrook built the Garden State's largest farm on the backs of those fleeing twentieth-century miseries. He treated them decently (though bitterly fought their attempts to unionize) and created "ethnic villages" for his different worker groups that even included a Buddhist temple for his Japanese laborers. At its height in the 1940s and 1950s, Seabrook was home to five thousand workers speaking thirty languages. In the scheme of things, the little camp Charles Seabrook built for the white city women of the Woman's Land Army was simply an early manifestation of his grander vision.

The New Brunswick farmerette unit had no financial worries, as the Johnson and Johnson laboratories profitably engaged it to pick belladonna, the highly poisonous but medicinally useful herb planted at the company's farm in central New Jersey. Belladonna was especially valuable during the war, as the usual supply imported from central Europe was no longer available and war injuries propelled demand. The farmerettes were issued gloves and stern instructions not to sample the sweet berries of the "deadly nightshade." The unit reported no casualties and no deficits.

New Jersey was host to still another unusual farmerette camp, this one sponsored and operated by the YWCA, not the WLA. The Polish Land Army Unit thrived as an ethnically homogeneous group of women recruited from the immigrant neighborhoods of Newark. Laura Patterson, an energetic YWCA Land Service organizer, worked with the Polish White Cross and Polish Ladies' Society to recruit its members, and found the women eager to enroll, but there was one hitch: these farmerettes were married and needed to bring their children to camp.

"The children formed the chief difficulty in recruiting the foreign-born woman,"

Patterson explained. "It was found necessary to take the children with their mothers. That accounted for our twenty-four children in camp."[5]

In the only documented example of providing child care at any farmerette camp in the nation, the YWCA-run Polish Land Army unit situated in Holmdel hired Miss Ida Apgar, principal of a local New Jersey school, to run a nursery at the camp. Apgar bathed, dressed, and fed the little tykes, told them fairy tales, and read them books. "The mothers left for the field knowing that their children would be well cared for in Miss Apgar's charge."[6]

While many married women joined the WLA's ranks, and some probably had young children, no other camp accommodation seems to have been made for their children. They must have made their own arrangements, leaving their sons and daughters in the care of family or friends. The YWCA's abiding concern for working women's welfare and its experience with their child care needs gave it a much better grasp of the kind of support working mothers required—certainly more sensitivity than the suffragists or the garden club ladies displayed.

Though the Polish women passed their required Land Army physical examinations with ease (the attending physician pronounced them the healthiest people he had ever seen), they had a harder time convincing their husbands that becoming a farmerette was a wonderful idea. Employed as mechanics and factory or mill workers in Newark, the husbands "thought the work too difficult for their wives and prophesied their return within a week," Patterson recalled. But "they found their prophesy unfulfilled."[7]

"The enthusiasm of our women was remarkable," Patterson reported proudly. "They were also desirous of showing the Polish colony of Newark and incidentally their own husbands what they were capable of doing for their adopted country."[8] They picked potatoes eight hours a day, and were paid ten cents a barrel. After the first week of "breaking in their backs" and learning the correct wrist movement, they became speedier pickers, and most could pick forty barrels a day "easily." One dynamo, Mrs. Laskowska, set a record, picking eighty-one barrels in one day.[9]

The women and their children lived in a spacious nine-room house donated by one of the farmers. They slept on cots, hauled water from a well, and bathed in a brook. Farmers supplied the kitchen with potatoes, apples, cabbages, and other vegetables that the camp cook, Mrs. Radenewcz (the president of the Polish Ladies' Society who signed up for duty herself), used to whip up favorite Polish home-style meals, including her famous sour beet soup.

The women paid a board charge of fifty cents a day for themselves and each of their children older than age three who lived in camp; the fees severely cut into their earnings. One poor mother of three children paid twice as much in board fees for her family as she earned picking five hundred barrels of potatoes. This effort was intended as a patriotic, not necessarily profitable, one, though most women did take home a small purse of earnings. The unit managed to meet its expenses and turn a small profit of

$54.06 but only because Laura Patterson served as camp supervisor and the Y paid her
salary, Miss Apgar donated her services, and the free potatoes helped keep food costs down.

What the unit accomplished, however, went beyond mere financial accounting.
The farmers found the women more conscientious and dependable than the typical
hired man, and the women felt well appreciated. One farmer even wrote a tribute to the
women's work for the local *Red Bank Register* newspaper.[10] The local farm agent for the
Federal Employment Bureau was impressed, telling his superiors at the Labor Department that the Polish unit's work was "most valuable help" and his office "would have
been in great difficulty to supply labor in that district without the aid of these women."[11]
All told, the women workers saved crops valued at nearly $40,000.[12]

The women's husbands were impressed. When their wives didn't quit after the first
week of work, they ventured by train from Newark to see for themselves, arriving at the
camp with older children, grandmothers, and other curious relatives. "They were very
pleased to hear that their wives were satisfied and making good," Patterson wrote. "They
all agreed that the children were greatly benefited by the change from city streets to the
freedom of the country."[13] The cook strained to feed fifty mouths a proper Sunday
dinner from her four-burner oil stove, but everyone enjoyed themselves so much that
the families' Sunday visits to the farm became part of the camp's rhythm.

The Polish unit also made another important point: "We proved that foreign women
could work in the fields," the chairwoman of the Land Service Committee reported. By
that she did not just mean that "foreign" women could manage the back-breaking
work. More important, the Polish unit proved that foreign women could be organized,
be regimented, obey orders, and work under supervision in an American-style structure. They were summoned to American patriotism and could be trusted.[14] The Polish
unit's success, however, did not ease the profound mistrust between the YWCA and the
Woman's Land Army.

The Young Women's Christian Association had a prickly relationship with the
Woman's Land Army. The much larger, more powerful, and accomplished YWCA was
sympathetic and supportive of the women's land service movement—the Y was, after
all, one of the WLA's founding organizations—but it insisted on maintaining an arm's
length distance, an aloofness that puzzled and annoyed the WLA officers. The YWCA
had a clear image of itself as a Christian force for the working girl's protection and
betterment, and carved its role in the women's war work movement within these distinct lines. Through its War Work Council, it provided housing and supervision for
women living near munitions and industrial factories and ran canteens and recreational
spaces for soldiers. Its Bureau of Social Morality catered to the spiritual, as well as
physical, well-being of its charges. Rivaling the Red Cross's sophisticated fund-raising
campaigns, the Y's public appeals for donations to its War Work Council kept it well

financed. The Y was well respected, supremely well organized, and did excellent work; moreover, it took care not to spread its efforts too thinly.

By early spring 1918, when the WLA was kicking into high gear, the YWCA's National Board was warning its members to go slow: "We would not deem it wise to become a part of the organization of the Woman's Land Army, but that we should hold ourselves in readiness to cooperate with any agency making a contribution to the problem, as definite and specific needs shall be presented to us."[15]

When the YWCA formed its Land Service Committee in April 1918, it invited several WLA-affiliated women to join, including Delia West Marble, Anna Gilman Hill, and Ida Ogilvie. The presence of these gung ho Land Army women seemed to alter, at least slightly, the Y's attitude. In May, the Land Service Committee published its policies in *The Girl on the Land* brochure, which gave tacit endorsement of the WLA by including a list of all state WLA chairwomen. But the Y still insisted that it would not become the Land Army's "sugar mommy," denying the WLA free access to its deep pockets. Over and over, when the WLA appealed to the YWCA to financially assist or take charge of a farmerette unit—often a troubled unit—the Y turned down the request. When Y staff members were dispatched into the field to evaluate these WLA pleas for help, they filed caustic reports that often questioned the reliability and even the motives of the WLA's request.

What comes through, in memoranda and letters, is the level of mistrust and even open hostility between the organizations. The Y regarded the WLA as a scatterbrained, spendthrift debutante with designs on the purse of her dowager aunt. The Y found suspect the WLA's nascent and wobbly organizational abilities, its selection procedures, and perhaps even its moral fiber for unlike the Y's Land Service Committee, the WLA did not open each of its meetings with a prayer.

A distinct difference between the two groups' missions also helped explain their frequent clashes: the WLA's purpose was war work and agricultural help while the Y's core mission was to protect the working women's morals: "Our object is not to promote agricultural work but to supervise and take care of girls, having the same relation to girls in farm work as we now have to girls in industrial work."[16] The Land Army, as an emergency response, wanted to meet urgent needs. The YWCA, as a permanent organization with a religious and social mandate, took the long view and saw its involvement in 1918 as a series of experiments in preparation for more extensive and effective work in the future. The Y found the experimental venture it was seeking in providing land service for the foreign-born woman in the New Jersey Polish unit and tried its hand at running a farmerette camp for young American women at Yorktown Heights, New York. It provided supervisors or chaperones for a few WLA-operated units around the country, but for the most part, while the Y and the WLA shared the goal of putting women on the land, the Y insisted on doing so in its own way.

As with so many WLA state organizations, the New Jersey branch initially encountered a high hedgerow of farmer mistrust and community skepticism that had to be faced and gradually surmounted. "At first only three farms gave support," reported the chairwoman for Burlington County. "The neighborhood was conservative and indifferent and in some directions even antagonistic." But attitudes began to change: "After two weeks of work in the district, the unit is creating a more and more favorable impression. Courtesy, interest, and co-operation are evidenced in rapidly increasing degree."[17] In another few weeks the WLA chairwoman could report that farmers were calling for larger units of women, and by harvest time the farmerettes had become part of the community fabric. Shopkeepers offered them special discount prices, tradesmen donated their services to the unit's camp, and farmers sent gifts of fresh vegetables, milk, and eggs to the WLA camp's cook.

The New Jersey WLA organizers could rightfully claim a portion of credit for the goodwill and community support the farmerettes enjoyed as the season progressed. Though the workers themselves convinced the farmers with their own muscles that they were capable, the WLA administrators did not simply sit back and wait for a change of attitude to occur. Taking a cue from George Creel and his war propaganda machine, the New Jersey WLA women created images in the public eye and perceptions in the public mind to fix the farmerette in the public heart.

Coupled with Mrs. Morgan's fund-raising schemes, the publicity campaign launched in New Jersey was perhaps the WLA's most sophisticated. A speakers' bureau brought the WLA into ladies' and men's clubs, patriotic gatherings, and community sings all around the state. A corps of trained "Four-Minute" speakers fanned out into movie theaters, popping up from their seats to inform their captive audiences about how the Woman's Land Army was helping avert worldwide famine, and concluding with a donation pitch. Ushers passed out WLA brochures and a hat for bills and coins.

Tacked up on pillars, walls, or trees was the handsome new poster the New Jersey WLA had printed, featuring the Charles Dana Gibson illustration of Uncle Sam tipping his hat and shaking the hand of a uniformed farmerette with the tagline "Until the Boys Come Back." The WLA made up versions of the poster for each major county in the state, intended for local fund-raising and recruitment drives, while giant billboards brought Uncle Sam and his helpful farmerette to New Jersey's cities.

Photographers hired by the WLA visited every unit in the state, all through the season, and took pictures of the women hard at work. These photos were distributed to the newspapers as well as collected in booklet form to show off to farmers still unconvinced of the merits of women's labor. Enlargements were displayed in public libraries and town halls. The state WLA commissioned a moving picture of the New Jersey units and produced lantern slides featuring a state map with each unit's location noted by a star. In a public relations maneuver even George Creel hadn't yet perfected, each New Jersey unit chose a member to act as a "journalist" and chronicle her group's life and work, forwarding her notes to the Trenton headquarters every week. This clever arrangement did not always work well, however, once the fatigue of long, hot days in the field set in; sometimes the journalist-farmerettes fell asleep before they could write their dispatches from the farm front.[18] But they did generate enough story ideas for the Publicity Committee in Trenton to write weekly press releases and send stories to all the local newspapers and big city Sunday editions, as well as articles specially tailored for the farm journals. The season's big print publicity coup was the month long coverage in the *Newark Evening News*, but even that could not compare to the buzz generated by WLA Day at Wanamaker's. Newark's largest department store put live uniformed farmerettes in its display windows, giving recruitment and fund-raising a big boost.[19]

One New Jersey county raised $700 from its community movie nights, and another farmerette unit put on a minstrel show, which was still considered an acceptable form of entertainment at that time. But as the season wound down, the more substantial contributions, those large private "subscriptions" Mrs. Morgan and her Finance Committee sought, became more difficult to secure. As Elizabeth Devery, the chairwoman of Burlington County, wrote:

> Dear Mrs. Morgan . . . I have not had the opportunity to personally
> interview any people in regard to subscriptions to our state treasury, but have
> written to nine wealthy men and women, six of whom I am acquainted with.
> I cannot hope for $250.00 from each one; but I feel sure something will
> come of it. I will report to you as soon as anything results.[20]

"I haven't anything yet for the State Fund," admitted the Bergen County chairwoman, Sarah Fuller Preston. "We are such a small community here and I have asked everyone I know to contribute to this unit. We are going to have a deficit in running expenses, I fear. That deficit I expect to assume myself."[21]

By early autumn a strange new impediment to Mrs. Morgan's fund-raising schemes emerged: the Spanish influenza epidemic hit New Jersey hard. "Epidemic has prevented getting contributions," said the terse telegram Mrs. Morgan received from a county organizer in early October.[22]

Instead of waiting for her wealthy contacts to write fat checks for the WLA, Mrs. Devery took a different fund-raising tack. On October 2, just before state health officials ordered a halt to public gatherings for fear of spreading the flu, she staged a benefit program for the WLA at the Mt. Holly Theatre. This opulent season finale gave the Land Army movement the kind of proper society standing that could turn into big checks later on.[23] The program featured two short plays, a wartime melodrama and a comedy, and a program note assured the audience that "each male member in both

plays has fulfilled all obligations in respect to military service." Between the stage per-
formances, a moving-picture screen unfurled, and the audience was treated to two
action-packed films featuring women on the land: the tried-and-true British WLA
documentary and then new footage of the American Woman's Land Army at work.

Audience members held in their laps a handsome program brochure, containing a
blunt reminder of why the WLA had to begin preparing for the 1919 season:

> Save Food—But you must Raise it first
> Help the Farmers of America WIN the WAR.
> If the soil does not produce abundantly next summer our soldiers
> will lack food; we will be hungry and our Allies will starve.[24]

The program also explained that New Jersey citizens could aid the cause either by joining
the WLA, with a membership fee of a dollar a year, or by recruiting a worker or loaning
houses, furniture, and automobiles to the Land Army.

The finale of the Mt. Holly Theatre benefit was a stirring "Allied Patriotic Tableau,"
which would also be staged at New York's Metropolitan Opera House a few days later as part
of the Fourth Liberty Loan campaign. Its pièce de résistance was a rousing rendition, with
full orchestral accompaniment, of "The March of the Land Army" written by Connecticut
farmerette Cornelia Brandreth (displaying rare rhyming talents) and dedicated to the women
of the Land Army.

There's an army that cannot go over there,
There's an army that will ever do its share—
From the East and from the West,
For the land that they love best.
From the South and from the North
All the girls come marching forth.
They come with loyal heart and willing hand,
To raise the food their Country will demand.
Their spirits never lag,
For they're working for their flag,
And as they swing along
You can ever hear their song:

(Refrain)
We are the Girls of the Land
And for Liberty we take our stand.
We'll fight for the right with our might
As we march with our hoe in hand
For the boys who have gone over there.

And for Belgium and France so fair
We'll sow the seed, our Allies to feed
Till Peace every land shall declare.

Mrs. Morgan tucked the benefit concert program into her files at her Princeton home, saving it as a memento of the imagination and ambition—if not overwhelming financial success—of her New Jersey Woman's Land Army.

18

GEORGIA COTTON

Southern white women did not pick cotton; it was not done. Very few white men did, either. Cotton picking was the province of black men and black women and, often, black children. In Augusta, Georgia, it would not be proper for the fluffy white boll to be plucked by a lily white hand. This was wartime, however, and Mrs. Clara Mathewson simply did not see why the white women of Augusta—the club women, the suffrage women, and the Girl Scouts—should not help bring in this most essential crop, the backbone of the local economy.

Although the idea went against all tradition, all expectations, Mrs. Mathewson would not be dissuaded. All other efforts to find adequate labor for the cotton crop had failed the previous year—even the outrageous ploy many of Georgia's white landowners used, refusing to allow their black sharecroppers to register for the military draft or to report for duty once they had been called. The planters simply did not deliver or, where necessary, read the conscription notices to their black tenant farmers and laborers; local sheriffs arrested hundreds of Georgia black men and threw them into army stockades for not responding to the draft notices they'd never received. The sheriffs then collected a fifty-dollar reward for handing over each "slacker." In some towns, sympathetic draft boards "resisted sending healthy and hard-working black males" to the military, where they were most often put to work in menial labor, because they were needed in Georgia's cotton fields.[1] Despite these schemes, valuable cotton went unharvested in 1917.

Cotton was still king in Georgia, especially around Augusta, where the fertile fields bordering the Savannah River were just perfect for growing cotton and where the deep-river port provided a great shipment hub. The state still relied too heavily on cotton, despite the best efforts of the agricultural colleges and even the women's clubs, who tried to convince farmers to diversify their crops. In 1914 the Georgia Federation of Women's Clubs had launched a series of agricultural rallies in all the counties to educate farmers on the need to diversify and plant more soybeans and peanuts on their land, but such change would be slow. Further, cotton was needed for the war. The Allied armies, our own troops, and even the Germans (who had paid well for Georgia cotton while America was still neutral) required cotton for all those bandages and all those uniforms. Prices were high.

Finally, it was a lowly insect, not experts' advice or concerned women's rallies, that would change Georgia's cotton economy. The boll weevil had arrived from Texas in 1915 and spread around the state, infecting the cotton shrubs. Although the 1917 and 1918 seasons marked the cotton crop's high point in Georgia's history, in the following six years, the boll weevil would eat 30 percent of the state's cotton crop.

But while the 1918 crop was ripening, Clara Mathewson was marshaling her resources. She was active in the Equal Suffrage Party of Georgia, and her Augusta suffrage sisters served as the nucleus of her WLA campaign. Still, there was a lot of explaining to do and some incredulous questions to be answered at the first organizational meetings. "Just what is a Woman's Land Army anyway?" asked one meeting attendee. "Are the girls really expected to work in the fields?" asked another.[2]

"When the committee of women met at the Soldier's Club on Thursday," the *Augusta Chronicle* reported, "some were inclined to scoff at the idea, to say it could not be done; others were inclined to doubt the necessity for forming such an army, while still others were positive that if it were successfully organized, the girls would not be physically able to stand the heat."

The group was assured that under the Land Army system, the women workers would be "adequately chaperoned and not allowed to work until exhausted or overheated." Understanding that a WLA camp, especially one housing women from other towns or cities or perhaps even other—northern—states, would never be accepted in Augusta, the plan was to recruit only local women who were known and trusted, and would do limited stints in the fields but sleep in their own beds at night.

Even before the meeting, Mrs. Mathewson, a seasoned organizer, had done the legwork necessary to assuage the concerns she knew would arise. She'd already approached several prominent farmers and plantation owners with her plan. Desperate not to leave cotton rotting in the field as it had in the 1917 season, they had endorsed this idea of carefully chaperoned squads of white women workers—even if they were their friends' and neighbors' wives and daughters. Mathewson then went to the Richmond County Agricultural Agent, Gus York, for a letter of recommendation. He obliged with an enthusiastic reply.

"As to the practicability and value of the woman's land army in harvesting the present cotton crop," York wrote, "I will say that I am glad to co-operate with you, and believe if carried out according to your plans it will be of great value." The labor shortage was more acute than in 1917, "with men being called every day by the draft," York explained. "It would seem unless we get more force behind this crop a great part of it will go unharvested," he warned. "Besides the material benefit such a movement will engender, the moral effect will be greater," York wrote to Mrs. Mathewson. "I feel sure that the farmers will cooperate in every way possible with your land army workers and I shall be very glad to lend my assistance."[3]

Hoping to overwhelm any possible community opposition to her Land Army of white women, Mathewson also solicited the help of one of the most respected men in town, Judge Henry Hammond. An ardent suffrage supporter and featured speaker at all the Augusta Equal Suffrage rallies, he and Clara Mathewson were comrades in suffrage. He agreed to lend his prestige and flowery pen to her Land Army cause and wrote an open letter that was published in the *Chronicle*:

> Think, city girl! You can pick a bag of cotton after dinner that will make
> warm socks and underclothes for a first-class fighting man, or a suit of khaki
> so dear to your eye for a brave soldier boy. Go to the work at hand. Put
> yourself in close touch with the big labor of the world right here. There
> never was such a time.[4]

The *Chronicle* also became a civic booster of the Woman's Land Army effort, covering it extensively and approvingly in the paper's pages. From its formation ("Augusta Women Form 'Land Army', Will Pick Cotton and Gather Crops") to its march into the fields ("Young Ladies Go Cotton Picking") and record of accomplishments ("Hephzibah Unit of Land Army Has Picked 13 Bales Cotton"), the *Chronicle* offered its readers complete coverage of the venture. "*The Chronicle* will carry a full account each day of the place, time of starting, and number of pounds of cotton picked by the Woman's Land Army," the editors promised.[5]

When Mrs. Mathewson and her committee put out the call for the first set of Land Army volunteers, thirty-two women from the finest Augusta families signed up, and the *Chronicle* printed their names as "Cotton Patriots." Subsequent volunteers were directed to apply for duty at the WLA office in the Augusta Soldier's Club. Recruitment expectations were high: "It is the desire of the committee that every unemployed woman or girl in Augusta will enroll immediately."[6] But prospective farmerettes had to be in earnest about their commitment. The Augusta WLA leaders warned that service was no lark: "It would not be in keeping with the patriotic mothers who inspired the organization of the Woman's Land Army, neither would they be of any service to the farmers, if it is undertaken in a spirit of fun, rather than a spirit of patriotism."[7]

The Augusta and Richmond County communities rallied around the farmerettes. The WLA formed a Transportation Committee to carry them to and from the fields and sent out a call for the loan of cars and drivers. Grocers were asked to cooperate by saving flour, sugar, and crocus sacks for the cotton pickers' use. Those men younger than draft age were asked to serve as escorts and accompany the women into the fields. They would be armed with guns, ostensibly to keep the workers safe, with the unspoken danger being the black laborers who still remained in the cotton fields.

"Proof positive that the Woman's Land Army of Augusta is an assured fact and not just 'patriotic talk' will be given this afternoon when the first squad of young women goes out to the Beech Island plantation of Mr. Paul Dunbar armed with cotton sacks and enthusiasm to help gather the cotton crop of Richmond County," the *Chronicle* reported on August 27. "Dressed in blue overalls, khaki suits and motor corps uniforms, or the discarded suits of last summer," the first squad of farmerettes "presented the true picture of the modern American womanhood which adapts itself to any sort of necessity and lends to it her own feminine charm."[8]

Some time-honored customs of cotton picking needed to be bent to accommodate this new class of laborers. "It is customary for the farmer to give each laborer a sheet to put his pickings in," the newspaper reported, "but owing to the fact that the girls will probably not pick as much as a day laborer," they could share the collection sheets and required fewer. One break with custom was most welcome: "An interesting feature of the Woman's Land Army labor for the farmer's wife will be the picnic dinners which the girls are to carry with them. Heretofore the cotton picking season meant long hours in the kitchen, preparing the dinner for the hands; the picnic dinner solves this problem."[9] Yet some customs were sacred. While the farmerettes picked, they still mopped "their faces with the traditional red bandana handkerchiefs."[10]

Even more so than in other states, the Georgia farmerettes were a novelty. "Cotton picking has always been a subject of interest to the people of Augusta—to all the South for that matter," the *Chronicle* told its readers, "but never have the 'pickers' attracted so much attention and been the subject of so much comment as they were yesterday afternoon."[11] These farmerettes, blasting years of southern agricultural tradition and rigid racial roles, made for great newspaper copy, and the *Chronicle* editors knew it. "The people of Augusta will await with interest the account of the success which the Woman's Land Army is sure to meet."[12]

The farmerettes were sent out to the fields only in the early morning or early evening, the cooler parts of the day. They worked at the back-breaking task for only two or three hours at a time, unlike the impossibly long hours the typical black man or woman cotton picker kept during harvest season. The farmerettes also enjoyed a brand-new custom in the treatment of cotton pickers when they were invited into a plantation owner's home and served cold ginger ale for refreshment.

But those farmerettes did work. Fueled by enthusiasm, the first squad picked three hundred pounds of cotton in ninety minutes on the farm owned by Mr. Dunbar. Mrs. James Farr set the highest record, picking twenty-eight pounds, and Miss Julia Moore came in second, picking twenty-four pounds.

"That Mr. Dunbar is satisfied that girls can pick cotton as efficiently as men was proven," the *Chronicle* reported, "when asked by Mrs. Mathewson, the leader of the Land Army, when he wanted another squad to pick, he unhesitatingly replied: 'Tomorrow.'"[13]

Groups of ten to twenty farmerettes—club women, school teachers, Girl Scouts, and their leaders—came from every section of Richmond County and set off three or more times a week for fieldwork stints. They were paid the going rate for average-ability cotton pickers, or seventy-five cents for each hundred pounds, and many donated their earnings to the Red Cross. The Augusta Motor Corps offered its trucks, augmented by a caravan of volunteers driving their own cars, to transport the farmerettes to the field.[14]

As the cotton harvest progressed Mrs. Mathewson continued making logistical corrections to her plan, tweaking it to "make the army more efficient" and responsive to the farmers' needs. Her strategy worked. "The farmers have expressed themselves as being thoroughly satisfied with the results" of the Land Army, the *Chronicle* reported. "It has passed the experimental stage and proven itself worthy of being taken seriously, and it is in this spirit the farmers of Richmond County are asking for their [the farmerettes'] help."[15]

Augusta was not the only Land Army site in Georgia in the summer of 1918. Women students of the Berry School in Rome were farming on their property as well as helping neighboring farmers, all under the leadership of a Bedford Camp–trained unit leader. They were not, however, picking cotton.

Though for the most part the southern states were not receptive to farmerettes in the summer of 1918—the social taboos were too powerful—there were some other notable exceptions. In Greensboro, North Carolina, women studying to become teachers at the Greensboro Normal School worked on the three hundred–acre college farm and helped on neighboring private farms. The Greensboro farmerettes hoed corn, threshed wheat, pitched hay, and cultivated sweet potatoes and tomatoes in their khaki uniforms. "Our uniform consisted of khaki suit—middy, skirt, and bloomers we made up in the sewing lab," recalled Marjorie Craig, one of the Greensboro farmerettes, "leggings, coarse brown stockings, boy's square-toed shoes, cotton gloves, and a big straw hat. We rode to and from the farm on the College truck. Our passing thru town never ceased to attract attention."

The Greensboro farmerettes also gained renown for their singing. "We often sang together as we worked," Craig explained, "all the popular war songs, and college songs, and for good measure we had the farmerettes' specialty—Negro spirituals." It must have been quite a sight and sound as a squad of white women, in their khaki uniforms, toiled in the fields of North Carolina and belted out their favorites—"Standin' in the Need of Prayer," "Little David, Play on Your Harp," and "I Got Shoes." The harmonizing farmerettes were even invited to a local home to sing their rendition of the spirituals. "We went late one evening and sang and sang," said Marjorie Craig.[16]

The Virginia division of the WLA had only twenty farmerettes in its jurisdiction in 1918, but their efforts "surprised and pleased" the local farmers.[17] "The work of these girls was altogether satisfactory; it was highly efficient and greatly appreciated," wrote one of those pleased farmers, G. C. Stone, of Pittsylvania County, in an appreciative letter to the WLA.

The girls came here "green and ignorant" knowing practically nothing of farm work, or even of farm life except in a vague sort of way. They came direct from College and were unaccustomed to exposure to heat of sun, or to any kind of long drawn out exertion, [but] while here they assisted in the handling of live stock, harnessed and cared for teams, hauled with wagons, shocked, stacked and threshed wheat, hoed tobacco and corn, built fences, and assisted in surveying.

While the work of these girls was to me a sort of experiment, I am glad to say that I consider the experiment entirely successful, nor should I hesitate to employ them again.[18]

But not many Virginia farmers followed his lead.

Given the southern states' social climate at the time, it is all the more remarkable that the city of Augusta took such unabashed pride in its Land Army and eagerly pointed to its spreading fame. The *Chronicle* boasted,

That the Woman's Land Army of Augusta and Richmond county is creating favorable comment, even in cities as far away as New York, is evident from the following paragraph which appeared recently in the *Textile World Journal*.

"Ten of Augusta's best known young society girls have been engaged during the last few days in cotton picking on the nearby farms. Twenty other like units are being organized, and the plan seems to be working to the benefit of the cotton industry and the enjoyment of the girls."[19]

Clara Mathewson playfully corrected the *Textile World Journal's* account. She told the hometown paper, "The paragraph referred to, is true, but limited in its scope. The ten young society girls picked cotton, but so did the older women."[20]

While the *Chronicle* lavished attention on the Woman's Land Army, the paper never printed a photograph of the farmerettes at work, of the white women picking cotton in the fields. One such photograph did appear, however, in the *Woman's Journal*, the national suffrage newspaper. It did not actually show the women stooping and picking; instead, the squad of twenty women—some wearing overalls, some long skirts, all with straw hats—simply posed and smiled for the camera. In their accompanying comments, the *Woman's Journal* editors, while admiring of the ability of the Woman's Land Army to breech southern racial and social barriers, also put in a sly dig:

"Win the war by picking cotton" is a new cry in Georgia, and of course the women are doing it. The world has never needed cotton more than now, and so it is again an unenfranchised class that is saving it for the sake of humanity, and it is the leaders of women's struggle for enfranchisement who are the leaders of the Woman's Land Army Corps to come to the rescue of the cotton.[21]

The *Chronicle* supplemented its coverage of its home WLA units with pictures of other farmerettes around the country and comic strips featuring farmerettes. It also included this little ditty:

> The "Man with the Hoe" must take a back seat;
> His ways are too slow for now!
> The "Land Army Girl" is out in this war,
> Armed with a tractor and plow.[22]

As the long harvest season extended into October, the Augusta WLA set new picking records. Like sports scores, they were reported in the newspaper. The unit at Hephzibah picked 13 bales (each bale weighing about 500 pounds), with Miss Rosa Reynolds packing in 175 pounds in one day; Miss Lottie Henderson tipped the scales with sacks weighing 170 pounds; and the Augusta Girl Scouts amassed a cumulative total of 4,000 pounds of cotton by early October.

"Whether or not the girls have derived much 'enjoyment' from the work," the *Chronicle* concluded, "could not be ascertained. But certainly they have been instrumental in serving their country, by going out into the fields and doing their 'bit' to save the cotton crop of Richmond county from ruining."[23]

When the war was over and the soldiers returned, Augusta held its big victory parade down the city's main street. "The car that won the prize for 'most unique' was the Farmerette Car," the *Chronicle* reported. "Even the running board of the car was made of vegetables, and the dainty little farmerettes on the car completed the charming effect."[24]

19

HARSH TERRAIN

In certain sections of the country the idea of tanned, muscled women wearing uniforms, riding tractors, and living communally was just too unseemly, too dangerous—too Amazonian—to be acceptable. Even in states where the Women's Committee was enthusiastic and the WLA was well organized, community opposition sometimes prevented any extensive use of women's farm labor. Yet the Land Army sometimes managed to take root in such harsh terrain.

Michigan should have been an easy place for the WLA to grow, but it wasn't, despite the best efforts of Caroline Bartlett Crane, who mobilized the woman power of her state so effectively. The farmers' blanket rejection of women workers was impenetrable in most areas of Michigan, she found, but not all them. So she encouraged her local leaders to move quickly and plant WLA seeds wherever the hard ground might yield.

One of Michigan's most important crops, cherries, provided a soft spot. It required many hands and quickly. Ann Arbor became the recruitment base, and the University of Michigan coeds became the standard-bearers for the state's Land Army effort. One university unit dispatched to pick cherries in the Traverse Bay region grew into a gigantic camp of eighty-five women, seven supervisors, a cook, and a nurse.[1]

Michigan could claim some small victories for the Land Army elsewhere in the state, The Woman's Committee of Midland County secured a unit of the WLA to gather cucumbers for pickles, and "this unit gave perfect satisfaction and received favorable press notices," reported the county chairwoman.[2] Where importing city or out-of-state women was frowned upon, the state's local Women's Committee appealed to neighborhood women to sign up for farm duty. "Kalamazoo County women were induced to help in harvesting grapes and potatoes," Caroline Crane reported. "St. Clair County women did much light harvesting work. Oceana County helped to harvest a heavy fruit crop."[3] In truth, though it had so much potential, Michigan was a disappointment to the WLA.

The Land Army did manage to blossom in the arid plains of New Mexico, thanks to the daredevil spirit of a woman with a fondness for Rough Riders. Isabella Selmes Ferguson was a friend of Theodore Roosevelt, and she married two of his Rough Rider veterans during her life. Like her friend TR, Ferguson was an advocate of preparedness before the war, and when America entered the fray, she joined the state Women's Committee and volunteered to lead the Woman's Land Army in New Mexico. The state's frontier spirit bode well for introducing women workers, but it wasn't easy.

Ferguson built a sturdy framework of county WLA committees and conducted a survey of each county's labor problems in the state. She pinpointed the orchard areas around Mountain Park, not far from the Texas border, as a most promising site to develop the Land Army. "After visiting Mountain Park at this time, I am quite convinced that there is no better opportunity in the State this year for effectively using the Woman's Land Army," a WLA field scout reported back to Ferguson, "and thus paving the way for probably much greater usefulness next year and possibly longer."[4]

For Mountain Park, Ferguson helped muster a WLA unit of about fifty women who hailed from ten counties within New Mexico. The unit "practically solved the problem of labor shortage and saved the fruit crop," according to a historian writing just a few years after the war.

> Most of the workers slept on the floor on alfalfa or pine boughs; the heat in
> the harvest fields where these women worked was often 100–116 degrees at
> noon, yet all not only survived the work but were physically benefited by it
> without exception. During the excessive heat the working hours for the
> 'harvest hands' were from 6:30 to 11:30 A.M., and 3 to 8 P.M., with a short
> interval at five o'clock for tea.[5]

How civilized.

Isabella Ferguson's own mother, whom she lassoed into service to the Land Army, had a distinctly less civilized experience when she agreed to escort a WLA unit through rugged terrain on an emergency crop rescue mission. Martha (Patty) Flandrau Selmes must have been quite a feisty lady to take on this assignment at a remote ranch. As she explained in a hastily written note carried back to Isabella:

> They seem to have made no preparation for us whatever. We have lost our
> bedding because the Mexicans weren't told where they were going and will
> probably keep on as long as the gasoline lasts. (They had gone forty miles in
> the wrong direction). If they turn up, I am sending this in by them. There
> are no cups here and about eight plates—there are twenty girls. No one was

told to bring table things, so bring cups and plates and some good coffee.
The prospect of food looks rather dubious . . .

Bring part of the sugar we had on the last trip, and some cold cream, two
big tubes. The corn is like the ocean and endless. For Heaven's sake be
careful on the road after you turn just before 'R. You have been over part of
it but not the worst. I never saw such roads and such cliffs. Please bring a
gallon of vinegar. We have no butter but we'll have to take things as they are.
We take in hay tomorrow, prepared for a tough job.[6]

Mrs. Selmes and her unit amply met the call for help in harvesting the ranch's
alfalfa and corn; they harvested thirty acres of alfalfa in four days. Another unit, in
Mimbres, Grant County, reported that eight women mowed, raked, and stacked sixteen tons of hay.[7]

Isabella was clearly a hands-on administrator who did not flinch when she—or her
mother—needed to accompany and supervise the farmerette units in the field. Whether
at the reins of her horse-drawn buggy, wielding a pitchfork on piles of hay beside her
workers, or laughing with them as they bathed themselves clean in a horse trough,
Isabella Selmes Ferguson stood with her troops, a farmerette's farmerette. Taking command of the Woman's Land Army in New Mexico was her own sort of Rough Rider
experience.[8]

In Colorado, the Land Army was nimble, alighting where and when most needed.
"A flying squad of girls to save the crops of Colorado has been organized," it was
reported in mid-summer. "In June women were working in twenty four counties. Their
picking average was 125 pounds a day of gooseberries, strawberries and cherries. In one
week the Denver squad had turned in $1,500."[9]

The orchards of Oregon were filled with farmerettes, who found a warm welcome in
certain sections of the state. At the University of Oregon, thirty members of the Tre Nu
sorority organized themselves into an agricultural unit, going from place to place during the summer to perform farmwork.[10] In Medford, a WLA camp was established on
the grounds of a large woman-owned orchard, and an announcement in the local newspaper reported on recruitment progress.

Enrollment for the Woman's Land Army will be received all day at County
Pathologist Cate's office and at the office of the Rogue River Fruit and
Produce Association on Main St. for residence or day work from WLA
Camp at Hollaway Orchard, to work in surrounding orchards. Articles

concerning the project have been reprinted in the Portland papers and applications are being received from out of town people who are anxious to enlist in the movement.[11]

Some prospective farmerettes took preliminary training at the Oregon Agricultural College in Corvallis before their deployment. Others wanted to enlist in the Land Army but worried about the physical toll the work might take on the bodies of those with sedentary habits. A schoolteacher in Portland, Oregon, wrote to the WLA recruitment office:

> Our association is enrolling teachers who for patriotic reasons are anxious to help this summer in the farm work. Many of them would be unable to put in 10 hours a day of hard manual labor but all are very anxious to do something in this great movement. Do you think that there would be any place in your contemplated campaign for earnest women who will attempt any kind of work which will not render them physically unfit for returning to the school room in September? We have over 100 enrolled and each has signified her aptitudes and preferences.[12]

Washington State fruits were also tended by farmerettes, with more than four hundred of them working in the orchards; however, they could work only in a handful of locations, where the community approved of women workers. Bedford Camp alumna Harriet Geithmann, a Washington native daughter, returned home and led a unit of orchard workers in Cashmere, Washington.

Ohio was home to 125 farmerettes in five units as well as a campus contingent at the College for Women of Western Reserve University in Cleveland and another at Oberlin College. In Ohio, as in other states, popular sentiment toward the farmerettes was initially cool, hindering expansion. Once a farmer consented to employ a few Land Army women, though, his neighbors usually followed.

"I employed eight girls from the Woman's Land Army and am well pleased with the results," said T. D. Morley, a farmer in Mentor, Ohio. "They worked with enthusiasm and determination. Each worker did her best and they added new energy to the other employees."[13]

Missouri had a promising start to the season when women were called for the early strawberry crop in April. "The University of Missouri girls came to the rescue," reported the chairwoman of the Missouri Women's Committee Food Production task force. "Twenty-seven went down to S.W. Missouri and spent the entire time." But "there were numerous obstacles and disappointments" in deploying women into the Missouri fields, and the best-laid logistical plans sometimes went awry, forcing some quick-witted improvisation. "The situation of the committee on the ground was very difficult," admitted the Missouri WLA leaders, but "some of the growers stated that the girls were the best pickers they ever had. It was necessary to prove this to the growers before we could secure from them the proper equipment for housing and caring for the girls."[14]

A total of 350 women in nineteen Land Army units worked in the Missouri strawberry fields in the spring of 1918. Three additional units of women were eager to join, but the committee was unable to place them, owing to an unusually short season and poor crop. While plans were in place for at least some of the units to stay in the field the entire summer, no further records of the Missouri WLA experience can be found. The state's efforts later in the season do not appear in the national organization's reports.

"From the standpoint of money made it was a failure," concluded the WLA chairwoman, but as an experiment in community service, the Land Army served a larger purpose. "We know that rural life in Missouri is somewhat behind that of many of our sister states," the WLA chairwoman explained. "The University girls are going back into cities and richer parts of the state, taking with them an interest in the laws regarding country schools, sanitation, etc. . . . and plans to lighten the burden and enlighten the mind of the farm woman, will command their attention and support."[15] This broadening of sympathy between city and rural women was certainly one of the Land Army's goals.

Even socially conservative Utah used some women farmworkers, referred to as "camp girls," to help gather fruit in the fall. The Utah Farm Bureau and the Women's Committee also organized automobile convoys to take those local women who had volunteered to help in the harvest crunch from their towns to the fields.[16]

Of all the tales of tribulation and triumph recorded in the WLA's scattered annals, the saga of the women of Kansas is the most dramatic. In January 1918, long before the Kansas spring wheat crop was planted, a group of patriotic Kansan women wrote to the Kansas War Council and volunteered to help harvest the state's essential wheat crop. If the farmers of Kansas could be assured that they would have adequate harvest labor, the women reasoned, they might be able to plant a larger crop of the all-important grain. The women received a curt "no thanks" from the War Council. By harvest time, however, the council was forced to change its tune.

One contemporary news account explained,

> When the matrons and the ladies and the "flappers" . . . offered last January
> to aid in the harvesting this summer, the Kansas War Council declined their
> proffered help. The thing seemed impossible. The offer had a far different
> aspect a few weeks ago, when the War Council faced the situation of a
> bumper wheat crop and manpower entirely inadequate to handle it. The fate

of the crop hung in the balance. Then thousands of women—the same
women whose January offer of aid had been scorned—sprang up from all
over the state, and the wheat crop was saved.

"If this volunteer army had not, unbidden, come to the rescue, a great part of this
tremendous crop would have been lost," the article concluded, calling the incident "one
of the most romantic battles of the Great War."[17]

At that same time in August, a Western Union telegram arrived at the White House.
Cabled from Salina, Kansas, it was addressed to President Wilson:

> Beg to inform you big organization perfected here which will have member-
> ship of several thousand, known as Kansas Tractor Girls, provide tractioneers
> for farmers of country in helping to increase production of nation's food
> supply. What brave women of France and England can do we can do.
> Training already begun. Arrangements being made for schools of instruction
> throughout State. We need your counsel. Please Answer.[18]

The president and secretary of the Tractor Girls signed the telegram. Within days, newspapers around the nation were running stories about how the "Jayhawker Tractorettes"
had pulled a prairie schooner to the Kansas State Fair and recruited women to join the
tractor service. As one Topeka newspaper explained, "It will be up to the girls to plow
the fields next spring."[19]

20

MISS DIEHL AND THE WELLESLEY
EXPERIMENT STATION

The great outdoor laboratory of the Woman's Land Army of America sprung up on the Wellesley College campus. Transformed into a quasi-military base, it had straight rows of white tent triangles flanked by square wooden structures, all set on a precise grid on the manicured college lawns. Trenches and water pipes zigzagged through the compound, tractors and tools ringed the perimeter, and the mess tent's cooking smoke wafted over the college buildings' Gothic Revival spires. A pig named Zelda waited patiently outside the kitchen for his garbage breakfast while women in green khaki uniforms practiced marching steps on the college playing fields, turning smartly to a U.S. Marine Corps drill sergeant's commands.

These tender ladies, who were learning both how to salute and how to plow, were the future officers of the Woman's Land Army of America, and this camp was their West Point. Chosen for their leadership potential, they'd signed up for this most innovative and audacious undertaking of the Land Army yet: the Wellesley College Training Camp and Experiment Station.

Before reporting for instruction in the ergonomically correct posture for hoeing, the cadets heard the bugle call summoning them to the raising of the colors. At the flagpole a petite woman in a pressed uniform stood at rigid attention, her hair pinned up under her hat and pince-nez glasses on her nose. Her eyes darted from one Land Army soldier to the next as they assembled around the pole and took mental note of their movements—how fast, how fluid, how deliberate they were. Those women who had the nerve to meet her gaze slightly bowed their heads in greeting; those who straggled in last, bumping shoulders to join the circle, avoided glancing her way. It was not wise to be tardy when Miss Edith Diehl, the director of the Wellesley Training and Experiment Camp, was watching. And she was always watching, taking notes in her red leather notebook.

The Wellesley Camp was set up to train a new cadre of unit leaders, the commissioned officers of the Land Army who would organize and run units of their own the next season. The movement had a scarcity of qualified unit leaders—it was the common complaint of all state and county organizers—and this shortage threatened the ambitious plans to expand the Land Army and perhaps keep it going in peacetime. While thousands of women nationwide were working under the banner of the Woman's Land Army, another of this training camp's functions was to work out kinks in the unit management system—for example, housing, rations, and governance questions—that would be "both uneconomical and inefficient" for each Land Army unit to work out for itself. This grassroots movement needed to be cultivated, pruned, and standardized.

These goals were certainly reasonable and laudable, for the Land Army prided itself on its brains as well as on its newly developed brawn. But WLA executives at the highest levels, women who were established in their own professions in academe, the sciences, philanthropy, and the arts and who took a distinctly cerebral approach to the cabbage patch, harbored loftier ambitions for the Wellesley Camp. They felt this camp could be a place where the newest ideas in science, technology, psychology, nutrition, and industrial management could be synthesized and applied. They wanted to see the theories of the women's land service movement grafted to the practical lessons already learned in the field and new concepts put to the test.

In Diehl's mind, the camp would be a great outdoor laboratory for testing, probing, and measuring the capacity of women to undertake strenuous labor, quickly master new skills, and assume leadership roles. Women would need these aptitudes to lead the Land Army and, as Diehl believed, to dispatch their duties in the greater war effort and ultimately to assume their proper place in the unfolding twentieth century.

The camp would take not an intuitive but a genuinely scientific approach to Land Army work. It would experiment, compare, measure, and carefully record results. It would combine military rigor with feminist ardor, practical mechanics with the scientific method. It would be a boot camp, officers' training school, ag school, home ec kitchen, and psych lab all rolled together. The experiments conducted in this Experiment Station would not be the traditional ones dealing with varieties of soils and plants; instead, they would involve the women themselves.

The idea for such a camp found a sympathetic friend in Ellen Fitz Pendleton, Wellesley College's president. Trained as a mathematician, she spent her entire professional life on the campus, taking her baccalaureate diploma, studying as a graduate student, rising to join the faculty, and then becoming the first alumna to lead the college. When Wellesley alums active in the Land Army approached her, she asked her Board of Trustees for permission to host a WLA training camp on the college grounds. After all, Wellesley's sister schools had already donated their campuses and faculty to the war work movement. Vassar was training farmerettes and nurses this summer, Barnard was staffing the WLA Bedford Camp and a serviceman's canteen, Smith was training psychiatric social workers, Mount Holyoke was holding classes for public health workers, and Bryn Mawr was conducting a summer institute for female industrial managers. Pendleton convinced the board easily, finding the members were intrigued by the idea. Even better, four of her trustees stepped forward, said they would personally subsidize the camp, and pledged $10,000 if their fellow board members would commit the college facilities to the endeavor.

This undertaking would require even broader support and deeper resources, so a well-connected Advisory Board was formed, heavy with such Boston Brahmin names as Adams, Endicott, Ware, Blodget, and Bowditch—names that could open doors and wallets. The Advisory Board also put out the call for a director of the camp,, someone practical, organized, and committed, a leader of women; also, ideally, a bean counter. The appeal hummed through the network of women devoted to the new profession of war work, and they found the perfect woman for the job in Miss Edith Diehl.

By the time Miss Diehl agreed to don the Woman's Land Army uniform at the age of forty-two, she was already famous as one of the foremost hand bookbinders in America. One of the few women in the world to own her own bindery, she'd earned a reputation as a master craftswoman, a savvy businesswoman, and successful entrepreneur. Earlier in the war, she'd single-handedly reorganized the Red Cross's medical supply efforts in New York City, where she served as director of workrooms, and had invented a new, highly efficient technique for cutting bandages with electric scissors, greatly improving production. She radiated confidence and competence. She was also a Wellesley alum. Truth be told, many found her somewhat intimidating, but she won their admiration.[1]

Miss Diehl, as she was always known, exhibited the enviable, easy poise of a woman who knew her own mind. Born into a well-off family in Brewster, New York, she was the strong-willed child of a self-made, immigrant father and a socially prominent mother. While still a teenager, Edith decided that her hometown needed a proper library, so she founded the Brewster Public Library. She solicited money, found donors to give hundreds of volumes from their private collections, incorporated a board, and served as its chair. She also served as volunteer librarian and, with two other young women, kept the library open for three hours every day. She loved handling the books.

Edith wanted to study philosophy; she was fascinated by its melding of logic and spirit. Her father gave his headstrong daughter permission to study in Germany, and in 1898 she became the first American woman to enroll at the University of Jena, studying with some of the era's great philosophy professors. She was also fascinated by the aesthetics of finely made books, and studied bookbinding with Evelyn Nordhoff, the most distinguished American woman bookbinder of the day. She continued her philosophy studies at Wellesley, but after two years, to her parents' consternation, Edith dropped out of college to study bookbinding with Europe's great masters. She sailed for England, and apprenticed at the workshop of Thomas James Cobden-Sanderson, a friend and collaborator of designer William Morris, who was creating artistic specimens of the book craft. She also studied with the expert book restorers at Westminster Abbey. Next she went to Paris, working ten-hour days at the benches of the best French craftsmen, and then to Brussels to study new techniques. Surrounded by men, she was known for asking incessant questions—sometimes annoyingly so—and staying after hours to learn more about leathers, papers, threads, and adhesives. She gained a reputation for "extreme thoroughness" and attention to detail. Details thrilled her, as did experimenting with new ways and improving techniques and materials.

After five years' apprenticeship in Europe, she finally opened her own two-room bindery in 1907 on Twenty-third Street in Manhattan. Orders came in so fast and her bookbinding classes filled so quickly that within a few months she had to move to larger quarters. Within a year she'd outgrown that space and purchased her own building, where she used two floors as a bindery and two floors for living quarters. When the war began in Europe in 1914 Diehl decided that binding books was not the way she should be spending her time. Perhaps it was her innate sense of duty, perhaps it was her father's German accent, but she heard the call to war work before most Americans were ready to listen. She closed her bindery, put her equipment in storage, and volunteered her full-time services to the Red Cross.

She went to work in a medical supply workroom, where volunteers cut, rolled, and prepared bandages for shipment to the front lines, but she found the operation of the workrooms inefficient. Cutting bandages by hand was woefully slow, so Edith devised a new way, using electric cutters, and increased production dramatically. She drew up a work flow and organization chart, carefully plotted on blueprint paper, to streamline workshop operations. Recognizing her extraordinary organizational abilities, the Red Cross soon made her the director of all its workrooms in the city. She supervised the work of nearly six hundred auxiliaries, where volunteers pledged their time and fingers to the cause of European relief.[2]

As America entered the war, Diehl left the New York supply workrooms to devote her energies to the Red Cross's rehabilitation work with soldiers. Believing that bookbinding could be a therapeutic outlet for wounded soldiers and perhaps a new vocation for those who'd lost legs, she organized bookbinding training classes at the Mansfield Rehabilitation School. She also trained the first group of women rehabilitation workers the Red Cross sent to France. Then the Woman's Land Army called her.

Edith Diehl was not someone who liked to fly by the seat of her skirt. Although confident in her organizational and administrative abilities, she was uneasy with her complete ignorance of agriculture. Her companion, Marie Miner, an expert botanist, had helped her draw elaborate plans for the house and gardens they shared in Brewster—the place they called "Our Acre"—but Edith didn't know the first thing about the mechanics of commercial farming. In everything she undertook, she wanted to have the best possible grounding, so she signed up for a crash course in scientific agriculture at Cornell and spent part of her spring in Ithaca, learning the lay of the farmer's land.

At the end of the course, Diehl moved to rooms at Wellesley and began assembling her staff and drawing up plans. She had to work fast, inventing this complex camp from scratch in just a few weeks. She drew inspiration from the National Service School, especially the original camp near Washington, D.C., and consulted closely with its commandant, Elizabeth Poe. Diehl liked the military orientation that Poe had taken for her camp and adopted it at Wellesley. She liked precision.

When it came to soliciting expert advice, Diehl went straight to the top. She insisted on the best minds and the most modern practices. While looking to build and equip the camp, she turned to the military and relied on the expertise of Col. N. H. Hall of the Charleston Naval Yard in Boston for help in "camp science and placement." When it came to agricultural training, she looked to Dr. Kenyon Butterfield, president of the Massachusetts Agricultural College at Amherst, to provide the camp's instructors. As for physical training, she called in the Marines. Three times a week two drill instructors came to camp and led the women in calisthenics, foot movements, and drills. They also conducted inspections, keeping the recruits up to military snuff.[3]

As a firm believer in the importance of efficiency and a devotee of the new concepts of "scientific management," Diehl also recruited Frank Bunker Gilbreth as the camp's "consulting efficiency specialist." The most famous practitioner of the day, Gilbreth's manic devotion to efficiency in both labor and life was later made famous by his children's memoir, *Cheaper by the Dozen*, and Edith Diehl made sure the Land Army trainees got a goodly dose of Gilbreth's contagious zealotry.

Diehl's choices for her resident staff made clear her intentions for the camp. She wanted only experts in their field and, where possible, expert women. She recruited a physician, Dr. Katherine Raymond to tend to the cadets' health, supervise the camp's sanitation and hygiene, and design and conduct the physiological experiments Diehl was so eager to pursue. A "psychological investigator," Dr. Hermione Dealey, conducted the psychological testing. Miss Stena Holdahl agreed to be the nutritional expert and "household economist" for the camp. Marion Nute, a woman physician from Boston who was also a crackerjack automobile driver as well as an "expert mechanician," was brought on as the camp's motor instructor.[4]

The ultimate micromanager, Diehl oversaw every detail of setting up the camp. In consultation with her military advisers, she decided on everything from the design of the latrine (opting for the Marine Corps model) to the type of tent (U.S. Army design) to the kind of tent fabric (as canvas was too scarce and expensive in wartime, she went with cotton duck). As to the kind of work shoe to be worn, she decided sturdy Boy Scout boots worked best, as they came closest to fitting a woman's foot.

Diehl also personally designed the Wellesley Camp uniform, a slightly snazzier version of the standard WLA attire. She threw out the overalls and bloomers favored by many units ("ugly and unserviceable," she called them) and went for riding breeches with ample room in the seat and knee. "There is no need of our being frumps just because we are in this work," she explained.[5] Diehl discussed uniform ideas and options with the cadets and asked for their input. "Hats were discussed. Leggings discussed. Gloves howled down," wrote Carol Maynard a recruit from Worcester, Massachusetts, in her camp notebook.[6]

The Diehl haute couture line combined the English Land Army style with "elements of the French army uniform adapted to a woman's figure and cut by the best tailor in New York," as one newspaper reporter described it. Matching leggings; a knee-length, belted coat for town wear; a man's tan cotton shirt, and black, knotted tie completed Diehl's costume. ("If the weather is warm, the tie can be hung on a fence while working.") A ten-cent straw hat for laboring in the field and a "sensible, but very becoming" green cloth hat for dress wear accessorized the outfit.[7]

"Two months intensive training is a very small price to pay for the privilege of wearing such a costume," announced one newspaper columnist who previewed the Diehl label. "If any recruits are needed for the Wellesley camp, I would suggest that the director exhibit that officers' uniform, and I will guarantee that there will be no dearth of volunteers."[8]

Fashion plates were not exactly the recruits Diehl had in mind. She and the camp adviser were looking for women who were older than the typical Land Army recruit, women "with collegiate, professional or executive experience" between the ages of twenty-one and forty-five. "Middle aged women are preferred," as one newspaper account put it.

The word went out. Notices in newspapers, college publications, suffrage magazines, gardening club bulletins, and YWCA war work circulars around the country stirred up interest, and WLA state organizers were urged to recommend worthy candidates. As in any military academy, the applicants' subsidized education was conditional on their promise to serve in the WLA corps in the 1919 season. Scores of women applied, but the camp was kept small. Initial plans called for sixty trainees, but for financial and logistical reasons, this target was pared down to fewer than three dozen. Poring over the applications, Diehl and her Executive Committee made an effort to enroll women of different ages, of different levels of education, of various occupations, and from all parts of the country.

Diehl's drive for diversity probably had less to do with progressive social thinking than with expedient scientific strategy. Diehl said in describing the selection criteria,

> Our object was to provide material for experimenting in regard to the
> desirable qualities of leaders, to investigate the capacity of women workers
> on the land, and to define the physical requirements for such work. We were
> both experimenting and training—and in fact it may be said that the
> training was the secondary object of the Camp, for the sake of developing
> some scientific results. [9]

Diehl selected thirty-two women hailing from fourteen states. They included eleven college graduates and one woman with a doctorate who was a faculty member at the University of California at Berkeley. Among the recruits were a neurologist, a chemist, an interior decorator, several teachers, and a suffrage organizer. Five of the women were married—a few were war brides who wanted to do their bit while their husbands were in the service—and several were mothers. The camp did not provide day care facilities. Lillian Hayes traveled to the camp from Salem, Ohio; Jessica Sherman from Sioux Falls, South Dakota; Leonore Callahan from Jersey City; Emerson Lamb from Baltimore; Caroline Bates Singleton from California; and Zelda Knowlton from Colorado—all arrived with confidence that Uncle Sam and Edith Diehl wanted them.[10]

They arrived at Wellesley in the last days of July and immediately lined up to undergo a battery of physical and psychological tests. Dr. Raymond conducted the medical exam on each woman, covering everything from her mucous membranes to heart rhythms, lung function to bowel workings, and muscle strength to menstrual cycles.

"It was most important that we should know thoroughly the physical condition of each woman in order to make the comparative tests of endurance and fitness that were part of our experiment," Diehl explained. They were rated from A for "unusually strong, absolutely sound," to C for organically sound but below the desired health standard. Diehl accepted these C-ranked women into camp, "as we wished to test their endurance in this work, in order to establish a line for rejection," as Diehl explained. They were all part of the experiment.

Next, the recruits were subjected to a set of "simple psychological tests" consisting of a battery of intelligence-measuring exams and ranked again. Tabulating their psychological test scores together with their physical exams, Dr. Dealey claimed to see a correlation between a woman's aptitude in certain complex psychological tasks and her muscular ability.

Before they could even begin training at the Wellesley Camp, the women had to build it. After all, if a Land Army unit was needed in an area where no existing housing was available, the workers would have to create a place to stay and organize themselves into a living community. They would have to build a base camp, a tiny, self-sufficient city plopped down in a field that would be capable of providing food, shelter, sanitation, transportation, and even governance to its inhabitants. The ability to build a camp would make the Land Army more flexible, portable, and self-reliant. So construction skills were part of the survival curriculum Diehl designed.

Diehl and her Marine advisers drew up the camp's site and plans. They placed it "in accordance with the scientific methods used by the Marines, with due consideration of the matter of drainage and prevailing winds, and with the tents lined up so that the breeze would blow through them from end to end," Diehl reported. The women became building apprentices under the tutelage of a master builder from Boston's Rindge Training School of Mechanic Arts and constructed the camp's four buildings, the wooden tent platforms, and the dining tables. They hammered down almost a hundred pounds of nails into nearly a thousand feet of two-by-four lumber, hundreds of feet of tongue-and-groove flooring, and an acre of tar paper roofing. They dug trenches for pipes and a pit for the cesspool. They also got a dose of plumbing, learning to cut, thread, and join the metal water pipes. Working in squads, they rotated to new construction chores each day to gain an appreciation of the labor involved, "to make them somewhat intelligent about building processes, and rid them of the awe connected with a job concerning which they were ignorant," as Diehl put it. While the camp was being constructed, the women lived in what they called the "barracks," one of the Wellesley dormitories. They pushed hard; the camp was up within two weeks.

For a woman who inhabited the rarefied world of fine books and moved in New York City art circles, Miss Diehl certainly had a keen taste for military order and discipline. From the first day, Diehl imposed a military-style chain-of-command structure in the camp. Acting as commandant, Diehl appointed a supervisor, and she gave orders to squad leaders, who were responsible for squads of eight women. Diehl wrote up the day's work plans and handed them to the supervisor, who posted them on a bulletin board and "translated" them to her squad leaders, who, in turn, assigned the tasks to their workers.

Diehl also instilled a distinctly egalitarian spirit into the camp. Every three days these leadership positions rotated to a new set of women. "The object of this rotation was to test each girl's ability to lead, and to develop her powers along the line of leadership by friendly criticism and by first-hand experience," said Diehl. "A nice spirit of unquestioning and ready response was developed towards those in authority, and the Camp became a cheerful cooperative society of working women." Diehl recognized that just as in the military, when running a Land Army unit, a clear authoritarian structure was simply more efficient, and efficiency was the goal. Any tendencies toward dictatorial powers were tempered by Diehl's boisterous weekly Camp Conferences, Sunday afternoon meetings where cadets and staff openly discussed policies and procedures and offered pointed criticism. "This interchange of viewpoints is most valuable and even essential for the promotion of happiness and contentment in the camp," Diehl explained.

Diehl even used the Camp Conference to put to a vote whether to introduce military drills into the curriculum. "I personally was not certain that it would be advisable or profitable," Diehl said, but the women voted for it. So Sergeant Young of the Charleston Navy Yard conducted maneuvers and drills three times a week, with practice in "simple foot movements and line formations," a genteel version of marching, turning, and parading. The drill sergeant also led the women in exercises "to limber and harden them" on the Wellesley lawns. "The drill was greatly enjoyed by the women," Diehl reported, "and they all said it sharpened and coordinated their powers of thought and action." Diehl took pride in the press descriptions of the Wellesley Camp as "The Land Army Plattsburgh." Further, she was delighted when a Boston newspaper ran the head-line "Wellesley College Adopts Military Life" with photos of a straight line of uni-formed WLA women saluting their Marine drill instructor, "who is instructing the girls in the Manual of Arms" and providing intensive drilling "almost as strenuous as that in train-ing camps of soldiers."[11]

Once the camp was built the Wellesley Camp farmerettes were plunged into a cur-riculum on the theory and practice of farming, and the foremost agricultural experts came to lecture. The women sprawled on the ground with notebooks in hand and received lessons on soil types and fertilizers, apple tree pruning, egg production, and swine management. They traipsed into the fields for hands-on demonstrations regard-ing the proper use of the six-tined manure fork and the spike-tooth harrow. Using the latest educational technology, they watched moving pictures that demonstrated the workings of farm machinery and then went outside to use those machines. They spent five days at the Massachusetts Agricultural College in Amherst as the guest of President Kenyon Butterfield, who was both an enthusiastic camp supporter and close adviser to Edith Diehl. The recruits were introduced to the latest advances in agricultural science and received an intensive course in tractor maneuvers. They took field trips to working farms in the area and then brought home their knowledge to try out on Wellesley's practice gardens and furrows. And they learned about the wonders of efficiency from the great evangelist himself.

Maj. Frank Bunker Gilbreth brought his magic lantern slides with him, projecting them on the wall of the mess hall as he spoke. He was a large, burly man and spoke in a booming, authoritative voice tinged by his native Maine accent. But he was jolly, too, and not at all boring. Gilbreth was not what the women had expected of an industrial engineer who specialized in "efficiency."

The push for efficiency was all the rage in America. It was what would win the war, and it was what would make America great, strong, and prosperous afterward. "Scien-tific Management," the amalgam of theories for analyzing and improving how work got done, was the vehicle that would carry the world toward efficiency. Gilbreth and his wife, Lillian, had been bringing the good news of scientific management—sometimes called "Taylorism" after its most celebrated proponent, Frederick Winslow Taylor—to factories, construction sites, and even kitchens around the globe. They were both in-dustrial engineers, specializing in time- and labor-saving processes, and they employed photography, moving pictures, and stopwatches to do their "motion studies" of people working.

The day America entered the War, Gilbreth sent a telegram to Secretary of War

Netwon Baker announcing, "I am on my way to Washington on 7:03 P.M. train to offer my services. If you do not know how you can use me, I can tell you."[12]

He was met at the train, whisked to the War Department, mustered into uniform, and assigned to put his motion studies to work, improving how soldiers could be trained to assemble and disassemble machine guns more efficiently and to perform other essential battle tasks. Major Gilbreth of the Army Engineering Corps was stationed at Fort Sill, Oklahoma, and set to work formulating "the One Best Way for the soldier," as his wife described it. Overwork and camp conditions quickly took a toll on Major Gilbreth, and by early 1918 he suffered from double pneumonia and uremic poisoning. Gilbreth was not expected to pull through. He did, but his recuperation was very slow. He was transferred to Walter Reed Army Hospital in Washington, D.C., where he helped with the occupational therapy classes for wounded soldiers while he regained his own strength. In July, he reluctantly accepted an honorable discharge and returned to his family's summer home on Nantucket Island, where he was welcomed by his wife and children. Although he was still weak, he was eager to rejoin the war effort.

Edith Diehl had read Gilbreth's books, kept copies on her shelf, and admired his approach. Her work in the Red Cross workrooms had taught her the value of efficient organization and practiced motion. Even in bookbinding, though the craft was slow and exacting, she'd found room for greater efficiency: she arranged her tools and supplies in her studio so they were more readily at hand and in the order she needed them. Diehl was a scientific management devotee, so she invited Major Gilbreth to bring his message to the Land Army women.

When he received Miss Diehl's invitation to lecture her Woman's Land Army cadets about efficiency, he accepted with glee. It wasn't such a long trip to Wellesley from Nantucket, though he still had to walk with a cane. Lillian came with him. Lillian had just designed for the War Department an efficient kitchen layout for wheelchair-bound soldiers returning home, and she gave her own lecture to the women on "the Science of Learning." In the camp's mess hall Frank set down his cane, took up his lantern slides, and brought the "One Best Way" to the farmerettes.

The lantern images were photographs of some of his famous "motion studies" featuring people at work. Each series of frames captured the complex bodily motions of a person performing a single task, such as tooth brushing or bricklaying. In the darkened hall, Gilbreth analyzed each of the motions involved, breaking down each movement into its parts and purpose. He gave them the pseudoscientific name for each of these constituent parts—a "hterblig," or Gilbreth spelled backwards—and made them giggle. Then he told them how wrong the conventional way of doing most things was—how wasteful in terms of time and effort—and how it could be trimmed down to a more compact essence, or rhythm. He told them that in each task on the farm, in the camp, and in life, they needed to search for that holy grail—that is, the one best way. That was his gospel message. His presentation was not unlike a revival meeting.

"All activity is in two parts," he told them. "Number one is decision. Number two is motion." Carol Maynard took careful notes and reproduced Gilbreth's chalkboard drawings in her notebook.[13] He listed the sixteen subdivisions of motion—search, find, select, grasp, transport, load, assemble, and so forth—and drew a graphic symbol for each on the board. He showed them the lantern slides of his motion study experiments and offered his interpretations of what they demonstrated. He talked about "necessary" and "unnecessary" fatigue and even brought out photos of his own desk, marked off with rubber bands into a series of grids, to analyze his own desk work motions. He gave them an exhibition of "faulty and perfect motions in working operations." The women asked a great many questions. Gilbreth's tawny mustache moved up and down as he gave them detailed, but sprightly, answers. His enthusiasm was contagious.

"Dr. Gilbreth interested the women to experiment independently along the line of efficiency methods in their work," reported Edith Diehl, "and as a result a number of women came to me with suggestions of improved methods in doing things. The theory of eliminating waste motion was put into practice at once in our household work."

Everything became a system at the camp, right down to the way meals were served in the mess hall. Stewards were appointed for each table, and they brought the food from the pantry to the table. Then the meat dish was passed from one end of the table and the vegetables from the other, with each hungry soldier helping herself as the bowls passed. "This method avoided waste, hastened service, and required less room," Diehl reported happily. Even drinks were poured at one end of the table and passed along. "This insured hot drinks for all, with fewer steps in the service."

This was scientific management. And if it was taken seriously in the camp, it was raised to nearly religious importance in the field. Great emphasis was placed on the ergonomics of farmwork, both for the sake of efficiency and to avoid straining the female body. Consider these lecture notes on the correct posture for spading:

> The right hand grasps the hand of the spade from beneath, the left foot is
> placed on the left side of the blade, the left hand grasps the shanks of the
> handlebar . . . as the body bends forward so as to fling a maximum pressure
> of weight upon the blade, the left hand slides upward towards the handle.

No doubt this description would have elicited a great belly laugh from the poor farmhand, now a soldier, whom the Land Army women were preparing to replace. This method was the right way, the One Best Way, to spade, and the Land Army recruits were to learn it and practice it. "The amount of work accomplished by the worker after being instructed in the scientific way of handling a tool, and in the scientific method of procedure, was appreciably greater than the output before instruction," Diehl wrote in her camp report. "And in a few cases nearly doubled."

This improvement in efficiency was not simply described it was measured with a stopwatch. Dr. Dealey, the camp's psychological investigator, often held the stopwatch. Not content simply to allow the Land Army trainees to take a coffee break or stretch every so often, she conducted extensive experiments to determine the spacing and duration of optimal rest periods for fighting fatigue and maximizing productivity. Her findings: ten minutes of "good, intensive relaxation" during each hour of work yields 33 percent more rows of peas hoed.

Another set of experiments explored whether women needed specially sized farm tools, ones better suited to the smaller female frame. After many hours of careful observation, the conclusion was that ordinary tools were not too large or heavy for women to use "when they learned the professional method" of handling them.

Driving tractors was a different story. While "each woman in camp served her apprenticeship in tractor driving," Diehl explained, and even gave public demonstrations of their tractor prowess at a Labor Day open house, "my opinion is that few women are physically fitted to drive tractors, though some of our workers believed themselves quite able. The strain on the muscular system is very great in handling certain types of tractor, and the frequent and intense joltings, I believe, might be injurious to women."

Diehl insisted, however, that the women learn to drive a motorcar. Hadn't Miss Diehl herself driven one of the first automobiles to appear on the roads of Brewster, her 1912 model, five-passenger Cadillac? Driving was an important skill for a woman to master, for it gave her mobility and independence. Knowing how to drive was essential in the Land Army, where the unit plan depended on transporting farmerettes from the unit's camp to various farmers' fields.

Diehl herself took the wheel of the camp's Ford one-ton truck to give a demonstration. Then she handed over the drivers' ed lessons to Dr. Marion Nute, the camp's resident auto expert, who gave each woman a half day of personal driving instruction.

"On highway go to right," Carol Maynard jotted down during her lesson. "Keep right wheels so they aren't in gutter. In passing vehicle go to left. On stopping—stop slowly—quick stop and start wears out tires. For stop or turn put out your arm. Honk at cross roads."[14]

In true Wellesley Camp fashion, the hands-on behind-the-wheel course was supplemented by lectures on the theory of the four-cylinder gasoline engine and the workings of gears in automobile transmissions. "Differential box has to have solid grease," Carol Maynard dutifully recorded. "Always have pliers with you. Pound with hammer to be sure that valve is not pinched."

The camp farmerettes experimented with everything from types of mosquito netting to nutritionally sound recipes, from bed types to barrel shower designs, and came up with a few technological breakthroughs in the outdoor kitchen appliance department. One was an improved version of the "fireless cooker," a type of slow-cooking crock that used hot soapstones, which saved on fuel and didn't require a live fire. They also perfected a design of the "iceless refrigerator," which utilized simple evaporation to keep food cool. Constructed of nothing more than a wooden box, screen mesh, a pan of water, and strips of flannel wicking moisture into the sealed box, the design was so elegant that the YWCA asked permission to use it at its summer camps. The Boston Health Department placed a model of the refrigerator in the Boston Common and had a demonstrator on hand to extol its economical virtue.

The Wellesley officers in training also received instruction in camp management skills. They covered negotiating credit with the local grocery store, keeping card file records on each worker and each farmer, basic financial bookkeeping, camp sanitation and hygiene, dietetics, and nutrition. Even the camp's recipes were compiled into a cookbook supplement to Diehl's official camp report.

While Edith Diehl reveled in refining the nuts and bolts of Land Army life and work, she did not neglect the broader, more philosophical aspects of a Land Army liberal education. Leaders needed to understand "Land Army principles and standards" and what the Land Army stood for and its ideals. Director Diehl invited Professor Ogilvie to speak about the lessons of her Bedford Camp and the Land Army movement.

"This is the first time women have had the opportunity to work hard with their muscles," Ogilvie told them in an inspiring pep talk. "We must not let the world go hungry. No task could be more important to set yourself to."[15]

Diehl also invited Professor Ethel Puffer Howes to deliver a series of lectures. In a somewhat strange combination, Howes brought together both her deep knowledge of the WLA organization and her academic specialty, the philosophy of aesthetics. In one memorable afternoon talk, she offered a disquisition on the aesthetics of the Woman's Land Army.

"Aesthetics is the study of the science of beauty," Carol Maynard copied earnestly into her notebook as Howes spoke. "I want to express to you some of the elements of beauty in the idea of the Land Army and the Wellesley Training Camp." Professor Howes spoke of "the romantic idea of women dealing with crops" and the "element of the picturesque as expressed in Land Army posters." She spoke of freedom of will and moral law in the WLA's development; its Platonic ideal; the beauty of the uniform, which offered freedom from personalities; and the beauty of the work shoe, so perfectly functional.

How the farmerettes, who'd risen before dawn and spent the day with their backs bent perfecting their hoeing technique with a stopwatch, took to Dr. Howe's rather esoteric approach isn't really known. One Wellesley Camp recruit from Connecticut wrote home to her family, however, complaining that the training was "a bit too scholastic."[16]

"The idea of the Wellesley Camp is to make incarnate the elements that are going to make the Woman's Land Army," Professor Howes said in conclusion. "I have faith that we can do something to change the whole status of the working woman."

From Platonic ideals to latrine disinfection, the Wellesley Camp cadets received a broad education. And Edith Diehl, in her Land Army uniform, took on the scientist's role, simultaneously testing theories, making postulates, and assembling data to support or refute them. She took the experimental process seriously. Diehl's meticulously detailed report on the camp—every nail, every ounce of food, every penny accounted for—resembles a laboratory notebook. It is precise, but also broad and thoughtful, almost philosophical. From her findings and the trial-and-error process of her grand experiment, Edith Diehl drew a blueprint for a permanent land army of women.

21

Tiller, Planter, Gleaner:
New York

In a delicious reversal of roles, American soldiers and sailors eagerly signed up as contributing members of the Woman's Land Army. They took dollar bills out of their own uniform pockets, signed membership forms, and offered their moral support to the cause. American fighting men rallying to the aid of farmerettes was one of the more remarkable scenes in a ten-day recruitment and fund-raising drive that the New York State WLA mounted in mid-September. It was an especially touching and useful gesture during the New York WLA's wildly ambitious effort to enroll a million contributing members and raise more than half a million dollars to further the movement's work.[1]

Farmerettes fresh from the fields and decked out in their uniforms of blue denim smocks and bloomers were everywhere. They appeared in all the big cities and small towns of the state, making speeches, handing out WLA literature, collecting donations in buckets, and parading in horse-drawn hay wagons down city streets. New York City was teeming with farmerettes and WLA volunteers—men, women, and Girl Scouts—who marched into hotel lobbies, office buildings, department stores, and movie palaces to find sympathetic citizens willing to plunk down a dollar donation or sign up for late-harvest farmerette duty.[2]

The exquisitely tuned donation machinery of the Liberty Loan and War Savings committees of New York was turned over to the WLA for the campaign. All the War Savings Stamps bureaus and booths in Manhattan were put at the Land Army's disposal, and forty-five experienced War Savings solicitors were assigned to make the pitch for WLA donations. A thatched hut set up on a corner of Broadway and decorated with vegetables did a brisk registration business.[3]

The power of the Four-Minute Men was also thrown behind the Land Army. For a week, all the state's Four-Minute Men—and New York City alone had fourteen hundred of the volunteer speakers—devoted their presentations to the Woman's Land Army and exhorted their audiences to support the organization. WLA representatives accompanied

213

every Four-Minute Man (and several Four-Minute Women) into the cinemas and vaudeville houses, enrolling new contributing members and farmerette recruits on the spot.[4]

The governor's wife, Olive Hitchcock Whitman, agreed to become the campaign's
honorary chairman and went on the stump for the WLA. A vice president of the New
York Telephone Company, Mr. Frank H. Bethell, took charge of the actual workings of
the campaign and brought corporate clout to the effort.[5] Even the U.S. senator from
New York, James W. Wadsworth, a vociferous opponent of woman's suffrage (his wife
was president of the National Association Opposed to Woman Suffrage), fully approved
of the Woman's Land Army's work. A gentleman farmer himself, Wadsworth consented
to join the campaign committee. From the campaign headquarters office in the Biltmore
Hotel, the WLA mailed literature to clergymen, farmers, bankers, merchants, produce
dealers, and farm implement sellers throughout the state, urging them to lend their
financial and moral backing to the Land Army. A public plea was issued for trained
clerical workers "who are patriotically interested in helping to increase food production" to help type and mail the WLA campaign materials.[6] Even the *New York Times*
discussed the campaign in an editorial:

> No movement is more worthy of support than the "drive" of the New York
> State Woman's Land Army for new members. It wants a million more, and
> should get them .
>
> The "farmerette" is not a joke; she is a factor in the fight. The
> Woman's Land Army copes with the problem of raising food . . . and
> with a need of 50,000 laborers on the farms of New York and no other
> way in sight to get them, the Army should have every assistance the
> public can give.[7]

Such public enthusiasm was the sweet fruit of an ample harvest in New York, which
was achieved, in no small part, by the work of the Woman's Land Army.[8] From the
Niagara fruit belt and the Finger Lake orchards to the truck farms of Long Island,
farmerettes had brought in a record harvest. The apple crop was nearly five times the
size of the state's 1917 harvest, and only the blight-stricken potatoes proved disappointing.

Forty-four official WLA units were active in the state's fields during the 1918 season, employing well over a thousand women. Several thousand more women worked in
emergency squads or units not under direct WLA auspices. Even with the last fruits of
the season still on the trees and vines, satisfied farmers were already requesting WLA
units to return to their fields and orchards the next year.

While the New York WLA tasted success in the fall, it had experienced a sour start
back in the spring, when it grappled with a fundamental structural question of its
relation, as an emergency labor initiative, to the existing state labor employment
system. This relationship took a different shape and tone in each of the states depending

on the degree of cooperation and enthusiasm state leaders offered. The New York WLA had an easier time than many of its sister organizations, as Governor Whitman was receptive toward women taking men's places in the workforce and didn't doubt women could work productively in the fields. He welcomed the WLA and, more important, instructed his state's Employment Bureau to work with the Land Army.

With good intentions and even a budget allotment, the Employment Bureau collaborated with the New York State Food Commission to introduce women into the farming workforce. The state was divided into six districts, and six women "farm-labor specialists" were appointed to investigate where women's labor was needed and wanted in their districts. The labor specialists were then expected to find proper accommodations for a unit of women, engage a suitable supervisor for them, outfit a camp, and then turn over the recruitment and selection of women farmworkers to the district employment office.

In this scheme, New York State was, in essence, embracing the Land Army concept, assuming its field functions, and making women's land service a government enterprise, just as it was England. But this arrangement did not sit well with the New York State and county divisions of the Woman's Land Army. It tangled the lines of authority and responsibility and left room for wasteful duplication of effort. The New York WLA called on Virginia Gildersleeve to come to the rescue, to negotiate a compromise and soothe bruised toes.

But by spring of 1918 Virginia Gildersleeve wanted out of agriculture. She felt she'd done all she could to establish the WLA and was proud of the organization, but her attention had turned to other war work endeavors. As a leader in women's education, she wanted to help prepare America's college women for tasks that required trained brains—especially in the sciences, medicine, law, and management—and would open up careers for them after the war. Though she was intent on resigning gracefully from her Woman's Land Army post, she realized that cooperation between the WLA and various government agencies was essential for the Land Army's future. When the New York chapter asked her to use her diplomatic skills to forge an agreement, Citizen Gildersleeve couldn't bring herself to say no. Whatever settlement she might be able to draw could serve as a template for relations between the WLA and public employment bureaus at the state and national level. Establishing good working terms with the government was imperative "so that permanent machinery may be developed to carry on this important work in years to come," Gildersleeve concluded.[9] (Years later, Gildersleeve displayed her diplomatic talents as a member of the U.S. delegation to the United Nations Charter Committee, where she helped frame the new institution and served as an alternate delegate in the first UN General Assembly.)

Gildersleeve mediated between Ida Ogilvie, representing the WLA, and Louise Odencrantz, chief of the Women in Industry office of the New York State Employment Bureau, to "adjust relations" and coordinate the two bodies' work. They managed to set out some basic ground rules, but the most contentious issue of figuring out which organization was in charge of establishing and running the units, was left vague and unsettled. Even the definition of an "official" WLA unit was left in limbo.

Both sides agreed to run their emergency farm labor efforts on separate, parallel tracks and try to avoid dangerous intersections and crashes. In the end, it was not diplomacy but exigency that solved the impasse. The Employment Bureau's six farm labor specialists were so quickly swamped with farmers' requests for women workers and so overwhelmed by logistics that they welcomed the county WLA committees's help in their territories. The agents were especially eager to hand off all funding and operational responsibilities and simply act as recruiters.

Still, the WLA fretted that the same high-caliber farmerette recruit who exemplified the movement—that plucky patriotic woman—might not be attracted to land service if ushered through the door of the Employment Service. The WLA felt that was not how refined women found their war work. Even Helen Kennedy Stevens, on her early recruitment tour through the state in the spring, reported that "in Albany, no respectable girl would register at the State Employment Bureau," according to Virginia Gildersleeve's handwritten notes.[10]

But the Employment Bureau was able to reach into different pools of prospective recruits, beyond the grasp of the typical club and college networks, and bring the city working girl's vigor into the farmerette camp. During the spring and early summer of 1918, the bureau signed up more than a thousand women from the rolls of Manhattan's Working Women's Protective Union and sent them to work on downstate farms.[11] In addition, the New York League of Women Workers donated the use of two of their vacation houses for farmerette training farms, and Manhattan Trade School students practiced the agricultural arts there.[12]

The Employment Bureau reported that between May and October 1918, New York farmers filed requests for 7,738 women workers. While it managed to place more than 3,000 women into agricultural jobs, it clearly could not meet the farmers' surging demand. As happened in other states, as the season wore on and the farmers' distrust of farmerettes metamorphosed into enthusiasm for them, farmers clamored for more women workers, outstripping the WLA's ability to quickly form and staff new units. The demand lag, which the WLA had tried so hard to avoid in this second season, again hindered progress. Some New York farmers even expressed anger about the WLA's "failure" to meet their post-conversion farmerette needs.[13]

Not all of these farmerettes worked under the WLA's banner, however. The Employment Bureau reported about eighty units in New York fields, but the WLA claimed only forty-four of these. The WLA had refused to certify the other units, because it could not adequately supervise them. Nor did the Employment Bureau's recruits necessarily meet the stringent physical and character requirements the WLA imposed. Further, the WLA openly voiced these concerns: were the farmerettes enrolled by the Employment Bureau motivated more by a paycheck than by patriotism? Did they undertake land service as a duty or just another job? Did they bring the same enthusiasm for the work and spirit to the camp? While eager to get more women in the fields, it was a matter of quality control. The movement's reputation depended on it. These "unofficial" Land Girls didn't wear official WLA uniforms—they usually worked in overalls—and they didn't wear the brassard of a WLA veteran, though they were eventually afforded this honor.

With state employment bureaus trying desperately to fill farm labor requests—and perhaps lowering recruitment and supervision standards in the process—and as state WLA divisions worked frantically to set units in place while maintaining the movement's character, friction between the two groups occurred in several states, but it was most pronounced in New York. Nevertheless, the work of the state's farmerettes, official or not, won applause.

Ida Ogilvie and Delia West Marble together ran the Bedford Camp again, a greatly expanded enterprise of 160 farmerettes in a main camp in addition to five satellite units placed strategically in the vicinity. Farmers' demands for workers had doubled since the previous year. In the six months the Bedford Camp operated in 1918, spanning planting time to the last fall harvest, more than 434 women labored there, representing an increase of 400 percent over the 1917 season.[14] The Bedford Camp alumnae of the 1917 inaugural season were deployed to lead WLA units around the country, from Mount Berry, Georgia, to Newport, Rhode Island, to Painesville, Ohio.

About sixty miles away, in Poughkeepsie, the Vassar College Farm effort was also expanded. Nearly 200 "Romperettes" shared the Vassar campus with 430 Red Cross nurses in training, and college women from forty-six states took part in President MacCracken's two-track war-training initiative. Sharing dormitories and attending evening entertainments together, both sets of women also joined to publish *The Thermometer*, their own weekly newspaper. (They cheekily rejected other journal titles reflecting their wartime bond, such as "The Bed Tenders," "Homestead and Bedstead," or the "The Grave Diggers.") In a spirit of sublime cooperation, the farmerettes provided the nurses with frogs and mice they had bravely caught in the field for medical dissection labs. Two six-week shifts of Vassar farmerettes worked on the college farm and for surrounding Dutchess County farms. On their days off, the Vassar farmerettes and the nurses enjoyed such wholesome diversions as organ recitals in the college chapel and Virginia Reel dances in the gymnasium. While listening to Bach or resting between dance sets, they also knitted mufflers to send overseas.

Alice Campbell, that colorful chronicler of farmerette life, contributed sassy dispatches to *The Thermometer* from her new WLA assignment as a unit captain on a Connecticut dairy farm. "We are profiting by last summer's training on the Vassar farm and . . . working ten hours daily, helping Uncle Sam 'win the war' and 'doing our bit' by ruining our lily white hands," she reported. "As one farmer to another we wish your crops and cows success."[15]

By almost any measure, the New York Woman's Land Army enjoyed enormous success in the 1918 season. "Farmerettes, Tractors, and Volunteer Workers Make Up Man-Power Shortage," announced the *New York Times*.[16] "Farmerettes Declared to Excel Men under Agricultural Labor Conditions," trumpeted the *New York Tribune*.[17] And two weeks later, the *New York Times* reported, "Women on Farms Prove a Success."[18]

"The farmerette is the only solution of the food crisis," was the testimony of John C. Curtis, the Farm Bureau manager of Westchester County and member of the New York State WLA's Board of Directors. He was hardly an impartial observer, but he was an influential voice, and the WLA handed him a megaphone at every opportunity.[19]

By late summer the farmers were calling for more women workers, and more women were eager to serve. The limiting factor was money for establishing more unit camps. State farmers requested at least thirty more camps than the WLA could finance and support. For the next season, a confident WLA wanted to set up at least two hundred camps around the state, or one in every farming community. This expansion would require broad public support, political will, and cash. That reality was the rationale behind the WLA's bold fall membership campaign.

"With the farmers wanting the work done and the girls longing to do it, it seems unpatriotic that we cannot raise enough money to start the camps," WLA campaign chairman Frank Bethell lamented during one of his many stump speeches. "It takes $2,000 to start a camp and keep it going."[20]

The governor's wife enjoyed her role as the campaign's drum majorette. As Mrs. Whitman explained,

> We do not need merely an army of devoted young women such as those who
> have done the actual farmwork this season. What we wish to obtain in this
> drive is an army of supporting members back of the line, members who will
> contribute a little of their money and a great deal of their moral support
> toward expanding the movement. City dwellers and country dwellers alike . . .
> will be asked to become supporting members of the Land Army.[21]

Supporters could sign onto one of four "membership classes" and become a "Tiller" for a token dollar donation a year, a "Planter" for $5, a "Gleaner" for $25, and a "Harvester" for $100. "Obey your impulse," the membership flier urged. "Get behind the girl he left behind him."[22]

Each district in the state was issued a membership goal, the quota of members, money, and farmerette registrations the local campaign committee was expected to meet. On the campaign's first day Ulster County reported "going over the top" and obtaining its quota of six thousand new members by four o'clock in the afternoon. Albany County was well on its way to meeting its goal of seventeen thousand supporters early in the campaign.[23] Though the million-member goal was unrealistic, the campaign itself effectively stimulated broad-based "moral" support.

Still touring the States as a representative of the National Land Council of Great Britain and still barnstorming for the Land Army's cause, Sophia Carey was dispatched by the New York WLA's Campaign Committee to speak around the state. Carey went to a wide variety of locales. She traveled from the marble steps of the Sub-Treasury Building in Manhattan to the canvas tents of late-summer county agricultural fairs. Often accompanied by uniformed farmerettes from the vicinity, she brought the Land Army's glory to both bankers and the blue-ribbon pickle set.[24] While attending one county fair in Hornell, in the southwestern section of the state, Carey learned that more workers were desperately needed in the local potato fields. A beguiling pied piper, Carey marched through the town's streets and coaxed a large crew of neighborhood women to untie their aprons, to take up their hoes, and to bring in the vital spuds.[25]

The climax of the New York WLA season, and the springboard for the fall membership campaign, was an "upstate" conference that was held in Albany during the third week of August. Though it was a state affair, it took on larger significance as one of the only official Woman's Land Army conferences since its founding eight months before. (California had also held such a meeting.) It gave WLA leaders a rare opportunity to reflect, report, and strategize. They could take the time to take a deep breath and look ahead.

Hundreds of printed invitations were sent to those involved in food production in the state, from farmers and Grange leaders to "potato club" members and representatives of war emergency food committees. "It is expected that every man and woman in the city of Albany and vicinity that can possibly arrange to be present will do so," reported the *Albany Argus* on the day before the conference opened.[26]

The future of the WLA in New York shimmered with promise. Governor and Mrs. Whitman personally welcomed the delegates as they entered Chancellor's Hall. They gave them warm praise. "In the land army movement that has swept the State during the past few months, the women of this State have been given an opportunity to make themselves felt and to show that they are able to do a work worth while," said the governor, who was locked in a tight reelection campaign and was eager to win the votes of New York women, who could cast their ballots in state elections for the first time. "The organizing of the Woman's Land Army is in itself significant of the fineness of the womanhood."[27]

Ida Ogilvie spoke to the attendees about the Bedford Camp's accomplishments. Edith Diehl, taking a brief leave from her duties at the Wellesley Camp to speak to the conference, outlined her vision of the WLA future: she saw one that would bring a "scientific basis," "efficiency," "standardization," and "military lines" to woman's farm labor. "Skill in women can be made to take the place of strength in men," Diehl told the conference.[28]

Diehl also promised a new kind of Land Army unit for the next season, a "movable unit." Under development at Wellesley, it would be a self-contained camp packed onto a truck and be as useful in peacetime as in wartime. Diehl announced,

> The methods we are working out at Wellesley, will enable the farmer to pick
> up his telephone, send out an S.O.S. call for farmerettes . . . and have the
> call answered at once by an efficient army of trained and able bodied women
> workers, who will bring their own portable houses and mess tent with them,
> set up the same with military precision, provide their chef and manage their
> household while doing the work he wants done on his farm.

The movable unit would even contain sanitary accommodations and an incinerating plant for camp waste.[29]

Arthur Lawrence, the Food Administrator for Westchester County, offered his own testimonial to the Land Army. "The farmerette movement has swiftly passed from theory to fact," Lawrence told the conference. "It is not a picturesque form of patriotism of a few women faddists. It is a necessary effort on the part of the only people in the country who can relieve the food shortage."[30]

In a pragmatic but poignant testimony of just how far the WLA had passed beyond "picturesque patriotism," scores of farmers and farmers' wives attending the conference took part in a discussion forum, conducted by the Westchester Farm Bureau manager, on the logistics of using farmerette labor. The farm families eagerly raised their hands to ask nuts-and-bolts questions about adapting farming methods to women workers and about establishing farmerette camps in different localities.

On behalf of the Champlain Valley district farmers, one woman in the audience stood up and requested that a farmerette camp be established there immediately. The Land Army was, indeed, no longer a theory.

Capping the first day of the Albany conference, a fleet of borrowed cars and trucks constituting the "Woman's Land Army Motor Corps" transported two hundred delegates from the meeting hall to the WLA camp at Colonie in a near suburb of the city. The delegates took a guided tour of the camp, and the uniformed farmerettes stationed there served them a picnic supper on its grounds. After dinner, all joined in a "community sing" of patriotic songs led by the Land Army girls and grateful local farmers.[31]

Former U.S. representative Peter Ten Eyck, who employed farmerettes on his own Indian Ladder Farms near Albany, delivered the conference's closing speech. "This meeting is historic in that it serves as an opener to the door of opportunity to women," he declared. "The Land Army movement should prove an answer to the critics of Equal Suffrage. The Land Army is one of the most important movements ever started in this country."[32]

22

MARRIAGE OF CONVENIENCE

Theodore Roosevelt was supposed to be the keynote speaker at that New York State Woman's Land Army conference in Albany. He had been invited, and he accepted with pleasure. U.S. Secretary of Labor William B. Wilson also received an invitation to speak, but he refused. U.S. Secretary of Agriculture David Houston, invited to say a few words or at least to send a letter of greetings, also declined.

As an advocate of women's war work, as a friend of suffrage, and as a former governor of New York, TR was the natural choice to headline the Albany conference. His name on the tentative program made a loud, profound statement about the stature the Woman's Land Army had achieved. The cabinet members' refusal to attend the conference made its own statement.

During the late summer and early fall of 1918, it suddenly became politically advantageous to support the Land Army, to extol the movement with a rip-roaring speech, to pledge the power of government agencies, and to promise to help the beleaguered farmer by embracing (figuratively) the curvaceous farmerettes. Enough newspaper editorials singing the Land Army's praises had already appeared to give governors, mayors, and other politicians a certain comfort level in becoming outspoken supporters. New York governor Whitman, along with the governors of Illinois, California, Connecticut, and Pennsylvania, appreciated the farmerettes' new political cachet.

TR never gave that keynote address in Albany, however; by August he was in mourning. Just a few weeks before the conference, in mid-July, he lost his youngest and favorite son, Quentin, an American Expeditionary Force pilot, in a dogfight over France. The former president withdrew from all public appearances for the rest of the summer, and some say the old Rough Rider was never the same. He died barely six months later.

The organizers of the Albany WLA conference sent their condolences to Roosevelt and hoped that their invitation to Secretary Wilson or Houston might pan out. They had even placed Wilson's name on the tentative program. That was a mistake. While the nation was happily whistling the farmerette's tune, the federal government was still biting its tongue.

Through the summer, while thousands of farmerettes proved themselves in the field and tackled tons of crops, the administration averted its eyes. In the July 23 issue of the Department of Labor's Employment Service Bulletin, in an analysis of emergency labor sources, the agency said dismissively, "While the 'Land Army' (of native-born women working for patriotic motives) has been incorporated in the Eastern States, it cannot this year be described as a fully organized and mobilized force. There is no great need for women yet."[1]

The Department of Labor may have felt some chagrin just a few weeks later when Great Britain's Women's Land Army, a force of seventeen thousand women in official uniform and another quarter million women working part-time, sent a salute to their American cousins. The British Land Lassies wrote in an official communiqué,

> Your vigorous young organization has created a new source of inspiration in us, who have labored since the beginning of the war. The American Land Army is facing its responsibilities in a manner worthy of the strength of a great democratic country . . . and we in Britain are proud to have been the means of inspiring action so far-reaching.
>
> In the land trenches, behind your armies and our own, a fight is being bravely waged, fraught with issues no less grave than on the seas and battle fields of Europe.[2]

This tribute brought a lump to the throat, and the WLA immediately distributed it to the press. It ran in newspapers large and small across the country, even as federal labor and agriculture administrators continued to deny the Land Army had any role to play.

Likewise, Clarence Ousley could not have been pleased when a motion picture script arrived on his desk that summer, circulated by an editor at the Committee on Public Information's Division of Films. "We're putting together a scenario about new lines of industry in which the war has carried women," wrote Rufus Steele, the Scenario Editor for the CPI , and he had included a list of "picturesque ideas" for the film. Taken from existing film footage, many of the film's proposed scenes featured that most picturesque working woman, the farmerette. From women in Missouri saving the strawberry crop to Land Army women on a Connecticut estate and the WLA Libertyville Training Farm in Illinois, Land Girls figured prominently in this women-at-war documentary.

The film's spectacular finale called for "a triumphant procession of women with victorious trumpets and banners, led by one representing Democracy. The women in the costumes of farmers, policewomen, etc. The women marching joyously, with their faces upturned to the light."[3] This finale obviously would not be taken from existing newsreel footage.

This cinematic tribute to women's war work glossed over some troubling realities, at least from the perspective of the chairwoman of the Women's Committee of the Council of National Defense, Dr. Anna Howard Shaw. By summer of 1918 Shaw was suffering from physical exhaustion—she was under doctor's orders to cut down on her punishing travel and speaking schedule—but she was also feeling the strain of political frustration. She was no longer able to conceal her disillusionment and anger about the impossible and powerless position of the Women's Committee.

Not only did the committee still lack executive powers and spending authority, but it also found itself superseded and circumvented by the "women's committees" various federal departments had established. The Treasury Department had its own Women's Liberty Loan Committee at the national and state levels, and the Food Administration appointed its own women's section to handle conservation work. These bodies were accorded such instruments of governmental authority as an ample budget line and the postal franking privilege. This duplication of effort eroded the mandate and the authority of the Women's Committee. Even some of the large women's organizations, such as the National League for Women's Service, the Red Cross, and the General Federation of Women's Clubs, commanded their own members and conducted their own projects with little deference to Shaw's committee or even coordination with it.[4]

Matters became so untenable that the Women's Committee members seriously considered a "mass resignation" to protest their organizational impotence, but they decided such a gesture would endanger American women's unity behind the war. Instead, they voiced their frustration directly to the administration. Shaw wrote to Secretary of War Newton D. Baker, who also held the chairmanship of the Council of National Defense, and questioned whether the Women's Committee was still a useful and viable body, or just an empty shell. Should its functions be redefined and strengthened, she wondered, or should it just disband?[5]

Secretary Baker forwarded the memorandum to President Wilson, who replied, "I agree that the Women's Committee is still very useful, but it is indispensable that the Women's Committee continue to exercise the functions originally assigned to it."[6] In other words, while the committee was still politically useful, it was never intended to wield any power.

Shaw wrote a scathing reply to Secretary Baker. "The Committee began its work of organizing the women of the nation for war work under a misapprehension of its status and functions," Shaw fumed. She proposed a total restructuring of the Women's Committee. She felt the committee should have more authority and its own funds, be allowed to coordinate the work of the various federal agency programs aimed at women, and be accountable only to the president, not to the Council of National Defense. Shaw's demands were ignored.[7]

All the more galling to Anna Shaw was that she had to admit that Harriot Stanton Blatch's critique of the subservient role given the Women's Committee had been correct. Now, at the end of the summer of 1918, she was finally willing to say so herself, and a bitter tone crept into her discussions about women's role in the war. When journalist Mabel Potter Daggett sent Dr. Shaw a copy of her new book with the bombastic title *Women Wanted: The Story Written in Blood Red Letters on the Horizon of the Great World War* and said it was a celebration of the wonderful opportunities the war opened for women, Anna Shaw wrote her a note of thanks. With an unusual dose of vitriol, Shaw let her frustration pour out:

> I hope that you have stated in this book that while women are wanted, they
> are wanted for work and for nothing else. I earnestly trust that you brought
> out the facts of an enormous demand for woman's work without a corre-
> sponding appreciation of the value of that work, or recognition of its
> relative worth to the Government. The farther I get into this experience
> of war and government, the more I realize that unless we women stand
> together and stand up for a principle of justice and fair play, the more we
> are going to be swamped instead of released from dictation and subordi-
> nation.[8]

By the end of September, Shaw would see her Women's Committee dissolved and its functions folded into a new body called the "Field Division of the Council of National Defense."[9]

Perhaps the women planning the New York Woman's Land Army Conference in Albany should not have expected any kind of enthusiastic response from Secretaries Houston and Wilson to their invitations, nor should they have been shocked when Uncle Sam did not answer their appeal for a letter of acknowledgment. Once again, the WLA organizers had to ask their powerful male friends to intercede on their behalf, and letters written on the stationery of Wall Street firms and influential civic boards landed on the cabinet secretaries' desks: Would they not offer a few words of encouragement, a bit of congratulations, to be read at the conference? Agriculture Secretary Houston's secretary replied saying that he was sorry, but he was planning to be out of town and could not possibly comply with their request. All the while, the administration was quietly, hesitantly beginning to discuss the possibility of incorporating the Woman's Land Army into a federal government agency.

It's fair to say the Wilson administration was woefully conflicted about the farmerettes. On the one hand, the whole concept was anathema—well-bred American white women stooping in the fields like peasants or Negroes. "I will despise American manhood if the great body of our men permit our women to be drafted for the hard tasks of agriculture until we have sent every able-bodied creature in breeches to the trenches or driven him to the fields," Clarence Ousely told an audience that summer.[10] But it was true that the city and townsmen, if they went into the fields at all, were willing to do only short stints. The Boys' Working Reserve had been something of a disappointment, for the lads could be troublesome and required such constant supervision. The "Work or Fight" state laws had "driven into the fields" some shirkers and slackers, but the statutes were unabashedly racist, targeting Negroes, and brought reluctant workers into the fields. Even the skeptics had to admit, though, the women of the Land Army were eager and reliable. The farmers seemed to think they really were helpful and even wanted the singing farmerettes to return to their fields the next season.

By midsummer, however, some rumblings could be heard in Washington regarding the Woman's Land Army. Perhaps, some said, it would be better to harness the Land Army's energy and steer it where the administration would like it to go. The government could take the WLA's direction and governance out of the hands of those capable—but sometimes impossibly pushy—women and put it under the safe yoke of the Labor Department or maybe the Agriculture Department or somewhere else.

Rumors began circulating among WLA leaders toward the end of July. "The Land Army is to be 'taken over' by the Federal Department of Labor—but nobody knows what this means," Grace Schenck, chairwoman of the Connecticut division of the WLA, wrote to her colleague Corinne Alsop.[11]

"There is a difference of opinion among the state chairmen as to just what form this cooperation should take," Schenck admitted to another correspondent at the same time. The WLA's National Board dispatched one of its officers, Juliet Morgan Hamilton, to Washington to consult with the Department of Labor.[12]

Laura Crane Burgess and the rest of her New York WLA colleagues were astonished when, just days before the Albany conference was to open, they were notified that the administration was sending a representative to the conference after all—someone from the Department of Labor. And she was going to bring a message of endorsement.

The wire services carried this dispatch the day before the Albany Conference opened on August 20:

U.S. PRAISES FARMERETTES:
Wilson and Aides Pay Tribute to Girl With Hoe.

The Girl with the Hoe has been officially endorsed as a great help to the farmer and a credit to her country by President Wilson, Secretary Wilson and Secretary Houston—this is a news item dropped by Mrs. Margaretta Neale, director of the Woman's Division, United States Employment Service, on her way through New York to the convention of the New York State Woman's Land Army.

"The need of women for war service on the farms is a vital one and must
be met," said Mrs. Neale. "The farmerettes have rendered splendid service
and the farmers are beginning to appreciate their value."[13]

At the conference Mrs. Neale announced that the U.S. Employment Service would
begin maintaining a recruiting agent at the WLA headquarters in Manhattan and at
state WLA offices as well to coordinate recruitment activities. The Employment Service
would also accept applications for and registrations from farmerettes at its own bureaus.
Finally, the Department of Labor would extend the postal franking privilege to the Woman's
Land Army of America.

Then the negotiations on the prenuptial agreement for this marriage of convenience
began. But who the lucky bureaucratic bridegroom would be remained strangely unsettled, for neither agriculture nor labor wanted to be betrothed to the farmerette.

At just this time President Wilson received a letter from a close personal friend, Mrs.
Edward P. Davis, wife of his Princeton classmate, concerning the Woman's Land Army.
Addressing the note to "My dear Friend," Mrs. Davis, a WLA state organizer, com-
plained to the president about the federal government's lack of interest in the Land
Army. "It is my judgment that some direction or control should be exercised by the
Government," she wrote to the president. She felt the farmerettes, no less than their
brother doughboys, needed their commander in chief. "More women will enlist in the
Land Army if they know they are serving their country" and can get government recognition, Mrs. Davis argued. "Now many feel it is only an experiment and they pass it
by. . . . We need the authority from you to enlist the women who cannot work at
munitions, etc. for farm work. A word from our Commander in Chief recommending
that women work out doors will do a world of good."[14]

Mrs. Davis also gave her friend some advice:

> We all here feel that if the 'Army' could be organized under the Depart-
> ment of Agriculture, *not* under Labor, it would be better for all con-
> cerned as now the two Depts. get mixed up in placing the women on
> farms and the farmers have to be educated to making use of women
> workers outside the house.

Mrs. Davis's personal plea brought the Land Army to the president's attention, and
he responded promptly, assuring his friend that he would look into the matter. He
forwarded her letter to Secretary of Agriculture Houston, along with a probing note.
"Tell me what you think of her suggestion that the Woman's Land Army (which does
not seem to be coming along as it should) should be transferred to your Department from
the Labor Department, which has only a chaperone's interest in it," the president wrote.[15]

No cabinet officer could fail to notice the president's mild impatience and implied
directive: get these women settled somewhere. Not in my department, Secretary Hous-

ton told the president. "It seems to me that it would not be desirable to transfer the Woman's Land Army from the Labor Department to the Department of Agriculture," said Houston. "So far as I have been able to ascertain, the women whose services are secured through this Organization come largely from towns and cities," he explained, and mobilizing urban women is labor's bailiwick. "It would seem that it would be desirable for [Labor] to continue to have contact with this Woman's Land Army," Houston concluded.[16]

With his hands full of other, more pressing wartime emergencies, the president was not about to step into this hot-potato game between agencies. He could see it was a sort of negative turf war, where neither side wanted the prize. President Wilson simply told Houston, "I agree with your judgment in the matter."[17] The Woman's Land Army would enter the Labor Department's household.

September was a hectic time for the Land Army, for it was the peak of the harvest season, when farmers' calls for more women workers ricocheted around the nation. WLA organizers hardly had time to catch their breath, filling requests for emergency squads, driving the occasional farmerette with influenza symptoms to see a doctor, closing up units whose work was done, or piloting a fund-raising campaign. Weeks had gone by since Mrs. Neale's announcement that the WLA would enter into some affiliation with the government, and some soft voices of doubt could be heard. Several national and state WLA officers, eager as they were to gain government endorsement, support, and much needed funding, began to express wariness about the affiliation's terms and got cold feet about this new partnership.

Exactly what would this proposed relationship with the federal government mean to the Woman's Land Army, they wondered. Would it strengthen the WLA, or change it fundamentally? The new kinship began to be referred to in various ways: as an "affiliation," a "partnership," perhaps a "coordination," just an "agreement," or possibly a complete "takeover." The WLA's state and national officers, the women who had created, nurtured, and financed the army were confused and ambivalent.

Ida Ogilvie feared that in any merger arrangement women would lose control over their Land Army. "The Land Army as yet owes its existence to private effort," she wrote in September, "but indications are that soon it will be under Federal control. How that will affect their work, no one can tell." For women to lose control of the organization would be a shame, Ogilvie believed. "The Land Army camp is the first institution founded by and for women, for the work women can do, not modeled on any preexisting institution for men, nor made by men for what they think women need."[18]

Money and control, as ever, would be the sharp bones of contention. Grace Schenck, the Connecticut WLA chairwoman, understood this situation. She wrote to her WLA colleague Corinne Alsop that accepting government funds would not be wise unless the WLA could be in control of them, "unless these appropriations can be spent by the WLA, rather than through state employment bureaus, such as they have in New York state—where politics has entered very actively into the work, and the WLA has been unable to control in any way living conditions, moral surroundings, or the details of labor. It is vital to avoid this," Schenck warned.[19]

Grace Schenck took some comfort in Juliet Morgan Hamilton's deputization to lead the new Federal Relations Committee and represent the WLA in exploratory talks with the government. "Mrs. Hamilton is going to D.C. to negotiate with the Secretary of Labor," Schenck wrote to Alsop. "She has good sense and appreciates the economic side of the work more than some others."[20] She was the daughter of financier J. P. Morgan, after all.

Juliet Hamilton and her WLA Federal Relations Committee's negotiations with John Densmore and Margaretta Neale for the Department of Labor's Employment Service extended through September and October. As might be expected, they did not bargain as equals. The Labor Department set the terms, requiring the Land Army to trade its independence for the promise of financial security and social respectability; it was so much like a marriage. The government affiliation seemed to promise what the WLA needed and longed for—a sense of stability, professionalism, and recognition. In return, the proposed partnership offered the Employment Service reliable warm bodies willing, even eager, to take on monotonous, poorly paid work in a time of labor emergency. It was a fine match.

As the agreement began to take form, the WLA leaders realized that the new relationship would demand a complete overhaul of its organizational structure, its methods of operating, and its corporate constitution. A subcommittee of the WLA's Board of Directors began recasting the structure to meet the demands of affiliation. This new document placed the WLA firmly under the wing—some might say, under the thumb—of the Department of Labor, which would have final say over appointments, funding levels, deployment, working terms, and wages of units.

What emerged was a strange, two-headed organism—one part private association and one part government agency. In the new Woman's Land Army division of the U.S. Employment Service, the U.S. Secretary of Labor would appoint the WLA's federal director, but the private association, the Woman's Land Army of America, would nominate the candidate. This federal director of the WLA also had to be approved by, and then had to report to, the Employment Service's director general. Upon her appointment, she would then become a government employee. This process was replicated at the state level, with a state Land Army director nominated by each state's WLA board but only with the advice and consent of the U.S. Employment Service chief in that state. No troublemakers, please.

The Employment Service bureaus in every state would help recruit farmerettes and decide where the Land Army units should be placed, but the state WLA branches and their county committees were still responsible for organizing, equipping, and managing all the units in their area. And, perhaps more significant, the state Land Armies still had to foot the bill for equipping and running the units and had to raise their own funds for these expenses. The state Land Armies had to keep soliciting significant donations from members to underwrite their units and camps; this burden was not taken off their shoulders.[21]

In the new arrangement the WLA would still recruit among college students and women's club members and devise training opportunities and curricula. It had to relinquish control over the farmerettes' employment and housing conditions. The government wanted more flexibility and did not necessarily want to be bound by the eight-hour-day and equal wage policies the WLA adhered to so carefully. The function of the private WLA organization was boiled down to the work of four committees—publicity, camp management, training, and finance, with a director for each—and state representatives served on these task forces. The women at the New York headquarters were reduced to compiling statistics and writing press releases as decision making shifted down to Washington.

After dozens of meetings among themselves and with Department of Labor negotiators, the Woman's Land Army finally called a conference of state and national officers to approve the new design. Meeting at the Cosmopolitan Club in Manhattan on October 23 were eleven members of the National Board and fourteen state delegates. Many of the women who had attended the WLA at its birth were present: Hilda Loines, Ethel Puffer Howes, Ida Ogilvie, Emma Winner Rogers, and Delia West Marble, with WLA president Helen Gilman Brown holding the gavel. Edith Diehl was there, and listening intently were most of the eastern states' leaders, plus representatives from California and Kansas. Telegrams were read from those states unable to send a delegate, including Oklahoma, Georgia, and Virginia. Juliet Hamilton moved that "the plan of the Government" be accepted, and Grace Schenck seconded it. After Margaretta Neale explained the plan in detail, it was approved unanimously.[22]

It was something of a Faustian bargain, with the WLA trading away its independent soul for the government's "recognition" and approval, for salaries and postal stamps, and the promise of long-term security. "Women Farmers Are Recognized" was the *Christian Science Monitor*'s headline announcing the WLA's vote. "The request of the United States Department of Labor, asking the Woman's Land Army to affiliate with it, was granted by a unanimous vote," the *Monitor* reported, as if it were covering a proposal on bended knee accepted by a coy maiden. Now, the paper claimed, the Woman's Land Army would have the commander in chief as its star recruiter. As the *Monitor* envisioned it, "Henceforth, President Wilson, through the federal employment office, will assist in the recruiting of farmerettes."[23]

But that's not exactly how it turned out.

Like one of those new fangled mechanized farming contraptions, which could perform two tasks at once with the help of pulleys and pinions, the Woman's Land Army was able to operate on two separate levels during the fall of 1918. While one set of mechanical arms was wrestling with the Department of Labor to secure the organization's future, the other was fashioning ambitious new plans for the Land Army in the 1919 season.

Edith Diehl, now the national director of training, began writing her exhaustive report on the Wellesley Camp's experiments and experiences with the intention of drawing lessons from the findings and codifying, in a field manual, the way Land Army women ought to work and live in units and camps. Diehl also began planning the curricula for regional Land Army training centers for workers and, replicating the Wellesley model, for WLA leaders and supervisors. At the same time the Camp Standards Committee was compiling another manual, based on the reports local WLA organizers, unit supervisors, and camp directors submitted on what worked and what didn't in the field. The goal of the *Handbook of Standards* was to learn from past mistakes and standardize future endeavors and to eliminate the reinvention of the Land Army wheel each time a new unit was required.

Under the auspices of the American Committee for Devastated France, arrangements also got under way to send a unit or two of experienced farmerettes to France to work on the ruined French fields and teach French women to use modern farm machinery. Work at the Libertyville farm in Illinois continued into the fall, with a crew of farmerettes putting fifty acres of hay and alfalfa into the barn, while a Saturday morning course gave high school girls in the vicinity a chance to learn practical farm skills. One hardy unit of New England farmerettes proposed to relieve the nation's sugar shortage by tapping Vermont's and New Hampshire's maple trees the next spring.

Ida Ogilvie, now the WLA's director of recruitment, and Director of Publicity Helen Kennedy Stevens began another tour of college campuses. Meanwhile, Olga Ihlseng, a Bedford Camp veteran, assumed the national field secretary's responsibilities and began plotting a swing through the southern and western states to mobilize the state WLA divisions there and pump up excitement for the next season.

Delia West Marble began gathering articles and photos for a newspaper to be published periodically called *The Farmerette*. She also paid for and leased rooms for a "clubhouse" in midtown Manhattan, where farmerettes could meet, talk, reminisce, and sing around the piano. WLA alumni clubs were established on women's college campuses, offering a sense of belonging among veteran farmerettes and encouraging future recruits. A three-reel farmerette moving picture also began production on the farm of G. Howard Davison in New York State.

And then came peace.

The Fair Farmerettes and Their Shameless Chauffeurs

When lonely ladies cease to loaf
Their chauffeurs do not have to chauf.

Dora, for her country's sake
Labors till her muscles ache.

Joseph, always wide-awake,
Wishes he might be a rake.

Rhoda, loyal to the nation,
Does her bit for conservation.

Adolph, though of lowly station,
Quite approves her cultivation.

Cynthia, too forsakes her beaus
For the care of garden-rows.

Anatole his interest shows
Both in Cynthia and her hoes.

Puck magazine published this satire of "society farmerettes" in January 1918.
The drawings are by artist Rockwell Kent, using a psuedonym.

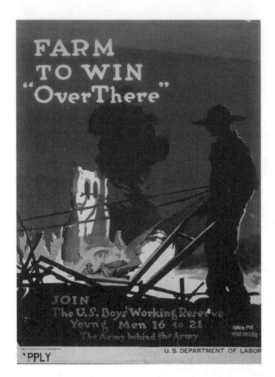

The Boys Working Reserve recruited males too young to enlist in the military to sign up for farm work, but disciplinary problems plagued the program. *Library of Congress*

Several WLA State divisions issued their own recruitment posters like this one for the Ohio WLA. *Cleveland Public Library*

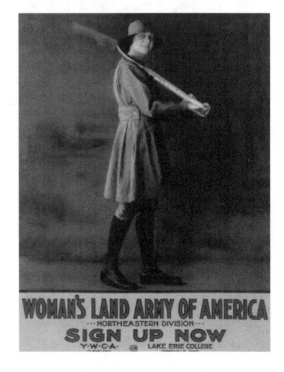

This poster, by illustrator Herbert Paus, was used for national, state and and local WLA recruitment. *National Museum of American History, Smithsonian Institution*

The U.S. Department of Agriculture refused to endorse the WLA, preferring to rely on the recruitment of boys and city men for volunteer farm service. *National Archives and Records Administration*

The northern and southern divisions of the California WLA enrolled thousands of women to handle the state's many crops. *Library of Congress*

California welcomed the Woman's Land Army with brass bands, accepting the farmerettes more readily than other parts of the country. *Library of Congress*

Images of hearty and happy farmerettes filled American newspapers and magazines in 1918. These women served in the Newtown Square, Pennsylvania unit. *National Archives*

WHAT IF THE GERMAN PROPAGANDISTS HAVE STARTED A CAMPAIGN TO INTIMIDATE OUR
FARMERETTES?

Farmerettes enjoyed the affection of the American public, and the attention of
cartoonists, as in this spoof in a July 1918 issue of *Life* magazine.

Students studying to become teachers at the Greensboro Normal School worked
as farmerettes in the summer of 1918. *University of North Carolina at
Greensboro Archives*

The YWCA joined the Land Army movement, recruiting for workers and supervisors, as well as operating its own units in the field. This poster was drawn by artist Edward Penfield. *Library of Congress*

The goal of the Illinois Training Farm for Women was to equip women with the skills needed to run a farm and make her home on the land. *Illinois State Archives*

Charles Dana Gibson created this recruitment poster for the New Jersey Woman's Land Army. *Library of Congress*

The southern states were slower to accept the farmerettes in 1918, but WLA units thrived in Greensboro, N.C.(shown in this photo), Augusta, Georgia, and sections of Virginia. *University of North Carolina at Greensboro Archives*

A New England farmerette in her "town" attire shows off the tools of her trade. *Schlesinger Library*

Alice Holway (second from left) posed with her comrades in the Naulahka Unit of the WLA near Brattleboro, Vermont. Schlesinger Library, Radcliffe Institute, Harvard University

Vassar College became a training center for both farmerettes and nurses in the summer of 1918. Here the farmerettes pose for a group photo. *Vassar College Special Collections*

A farmerette in full WLA uniform. There were many regional variations of the uniform, but almost all eliminated skirts. *Library of Congress*

Mildred Buller Smith left her studies at the University of Chicago to join the WLA. Here she dusts potatoes on the Dimock farm in East Corinth, Vermont. *Schlesinger Library*

23

A HUNGRY WORLD

The day after the armistice was declared on November 11, Mabel Jacques Eichel was at her desk in the New York State Woman's Land Army offices at Thirty-first Street and Fifth Avenue. The victory celebrations had gone on all day and far into the night, marking the silencing of the European guns at the eleventh hour of the eleventh day of the eleventh month of 1918.

On this glorious morning after, Mrs. Eichel, chairwoman of the New York State WLA, was working when a visitor walked into the WLA office, sharing glad tidings of peace. Then, recalled Mrs. Eichel, the visitor remarked, "in a rather consoling manner, 'Now your work is over.' The soldiers will be returning, there will be plenty of men to cultivate the land. In addition, it will of course no longer be possible to obtain women to do this work because the patriotic spirit inspiring them to enlist in your Army has gone."

"But," Mrs. Eichel noted in polite disagreement, "the officers of the Woman's Land Army had an entirely different idea of what the signing of the Armistice really meant to their organization."[1]

"There is still a hungry world to be fed," insisted WLA president Helen Gilman Brown, in a letter to all the WLA state and county divisions. Even in peacetime, hunger was dangerous.[2]

"We have to consider a new world situation in food," U.S. Food Administrator Herbert Hoover announced the day after the armistice. "We have to survey Europe of which a large part is either in ruin or in social conflagration, and its population on rations or varying degrees of privation, and large numbers actually starving."[3]

Within days Hoover pledged that twenty million tons of food must be sent to Europe to prevent starvation and civil unrest that could threaten the peace. He wanted to send food not only to our European Allies in the war—England, France, and Italy—but also to those smaller nations who'd fallen under Germany's yoke: Belgium, Serbia,

231

Bohemia, Romania, Armenia, and Greece. Hoover estimated there were between two hundred million and three hundred million hungry mouths to feed in Europe.

Hoover called upon Americans to continue practicing voluntary pantry austerity—restricting consumption of butter and fats, sugar, and condensed milk, among other staples—though Wheatless Wednesdays would no longer be necessary and white bread was no longer considered unpatriotic. "We must realize that the spectre of famine abroad now haunts the abundance of our table at home," Hoover warned. "Famine is the mother of anarchy."[4]

Russia, in the throes of civil war, also needed our help, Hoover explained. Food was especially needed in the northern sector of the country, where fifty million people were facing starvation while trying to resist the Bolsheviks. His message was, bolshevism thrived on hunger and had to be contained. "We see the threat of the red flag in Holland, Switzerland, and the Scandinavian countries," the *Wall Street Journal* warned. "Hunger causes it."[5]

In a deeply unpopular move, the administration also said that Germany would have to be fed.[6] Within hours after signing the armistice agreement, the German foreign secretary warned that starvation was threatening to break out into riots and anarchy in his defeated nation. With his navy already in full mutiny, he appealed to President Wilson to provide food. Even German women's organizations wrote to Mrs. Wilson and to Jane Addams, begging their help in securing food.[7] In his message to Congress announcing the armistice, Wilson tried to prepare the American public for the necessity of feeding Germany as a preventive measure. "Hunger does not breed reform; it breeds madness," Wilson told Congress, "and all the ugly distempers that make an ordered life impossible." Furthermore, Wilson cast Germany's devastation as a financial issue as well. The president reminded Congress that a starving Germany not only would be a breeding ground for anarchy, but also would leave it unable to pay its massive war reparations to France and Belgium.[8]

Still, a public wail of protest greeted the prospect that American sacrifices at the dinner table might go to feed the "Hun." "The problem of food conservation asked of Americans in the postwar period will be complicated," admitted the *New York Times* in an analysis of the situation, "and those who deny themselves will not know what fraction of their saving will go to Germany."[9] But the *Times* emphasized another reason why "feeding our beaten foes is not merely humane, but expedient": it would bring the two million American soldiers stationed overseas home sooner. If faced with continuing food shortages, the American Expeditionary Force (AEF) might have to remain overseas for a year or more, "with our soldiers facing wild armed mobs in various countries in Europe," the *Times* warned. The well-intentioned arguments were moot, at least for the foreseeable future, however, as our European Allies stubbornly refused to allow food to go to Germany or the naval blockade to be loosened.

Barely a week after the signing of the armistice, Hoover was on to Europe to inspect the situation for himself, and 200,000 tons of food, a first installment, were launched across the ocean to avert anarchy. Hoover worked in Europe for another six months, establishing the American Relief Administration and overseeing a massive food distribution and reconstruction effort. "Food, it has been said, will win the war," the *New York Times* said. "Food, it now turns out, is the one necessary bridge that will carry Europe over from the state of war to an orderly productive peace."[10]

The Woman's Land Army made the same argument. "Our food obligations have been increased enormously with the ending of hostilities," the chairwoman of the WNF&GA's Land Service Committee wrote to her state leaders, urging them to continue their work. "Secret promoters of revolt urging the doctrines of anarchy are at work in many places," she warned. "These look to privation and want to kindle the flames of insurrection. . . . By raising sufficient food to feed Europe, the danger of riots, anarchy, Bolshevism, etc, will be averted and the stay of our boys 'over there' will be shortened."[11]

Without question, America's food production responsibilities would increase in 1919. But would the boys be back in time for spring planting? Demobilization promised to be slow. Not only was the A.E.F. needed to patrol those volatile areas of Europe where spasms of insurrection erupted, but the influenza epidemic complicated matters everywhere—in the military bases abroad, in the camps at home, and in the general population. The fall of 1918 witnessed the most virulent sweep of the pandemic. Within just a few months, almost 60,000 American soldiers would die from the flu, more than fell in battle during the war, and nearly half a million of their kinfolk at home would also succumb to the postwar plague.

And of those farmer-soldiers who did return—who were not among the 230,000 wounded—would they go back to farm life? Had their worldly experiences soured them on the hard, solitary, weather-beaten life on the soil? Would the higher-paying city jobs continue to draw them away from the land? Would their sweethearts want to live an isolated farmhouse existence after they had been war workers? This dilemma was expressed in a favorite popular song of the moment, "How 'Ya Gonna Keep 'Em Down on the Farm (After They've Seen Paree?)" by Sam Lewis and Joe Young.

On the Friday after the armistice was signed, in an open letter published in the major national newspapers, the chairman of the National Board of Farm Organizations reminded his countrymen that "the problem of raising food enough to keep the world from famine is first of all a question of relieving the present shortage of labor on American farms."[12] Even in a world made safe for democracy, farm labor was still a problem in America.

The work of the Woman's Land Army was, most emphatically, not over. Many in the WLA leadership had already begun envisioning the Land Army as a continuing, even permanent, organization. They saw the institution as outliving and expanding on its wartime origins. Public sentiment bolstered their views. As Elene Foster, a reporter for the *New York Tribune*, wrote three months before the war ended:

> This land army is no temporary organization. It has come to stay, mark my
> words. Long after the treaty of peace is signed and that other great army has
> returned from over seas, the Woman's Land Army will continue to serve in
> the same efficient manner in which it is serving today. Their record is
> something of which we may well be proud and this is only the beginning of
> things.[13]

"Among the social organizations which, though brought to life in war time and for
war purposes, realize that their work must continue after peace has been restored, is the
Woman's Land Army of America," said the editors of *The Survey* magazine.[14] "The
Woman's Land Army has become an assured thing," the *Christian Science Monitor* also
insisted, a few weeks after the armistice, "an institution whose genuine worth and value
is recognized."[15] And the editors of the *New Republic* asserted, "The Woman's Land
Army is one of the organizations created by war which ought not to be disbanded, until
its possibilities of civil usefulness have been thoroughly canvassed."[16]

Just before the armistice, the WLA had talked of expanding significantly, with the
number 300,000 American women working on the land in the 1919 season bandied
about in the press. But the happy prospect of peace did raise some "sober questions"
that had to be confronted, according to a report in the inaugural issue of *The Farmerette*:

> Autumn found [enthusiasm] still at white heat, a steady flame to carry over
> till next year. Then came the Armistice, and sober questions began to be
> asked. Will the Land Army be needed next year? Will not enough man
> power be released to handle the agricultural situation? Will the courage of
> the farmer hold to his difficult task? No longer urged by patriotic fervor, will
> women desire to continue land work?[17]

In peacetime, would the farmerettes have the will to "carry on"?

Helen Fraser had returned to America for a second lecture tour, arriving just before
the armistice. She had been in New York City to witness the wild, premature celebrations of the "false armistice" on November 7, when an erroneous newswire report of a
cease-fire brought happy mayhem to the city. She greeted the coming peace an ocean
away from her long-suffering countrywomen. She was booked from coast to coast,
another six-month marathon tour. Now she'd gladly rewrite her lectures a bit to reflect
this new situation. Fraser had a new message to deliver: women's war work efforts would
simply have to be retooled for reconstruction work.

Assistant Food Administrator F. C. Walcott wrote to Fraser just two days after the Armistice:

> My dear Miss Fraser—Our Food Administration will be converted into a
> huge European Relief organization in the next week, and I take much
> pleasure in sending this message to you, hoping that you can help to
> bring the country to a proper realization of our national and interna-
> tional duty . . . in order to feed the starving millions in Europe. It is the
> greatest human appeal that ever existed, and you know so well what it means
> that you can give this message to the country as you go through it with
> wonderful effect.[18]

One message Helen Fraser emphasized was that Britain had lost nearly a million of its young men, a frighteningly large percentage of an entire generation, and British women would not have the luxury of returning to "normalcy" anytime soon. While they would soon be replaced in the factories and mines, they were still needed in the fields. The British Women's Land Army was carrying on, full speed, into the new year.

The Woman's Land Army of America, like its British sister, had an obligation to carry on into peacetime as well; there was no doubt in the WLA leaders' minds. But, as usual, there was still considerable confusion in the American government's mind about the WLA's role. Though the affiliation agreement between the WLA and the Depart-ment of Labor had been approved and signed by the WLA Board of Directors on October 23, the pact was not made public until November 10 and was buried in the news of the armistice. Further, the Department of Labor still had not officially signed the agreement. It was still sitting on the secretary's desk in mid-December, when a frustrated John Densmore, director general of the U.S. Employment Service, who would oversee the WLA as a division of his agency, prodded Labor Secretary Wilson to make a decision.

"The Woman's Land Army is very anxious to learn definitely whether we expect to go on with it [the agreement], and whether in your opinion it has a valuable function to perform this coming year," Densmore wrote to his boss on December 12.

> I would respectfully recommend that this agreement be made effective, and
> that you announce very simply that there will be such need for farm
> products next year as to make it a necessary matter of preparation that the
> Woman's Land Army be continued. I think that in many of the eastern states
> and in some of the western states it will probably be greatly needed during
> the coming year.[19]

While it was difficult for the WLA to plan for the spring without the assurance of government support and, more important, funding, the WLA leaders had grown accustomed to such neglect. They didn't let federal indecision stymie their forward motion. While pressing the Labor Department for a definite commitment to the merger, they pushed ahead with rewriting the WLA constitution and bylaws, planning the first national convention, and selecting new state directors. While the Women's Committees of state Councils of Defense disbanded in the capitals and local women's committees dissolved, the state and county Woman's Land Army divisions called new meetings and charted their roles in peacetime fields. "The Land Army is not ended with the return of peace," Delia West Marble told the farmerettes. "It's greatest task lies ahead, in the new era of reconstruction."[20]

Beyond their specific plans, deeper thinking was taking place wherever Land Army leaders huddled over luncheon plates and planning lists. They felt the Land Army must continue, but in what role and to what purpose? Now that it was no longer a wartime emergency response, what should the organization be and what could it aspire to be?

The women of the Illinois WLA envisioned it as the centerpiece of an educational enterprise, training women in the arts of farm life and preparing them for a lifetime on the land. "The coming of peace causes no turning away from the plow at the Liberty Training Farm," Margaret Blake and her colleagues explained. "Winter wheat must be planted, calves must be tended, cows milked and the chickens fed to lay. Reconstruction spells to the Woman's Land Army greater production and an extension of existing methods."[21] Adjusting to the training farm's recruitment appeal to postwar realities, the Illinois WLA took a new tack:

> It is expected that our returned soldiers are to be given an opportunity to take up free Government land, and many a girl who is looking forward to marrying her boy in khaki when he gets home will find a practical knowledge of farm opportunities and how to utilize them the best kind of a wedding present to offer her new husband.[22]

The WLA in California saw itself in the vanguard of a new agricultural labor movement, one that would provide a dependable source of seasonal workers, who in turn would enjoy fair pay, good working conditions, and comfortable housing. These were definitely not the usual conditions provided for migrant laborers; the women of the WLA could make such demands. New Jersey envisioned its WLA as gateway to "Americanizing" and protecting the many uneducated immigrant women who already did stoop labor in the state's truck farms and supplementing them with a new breed of farmerette.

Mabel Eichel's New York State WLA began drawing up an extraordinary planning document, painting a provocative portrait of an enduring Woman's Land Army that would play a multidimensional role in postwar American society. In this sketch of the

Land Army's future, a permanent WLA would help solve the intractable farm labor shortage, open a new vocation to women workers, and "offer a solution not only of our rural or country life problems, but those of the City as well," according to the New York WLA visionaries.[23] Quite the panacea. The plan was being written as 1918 drew to a close. So while Mrs. Eichel's husband, New York State's chief public health epidemiologist, was compiling the grim statistics of the influenza outbreak's toll, she was trying to craft a brighter future.

On December 18, 1918, Labor Secretary Wilson finally signed the WLA affiliation agreement. The Woman's Land Army became a division of the U.S. Employment Service. "The benefits of this affiliation are beyond question," Helen Gilman Brown wrote to her WLA officers around the country.

> We shall be assured of Government support; we shall have the inestimable help of expert advice as to the distribution of labor; we shall have the added authority and the larger opportunity that must follow such cooperation. To reap these benefits, we are asked to stand unitedly as a loyal group of American women, to prepare with conscientious thoroughness for the work we may be called upon to do, and to do it as efficiently as possible. We believe that the American woman must continue to be, not only a conserver, but a producer of food.[24]

"The end of the road upon which war has set our feet is not yet in sight," declared the editorial in the December 1918 inaugural issue of *The Farmerette*. "Food production must continue at high pressure. Upon the farmer still rests this burden and the Land Army must be quick to hold up his hands for years to come. The call to the Land Army is more urgent than ever."[25]

24

CARRY ON

When Helen Gilman Brown banged the gavel to convene the national convention of the Woman's Land Army of America in Philadelphia on January 14, 1919, she knew full well that trouble was on the agenda. The jolting changes of the past two months—the end of the war, the affiliation with the government, the restructuring of the organization, the new and uncertain role in reconstruction—had rattled the WLA and taken a toll. Excitement buzzed through the two hundred delegates gathered in the Art Alliance Club on Walnut Street, but it was mingled with the jangling, unnerving sensation of women moving at cross purposes.

The WLA organization's latest restructuring, intended to meet the demands of government affiliation, provoked a schism between those who wanted to give the state WLA divisions the autonomy and money to accomplish their goals and those who preferred that institutional decision making reside with a centralized national board. It was the American Federalism debate once again.

The dual—some might call it "schizophrenic"—nature of the new public-private WLA only made it worse. The new governing structure was an organizational nightmare, with both appointed and elected officials. It had an appointed federal director but an elected WLA president and National Board, with appointed state federal directors as well as elected state chairwomen and zonal directors thrown into the mix. Still to be determined was the bureaucratic mystery of how to synchronize WLA activities and finances with the gears of the U.S. Employment Service.

The altered atmosphere of peace proved disorienting for the WLA. No longer under the tension of war, the braid of political and social movements that had entwined to make the WLA strong and flexible during the war had suddenly loosened. The distinct strands plaited into the WLA—the patriotic, preparedness, suffrage, progressive, labor, country life, gardening, and professional women in agriculture movements—now began to unravel.

Many of the suffrage women who'd latched onto the WLA as a vehicle to propel American women toward the vote were now steering toward the finish line and driving the effort to force congressional passage of the "Susan B. Anthony Amendment" to the Constitution, affording federal suffrage for women. At the end of September President Wilson had urged Congress to approve the Nineteenth Amendment "as a war measure." While the House passed the amendment, the Senate rejected it, two votes shy of the required two-thirds majority. With the war ended, Wilson repeated his appeal, but when the Senate stonewalled and refused to bring it to the floor, the president would not expend his political capital to move it there.

Many suffragists were frantically lobbying while others were busy picketing and protesting. As the Land Army delegates assembled in Philadelphia, the Woman's Party held "watch fire" protests outside the White House, burning President Wilson's speeches under banners mocking the "democracy" made victorious by the war. Louisine Havemeyer, who joined the protests, would soon be arrested and imprisoned for burning the president in effigy in front of the White House. After serving her time (just a few days) she climbed onboard the "Prison Special" railroad train, a spectacular publicity stunt in which she and twenty-five other notable "suffrage-convicts" dressed in replicas of their prison uniforms, toured the country by rail, making impassioned speeches. Mrs. Havemeyer no longer had time to tour on the Woman's Land Army's behalf.[1]

And that other WLA trouper, Harriot Stanton Blatch, was onboard an ocean liner bound for Europe, heading for an extended tour of the devastated lands. She intended to research her new book on how the war opened great opportunities to women. She, also, was not available to the WLA.[2]

Those women of the temperance persuasion, the social reformers and members of the Woman's Christian Temperance Union who'd supported the WLA, were also preoccupied now. They were attempting to secure enough votes in the state legislatures to ratify the Eighteenth Amendment, which would usher in the era of Prohibition. Some of the more "patriotic" and "100 percent American" movement ladies within the WLA, members of the National Security League and American Defense Society, now turned their trowels toward rooting out "Bolshevism," or the political and labor radicalism at home. They helped usher in a dark era of nativism and "Red scares."

Of the other involved groups, the garden club ladies seemed eager to return to their petunias. Social reformers embraced new public health and "Americanization" causes. Labor advocates found their mission among the women who'd entered the industrial sector during the war—though returning soldiers quickly displaced them from assembly lines—and pressed for protective labor laws for those women who remained in the factories. They were encouraged by the transformation of the wartime Women in Industry office into the new Women's Bureau within the Department of Labor.

The Women's National Farm and Garden Association was still committed to promoting women's careers in agriculture, but it found the WLA's new government alliance made it a less congenial collaborator. The partnership was fraying, though many individuals and local WNF&GA branches remained involved with the WLA.[3] The YWCA also became more skittish about its relations with the WLA, which had never been particularly warm. The Y was confused by the WLA's still amorphous terms of affiliation with the government and disturbed by its loss of autonomy. The WLA was too unsettled, and the Y wanted to keep its distance.

Internal disputes within the WLA rose to the surface as well, with long-simmering philosophical differences, mixed with sharp political disputes, all spiced by an occasional pinch of personal animosity. Warning bells began to ring during the frenetic weeks between the signing of the armistice in November and the affiliation agreement in December and the opening of the conference in January.

"My Dear Josie," wrote WLA vice president Juliet Morgan Hamilton to her colleague and relative, Josephine Perry Morgan of the New Jersey WLA, at the end of December. "I hate to butt-in any more, but I want to tell you that your Chairman, Miss MacIlvaine, has been trying to arrange for four states, New Jersey, New York, Illinois and Pennsylvania to secede from the National Army."[4]

Anne MacIlvaine made no secret of her disdain for the national WLA leadership, and they never trusted her, either. MacIlvaine, the daughter of a prominent Trenton family, had solid good-works credentials to recommend her as head of the Land Army for her state, but she also had an abrasive personality and high-handed manner. Her own staff disliked her.[5] Moreover, the friction between her and the WLA leadership was baldly political: MacIlvaine was vice president of the National Association Opposed to Woman Suffrage—she was an "Anti"—and the national Woman's Land Army was dominated by committed suffragists, several of whom also served as officers of the National American Woman Suffrage Association. Though the WLA was not a partisan organization, sufficient historical animosity between the die-hard WLA suffragists and MacIlvaine kept relations frosty.

MacIlvaine had further alienated her WLA colleagues when, during the WLA and Labor Department negotiations in the fall, she used her political connections to try to secure for herself a plumb appointment as assistant federal director of the WLA. Knowing her WLA colleagues would never approve of her appointment, she wrote directly to the White House, complaining about the WLA national leadership.[6] President Wilson's private secretary, Joseph Tumulty, had nimbly bounced her letter off his desk and deflected her diatribe, but now it bubbled up again, in the form of a mild mutiny, on the floor of the convention.[7]

In truth, MacIlvaine raised legitimate structural and policy concerns about the new WLA—about control, money, and power— that several more level headed state chairwomen also shared. But her impolitic outbursts had already squandered her own New Jersey WLA delegation's confidence in her, alienated any likely allies, and undermined her cause.[8] Undeterred, MacIlvaine drew up a list of grievances and a set of amendments to the new WLA constitution and prepared to lead a rebellion from the convention floor. Yet, in the end, it was the smooth, sensible, and politically sophisticated Margaret Day Blake who actually convinced her state to secede from the Woman's Land Army of America.

Hers was a stunning, though dignified, revolt. In the first week of the new year, just days before the national convention, Blake sent a letter to WLA president Helen Gilman Brown announcing that Illinois would not be sending its delegates to the convention. Instead, it was quitting the national WLA. "The Illinois women have seceded from the national organization saying that agricultural problems of the west are not understood by the eastern women who drew up the constitution of the national body," the *Chicago Tribune's* reported.[9]

In her letter to the WLA, Blake put it this way:

> The decision was reached that it is inadvisable for the Illinois organization to unite with the national board under a constitution so detailed as to offer the probability of interfering with our development along the specific, educational path which our local needs seem to demand.
>
> The training farm project is not merely, or even primarily, an economic or industrial enterprise, it is not merely an agency to provide trained or semi-trained women in agriculture. The most important service of the training farm is to emphasize . . . women's opportunities in country life.[10]

The new WLA constitution, tailored to the Department of Labor's needs, accentuated the "conflicting aims" between the Woman's Land Army as a temporary employment scheme and the Illinois WLA's goal of training women for a long life on the land. Margaret Blake and her state committee simply didn't see any way to bridge this basic philosophical difference. The new, more centralized, less flexible WLA could not thrive in the Illinois climate. Mrs. Blake's goal now was to find a permanent home for the Illinois Training Farm for Women, which was continuing work through the winter, within the Illinois state university system. She left the Woman's Land Army to its own devices and its own dramatics at the Philadelphia convention.

So when Helen Gilman Brown rapped her gavel and brought the convention to order on that sunny and mild Tuesday morning in January, it was with the knowledge that one of the WLA's strongest state delegations had withdrawn, another was fomenting a mutiny, and several essential allegiances were splintering. She tried to smile.

The delegates glided through the reports of the credentials, elections, and federal relations committees, as well as all the standing committees. But when the new constitution and bylaws were presented for adoption, Miss MacIlvaine rose to speak.

"The situation of the Woman's Land Army has completely changed since October 23rd, when the proposed constitution was approved and recommended for adoption," MacIlvaine told her fellow delegates. "Since the signing of the armistice the character of our work has changed from an emergency task, meeting an emergency need, to that of a nation wide movement for food production which must prepare for a long future." When the Land Army started, it was expedient that it be run by a central committee, MacIlvaine admitted, "but at present the amount of actual and varied experience possessed by the State organizations is beyond comparison greater than that of the Board. In these circumstances it is clear that the actual shaping and development of policies must be done by the State leaders."[11]

The proposed constitution gave the federal director and an appointed national board "complete and arbitrary power over the most essential activities of the states." Instead, MacIlvaine insisted, the WLA executive body ought to consist of the chairwomen of all the organized states. A permanent WLA organization required "a council in which policies shall be determined by the people who are actually doing Land Army work—the State organizations," MacIlvaine argued.[12]

Heads nodded in the audience. Many within the state delegations actually agreed with her. They believed they'd shouldered the Land Army's burdens and expenses in the last season, they had learned the tough lessons, and now they wanted a stronger role; however, they were not prepared to follow Anne MacIlvaine. MacIlvaine also did not figure into her scheme the force of the hand now guiding the WLA—namely, the government. The Labor Department did not want strong, autonomous state WLA organizations making policy. Instead, the WLA's federal director would take orders, which the states would then receive and implement. That was, to put it bluntly, the price of government affiliation; with this new WLA constitution, it would be paid. While Anne MacIlvaine took the role of Cassandra, warning out loud that the Woman's Land Army would be undone by this arrangement, her voice was too shrill and her motives too suspect to be heeded. Helen Gilman Brown was a skilled political operator herself, dispatching Miss MacIlvaine's constitutional amendment to a quick negative vote and to the wastebasket. She then adjourned the convention for lunch.

With that unpleasantness behind them, the delegates tried to savor their land service victories and confront their many looming challenges. The state and county delegates participated in frank discussions about finances, wage and hour disputes, transportation woes, and the various problems of camp management. An "Experience Meeting of Farmers and Farmerettes" brought valuable additional dimensions to the analysis. They shared their frustrations, their failures, and their homegrown solutions. The honest exchange was cathartic, even invigorating. Together, they had accomplished some great things.

Dorothy Nicoll Hubert, who had served so diligently as the WLA's general secretary, was introduced as the new federal director of the WLA. Many in the audience knew and trusted her. Mrs. Hubert's suffrage movement comrades delighted in telling the story of how Dorothy met her husband, William, at a suffrage meeting in 1916, and their courtship commenced when he volunteered to drive the automobile for her suffrage campaign tour. She made forty-eight speeches in one week, impressing him mightily, and they were soon engaged. She would need such spunk and fortitude in her new position.[13]

Edith Diehl was named national director of training; Ida Ogilvie accepted the portfolio of director of recruiting; Olga Ihlseng, a Bedford Camp alumna, became field secretary; and Helen Kennedy Stevens took charge of publicity. Filling out the board of the WLA's private corporation, Helen Gilman Brown was reelected president. Juliet Morgan Hamilton of New York and Mary Schofield of New Hampshire (still in mourning for her son, who was killed in action in France) took the vice presidential spots, and Mary Potter Bush won the unenviable job of treasurer of the Woman's Land Army of America, Inc.

There was even a fashion show event at the convention, with a parade of models sporting different versions of a new "official" Land Army uniform. In this couture contest, the delegates were supposed to pick a winner, or the "one best way" for the WLA woman to dress for work. "The farmerettes of the Land Army spent several hours yesterday afternoon trying to pick out a suitable suit, a uniform, or something like that," reported one Philadelphia newspaper, "but could reach no agreement, although living models paraded up and down before the 300 delegates to select something 'fit' for farm work."[14] The delegates' goal was to choose a uniform design that could be adopted as "the" national WLA outfit, but reflecting the meeting's fractious spirit, they simply could not agree.

"Here are two of the proposed costumes," the newspaper caption explained, "which failed to meet unanimous approval." One was a puffy-legged, suspendered romper design, with cross-laced puttees, a collared shirt, and long tie topped off by a jaunty snap-brimmed hat; the other was more of a military cut, with cavalry-worthy jodhpur pants and tight leggings covered by a patch-pocket jacket, and topped off with a straw cowboy hat. Miss Diehl's fashion sense and her fondness for tightly knotted ties were strong influences on some of the uniform creations. "But what suited some were unequivocally rejected by others," reported the *Philadelphia Public Ledger*, and none of the eight uniforms ("ranging from sober black to merry lavender") pleased all the delegates.[15] The costuming matter was sent back to the Camp Standards Committee to decide.

At the elegant $2.50-a-plate banquet at the Ritz-Carlton Hotel that evening, more than three hundred delegates and guests enjoyed a celebration of the Land Army's short but glorious history and its sparkling future. Judge William Porter of Philadelphia was master of ceremonies and tickled the audience with tales of the "remarkable tasks" the farmerettes handled while in his employ the previous summer. Mr. J. Clyde Marquis, editor of the *Country Gentleman* magazine, a publication more likely to be found in a country manor house's den library than in a rural farmhouse, provided witticisms for the occasion.

Labor Secretary William Wilson was once again invited to give a keynote address and again declined to attend. Director General of the U.S. Employment Service John Densmore, who was the closest thing to a designated groom in this marriage of the WLA to the Department of Labor, did attend the banquet and offered an enthusiastic toast to the happy union. He strongly advocated the continued development of the Land Army movement, saying it was a big step toward the solution of the farm labor question, and prophesied that its affiliation with the government would prove advantageous to all. In this period of readjustment and reconstruction, he told the delegates, farmwork might offer a fine alternative for women suddenly thrown out of their industrial jobs by the soldiers' return. "Bolshevism and anarchism are fed on idleness," Densmore warned. The Land Army could occupy those dangerously idle hands.[16]

When Anna Gilman Hill, who had helped guide the WLA since its earliest days, took the podium, she hit upon a sensitive topic. Mrs. Hill reassured her audience that the Woman's Land Army was not working to take men's jobs away, and returning soldiers would find the farmerettes willing to give their jobs back. The farmerettes merely "exist to fill the gap," she insisted, but there were simply not sufficient returning soldiers to "make it unnecessary for women to help cultivate the soil." Unlike their sisters in industry, farmerettes were still needed on the land, at least for spring 1919.[17]

The evening's entertainment treat was the premiere screening of the silent, three-reel, farmerette moving picture, which the Land Army's faithful friend, G. Howard Davison, produced and filmed on his farm and other locations in Dutchess County, New York. With professional actors in the lead roles, it told the story of a farmer who doesn't believe women could be of any use to him, but his wise wife persuades him "to give the sex a trial." He calls in the Land Army, brings in a unit of nine farmerettes and a supervisor, and puts them to work in his fields from June until the October frosts.

"The pictures show the workers in bloomers and short skirts," said the *New York Times*'s description of the movie, "planting, hoeing, plowing, harvesting fruit on tall ladders, operating reapers and doing all the other things men do on a big profitable farm."[18] In the end the reluctant farmer is, of course, convinced of the farmerettes' value and converted to the WLA cause; the wife resists the temptation to say, "I told you so"; and all are happy and enlightened ever after.

This moving picture could not have had a more enthusiastic audience than the devoted WLA supporters in the hotel's darkened banquet room that night. But even they must have sensed that the film, earnest docudrama that it was, already seemed dated. It was a sunlit chronicle of a simpler time, when the biggest obstacle the WLA needed to surmount seemed to be the decent but stubborn farmer's resistance. Now the challenges facing the Land Army were subtler and more difficult.

Unhitched from the yoke of wartime, blinders removed, the WLA expanded its field of vision and set off in new directions. The early winter of 1919 was a time of exploration.

Dorothy Hubert moved her files into a new WLA office within the U.S. Employment Service suite in the Labor Department's building in Washington and tried to figure out how to mesh the soul of her Land Army with the machine of the Employment Service. Edith Diehl rented a Dupont Circle apartment for her stints at the Washington office and kept a desk in the New York WLA headquarters as well, though she still spent most of her time on the road, setting up farmerette training centers. A major new national training camp at the University of Virginia in Charlottesville seemed possible, as was another in New Jersey, and she also began sketching a proposal for a new kind of scientific experiment involving the farmerettes. Ida Ogilvie and Delia West Marble set out together on a tour of the western states to spark WLA activity there while Olga Ihlseng made her way, gingerly, through the southern states on a similar mission.

When New York called together all its WLA organizers late in January for a statewide conference, what emerged from the gathering was a stunning new design for the WLA in peacetime. The New York plan had both short-term practical and long-term socio political goals. Not only would Land Army work continue to provide healthful outdoor employment for the city women in the seasonal trades, in 1919 it could also offer paying work to those women who lost their war industry jobs to returning soldiers. A hot summer of unemployment for so many laid-off seasonal or tossed-out war industry women was dangerous at this moment, the New York WLA planners emphasized, echoing John Densmore's warning. Further, they touted the benefits of Land Army employment as "offsetting the tendency toward economic and social unrest and the opportunity for the spreading of Bolshevist propaganda."[19] The farmerette, having helped bring down the Hun, could now tackle the Red menace.

The imaginative, some might say "fanciful," New York document set its sights far beyond immediate labor needs. The plan's most ingenious aspect proposed that Woman's Land Army camps in each county be made into permanent rural community centers, where farmerettes from the city could be housed and dispatched for work in the summer months and the farmer and his family could be invited to participate in recreational and educational events, mingling with the farmerettes and forming sympathetic social bonds. This sort of gentle fraternizing between city girls and country folk, such as Saturday night community dances and sing-alongs, were highlights of the 1918 season in many WLA camps. This plan expanded on the concept and gave it an educational twist. The Land Army Rural Community Centre's circulating library, meeting room, community canning kitchen, and dehydrating plant, along with its menu of both practical and cultural classes, moving picture shows, and lectures, would enrich the country dwellers' lives. The Rural Community Centre's building would remain open for community use during the winter months, too, and help conquer the great menace to rural life—isolation and boredom.

Building on this idea of bringing new stimulation to country life, the plan suggested eventually broadening Land Army service to men, "encouraging young men recruited from the same walks of life as the young women to form Land Army Camps under the Unit system."[20] The planners envisioned a sort of Land Army summer Chautauqua— providing an infusion of fresh social and cultural blood into tired rural veins, while offering a healthful outdoor sanitarium for pale and weary city denizens—all with economic benefits and a progressive social bent. "We are glad to bring about a complete change in farm life," Ida Ogilvie announced to the *New York Times*. "Although colonization of farm help on a scientific basis will seem radical to some, it is the only way to provide that human companionship which will induce Young America to stay on the farm."[21]

Essential, nuts-and-bolts items were on the New York agenda, too: more training facilities needed to be established, transportation issues smoothed out, sanitation improved. Each Land Army camp had to be run on a sound economic basis and become "absolutely self supporting." Yet for Mrs. Eichel and her fellow visionaries on the New York WLA's Planning Board, the Land Army now stood poised to play a singular, significant role in a better America. "No one had dreamed that a group of patriotic young women, properly supervised, properly chaperoned, going out with their hoes in hand to fight the food shortage, would be the beginning of one of the greatest reconstruction movements which is today developing in this country," Eichel wrote, with unrestrained pride.[22]

Ida Ogilvie was even bolder in her depiction of the WLA's peacetime mandate. "The need of food production continues, but the Land Army has another and a higher duty in the reconstruction period that is at hand," Ogilvie preached to the faithful in the pages of *The Farmerette*.

> To it is presented the supreme opportunity of giving to large numbers of women the chance for the working out of one of the most interesting experiments in Democracy. . . . To break through class barriers has hitherto been easy for men; the Land Army camp shows to women the unreality of such distinctions, proves the imperative necessity for the subordination of the individual to the good of the whole, and illustrates these principles through the unhampered use of muscle and brain. The Spirit of the Land Army is the true substance of the democratic idea.[23]

The mantel that Professor Ogilvie draped onto the farmerette's shoulders—no longer made of khaki cloth but of a weave of American ideals—might have been a bit heavy for the farmerette's slender frame, but it lifted the Land Army's mission from digging dirt to upholding democracy.

The Pennsylvania division of the WLA took a more pragmatic, if prosaic, approach to preparing the land for 1919. Here the WLA was concerned about money and labor issues and understood that the rules of farmerette engagement would have to change. "Last year the girls were moved by patriotism, because they knew the world was starving for food," explained Myrtle Bargar, a veteran Pennsylvania farmerette. "Next year they will go out as a business proposition."[24] Miss Bargar spoke "with much frankness" at a meeting of the Brandywine Valley Farmers' Club, where the Land Army's place in the next growing season was the topic for discussion. "As the boys went overseas for $30 a month, so these girls went out to work on the farms for $15 a month," she explained, standing before the meeting in her WLA uniform. With peace, the girls would demand better wages. "They want a share of the profits in farming," Bargar explained.[25]

The terms of employment would have to improve, agreed Edith Ellicott Smith, now the state chairwoman of the Pennsylvania WLA and former president of the Pennsylvania Rural Progress Association. "Our girls are willing and industrious, and they have done well, but the farmers did not always give them a square deal," she complained. "In some places they have been quartered in houses where the plaster was falling off the walls and the bedbugs were plentiful enough to carry the girls away. On two farms we had to move the girls out into the barn while we had the house fumigated at our own expense."[26]

Expenses were definitely on the minds of the Pennsylvania WLA organizers, because even under the new government affiliation, the Department of Labor would not help with equipping camps, paying supervisors' salaries, or staunching any red ink. The pool of Land Army benefactors would surely shrink in the coming year, Mrs. Smith warned the Brandywine Valley farmers, and finding patrons to sponsor units or cover financial shortfalls was going to be ever more difficult. "The patriotic women who have been contributing thousands of dollars to support these girls while they are at work are not going to do it now that the war is over," she told them bluntly. "The support must come from somewhere else. I would advise you farmers to get together and talk the matter over and decide what you are going to do."[27]

There'd been some quiet grumbling about the farmers taking advantage of the Land Army volunteers' patriotism and reaping record-high prices for many of their crops while benefiting from the patriotic work ethic and subsidized labor of the farmerettes. The generosity of WLA sponsors—all those women and clubs writing big checks—had previously corrected any imbalances in the units' account books, usually caused by rainy-day downtime or expensive car maintenance. The farmers sacrificed nothing in this bargain and contributed little to the expenses of the farmerette camps that were run for their benefit. The WLA needed a radically different business model.

"The Woman's Land Army has helped to break down the silly taboo against women engaging in farm work," explained the *New Republic* in an editorial in January,

> but if the system is to have any chance of growing, or even of surviving, it is of the utmost importance that it should . . . be placed under expert leadership competent to work out and enforce proper standards of food, hygiene, social relations, hours and pay. Such an enterprise is peculiarly in danger of being shifted off a sound economic basis, since it appeals to so many vague ideals: the ideal of taking part in food production, the ideal of healthful labor under the open sky, the ideal of group association in work and living. These are of the soundest of ideals; but they must not be allowed to make easy the task of the would-be exploiter.[28]

Alice Graydon Phillips, speaking for the northern California WLA, took prideful exception to this analysis in her rebuttal letter to the *New Republic*. California had established itself on a sound business basis, she pointed out. Its farmerettes were protected by strong wage and hour rules, its WLA units didn't lose money, and the large farmers and orchardists they served shared the expenses of building the camps. It was indeed how the WLA should be run.[29]

Margaret Day Blake and her Illinois group, proudly independent but never impractical, decided that maintaining the Illinois Training Farm for Women would not be possible beyond the winter season. Blake struck a deal with the president of Blackburn College in Carlinville, south of Springfield, giving him the training farm's stock and equipment in return for a promise to enroll more women in Blackburn's two-year agricultural course. She also extracted a pledge from the college president to establish a special twelve-week summer course for women on the theory and practice of farming. In this way Blake hoped to ensure the continuation of the training farm concept.

The WLA's state and local branches held meetings all through the winter, taking the pulse of their communities as to whether Land Army units were feasible. The question of whether the Land Army was an employment service, a charity, or a business, kept arising.

"The work of the Land Army should go on," Josephine Perry Morgan wrote to one of the New Jersey WLA's benefactors, soliciting her patronage for the 1919 season:

> It will probably be on a somewhat smaller scale than last year. The Federal Department of Labor agrees that the Land Army is valuable as a solution of the chronic shortage of short term seasonal labor (the kind of jobs that the soldier refuses to take) and it is now affiliated with the Department. However, the private organization still keeps the responsibility of recruiting the

girls and providing for their housing and chaperonage. . . . Consequently the
organization will have to meet expenses for publicity and for equipment such
as blankets, dishes and cooking utensils. May we not count upon your
continued interest and financial aid?[30]

But ought the WLA ask for contributions at all? Some WLA organizers thought
absolutely not. "We made an experiment last year, to meet a patriotic emergency, at the
expense of private philanthropy," argued Elizabeth Packard of the New York WLA in a
letter to Josephine Morgan.

> The experiment was sufficiently successful to engage the cooperation of the
> Federal Bureau of Labor, under whose direct control (with us as advisors and
> volunteer overseers) all the future work will be inaugurated and adminis-
> tered. If, as we believe, our experiment established the Land Army on a basis
> of good economics—why is it any longer appropriate or possible to finance
> it on private charity? Is it any more reasonable to have a charity "drive" to
> support farm laborers than it would be to similarly propose to support our
> house-servants?[31]

If the farmers really want the women workers, they should agree to employ them
steadily, rain or shine, in an agreed contract and not day by day, Packard continued. "It
has been proven absolutely that wherever the farmers assume the same attitude toward
women's labor as they unquestionably must toward men's labor (I do not here speak of
wages, but of employment through all kinds of weather) a unit may be wholly self-
supporting and has no need of public subscription." The Land Army is not a charity for
farmers, nor is it a "fresh air fund" to bring city girls to the country, Mrs. Packard
maintained.

> If the Women's Land Army is an economic necessity it should (and may) be
> made to support itself without resort to private generosity. At this time—
> when our re-organization is placing the work under the Federal Labor
> Bureau—should we not answer this question once and for all? We can not
> launch it under government control as a charity, and hope later to change
> the policy.[32]

It was a fascinating debate but, alas, a moot one. These women would soon learn
that the federal government was not going to come through with any taxpayer funding
at all for the WLA. In partnering with the U.S. Employment Service, the WLA had
joined fortunes with an agency beset by powerful political enemies who did not wish to
see the bureau continue into reconstruction. They wanted it abolished.

With soldiers coming home by the shipload and looking for work, the Employment Service's offices around the country were working feverishly to place into jobs both demobilized doughboys and freshly unemployed munitions and shipbuilding workers. By all accounts, it was doing a fine job. Since the armistice the Employment Service reported placing an average of a hundred thousand returning soldiers and laid-off workers a week in new jobs.[33] But manufacturers' associations accused the Employment Service of pro-union tendencies, favoring union members over nonmembers for job placements and promoting closed, unionized shops. Continuance of the Employment Service became a proxy fight about organized labor's influence.

Industry's friends in the U.S. Senate set out to strangle—or rather, starve—the Employment Service to death. Although the House approved an urgent deficiency bill containing the $1.8 million the agency needed to keep running in the last quarter of the 1919 fiscal year, until the end of June, Senate Republicans filibustered and let the entire bill die before adjournment. In the new Congress, Republicans would be in control; the Republican majority was elected in November, barely a week before the armistice, as a rebuke to the Wilson administration's war policies. The new Republican leadership was flexing its muscles and moving aggressively to undo the wartime programs and structures the Democrats had rammed into place. Both the Employment Service and the Woman's Land Army became pawns in this congressional funding gamesmanship and reconstruction politics.

Labor Secretary Wilson appealed to the president to keep the Employment Service alive and give it an infusion of money from the President's War Emergency fund, but the president replied that fund had been depleted. Director General John Densmore telegraphed his federal directors in every state: prepare to shut down or limp along with a skeleton structure, for the 750 Employment Service bureaus would shrink to 56. Don't despair, Densmore told his directors; the service would surely regain funding in the new budget for the fiscal year beginning in July. Just hold on.[34]

Densmore also gave that message to the WLA leaders who were watching anxiously from the sidelines. WLA general secretary Vera Lane wrote to Josephine Perry Morgan on March 6,

> This morning Mrs. Hubert telephoned reassuring news from Washington. You probably saw by the newspaper that the Deficiency Bill failed to pass in Congress, and thereby imperils the continuance of the US Employment Service. Mr. Densmore assures Mrs. Hubert that the Land Army work will be continued at least until July first, and in his mind, without question, it will be continued permanently. We are to go on with our plans without anxiety, perfecting our organization and developing work.[35]

Carry on. Plan for spring.

In a display of wild optimism, the Camp Standards Committee unveiled the new, official, finally approved Woman's Land Army costumes—one uniform for field wear and another for "street" appearances. The field uniform adopted a clever "convertible" design, where the form fitting bib overalls could be transformed into a chic, after-work outfit ("pull up the trousers, turn down the bib, and don the coat, and you will have— a natty costume") suitable for a farmerette's fun night on the town. The street ensemble featured a tailored skirt, belted coat, Miss Diehl's favored four-in-hand tie, and a brown straw hat. On the belt buckle, buttons, and hat and lapel pins were the new Land Army bronze insignia, a stylized sheaf of wheat, designed by the celebrated American sculptor Paul Manship and struck by the Gorham company.[36]

A foldout fashion brochure was printed to publicize the new outfits, featuring a smiling young farmerette model striking dramatic poses. Those who ordered the uni- forms—the complete field outfit sold for $4.30, the officer's street attire for $21.50— were obliged to sign a contract. "I agree to wear sensible brown shoes and dark hosiery with this uniform," was one stipulation, along with a promise to wear a white shirt with "medium high turn-over collar." And "in order to preserve the integrity of the uni- form," the purchaser also had to promise that when she left the Land Army, she would remove and return the metal insignia to headquarters, "or see that such insignia does not come into the possession of any one not entitled to wear it."[37]

Wearing her officer's uniform, Olga Ihlseng, the WLA national field secretary, had a tough slog through the southern states. She recounted her lonely train journey in *The Farmerette*:

> I was asked for an amusing account of my trip through the South, but when
> I tried to look back on it from that angle, the humor of the situation seemed
> to vanish. I could see nothing but the worthy gentlemen who liked the Land
> Army idea exceedingly, but who would rather see their womankind doing
> beautiful feminine work (generally, on investigation, dishwashing and kindred
> amusements).[38]

The Land Army had taken root in a few places in the South during 1918, but for the most part it was not hospitable territory. "As far as the Land Army is concerned Mississippi is barren soil," Ihlseng said flatly. "Then I went on to Alabama and re- ceived still less encouragement," Ihlseng moaned. North Carolina was still equivocat- ing about the Land Army, even though the women students of the Normal School at Greensboro had acquitted themselves admirably as farmerettes that last season. There were glimmers of hope, according to Ihlseng, especially in the large orchards of the western part of the state.

Her trip through South Carolina started off gloomily, with one gentleman proffering the advice that "we would be doing better to stay at home to raise families." But when the state's governor, Land Army–friendly Richard Manning, joined her speaking tour attitudes seemed to change. "I felt that our stock had gone up 100%," Ihlseng chirped, and she had high hopes that units of Winthrop College farmerettes would pick cotton the next summer. As she moved southward, things looked brighter. In Georgia's peach orchard district near Americus, "we have been assured of a hearty welcome next summer," Ihlseng reported. Florida also gave her a warm greeting when she spoke at the Farmer's National Congress and showed lantern slides of farmerettes at work. "The next day I spent swearing on my honor that the pictures were not faked, and that we really had done all I said and then some." Units were already being formed in Florida for early spring vegetables. "The early vegetables you buy up North will probably be Land Army products," Ihlseng assured her readers.

Edith Diehl had her own plan to entice the southern states into a closer alliance with the WLA while supplying the rest of the country with a corps of properly trained workers and officers. She wanted to set up a national training center in Charlottesville, Virginia, on the grounds of the university there, that could be the movement's service academy and the flagship of a fleet of state training centers. Over the fall and winter, along with Ethel Puffer Howes and Bryn Mawr president M. Carey Thomas, Diehl had studied the Land Army's training needs and come up with a comprehensive, multi-tiered plan that would tap the educational resources and campuses of women's, coeducational, and agricultural colleges. Based on the results of the Wellesley Camp experiments, Diehl fashioned curricula for instructor, supervisor, and worker schools and courses of instruction ranging from agricultural methods to camp cooking, sanitation and hygiene, camp systems (including methods of efficiency and motion study), and camp welfare (recreation and discipline). In Miss Diehl's plan, there would never again be "green" farmerettes.[39]

Diehl had another plan in her pocket, this one of a "scientific" nature, that would expand on Wellesley's physical and physiological experiments. Consulting with what she called "the prominent Biologists, Physicians, Agriculturalists and with the experts who have been making a study of women workers in the various industries," Diehl was designing a "test camp" to investigate the kinds of farmwork suitable for woman workers and to measure the effects of such labor. The WLA gave her its blessing to pursue this groundbreaking work, and she hoped that President Ellen Pendleton would again allow Wellesley to become her scientific laboratory.[40]

Ida Ogilvie and Delia West Marble had a much easier time in their swing through the Pacific states, already fertile ground for the WLA. "In all of the colleges and universities where we have appeared," said Ogilvie, "women students and teachers have eagerly consented to jump out to the ranch or the orchard and do the work. We received the pledge of 75 per cent of the women we talked to."[41]

With the rush of returning soldiers swelling unemployment rolls—even if those unemployed men did not want to take up farmwork—Ogilvie and Marble were sensitive to the local labor tensions. "It is not intended that women should take the places of men," Ogilvie insisted in California. "There is work for every man. What the WLA emphasizes is that the women we send out are intelligent, not the class of cheap labor supplied heretofore where three Mexicans were required to do the work of one white man." (Clearly Ogilvie was not above exploiting prevailing ethnic prejudices for the Land Army's benefit.) "It will be the best organized, most compact and intelligent army of workers ever seen in this country," Ogilvie maintained.[42]

The WLA took a preliminary survey of the labor situation in each of its organized states, polling its chairwomen as to whether the Land Army would be needed and welcome again in 1919. The results were surprising. Some of the most well-established programs did not intend to continue, but other areas, where the WLA hadn't been able to penetrate the previous year, were clamoring for farmerettes.

The WLA asked its state chairwomen to estimate their budgets for 1919 and determine how much money it would take to keep going, with the tacit understanding that the Labor Department's promised money for salaries, travel, and postage expenses was probably not going to materialize. With the Employment Service's future still so unsettled, all fiscal responsibilities were going to fall back into the WLA's petite lap. The calculation was sobering: at least $83,000 would be needed to maintain the national and state WLA operations, and this estimate counted only the budgets of eleven state divisions and did not include sizable publicity or membership drive expenses.[43]

The Senate's assault on the Employment Service only intensified through the spring. State governments and social service agencies were forced to assume more of the load and place demobilized soldiers through their own job bureaus. The National Board of Farm Organizations pleaded with Congress to restore funding for the Employment Service, because farm labor was in such critically short supply again.

The WLA's national Board of Directors tried to hide its own mounting anxiety, but the members also tried to be sensible. Emergency meetings were called. President Helen Gilman Brown tendered her resignation before leaving on a YWCA-sponsored reconstruction inspection tour of Europe, and Mary Schofield took her place. Federal Directors Hubert, Ogilvie, Marble, and Diehl agreed to dollar-a-year honorariums rather than the promised government salaries for their work. Helen Kennedy Stevens left her WLA publicity director's post for a better-paying—or at least paying—position with the YWCA.

And yet the WLA kept chugging along, powered by the intrepid state divisions. New York and New Jersey designed their own publicity and fund-raising campaigns. The WLA published its long-awaited *Handbook of Standards,* providing an updated set of blueprints for running successful units based on a clear-eyed assessment of the previous year's mistakes and accomplishments. Besides the Charlottesville training camp, others were being readied in southern New Jersey, northern New York State, New Hampshire, and Ipswich, Massachusetts. At least thirteen states were poised to put farmerettes in the field, and the state WLAs would try to raise money on their own.

The great irony, of course, is that its affiliation with the federal government provided less security for the WLA, less flexibility, and no money beyond a few postage stamps. The grand scheme of centralized and streamlined control from Washington dissolved; however, the WLA already knew how to operate on its own. The state WLA divisions simply picked up the pieces and kept moving as best they could. Like a proud and defiant grass widow, humbled by circumstance, the WLA simply carried on.

25

FARMERETTE REDUX:
1919 AND BEYOND

The parades were over, the bands and banners gone. In the spring of 1919 the Woman's Land Army could not march into American fields with the same high step as in the previous year, but it could keep up a decent stride.

New York State kicked off its third season of farmwork with a Land Army "Field Day" on the streets of Manhattan, Brooklyn, and the Bronx, with uniformed farmerettes in straw hats collecting contributions in milk pails. Recruitment booths were set up in front of the Fifth Avenue library and in Times Square, with tractors and hay wagons parked at the curb.[1] The WLA in Maryland and the District of Columbia held a spring pep rally in the Department of the Interior's auditorium, where farmers and farmerettes together enjoyed a special "soil tillers" entertainment show. "Returning soldiers show little desire to go 'back to the soil,'" the farmers were told.[2] They already knew.

The farmers no longer needed any convincing. They'd seen with their own eyes what farmerettes could do, and those who still balked were beyond persuasion. The farmerette's reputation was sterling and secure, but the WLA's piggy bank was nearly empty. This season called for some creative austerity measures.

For starters, the WLA manufactured and sold a less expensive version of the official national uniform (only $4.30), and the Gorham-designed bronze insignia pin was offered as a separate fashion accessory ($2.50). Nonetheless, many state divisions ignored the national uniform or reused their 1918 costumes while many field units eliminated the uniform requirement altogether. The national office in New York was left with a pile of unsold stock.

That most compelling advertisement for the WLA, Herbert Paus's recruitment poster of a farmerette triumvirate bearing the flag and fighting the famine, was not reprinted in a new edition but simply dusted off and pasted over. The WLA treasury didn't have the money to print a new edition of the poster, but posters would surely be needed again for the spring recruitment and fund-raising drives. Like a good Hoover helper, the WLA figured out how to use the leftovers. By printing strips of paper with new slogans and pasting them over the outdated posters' "win the war" appeal, the posters could be easily used again.[3] Recycling the poster—saving the essential image while updating the message—was a clever and thrifty strategy and epitomized the WLA's revised yet familiar role in peacetime. But in hindsight, it was also a melancholy metaphor for how the WLA was forced to adapt to its reduced circumstances.

Free, or at least cheap, publicity was the byword. The Finance Committee engaged in negotiations to sell the Land Army moving picture to a commercial film distribution company "in order to get wider circulation without cost to the Land Army." Three thousand copies of Edith Diehl's final report on the Wellesley Camp, nearly a hundred pages long, were printed and distributed to a list of influential people, and Wellesley College underwrote the production costs.[4] The frugal publicity efforts were remarkably effective. Thousands of farmerettes signed up for agricultural deployment during the 1919 growing season—five thousand registered in New York State alone—though the WLA actually placed many fewer—probably between two thousand and twenty-five hundred—women in official units.

By the first of May, Ida Ogilvie and Delia West Marble opened their Bedford Camp for a third year and expected a very busy season. "We believe we will find ourselves called for help everywhere by midsummer," Marble predicted. Farmers in Pennsylvania, California, Colorado, Maryland, New Jersey, Vermont, New Hampshire, and Colorado again asked for farmerettes. Ohio's WLA raised $1,000 to sponsor special, short Land Army training courses for women at the state university, and WLA demonstration units were planned.[5] In Missouri, a unit of farmerettes was organized under the auspices of the Kansas City Gardens Association. The Oregon WLA issued a call to women to help save the fruit crops there, but other states were more reluctant. The Connecticut WLA wasn't sure it wanted to place women in the field again, as the tobacco farmers' pleas did not resonate with patriotism, only profit-taking, this year. There was no demand for farmerettes in Wisconsin "since the return of so many of our soldiers," reported the state chairwoman. "Maybe Wisconsin will need some camps in the future, but not this year."[6] Nor did the WLA have any demand in Delaware. In Michigan the WLA reported that "the labor shortage is severe, but the prejudice of Michigan farmers against employment of women is not yet overcome."[7]

But like a wind-blown seed, the Land Army now sprouted in places it had not managed to reach or take root in last year. Several hundred North Carolina women registered for Land Army work, and the national WLA suggested that its Virginia division organize "colored" women into their own WLA unit.[8] South Dakota began forming groups of women for potato picking and organizing women fruit pickers as Land Army workers. The Minnesota state agricultural college showed great interest in the Land Army and formed two trial farmerette units, and in Florida a demonstration unit in got under way. In Iowa the state director was attempting to place a demonstration unit in the western part of the state while groups of girls were organized to do light farmwork in the vicinity of Des Moines.

Yet the call for women workers made by a few Nebraskan farmers perhaps gratified the WLA most, providing sweet satisfaction in the state where even the Women's Committee had scorned the Land Army just the year before. The farmers of the upper midwestern states addressed their requests for farmerettes to the nearest U.S. Employment Service office, which was located in Omaha. The service then matched their requests with available female applicants, whom the WLA vetted. The Nebraska WLA director died suddenly in early spring, but with the Land Army's entrance into the plains region considered so important, the WLA's federal director, Dorothy Hubert, took over the state's organizational duties. She made several trips to Omaha herself and interviewed prospective farmerettes.

The Nebraskan venture got off to a shaky start when the first WLA unit was mustered for a farmer in Brownlee, only to have the farmer get cold feet on the eve of the farmerettes' arrival. "With nine farmerettes, the advance guard of Nebraska's women's land army, all dressed up in overalls and things and ready to go to work, the Brownlee farmer who asked for them has developed sudden coyness," an Omaha newspaper reported.[9] Once the Brownlee farmer reneged on the employment deal, the unit had to be disbanded and the farmerettes reassigned. The WLA organizers were disappointed but not deterred. "Once down is no battle, and we are continuing the work of the Land Army in Nebraska," they insisted.[10]

Other farmers in the region began requesting Land Army workers. J. D. Richards of Martin, South Dakota, wrote,

> I have a farm & cattle Ranch & can hire 3 women providing they can
> handle teams and do ordinary farm and ranch work. They must be healthy
> & fairly strong & not afraid of Indians. I live on Pine Ridge indian reserva-
> tion. I would not order them up here without seeing them & explaining
> what they will be up against when they come. Write me & I will come
> down. We have to begin haying & there is no men except I.W.W. [Industrial
> Workers of the World].[11]

Farmer Richards was asked to supply the names of two people who would vouch for him and to state the wages he was willing to pay the farmerettes.[12] Under the rules of the new *Handbook of Standards,* the WLA advocated a two-tier wage system, with women who were experienced or had gone through approved WLA training able to earn pay equal to the prevailing male wages, while novice farmerettes earned less. The eight-hour day was still the ideal, but a day of diversified work could stretch to ten hours if need be. Wages in the Nebraska region were quite good, often as much as $60 to $70 a month, with room and board included.[13] Some workers were offered the option of doing

housework for the farmwife and earning an additional $10 a week, but the WLA dis-
couraged this practice.

In the western states' wide-open spaces, the WLA had to be more flexible about the
unit system, for units were not as practical there. The WLA agreed to place small sets of
women workers directly under the farm family's care, if both employers and employees
could be checked carefully and monitored. Placing single farmerettes was frowned upon
and only tolerated if a woman was present in the farm family.

The Omaha office received queries from would-be farmerettes bearing postmarks
from places as close as Kansas City, Missouri, and Pacific Junction, Iowa, and as far
away as Pittsburgh, New York City, and New Hampshire.

> Sirs! I have been reading in the *Boston Globe* about women going to work in
> the wheat fields and I thought I would like to come out there and work. I
> can do all kinds of farm work. Can drive team any where in any place and
> like it. Am an American woman 34 years old. Am healthy and strong weight
> about 140. Never have headaches or backaches in my life. I should love to
> come out there to work. . . .—Mrs. May Kemp, Wilton, New Hampshire
>
> p.s. I have a little boy 2 years of age is there any place there where I could
> board him or is there any chance of my having him with me.[14]

The largest WLA contingent in Nebraska was placed on a thousand-acre corn and
grain ranch in Chadron, Dawes County, where Marcus J. Cain employed between five
and eight women workers. The WLA headquarters sent to Chadron three New York
City women, all farmerette veterans, and their adventures on a Great Plains ranch made
for amusing reading in the *The Farmerette*. They acquitted themselves quite well, and
Mr. Cain called for more women workers. Nebraska had finally come around.

With Edith Diehl holding the national director of training's baton, training
farmerettes became the WLA's primary focus in 1919. Training—providing the farmer
with skilled rather than casual labor while preparing women's bodies and minds for the
task—was the key to making the WLA into a permanent presence. Diehl approached
her training mission with characteristic zeal and precision. Just as bookbinding was a
craft, according to Diehl, farming was also a type of craft, and the craftsperson must be
properly trained in how to use the tools of the trade. So while Diehl negotiated for
training facilities to open in Virginia and New Jersey, she was also writing the lesson
plans for her practical ag schools. She tried out these lessons in a series of articles on
proper tool handling, written for *The Farmerette*:

> A girl does not need to know the scientific reason for using a hoe or spade in
> a certain way in order to be able to handle the tool correctly. After this way
> or knack is once learned, and the art of handling the tool is mastered, the

day's work will be finished with a clearer, happier mind and a much less fatigued body. There is a certain joy in tool handling to the master crafts-man, and every Land Army worker should aspire to master her craft.[15]

Diehl was able to put her curriculum into action when the "Woman's Cooperative Training Farm" in Leonardo, New Jersey, in the southern section of the state, opened in May 1919. Administered by the New Jersey WLA, the Leonardo Camp was established on the estate of Melvin A. Rice, the president of the state's Board of Education, who donated a large house and 225 acres of land for the training center. Repeated through-out the summer, the two-week training course taught the rudiments of agriculture, with a special emphasis on tool handling and machinery. The course was offered free of charge to women enrolling in the WLA—they had to pay only their $3.50 weekly board fee—and the graduating farmerettes were then placed in units. Fifteen students from the Trenton Normal School made up the first class at the Leonardo farm, which included an orchard, a small vineyard, a horse, and a cow named Pollyanna. Its large truck garden's produce would be sold to pay the training camp's expenses. Classes of about twenty women cycled through Leonardo's training regimen all through the sum-mer, and the farm was considered a great success.[16]

Not nearly so successful was the training camp at Charlottesville. Edith Diehl poured enormous energy into developing this national facility, which she intended would be the WLA's flagship academy, or an expanded successor to the Wellesley Camp. She convinced the University of Virginia to loan the military-style barracks that had housed the campus Student Army Training Corps during the war, along with an adjoining twenty-five acres of land, for the WLA camp's use.[17] Two courses were offered: a two-week "worker's course" in the "craft of farming" and with technical training in using tools and raising crops and a month long "short course in agriculture" designed espe-cially for schoolteachers who'd like to take up land work. Expert faculty from state agricultural colleges, a professional dietician, and a camp director were hired. Unlike the Wellesley or Leonardo training camps, there was a tuition and board fee at Charlottesville ($10 for the worker's course, $25 for the teacher's course), but its ac-commodations were deluxe, with electric lights and shower baths in the dormitories.[18] Edith Diehl expected six hundred students to enroll during the six semesters that sum-mer. Few came. In June, Diehl spent several weeks in the Virginia summer heat, trying to boost recruitment and save the camp, but by mid-July the Charlottesville camp had to be closed.[19]

If Miss Diehl was keenly disappointed by the Charlottesville Training Camp experi-ence, she was even more distressed by her inability to conduct her grand scientific experiment on the physiology of women's farmwork. Edith Diehl was not accustomed to failure. When she requested that Wellesley host a "Test Camp" where Diehl would personally supervise a special unit of women and gather experimental data on their work, Ellen Fitz Pendleton politely but flatly refused. President Pendleton expressed "real grief . . . not to cordially cooperate" with Diehl's appeal, but with the college facing a budget deficit, she could not provide the car and $500 in salary and expenses Diehl had requested. Pendleton could simply not go to her trustees again to find a WLA camp benefactor; she had to retain those wallets for campus concerns.[20]

Diehl responded that she would take her great experiment elsewhere. "It may be of interest to you to know that I have put my plan before Dr. Frederic S. Lee of the College of Physicians and Surgeons of New York (who has been making an investigation into the effects of war work on the women in Europe)," Diehl wrote to Pendleton. "He is entering into the project with me, and has offered me all the assistance I need for the physiological experiments and tests. Dr. Lee expresses the opinion that this investigation should prove of great scientific value, and has consented to act as my advisor throughout the investigation."[21]

Diehl did ask President Pendleton to save the Wellesley Camp's tents, tools, and equipment for her, as she hoped to establish her experiment elsewhere. Diehl also wrote to all the WLA state chairwomen, asking for their assistance in the scientific investigation:

> I am consulting scientific experts on the subject [of suitable farm work for
> women] and we shall need some careful records kept of the effect of all kinds
> of work on all kinds of workers. Will you . . . plan to have one or two of
> your best camps keep some sort of record to be sent in at the end of the
> season.[22]

Diehl was never able to form her experimental camp or pursue her scientific investigation. The study appears to have fizzled. Frustrated and still unable to draw any salary from the Department of Labor, Edith Diehl took a leave of absence from her post as director of training in July and never returned to the Woman's Land Army.[23]

California entered the season with a flourish, on the coattails of Ida Ogilvie's and Delia Marble's spirited recruitment tour. At the University of California in Berkeley, a training course for camp supervisors and unit leaders was planned, though it never got far off the ground. By mid-May forty women were picking and packing cherries at Farmington, under the auspices of the WLA's northern California division, and the Vacaville Camp opened again in June, with farmerettes working on eleven ranches in the vicinity. At Lodi, city trustees again granted permission to build a farmerette camp on municipal land. To cover the camp's $7,500 cost the Lodi growers went knocking on farm and ranch doors, imploring everyone to pay their fair share and warning that "no one will be given benefit of the Land Army labor unless he or she contributes to the support of the Land Army. The labor will absolutely not be given to those who refuse to aid the enterprise."[24]

The southern California WLA, for most purposes, had disbanded. Mexican male laborers were once again allowed to cross the border and work in the fields but without any of the wage, hour, or housing guarantees the WLA commanded. One unit of forty-five women was sent from Los Angeles to Hemet, where they were housed in the local grammar school and credited with helping save the apricot crop.

In the north, the late-season table and wine grape harvest promised to be large (though the wine from this grape crop would be the first vintage banned under Prohibition), and Alice Graydon Phillips, director of the Lodi Camp, promised the Lodi growers 150 farmerettes to handle the work. Recruiting farmerettes was becoming more difficult, Phillips found, as the allure of the Land Girl's life was beginning to pale. By mid-August the northern California WLA headquarters in San Francisco began "street recruiting" on the city's sidewalks. Miss Phillips, along with two tanned and experienced farmerettes wearing blue baggy jumpers and work boots, conducted "open-air recruiting," as the *San Francisco Examiner* described it, "endeavoring to induce their sisters to join them in land service work."[25]

The California farmerette strode into 1919 atop a vegetable-festooned float in the Rose Bowl Parade in January. By September, she was gone.[26]

The New York WLA had a bright beginning, too. April brought a Land Army "Field Day" in New York City. Farmerette veterans took to the streets, collecting coins in milk pails to help start the permanent rural community centers at the heart of the New York WLA's future plans. Nearly sixty farmerette camps were operating by late June, with forty units in Ulster County alone. Four training camps got under way—one for Land Army supervisors on the grounds of the Chautauqua Institution in the western section and others at Sterlington, in Rockland County, and in Schuyler Falls in Clinton County—in addition to the venerable Bedford Camp.[27]

The maddening problem for New York—almost the mirror image of California's situation—was that while five thousand women enrolled for farmwork and hundreds of farmers asked for their help, the WLA simply could not afford to organize or equip enough unit camps to meet the demand. Unlike California farmers, the New York farm owners would not contribute toward the camps. The numbers for July tell the tale: while 1,123 women registered for farmwork and the state's farmers asked for almost 1,600 workers, the WLA managed to place only 789 of those registered women in units, with another 170 working outside of units. "This is just half the number that the farmers have asked for," explained the New York division in its monthly bulletin, "but owing to our need of funds it has been impossible for us to meet the demands made upon us."[28]

In late July, New York governor Alfred E. Smith (who had defeated Charles Whitman in the 1918 election) proclaimed a "Governor's Day" on behalf of the New York WLA. He visited twenty-six Land Army camps, reviewing seven hundred farmerettes, and addressed a gathering of two thousand farmers, Land Army workers, and dignitaries in Ulster County. "The Land Army performed a splendid service to the Country in time of War and if we cannot profit by what we learned during time of War, then our efforts were very largely wasted," Smith said to the crowd. "But America is going to profit because America is composed of people who recognize the value of these new movements."

Responding to the WLA's desperate cries for financial support, Governor Smith also pledged his assistance: "I am willing and glad to promise to do anything in my power to help and encourage the Land Army. I, personally, do not see why the funds provided for Agriculture in this State should not be expended in part in supporting this movement."[29] Nothing, however, came of the governor's pledge.

By mid summer, the entire Woman's Land Army was falling apart. At the end of June, Congress again refused to reinstate funding for the U.S. Employment Service. As the new fiscal year dawned on July 1, the service, though not officially dead, became a bureaucratic ghost without substance or power. All hope of the Land Army achieving financial or organizational security within the federal government was lost. The affiliation seemed like a cruel joke now. Worse, it placed the WLA in an untenable situation.

"The unfortunate fate of the U.S. Employment Service cut off all hopes of an appropriation," a frustrated Mabel Eichel, the New York WLA director, wrote to her colleagues, "but the affiliation still remains and that affiliation commits us to the placing of all Units of women . . . the farmers have expected us to do this and we failed."[30]

The WLA women of New Jersey also found themselves stranded in midstream. During the last week of June, Josephine Perry Morgan wrote her final set of funding appeals on the Land Army's behalf, and even her smooth and practiced tone betrayed a touch of panic. She inquired whether the disbanded state Women's Committee might have an extra $500 or $600 left in its treasury to donate to the Land Army.[31] She wrote a more agitated note to the New Jersey State labor commissioner, demanding that he make good on the state's pledge of $1,000 toward supporting the New Jersey WLA camps. She reminded him that only half of that pledge had been paid, and the WLA needed the additional $500 quickly. "The farmers are asking us to provide women workers again this year, and the demand is becoming urgent," Mrs. Morgan told Commissioner Lewis Bryant. "Tents, cots and chairs are needed immediately for units now operating, but which are handicapped by this lack of equipment."[32]

No checks came in the mail. By the first week of July the New Jersey WLA officers came to a bitter decision: they felt they had no choice but to close down. Notice of an emergency meeting was mailed to all members. On July 11 the New Jersey division was to gather at the Colony Club in Manhattan "for the final settlement of affairs, and the placing of responsibility for the units already operating."[33]

Considering the financial and social pressures bearing down on the Land Army in the 1919 season, it is impressive that the WLA was able to operate in so many states, albeit on a small scale. Missouri boasted one unit of twelve farmerettes working in Parkville, Platte County. Vermont kept seven official Land Army workers busy, including Mildred Buller Smith and Elizabeth Clarke, but not counting "unofficial" farmerette Alice Holway working in Putney. Rhode Island had a WLA unit working at a peach orchard while Oregon and Washington used farmerettes in their apple orchards. North Carolina hosted two WLA units. One was called into a flooded tobacco region and, working in water ten inches deep, helped rescue the tobacco crop. The other Carolina unit at Valle Crucis did everything from road building to field and orchard work, and its success "has made many friends for the Land Army among the natives," according to a WLA Progress Report.[34] *The Farmerette* described the unit's achievement more pungently: "Their results were an eye-opener to the mountaineers, who called the Farmerettes 'boys' but were doubtful of the propriety of swearing before them!"[35]

Though there were no WLA units working in Massachusetts—disappointing the Smith College students who'd signed up in the spring to become farmerettes[36]—the New England branch of the WNF&GA teamed with the Massachusetts Agricultural College to operate a training station on Sagamore Farm in Ipswich. There women received instruction in all phases of practical farmwork, including farm accounting, and earned college credit for the course.[37] The training camp at Mary Schofield's farm in Peterborough, New Hampshire, graduated twenty-seven women from its worker's and supervisor's courses, and three other WLA units provided farmerettes to New Hampshire farms.

Pennsylvania employed about 125 farmerettes in six units, including a training camp at Wynnewood run by the National League for Women's Service. In addition to the Leonardo Training Farm, New Jersey had 75 WLA women working in seven units around the state.[38] And Maryland's WLA farm tapped government workers, who transformed themselves into farmerettes after office hours, to cultivate a ten-acre plot and provide produce to Red Cross and YWCA cafeterias.

It was a striking and even poignant irony that as the Woman's Land Army was faltering, it was invited to participate in the U.S. government's official July Fourth celebrations in Washington, D.C. As part of the "Call of the Land" pageant, held on the grounds of the Department of Agriculture, farmerettes performed in several tableaux. In one pose a uniformed farmerette on horseback carried an American flag while two others at her side hoisted harvest baskets in a living re-creation of the famous WLA recruitment poster.[39]

Despite many accomplishments in the field, the WLA was disintegrating at the national level. At the July 7 board meeting, the first since the Employment Service's collapse, the atmosphere was somber but still resolute. Federal Director Dorothy Hubert, no longer pretending she had any federal role to play, requested an unpaid leave of absence. Olga Ihlseng, whose federal appointment as field secretary was "recalled on account of the necessary retrenchment in the Employment Service," was hired onto the staff of the private WLA organization.[40]

Though the roof seemed to be caving in, the board methodically went about its business. Reports were read and filed, positions filled, and new state chairwomen and zonal directors named. Even when the New Jersey delegation stood up and announced that "owing to their inability to raise funds to cover their administrative expenses" they were closing their headquarters, the board managed to move on to the next item of business—assigning a new member to the committee writing a scenario for the Land Army Motion Picture Film.[41]

That summer Mabel Eichel wrote plaintively of the New York WLA's predicament:

> We have bravely tried to carry on our work with little or no funds, hoping
> against hope that some of the big minded men and women of this State who
> realize the seriousness of the food situation would step forward and give us
> financial assistance until such time as the State or the farmer might take over
> the support of the work. (Very few of such people have been found and
> those who have contributed have contributed in no way the sums that they
> have to other organizations.)[42]

The wealthy women who had so generously subsidized the WLA in the past had already turned their attentions elsewhere. The jubilant suffragists who'd supported the WLA as an auxiliary enterprise to their cause now concentrated on securing their ultimate prize. On June 4 the U.S. Senate had finally joined the House in passing the Nineteenth Amendment, and the suffrage campaign moved back to the states for the ratification fight. In this final push, every suffragist in the nation was mobilized to lobby her state legislature during the next several months, leaving no time or money for the Land Army.

By the end of July the writing was on the wall, and on August 5, 1919, the WLA National Board meeting took on the emotional trappings of a funeral. Several of the WLA's founders were present, the women who'd been midwives to the birth of the farmerette and raised her through the war—Delia West Marble, Ida Ogilvie, and Emma Winner Rogers—as well as the doting aunts who had helped nurture the "girl with a hoe," such as Mabel Potter Lewis, Grace Schenck, Mary Schofield, and Marion Davison. Margaretta Neale from the U.S. Employment Service also attended, out of respect and sadness for a lost opportunity. They gathered in the elegant Manhattan apartment of Juliet Morgan Hamilton and prepared the way for a dignified end.[43]

But the women determined that while the Woman's Land Army, Inc., might have to come to an untimely demise, the *idea* of a Woman's Land Army, the noble and practical essence of it, need not die and should not die. "It was the sense of the meeting that the

Woman's Land Army, having worked originally to increase food supply at the request of the government was now faced with a new aspect, that of supplying women with a new means of livelihood, for its work."[44] Reaching back to its roots, the WLA Board deputized a committee to consult with its original partners—the YWCA, Garden Club of America, and Woman's National Farm and Garden Association—"as to the best means of perpetuating the Land Army idea." And in a last burst of optimism, or perhaps self-delusion, a delegation of three was appointed to go to Washington and confer with representatives of the Department of Agriculture and the secretary of labor about "the continuation of the National Land Army, placing before them the impossibility of private financial support."[45]

In the last days of August, the U.S. government's official reply arrived in the WLA's mailbox—a pair of letters addressed to WLA president Mary Schofield. The first note, signed by Secretary of Labor William Wilson, was a perfunctory two sentences of thanks and farewell. The second letter, more personal in tone, came from John Densmore of the Employment Service. Expressing remorse for the bureau's promises of financial support for the WLA that it could not deliver, he conveyed his admiration for the Land Army, which despite this lack of support, "worked as steadily during the summer of peace as it did during the time of war." In his note, Densmore offered the WLA the kind of honest recognition the federal government had taken such pains to repress:

> The work done by the Woman's Land Army has not only been valuable in
> increasing the food supply when that was one of the most important
> questions before this country, but it has also demonstrated that women are
> able to do almost any kind of agricultural work and are specially fitted for
> certain branches of it. I therefore feel that your work has not only helped us
> in our need but has added to our knowledge and has opened a new means of
> livelihood for women.[46]

Densmore's kind words gladdened the hearts of the glum WLA leaders and in a small way fortified them for the disagreeable business of settling affairs. Things were in a bit of a mess. Though most of the units in the field kept going through August, some had to close early as salaries for supervisors, usually paid by the state divisions, dried up. Other smoothly running and happily self-contained units probably didn't even know that the larger organization was collapsing as its situation did not affect them yet.

At the beginning of September five hundred farmerettes still worked in twenty-seven units in New York. Mrs. Eichel had not yet closed her doors, keeping the state office functioning on borrowed money, hope, and adrenaline. In late August her New York State WLA launched yet another (increasingly desperate) fund-raising and recruitment campaign that featured farmerettes "in their working costumes, driving through the cities in truck loads, making cart-tail speeches in the interest of the work,"

as the *New York Times* reported. The organization also mounted a WLA benefit show
and rally at the New Amsterdam Opera House in Manhattan.[47]

Meanwhile, Pennsylvania was calling for more women to help with the fall harvest
to replace the teachers and students who had returned to school. North Carolina was
sending out additional farmerettes to help with the September apple picking. Olga
Ihlseng had her hands full when she assumed the oversight responsibilities for all the
New Jersey units. About three dozen women in five units worked through August, but
by the beginning of September the unit supervisors were shutting down their camps
and either storing the furniture and equipment or selling them to pay off bills. The
Richfield unit, in cooperation with the local Grange, put on a farmerette show and
gave its $45 share of the proceeds to the defunct but still indebted New Jersey WLA
treasury.[48]

The National Board of the WLA, in its final regular meeting on September 9, also
had to contend with financial unpleasantries. The board was liable for outstanding bills
and loan obligations amounting to a bit more than $6,000, and needed to make a plan
to meet these debts. Juliet Morgan Hamilton, who was comfortable handling large
sums of money and also knew where to find it, was asked to "go into the question of
finances," accompanied by Emma Winner Rogers, the capable and seasoned treasurer
of the National American Woman's Suffrage Association. To shrink the size of the financial hole in which the WLA found itself, Board Member Harriet Barnes Pratt offered to forgive the $2,600 in loans she had extended to the Land Army. Mrs. Pratt's
generous gift was met with "a rising vote of thanks" by her colleagues.[49] Other board
members rose to the occasion, too, agreeing to advance the money to pay the Kenilworth
Manufacturing Company's bill for the uniforms that had been ordered and delivered
but now were distinctly out of style. Finally, sadly, a motion was made, and seconded,
to hold a special meeting of the National Board of the Woman's Land Army on September 26. At that time, the members would vote on a proposal for the corporation's voluntary dissolution. The motion was carried.[50]

When the Women's Land Army of Great Britain was demobilized in the fall of
1919, a festive farewell ceremony in the opulent Old Drapers' Hall in London marked
the occasion. As the *Times of London* reported, an honor guard of 250 Land Lassies in
full uniform, "gallant-looking in their white overalls, their corduroy breeches, their
high boots, and their gay little felt hats," greeted Princess Mary and Lord Lee, president
of the Board of Agriculture, along with scores of other dignitaries who paid tribute to
the Land Girls' war service. Princess Mary presented Distinguished Service Bar awards
to fifty-five Land Girls who'd "performed deeds of quiet valour" in their land duty.
Then the Princess and Land Girls together sat down to "a gorgeous supper such as a
debutante at her first ball enjoys." A concert followed, where Land Army girls sang and

others performed country dances to the accompaniment of a Land Lassie playing the mouth organ. The festivities closed to the sound of hundreds of "crackers," those favorite British paper noisemakers, popping in boisterous celebration.[51]

The formal ceremony marking the end the Woman's Land Army of America took place quietly on Friday morning, September 26, in Mrs. Hamilton's apartment, when the proposal to dissolve the Woman's Land Army, Inc., was voted and approved. There were no farmerettes present, no ceremonies, no dignitaries, no honors. The WLA's official end, its legal demise, was equally subdued. It took place in New York State Supreme Court Judge M. Warley Platzek's chambers on February 2, 1920, when he signed the petition to dissolve the WLA Corporation. There was no fanfare, just a small notice in the newspapers.[53]

But the farmerette ideal was not dead. Even as the last rites for the national WLA were being administered in September, the Pennsylvania division was arranging for its own survival by bailing out of the national organization and clambering onto a life raft. "In regard to the future of the Land Army for Pennsylvania . . . As I see it, there is no future for us because of the expense," Virginia McComb, executive secretary of the Pennsylvania WLA, wrote to the division's treasurer Mabel Potter Lewis on September 22, 1919, "unless we can affiliate with or be merged into some other organization."[54]

Mabel Lewis thought merging with the National League for Women's Service would be a good fit. McComb, however, urged a partnership with the League of Women Workers, which already ran the Land Army camp at Whitford Lodge and was concerned with the welfare of working girls. This "self-supporting, non-sectarian, self-governing club was the one," explained McComb. "I have been trying to influence them to want us to affiliate and they need little urging, for they see the real thing in this Land Army work and want to keep it alive."[55]

"There seems now to be a prospect of a very happy adjustment for the Land Army girls in conjunction with the League," wrote Pennsylvania WLA chairwoman Edith Ellicot Smith to the state's farmerettes. "If we join with them as they request, we feel sure something worth while for the Land Army work will develop."[56]

After brief negotiations, the League of Women Workers of Pennsylvania extended an invitation to the Land Army to move in and become part of the League. It offered the Land Army a place on the League's executive board and an office in its building. The Pennsylvania Land Army agreed on October 17 and guaranteed to provide a $5,000 budget for its own work in the coming year. The Girls' Land Army Club, the Pennsylvania farmerettes' alumnae organization, voted to join the Girls' City Club of the League, "thus affiliating in the closest possible way the Land Army and League Girls."[57]

By February 1920, just as the judge was signing the legal forms to dissolve the Woman's Land Army of America, Inc., the first press announcements and advertisements

for the Land Army Committee of the League for Women Workers appeared in Philadelphia. "Do you want to become a producer rather than be a consumer only, during
this trying reconstruction period after the war?" asked the Land Army recruitment
brochure, aimed specifically at teachers and women office and factory workers on vacation. "The Land Army offers women the opportunity for community life in camps and
farm houses, under proper supervision . . . but with the greatest possible freedom from
restraint of any kind. . . . Try it a Summer and see for yourself."[58]

The Farmerette kept publishing, too. An "Honorable Discharge" issue appeared in
December 1919 (where the official Gorham-cast WLA insignia belt buckles, hat orna-
ments, and buttons were offered for clearance sale at deep discount) and a final issue in
May 1920. This last issue celebrated the indomitable spirit and occupational opportunities still open to the farmerette. It urged women to return to the fields in 1920—"Fall
In, Farmerettes, Fall In"—and told them where Land Army units were continuing au-
tonomously and where to apply for jobs or agricultural college scholarships. "Wherever
Land Army Units have worked there is an opportunity for a group of girls with energy
and initiative to get in touch with the farmers and form a Unit of their own," the
encouraging editors wrote.[59] To prove the point, Ida Ogilvie and Delia Marble continued to operate their own farm, employing only women workers, for more than thirty
years, keeping the Land Army's spirit alive.

The rebirth of the Pennsylvania WLA was a point of pride and optimism for the
movement, and *The Farmerette* also announced the reorganization of the New York
WLA veterans into a group called the Land Workers of America (LWA). (The British
WLA's veterans formed the National Association of Landswomen and continued their
Landswomen publication as an alumnae journal, under the auspices of the Women's
Institute.)

"The L.W.A. is an organization of WORKERS. Its purpose is to carry on and de-
velop the work and opportunities for women opened up by the Land Army," *The
Farmerette* announced. The Land Workers of America's honorary president was Ida
Ogilvie, and the group set its membership dues at a dollar a year, which included a
subscription to *The Farmerette.*[60] But there is no record of any subsequent issues of *The
Farmerette* or of any Land Workers of America activities.

In the spring of 1920, Monica Barry Walsh single-handedly tried to revive the
Woman's Land Army when she created the American Land Service. Miss Walsh, who'd
served as a field organizer for the New York State WLA in 1919, believed that the
concept of city residents helping the farmer was still sound and valuable. With the war
over, patriotism didn't enter into the equation, but she hoped to enlist workers from the
large pool of unemployed women and ex-servicemen eager to work and planned for a
coed "American Land Army."

In March 1920 Walsh leased an entire floor in the Lexington Theatre building in

Manhattan as a recruiting headquarters. Within weeks she had sent out press releases claiming that more than 1,200 young men and women had already volunteered to do farmwork and that farmers were already demanding 8,000 workers.[61] By late summer Walsh claimed that the American Land Service had sent 18,400 workers to farms in the northeast and mid-Atlantic states, as well as to the wheat fields of the west. Walsh said she had several camps in operation, though she did not specify their locations, and she appealed for public donations to continue the American Land Service's important work.[62]

Monica Walsh was a promoter, perhaps a well-meaning one, but she was more skilled in public relations than in public administration and better at generating hype than at providing real help. While newspapers eagerly printed her claims, no reporter seems to have ever found or visited an American Land Service camp. When Walsh applied for a grant from the Commonwealth Fund, her embroidered claims for the American Land Service came unraveled. "The project was the personal undertaking of Miss Walsh, a prepossessing young woman, apparently of some means, who was endeavoring to pick up the threads of the defunct 'Women's Land Army,' a war time organization," wrote Gertrude Springer of the Bureau of Advice and Information while conducting an evaluation for the Commonwealth Fund. "Miss Walsh frankly admitted that she had no real organization behind her. . . . As a matter of fact the American Land Service is Miss Walsh herself, and a few earnest, somewhat breathless young women volunteers," Springer advised the fund, calling Walsh's efforts "wildly directed" and "entirely beyond her depth."[63] The Commonwealth Fund did not support the American Land Service, yet Walsh was still trying to recruit thirty more women to fill places in two American Land Service farm camps in June 1922.[64]

In 1921, more than a year after the WLA disbanded, the *Woman Citizen*, journal of the League of Women Voters (the enfranchised successor of the National American Woman Suffrage Association) carried an article headlined "Where Does the Land Army Go From Here?" "Many people think that the Woman's Land Army, which claimed public attention during the war . . . was the very first blush of women's interest in agriculture in this country, and was a mere flash in the pan which died down when the boys came home."

Not so, reported *Woman Citizen*, for the farmerette has just turned professional: "The Land Army recruited for an emergency has been largely demobilized as an untrained national guard for food production, but has settled down into a permanent factor in the agricultural development of the country."[65] Though the Land Army had disbanded, the Women's National Farm and Garden Association was using its scholarship program to send the former Land Army girl to agricultural college and placing her in well-paying jobs in nurseries, orchards, and farms, where demand for her services outstripped availability. The Land Army's unit concept was still the WNF&GA standard, but now the farmer himself privately financed the camp, which hosted small groups of eight to ten women workers living together, as on the Dimock Orchard in Vermont.

Though the Woman's Land Army no longer existed, for some time to come it lingered in the public mind, and the farmerette continued to tickle the American imagination. In late 1919, the farmerette still appeared larger than life on the silver screen, with starlet Vivian Martin playing the sartorially splendid and silly farmerette heroine in *Little Comrade*, the movie adaptation of a short story that had appeared in *McCall's* magazine.[66] Another two-reel comedy called *The Farmerette* was released later that year, and untold vaudeville routines used the farmerette for laughs.

A uniformed farmerette who sang to her vegetables starred in a children's musical play, *The Farmerette,* composed by Claire Chapman in 1921.[67] Two years later, she was the subject, or target, of "a modern opéra bouffe" called *The Farmerettes*, which was written by a promising young American composer named John Laurence Seymour; his later creations premiered at the Metropolitan Opera House in New York.[68] And the popular songwriter Jesse Greer immortalized the farmerette in a boogie-woogie piano duet.

The Land Army's impact had a few weird ripple effects, too. In August 1920 the *Los Angeles Times* reported that the Crown Prince of Siam was sending a personal emissary to an American tractor show to buy thirty tractors for the Siamese woman's land army. "Three-fourths of the agricultural workers in Siam are women, and they have recently formed an organization similar to the women's land armies of the United States during the war, for the purpose of bettering Siamese agriculture," the *Los Angeles Times* explained, quoting the prince's emissary. "The Siamese heir-apparent, who is greatly interested in agriculture, is anxious to equip the Siamese woman's land army with the latest agricultural machinery."

"There are few tractors in that oriental country," the newspaper went on to say, "but the few that are there are greatly appreciated by the women, who propose to drive the iron steeds themselves."[69]

Later, Professor Ethel Puffer Howes piloted the concept of the Land Army into a new realm. In a pair of controversial essays published in *The Atlantic Monthly* in 1922, Howes denounced the choice that educated women were forced to make between family life and a career and their lack of support as they tried to balance these competing demands. Howes's novel solution was to adopt a version of the Land Army unit to bring domestic services to the beleaguered working mother and to protect the household worker from exploitation and elevate her status. Units of skilled household workers could live together in comfortable, self-sustaining units, offering cooking, laundry, housework, and child care services to busy career women in their area. Howes studied this and other innovative ideas in her Institute for the Coordination of Women's Interests, which she established as a graduate department at Smith College in 1925. Howes's working-woman think tank was undoubtedly too far ahead of its time, and funding difficulties forced its closure after six years. Nevertheless, Howes insisted that the social and economic "inventions" of the Land Army experience were applicable to other challenges facing the twentieth-century American working woman.[70]

By the time the Roaring Twenties were in full swing, the image of the picturesque farmerette had faded and was replaced by the striking form of the flapper, the young woman who dressed provocatively, smoked, drank, flouted convention, and threw off her corsets. Maud Muller succumbed to the Jazz Age. Women who took on seasonal farmwork were still referred to as "farmerettes" in news reports, and the farmerette continued to make occasional appearances in plays and cartoons, but for the most part the girl with a hoe became a hazy memory from the Great War.[71]

But then came another world war. Even before the Japanese attack on Pearl Harbor pushed America into World War II, farmers reported a dangerous shortage of available farm labor. Again, farmhands were attracted to lucrative war industry jobs, and again the specter of food shortages cast frightening shadows.

Once more, the Woman's National Farm and Garden Association saw the approaching threat and acted. In the spring of 1940, a year and a half before America's entry into the war, the WNF&GA began pushing for the revival of the Woman's Land Army of America. In Britain, already at war, a new generation of Land Army Lassies had been toiling in the fields for a year.[72]

First Lady Eleanor Roosevelt also began beating the drum to muster an American Woman's Land Army early in 1941, well before her husband, President Franklin Roosevelt, brought America into the war. She was keeping a close eye on Britain's war mobilization efforts and was particularly taken by its Land Army's accomplishments. "The United States, without a doubt, will need a Woman's Land Army," Mrs. Roosevelt told reporters at one of her weekly press conferences.[73] As assistant director of volunteer service for the Office of Civilian Defense (OCD), Mrs. Roosevelt unilaterally announced in November 1941, just before Pearl Harbor, that her department of the OCD would begin recruiting women to come to the aid of the crops.[74]

In early spring 1942, with universal military conscription under way and with more than two million men having already left agricultural jobs in just the past two years, Americans nervously asked how they could meet such a farm labor deficit. The New York State Assembly passed a bill excusing schoolchildren from school to work in the fields, Kentucky paroled its petty offense prisoners to work on farms, and Maryland dug up its old World War I "work or fight" statute to force "idlers" into farmwork.[75] All the while, the Office of War Information (akin to the Committee on Public Information) was waving the banner "Food Fights for Freedom" to rally the farmer to increased production. The possibility of raising a new Woman's Land Army began being discussed in earnest.

"With crops growing green and men busy with war, the farmerette may come back," *Time* magazine reported in April 1942. "If the U.S. [is] to feed the world, it must have a Land Army."[76]

Secretary of Agriculture Claude Wickard, however, remained firmly opposed to the idea. And American farmers, following in their fathers' footsteps, expressed great reluctance. "That's the silliest thing I ever heard of," exclaimed R. H. Vawter of the Kansas State Board of Agriculture when he heard about the American Women's Voluntary Services' intention to organize a Woman's Land Army. "Our wives would run them off the farms, even if the girls were so foolish as to consent to come."[77]

Nevertheless, in the spring of 1942 women's land armies began springing up spontaneously around the country. Women had learned how to organize themselves in the last war. Corinne Alsop, working with the University of Connecticut, created a Connecticut Land Army for her state while Hunter College students in New York City formed their own Volunteer Land Army. Dorothy Thompson, the popular syndicated columnist, became a cheerleader for the cause and herself organized a Volunteer Land Corps of twelve hundred young city women and men to work on New England farms.[78] In California the American Women's Voluntary Services placed a thousand women on farms to help save the fruit crops, and the YWCA also recruited its members to serve on the land. Henry Noble MacCracken, still the president of Vassar, sent his students out again to work on local farms.[79] Hilda Loines took charge of schoolchildren's Victory Gardens near her house in Lake George, New York. And Ida Ogilvie and Delia West Marble, who employed only women on their 680-acre dairy farm, helped rally a new generation to land service.[80]

Eleanor Roosevelt, the Land Army's most influential and tenacious champion, used her nationwide radio addresses to advocate for an American Woman's Land Army, pointing to the crucial role the WLA played in Britain and describing her recent tour of their camps.[81] Secretary of Agriculture Wickard, just as his predecessor David Houston during the last war, still would not authorize the government's formation of a Land Army of women. Even when, in the fall of 1942 (probably at Eleanor's prompting) President Roosevelt personally urged Wickard to consider using women to meet the farm labor emergency, Wickard resisted. Once senior USDA officials began making their own plans for a Land Army of women without his approval, Wickard was forced to acquiesce.[82]

Finally, in April 1943, the War Food Administration of the Department of Agriculture announced the formation of a Women's Land Army as a branch of the U.S. Crop Corps, which was already recruiting city men and student volunteers for emergency farmwork.[83] Almost immediately, Eleanor Roosevelt invited the newly appointed head of the WLA, home economist Florence Hall, to a White House press conference to unveil the new Land Army uniform for reporters.[84] The *Christian Science Monitor* ran a touching photograph of two generations of a farmerette family: a mother wearing her breeches and puttees and belted smock uniform from her days in the WLA of World War I and her daughter in the one-piece denim coverall, no longer such shocking attire, of the Women's Land Army of World War II.[85]

NOTES

CHAPTER 1: THE RIGHT TO SERVE

1. "The Women's March," *Times of London*, July 8, 1915.
2. Carol Twinch, *Women on the Land: Their Story During Two World Wars* (Cambridge, UK: Letterworth Press, 1990), p. 5.
3. "Great Procession of Women," *Times of London*, July 17, 1915, p. 3.
4. "The Woman's Right-to-Serve Demonstration: A Great Procession," *Illustrated London News*, July 24, 1915.
5. "How We Marched," *Times of London*, July 19, 1915.
6. Ibid.
7. Ibid., p. 9.
8. "Service for Women," *Times of London*, July 9, 1915.
9. "The Woman's Right-to-Serve Demonstration."
10. Twinch, *Women on the Land*, p. 2.
11. Ibid., p. 3.
12. In 1916 the Women's International Agricultural and Horticultural Union changed its name to the shorter Women's Farm and Garden Union.
13. Mrs. Chamberlain, letter to *Manchester Guardian*, dated Spring 1915, in Press Clipping File, Women's Work in Agriculture in World War I, Imperial War Museum Archives, London.
14. Newspaper clipping, dated February 19, 1915, in Press Clipping File, Imperial War Museum.
15. Helen Fraser, *Women and War Work* (New York: G. Arnold Shaw, 1918).
16. *London Evening News*, May 1915, in Press Clipping File, Imperial War Museum.
17. *London Evening Standard*, June 12, 1915, in Press Clipping File, Imperial War Museum.
18. *London Observer*, October 3, 1915, in Press Clipping File, Imperial War Museum.
19. David Lloyd George, *War Memoirs* (Boston: Little, Brown & Company, 1933–37).
20. Twinch, *Women on the Land*, p. 8.
21. Ibid., p. 10.
22. Barbara McLaren, *Women of the War* (London: Hodder and Stoughton, 1917), p. 102.

CHAPTER 2: FEMALE PREPAREDNESS

1. "To Train Women for War," *Washington Post*, January 23, 1916, p. 14.

2. "200 Women Soldiers Give a Public Drill," *New York Times*, March 25, 1916, p. 8.

3. Ibid.

4. Ibid.

5. "Women Ask Defenses," *Washington Post*, November 14, 1915, p. 19.

6. "Women to Occupy Tented Camp Today," *New York Times*, May 1, 1916, p. 6.

7. "Wilson War Slogan," *Washington Post*, May 2, 1916, p. 1.

8. "She Cut Cost of Living," *Washington Post*, June 11, 1916, p. 20.

9. "Women Offer War Aid," *Washington Post*, June 23, 1916, p. 4.

10. "Thirty New York Debutantes . . . Begin Camp as Soldierettes," *Washington Post*, June 4, 1916, p. ES5.

11. Bessie Rowland James, *For God, for Country, for Home, the National League for Woman's Service: A Story of the First National Organization of American Women Mobilized for War Service* (New York: Putnam, 1920), p. 8; and Ida Clyde Clarke, *American Women in the World War* (New York: D. Appleton, 1918), chapter 10.

12. James, *For God, for Country, for Home*, p. 16.

13. "Women Organized to Aid in Defense," *New York Times*, February 4, 1917, p. 11.

14. Ibid.

15. "Women's War Union in Vanderbilt Home," *New York Times*, February 7, 1917, p. 8.

16. "Women's Patriotic Meeting," *Christian Science Monitor*, February 21, 1917, p. 9.

17. "Wants All Women Included in Census," *New York Times*, March 19, 1917, p. 16.

18. "Brooklyn Women Interested in Gardening to Take Part in Horticultural Conference," *Brooklyn Daily Eagle*, May 2, 1915.

19. "There Is No Fortune in Farming for Women. . . ," *New York Evening Sun*, April 8, 1916, in Hilda Loines File, Records of the WNF&GA, Box 13, Folder 112, Schlesinger Library, Radcliffe Institute, Harvard University.

20. Examples of Loines's correspondence with British colleagues are evident in various issues of the Women's Farm and Garden Union Leaflet, Reading Room, University of Cambridge Library, Cambridge, England.

21. Minutes of the Council Meeting, March 12, 1917, Records of the WNF&GA, B-4, Box 6, Folder 35, Schlesinger Library.

22. Letter of Louisa Y. King to WNF&GA Members, March 1917, Records of the WNF&GA, B-4, Box 6, Folder 35, Schlesinger Library.

23. "Call Women to Flag," *Washington Post*, March 11, 1917, p. 8.

CHAPTER 3: AN AGRICULTURAL ARMY

1. "Pushcarts Burned in Riots Over Food," *New York Times*, February 20, 1917.

2. "Food Riot in New York," *Washington Post*, February 20, 1917; "Food Rioters Begin Looting," *Washington Post*, February 24, 1917; and "Storm New York Market and Manhandle Police," *Washington Post*, February 22, 1917.

3. "Federal Food Bill," *Christian Science Monitor*, February 23, 1917.

4. "Riots in Philadelphia," *New York Times*, February 23, 1917; "Food Rioters Begin Looting;" and "Emerson Attributes Food Rise to Exports," *New York Times*, February 26, 1917.

5. "Federal Food Bill;" *Christian Science Monitor*, February 23, 1917; and "Feed America First," *New York Times*, February 23, 1917.

6. "Trail 3 Germans in a Food Plot," *New York Times*, March 4, 1917.

7. "House and Senate Debate Food Riots," *New York Times*, February 22, 1917.

8. "Bread and Bullets," *New York Times*, March 30, 1917.

9. Ibid.

10. "Prison and Contract Labor Suggested for Farms in War," *New York Times*, April 8, 1917.

11. "Appeals to Nation to Send Food Here," *New York Times*, February 20, 1917, p. 11.

12. "Canada Wants Farmers," *Christian Science Monitor*, March 3, 1917.

13. "Suggests War Honors for Army of Farmers," *New York Times*, April 6, 1917, p. 19.

14. H. R., "Urges Chance on Farms for Physically Unfit for War," letter to the editor, *Washington Post*, April 9, 1917.

15. "Prison and Contract Labor Suggested for Farms in War," *New York Times*, April 8, 1917, p. 21.

16. Ludwig Fraenkel, "To Bring Over Prisoners," letter to the editor, *New York Times*, April 22, 1917.

17. George Sylvester Viereck, "Here Is a Way: Agricultural Bureau for the Unemployed," text of leaflet, April 1917. General Records of the Department of Labor, Record Group 174, File 20/28, National Archives and Records Administration.

18. Record Group, Estill R. Myers to Secretary of Labor, May 4, 1917. General Records of the Department of Labor, 174, File 20/28, National Archives.

19. Though Viereck's agricultural employment plan went nowhere, he was investigated by the Department of Justice and attacked by angry mobs several times during the war. During World War II, Viereck was imprisoned as an alien agent for his pro-Nazi propaganda efforts in the United States.

20. "Farm Labor Corps Proposed by Lane," *New York Times*, April 19, 1917, p. 4.

21. "Forbid Distilling Grain, Says Colonel," *New York Times*, April 22, 1917, p. 16.

22. "An Army for Agriculture," *Wall Street Journal*, April 11, 1917, p. 1.

23. "President Discusses the Food Problem," *New York Times*, April 12, 1917.

24. "Lever Urges Draft of Men for Farms," *Washington Post*, April 12, 1917.

25. "Asks Mobilization of Force on Farms," *Washington Post*, April 12, 1917.

26. "Enlistment for Crop Producing Work Is Urged," *Christian Science Monitor*, April 14, 1917.

27. E. R. Bathrick, U.S. House of Representatives, to Hon. W. B. Wilson, Secretary of Labor, April 26, 1917, Department of Labor, Farm Labor 1917–1918, RG 174, File 20, National Archives.

28. "Exempt Farm Workers," *Washington Post*, April 13, 1917.

29. President Woodrow Wilson, "Do Your Bit for America" Proclamation, April 15, 1917, First World War.com, Primary Documents, 1917 (www.firstworldwar.com).

30. "Michigan Acts on Farm Labor Supply Needs," *Christian Science Monitor*, April 14, 1917, p. 9.

31. Ibid.

32. "Schoolboys May Solve the Farm Problem," *Christian Science Monitor*, April 28, 1917, p. 8.

33. "Whitman Issues Call to Farmers," *New York Times*, April 16, 1917.

34. "Release Labor to Farms," *New York Times*, April 18, 1917, p. 14.

35. "Employers Send Labor to Farms," *New York Times*, April 22, 1917.

36. "Calls City Workers to Help on Farms," *New York Times*, April 20, 1917.

37. "Sunday Farming Measure Signed," *Christian Science Monitor*, April 28, 1917, p. 8.

38. "Volunteers Scarce for Work on Farms," *New York Times*, May 5, 1917, p. 9.

39. "Preparing for Food Harvest . . . Back to the Farm," *New York Times*, May 6, 1917, p. 33.

CHAPTER 4: SUFFRAGE AGRICULTURE

1. "Keeping Up With the Plow," *Woman's Journal*, June 2, 1917, pp. 10–11.

2. Caroline Bartlett Crane sketch by Martha Lohrstorfer, Library Staff, Local History Room, Kalamazoo Public Library (www.kpl.gov/local-history/biographies/caroline-crane.aspx).

3. "Women to Aid U.S. in Crisis," *Kalamazoo Gazette*, April 15, 1917, Council of National Defense, Committee on Women's Defense Work, RG 62.5, National Archives.

4. William J. Breen, *Uncle Sam at Home: Civilian Mobilization, Wartime Federalism and the Council of National Defense, 1917–1919* (Westport, CT: Greenwood Press, 1984), p. 117.

5. Harriot Stanton Blatch to Dr. Shaw, May 8, 1917, Women's Committee, Council of National

Defense, Correspondence of Dr. Shaw, RG 62, National Archives.

6. "High School Girls to Plow," *New York Times,* April 22, 1917.

7. Training Course for Women brochure, Spring 1917, Papers of Mary Lyon Schofield, Peterborough Historical Society, Peterborough, NH.

8. "To Teach Women Plowing," *Christian Science Monitor,* June 13, 1917, p. 2.

9. The committee used the terms *chairman* and *chairmen.*

10. "Women's War Union in Vanderbilt Home," *New York Times,* February 7, 1917.

11. "Keeping Up With the Plow," *Woman's Journal.*

12. Ibid.

13. Ibid.

14. Ibid.

15. "Girl Farmers Drive in a Muddy Parade," *New York Times,* June 16, 1917, p. 6.

16. Ibid. A version of this verse is also in the Emma L. George Papers, Manuscript Division, Library of Congress, Washington, DC.

17. "Girl Farmers Drive in a Muddy Parade," *New York Times.*

18. Ibid.

CHAPTER 5: SOIL SISTERS

1. Virginia Crocheron Gildersleeve, *Many a Good Crusade* (New York: Macmillan, 1954), p. 118.

2. Ibid.

3. Breen, *Uncle Sam at Home,* p. 3.

4. Mayor's Committee of Women on National Defense, Semi-Annual Report of the Committee on Agriculture, May–December 1917. Office of the Mayor, John Purroy Mitchel Papers, Committee on National Defense, Women's Auxiliary, Box 63, Folder 659, New York City Municipal Archives.

5. Ibid.

6. Ibid.

7. Ibid.

8. Ibid., p. 3.

9. Ibid.

10. "Women to Raise Budget," *New York Times,* June 12, 1917, p. 4.

11. "Miss Ogilvie Addresses Students," typescript (late Fall 1918), Barnard College Archives,

12. Mayor's Committee of Women, Semi-Annual Report, p. 5.

13. Women's National Farm and Garden Association, *Bulletin,* January 1918, WNF&GA Papers, Schlesinger Library.

14. Advisory Council of the Woman's Land Army of America, *Women on the Land* (New York, January 1918), p. 3, in Circulars and Pamphlets Relating to Women's Work on the Farm, New York Public Library.

15. Alice M. Campbell, "Eight Hours a Day on the Vassar Farm" brochure, October 1917, Vassar College Archives, Poughkeepsie, NY.

16. Ibid.

17. Advisory Council, *Women on the Land,* p. 3.

18. Campbell, "Eight Hours a Day on the Vassar Farm."

19. Advisory Council, *Women on the Land,* p. 3.

20. Ada L. Snell, "Farming at Mount Holyoke," *Mount Holyoke Alumnae Quarterly,* July 1917, pp. 57–60. Mount Holyoke College Archives and Special Collections, South Hadley, MA.

21. Ibid.

22. Ibid.

23. Ibid.

24. The Committee on Public Information, "War Work of Women in Colleges" (Washington,

DC, January 1918), Special Collections Division, Jackson Library, University of North Carolina at Greensboro.

25. "Mount Holyoke's War Garden," *Mount Holyoke Monthly* 27 (October 1917), Mount Holyoke College Archives.

CHAPTER 6: A FEMININE INVASION OF THE LAND

1. Gildersleeve, *Many a Good Crusade*, pp. 118–19.

2. Biographical details from "Ida Helen Ogilvie" memorial sketch, Barnard College Archives; Lois Barber Arnold, "Ida Ogilvie, Geologist," *Barnard Alumnae Magazine,* Spring 1978; and Edward H. Watson, "Geology, Florence Bascom, and Ida Ogilvie," *Bryn Mawr Alumnae Bulletin,* Spring 1965, Bryn Mawr College Archives, BrynMawr, PA.

3. Ibid.

4. Woman's Land Army (WLA), *First Annual Report of the Women's Agricultural Camp* (Bedford, NY, 1917), Mildred E. Buller Smith Papers, A-49, Schlesinger Library, Radcliffe Institute, Harvard University.

5. Helen Kennedy Stevens, "City Girl as Farm Worker—Her Own Story," *New York Times Magazine*, February 24, 1918.

6. "Girl Farmers Make Good," newspaper article, n.d., Barnard College Archives.

7. Harriet Geithmann, "Chronicles of Woodcock Farm," *Overland Monthly* 71 (June 1918).

8. WLA, *First Annual Report of the Women's Agricultural Camp*, p. 7.

9. Mayors' Committee of Women on National Defense, Report of the Committee on Agriculture, December 1917, p. 6.

10. Stevens, "City Girl as Farm Worker."

11. WLA, *First Annual Report of the Women's Agricultural Camp*, p. 7.

12. Ibid., p. 5.

13. Geithmann, "Chronicles of Woodcock Farm."

14. WLA, *First Annual Report of the Women's Agricultural Camp*, pp. 9–11.

15. Ibid., pp. 3–4.

16. "The Woman's Agricultural Camp," *Barnard College Bulletin*, October 18, 1917.

17. Geithmann, "Chronicles of Woodcock Farm."

18. WLA, *First Annual Report of the Women's Agricultural Camp*.

19. Ibid.

20. Mayor's Committee of Women, Report of the Committee on Agriculture.

21. "Results Show That Women Have Made Good as Farmers, Says Vrooman," *Evening Sun* (New York), September 15, 1917, Barnard College Archives.

22. Mayor's Committee of Women, Report of the Committee on Agriculture.

23. Geithmann, "Chronicles of Woodcock Farm."

CHAPTER 7: FARMERETTES AND HOOVER HELPERS

1. "Results Show That Women Have Made Good as Farmers."

2. "Farmers Not Exempt," *Washington Post*, August 31, 1917.

3. "Statement Regarding Camp Organized by Mrs. Camilla Short, Near Mt. Kisco," Memo to Secretary Carl Vrooman, n.d. (Fall 1917). Department of Agriculture, RG 16, Records of the Secretary, Women Labor, National Archives.

4. "Results Show That Women Have Made Good as Farmers."

5. Virginia Gildersleeve, "Women Farm Workers," *New Republic*, September 1, 1917.

6. James, *For God, for Country, for Home,* chapter 8.

7. "State Suffragists Condemn Picketing," *New York Times,* August 31, 1917.

8. "Women and Waste," *Woman's Journal*, July 14, 1917.

9. "Cheerful Women Workers," *Woman's Journal,* September 1, 1917.

10. "Be a Hoover Helper," *Woman's Journal,* July 14, 1917.

11. William L. O'Neill, *Everyone Was Brave: The Rise and Fall of Feminism in America.* (Chicago: Quadrangle Books, 1969), p. 191, as quoted in David M. Kennedy, *Over Here: The First World War and American Society* (New York: Oxford University Press, 2004), p. 286.

12. Harriot Stanton Blatch and Alma Lutz, *Challenging Years: The Memoirs of H. S. Blatch* (New York: G. P. Putnam's Sons, 1940; repr., Westport, CT: Hyperion Press, 1976), p. 92.

13. Harriot Stanton Blatch, *Mobilizing Woman-Power* (New York: Womans Press, 1918; repr., Whitefish, MT: Kessinger Publishing, 2004), chapter 6, p. 41.

14. Ibid., foreword by Theodore Roosevelt.

15. Clipping from *Boston Herald,* December 31, 1917, in a letter from Grace Burt, Massachusetts Committee on Public Safety, to Anna Howard Shaw, December 31, 1917, Council of National Defense, Records of the Committee on Women's Defense Work, Correspondence of Anna Howard Shaw, RG 62, National Archives.

16. Anna Howard Shaw reply to Grace Burt, January 8, 1918, Council of National Defense, Records of the Committee on Women's Defense Work, Correspondence of Anna Howard Shaw, RG 62, National Archives.

17. Anna Howard Shaw to Harriot Blatch, June 8, 1917, Council of National Defense, Records of the Committee on Women's Defense Work, Correspondence of Anna Howard Shaw, RG 62, National Archives.

18. Ibid.

19. Ida Clyde Clarke, *American Women and the World War* (New York: D. Appleton, 1918), chapter 1.

20. Report of Miss Anna Clark to Committee on Organization and Extension, December 17, 1917. Young Women's Christian Association, Land Service Committee Papers, Sophia Smith Collection, Smith College, Northampton, MA.

21. Minutes of the WNF&GA Council Meeting, December 8, 1917, WNF&GA Papers, Schlesinger Library.

22. Program of special WNF&GA conference on war work, Chicago, October 3–5, 1917, WNF&GA Papers, Schlesinger Library.

23. Account of President Henry MacCracken's remarks in Report of Anna Clark, p. 2, YWCA Papers, Sophia Smith Collection, Smith College.

24. Blatch, "A Land Army," in *Mobilizing Woman-Power.*

Chapter 8: Women on the Land

1. "On the 21st of December, 1917," typescript description of meeting participants, Barnard College Archives.

2. Report by Hilda Loines, Field Secretary, to the Meeting of the WNF&GA Executive Council, January 1918, WNF&GA Papers, Schlesinger Library.

3. The change in spelling from the British plural possessive "women's" to the American singular "woman's" was never explained, but it was probably just a grammatical difference of custom between the two Anglophone siblings.

4. Prospectus of the Woman's Land Army, Ethel Puffer Howes to David Houston, Secretary of Agriculture, February 27, 1918, RG 16, Records of the Secretary, National Archives.

5. Letter from the Advisory Council of the Woman's Land Army of America, January 10, 1918. Special Collections, Vassar College Library.

6. Ibid.

7. Minutes of Executive Council, WNF&GA, January 1918, WNF&GA Papers, Schlesinger Library.

8. Hilda Loines to Caroline Ruutz-Rees, February 2, 1918, Connecticut Council of National

Defense, Women's Division, RG 30, Box 375, Connecticut State Archives, Hartford.

9. The Woman's Land Army of America, "Help for the Farmer" (New York, February 1918), in Circulars and Pamphlets Relating to Women's Work on the Farm, Reserve Library, New York Public Library. Microfilm (MN ZZ-28,038).

10. Advisory Council, *Women on the Land,* in Circulars and Pamphlets Relating to Women's Work on the Farm, New York Public Library.

11. Woman's Land Army of America (WLAA), "The Organization of Agricultural Units" (New York, February 1918), in Circulars and Pamphlets Relating to Women's Work on the Farm, New York Public Library.

12. WLAA, "The Woman's Land Army of America," (New York, February 1918). Barnard College Archives.

13. Ethel Puffer Howes, lecture at Wellesley Training Camp, Summer 1918, from notes by Carol Maynard, WNF&GA Papers, Schlesinger Library.

14. "Land Army Incorporated," *New York Times*, April 25, 1918, p. 24.

15. WLAA, "The Woman's Land Army of America."

CHAPTER 9: A HYSTERICAL APPEAL

1. Memorandum for Mr. Harrison from R. Pearson, February 18, 1918, Correspondence of the Secretary of Agriculture, RG 16, Women Labor, National Archives.

2. "Statement Regarding Camp Organized by Mrs. Camilla Short, near Mt. Kisco," Correspondence of the Secretary of Agriculture, RG 16, National Archives.

3. Harry B. Shaw to Mr. C. L. Marlatt, U.S. Department of Agriculture Federal Horticultural Board, February 4, 1918, in Correspondence of the Secretary of Agriculture, RG 16, Women Labor, National Archives.

4. Memorandum for Dr. Marlatt from Clarence Ousley, February 21, 1918, Correspondence of the Secretary of Agriculture, RG 16, Women Labor, National Archives.

5. Memorandum for Assistant Secretary Ousley from E. Merritt, February 21, 1918.

6. Memorandum for Assistant Secretary Ousley from E. V. Wilcox, February 18, 1918.

7. Memorandum for Dr. R. A. Pearson from Clarence Ousley, February 21, 1918.

8. Papers of Ethel Puffer Howes, within the papers of her sister Laura Puffer Morgan, Schlesinger Library. Bryn Mawr president M. Carey Thomas, Howes's colleague on the board of the National College Equal Suffrage League, had marked the birth of Howes's younger child, Benjamin, Jr., in 1917 with this greeting: "Congratulations on the birth of your child of the suffraged sex."

9. Ethel Puffer Howes to Secretary David Houston, February 27, 1918.

10. Ethel Puffer Howes to Secretary Houston, March 15, 1918.

11. Dean James E. Russell to Secretary Houston, March 21, 1918. The Women's Agricultural Camp at Bedford's location was sometimes referred to as Mt. Kisco, a nearby and larger town in northern Westchester County.

12. George Creel to Secretary Houston, March 19, 1918.

13. Secretary Houston to George Creel, March 25, 1918.

14. U.S. Employment Service Bulletin, Department of Labor, March 18, 1918, Department of Labor, RG 174, National Archives.

15. U.S. Employment Service Bulletin, March 25, 1918.

16. Papers of Ethel Puffer Howes, Schlesinger Library.

17. Clarence Ousley to P. P. Claxton, Commissioner of Education, Washington, DC, April 9, 1918, Correspondence of the Secretary of Agriculture, RG 16, National Archives.

CHAPTER 10: A FINE PROPAGANDA

1. George Chappell and William Hogarth, Jr., "The Fair Farmerettes and Their Shameless Chauf-

feurs" in "Nonsense, Preferred," *Puck*, January 20, 1918.

2. *New York Herald,* n.d. (early January 1918), Council of Defense, Women's Division, RG 30, Box 375, Connecticut State Archives.

3. "Women and the War," unidentified newspaper clipping, Connecticut Council of Defense, Women's Division, RG 30, Box 375, Connecticut State Archives.

4. "Girl Laborers on Small Farms at $2 a Day," *New York Times Magazine*, February 3, 1918.

5. "Women on the Farms," editorial, *New York Times*, February 3, 1918.

6. Louisa Yeomans King, "The Woman's Land Army," letter to the editor, *New York Times*, February 25, 1918.

7. Stevens, "City Girl as Farm Worker."

8. Geithmann, "Chronicles of Woodcock Farm."

9. Mrs. Henry Wade Rogers, "Wanted—The Woman's Land Army," *Forum*, May 1918.

10. Mrs. H. O. Havemeyer, "The Woman's Land Army of America and What It Can Do for the Farmer," *Touchstone*, May 1918.

11. "She'll Work Vermont Farm," *Washington Post,* March 19, 1918.

12. Helen Taft, "The Six Weeks I Spent on a Farm," *Ladies' Home Journal*, June 1918.

13. Memo from Assistant Secretary Clarence Ousley to Mr. Wharton, Re: Request of *Ladies' Home Journal* for article on Woman Labor, February 18, 1918, Correspondence of the Secretary of Agriculture, RG 16, National Archives.

14. Dudley Harmon, "Is the Woman Needed on the Farm? What the United States Government Has to Say About Farm Work for Women This Summer," *Ladies' Home Journal*, May 1918.

15. Reinette Lovewell, "A Woman Who Needs You," originally published in *The Designer,* May 1918. Republished, with comment, by the U.S. Department of Agriculture, General Records of the Secretary of Agriculture, RG 16, National Archives.

16. Penciled corrections by Clarence Ousley on script submitted by Committee of Public Information, Division on Women's War Work, May 6, 1918, General Records of the Secretary of Agriculture, RG 16, National Archives.

17. U.S. Employment Service Bulletin, "The Farm Labor Problem," April 9, 1918, U.S. Employment Service, Department of Labor, RG 174, National Archives.

18. Editorial, (Philadelphia) *Evening Star*, May 8, 1918, Correspondence of the Secretary of Agriculture, RG 16, National Archives.

19. Editorial, (Philadelphia) *Evening Star*, May 9, 1919, Correspondence of the Secretary of Agriculture, RG 16, National Archives.

20. "Farmerette Play by Bessie Tyree," *New York Times*, May 23, 1918.

21. "The Society Farmerettes," lyrics by P. G. Wodehouse, music by Victor Herbert, in "Miss 1917," presented by Florenz Ziegfeld, Jr., and Charles Dillingham at the Century Theatre, New York (November 1917). Other musical numbers in the show were written by Jerome Kern; the rehearsal pianist was nineteen-year-old George Gershwin. In *The Complete Lyrics of P. G. Wodehouse,* edited by Barry Day. (Lanham, MD: Scarecrow Press, 2004), p. 113.

22. Ibid.

Chapter 11: Enlist Now!

1. For examples of Liberal members of Parliament relying on Fraser, see John W. Eulland to Helen Fraser, November 20, 1909, and May 16, 1912, Helen Fraser Papers, Suffrage Collection, Museum of London Archives.

2. Mary Shachan, Divisional Office for Labour Exchanges, Cardiff, to Helen Fraser, May 17, 1916, Helen Fraser Papers, Suffrage Collection, Museum of London Archives.

3. Harriot Stanton Blatch to Anna Howard Shaw, May 8, 1917; and Anna Howard Shaw to Harriot Stanton Blatch, June 8, 1917, Correspondence of Anna Howard Shaw, Council of National Defense, Women's Committee, RG 62, National Archives.

4. Advertisement for Helen Fraser's American lecture tour, Helen Fraser Papers, Suffrage Collection, Museum of London Archives.

5. Quote from the Vassar student newspaper in Henry Noble MacCracken's foreword to Fraser's book, *Women and War Work.*

6. Advertisement for Helen Fraser's American tour, early March 1918, Helen Fraser Papers, Suffrage Collection, Museum of London Archives.

7. Fraser, *Women and War Work,* p. 170.

8. G. Arnold Shaw, University Lecturers Association, to Dr. Anna Howard Shaw, August 26, 1918. Correspondence of Anna Howard Shaw, Council of National Defense, Women's Committee, RG 62/13A, National Archives.

9. Ada Comstock, Smith College, to Helen Fraser, January 28, 1918, Helen Fraser Papers, Suffrage Collection, Museum of London Archives.

10. "Food Will Win the War" program, Lansing, Michigan, March 12–13, 1918, Council of National Defense, Women's Committee, Reports of State Activities, RG 62.5, National Archives.

11. Harriot Stanton Blatch to Helen Fraser, June 3, 1918, Helen Fraser Papers, Suffrage Collection, Museum of London Archives.

12. Fraser, *Women and War Work,* introduction by H. N. MacCracken.

13. Laura Crane Burgess, WLA, New York Executive Committee, February 9, 1918, RG 30, Box 375, Connecticut State Archives.

14. California Women's Committee, Department of Women in Industry, Katherine Philips Edson, Chairman, instructions to County Chairmen, San Francisco, Spring 1918, National Council of Defense, Women's Committee, Reports of State Activities, RG 62/13b, National Archives.

15. "Council Opposes Drafting Women for Farm Work," unidentified Nebraska newspaper clipping. National Council of Defense, Women's Committee, Reports of State Activities, RG 62/13b, National Archives.

16. Nebraska Women's Committee Four-Minute Speech Topics, early Spring 1918, Council National of Defense, Women's Committee, Reports of State Activities, RG62/13b, National Archives.

17. "They Are All Pushing for Pershing," *Woman's Journal,* October 12, 1918, quoting a Kansas newspaper article.

18. Mrs. T. G. Winter, "What Minnesota Is Doing for the Woman on the Farm," *The Farmer's Wife* (St. Paul), n.d. (probably April or May 1918), Council of National Defense, Women's Committee, Reports of State Activities, RG62-13b, National Archives.

19. Minutes of the Missouri Council of National Defense, Women's Committee, May 17, 1918, Council of National Defense, Women's Committee, Reports of State Activities, RG 62-13b, National Archives.

20. Ibid.

21. Report of Prince George's County, Maryland Council of Defense, Women's Committee, December 1917, Council of National Defense, Women's Committee, Reports of State Activities, RG 62.5, National Archives.

22. Circular No. 128A, Council of Defense, Women's Committee, Department of Food Production and Home Economics, Katharine Dexter McCormick, Chairwoman, April 3, 1918. RG 62-13d, National Archives.

23. Anna Howard Shaw to Helen Fraser, February 25, 1918. Helen Fraser Papers, Suffrage Collection, Museum of London Archives.

24. Carrie Chapman Catt to Helen Fraser, February 13, 1918. Helen Fraser Papers, Suffrage Collection, Museum of London Archives.

25. Louisine W. Havemeyer, "Memories of a Militant" series, "The Suffrage Torch," *Scribner's Magazine,* May 1922.

26. Ibid.

27. Letter to Dean Virginia Gildersleeve from Harriot Stanton Blatch, April 23, 1918, Barnard

College Archives.

28. "Farmerettes Told to Stifle Fears," *Baltimore News,* n.d. (Spring 1918), Goucher College Archives, Baltimore, MD.

29. *Goucher College Weekly,* Baltimore, April 11, 1918, Goucher College Archives.

30. "Barnard to Train Women for Farms," *New York Times,* April 27, 1918, p. 17.

31. "The College Girl With a Hoe," *New York Times,* March 31, 1918.

32. *Goucher College Weekly,* Baltimore, April 11, 1918, Goucher College Archives.

33. Agnes E. Wells, University of Michigan, Ann Arbor, to Virginia Gildersleeve, March 29, 1918, Barnard College Archives.

34. "The College Girl With a Hoe."

35. Edward N. Hurley, *The Bridge to France* (Philadelphia: J. B. Lippincott, 1927).

36. Ibid.

37. "Woman's Land Army of America—Fight the Food Famine" recruitment poster, Herbert Paus, 1918. Princeton University Poster Collection, Archives Center, national Museum of American History, Smithsonian Institution, Washington, DC.

38. "The Girl on the Land Serves the Nation's Need," YWCA Land Service Committee, Edward Penfield, 1918. Princeton University Poster Collection, Smithsonian Archives.

39. "Help! . . . Until the Boys Come Back," Charles Dana Gibson for WLA, New Jersey Division, Trenton, 1918. Princeton University Poster Collection, Smithsonian Archives.

40. "Get Behind the Girl He Left Behind Him" by Guenther (New York: American Lithographic Co., 1918), New York State Land Army Membership Committee. Prints and Photographs Division, POS-WWI-US, no. 156/ LC-USZC4-7809, Library of Congress..

41. From the papers of Emma L. George, ed., *The Farmerette,* Manuscript Division, Library of Congress.

Chapter 12: In Bifurcated Garb of Toil

1. "Intrepid First Fifteen Start Out Tomorrow," *Los Angeles Times,* April 30, 1918; and "America's First Organized Women Farmers Take Field," *Los Angeles Times,* May 2, 1918.

2. "Women to Till Thousands of Southern California's Acres," *Los Angeles Times,* April 14, 1918.

3. "Report, Women's Committee of the State Council of Defense of California from June 1917 to January 1919," California State Library, Sacramento.

4. "America's First Organized Women Farmers."

5. Ibid.

6. "Want Teachers for Land Army," *Los Angeles Times,* May 22, 1918.

7. "Court Martial Is Approved," *Los Angeles Times,* May 9, 1918.

8. "To Turn New Earth in History of the American Woman," *Los Angeles Times,* April 30, 1918, p. II 1.

9. "America's First Organized Women Farmers." *Los Angeles Times,* May 2, 1918.

10. Ibid.

11. Idella Purnell, "The Woman's Land Army," *Westways* 72 (October 1980).

12. "Woman's Land Army," *San Francisco Examiner,* May 14, 1918. Newspaper Room, Library of Congress.

13. Unidentified San Francisco area newspaper, n.d. (early Summer 1918), Mills College Archives, Oakland, CA.

14. *Sacramento Bee,* June 5, 1918, in Catherine Gabriel Kipp, "Women on the Land: The Woman's Land Army, California Northern Division, 1918–1920," master's degree thesis, Sacramento State College, 1960; and "175 Women in Land Army," *San Francisco Examiner,* June 30, 1918.

15. *San Francisco Examiner,* June 23, 1918.

16. Purnell, "The Woman's Land Army."

17. Ibid.

18. Alice Prescott Smith, "Battalion of Life," *Sunset,* November 1918, in Kipp, "Women on the Land," p. 58.

19. Alma Whitaker, "Is New Woman Farm Labor Movement Practicable One?" *Los Angeles Times,* May 26, 1918.

20. "Woman's Land Army," editorial, *Los Angeles Times,* May 31, 1918.

21. "Woman's Land Army," *San Francisco Examiner,* May 14, 1918.

22. Smith, "Battalion of Life," p. 43.

23. Whitaker, "Is New Woman Farm Labor?"

24. "Woman's Land Army," editorial, *Los Angeles Times.*

25. Susan Minor, "Sisters All," *Overland Monthly,* May 1919.

26. "The California Woman's Land Army," *New Republic,* March 1919.

27. Ibid.

28. Minor, "Sisters All."

29. Purnell, "The Woman's Land Army."

30. "Court Martial Ousts Land Army Member," *Los Angeles Times,* May 8, 1918.

31. Ibid.

32. Ibid.

33. Ibid.

34. Ibid.

35. "Break Occurs in the Ranks of the WLA," *Sacramento Bee,* August 3, 1918, and August 17, 1918. Both in Kipp, "Women on the Land," pp. 75–76.

36. "Crisis Near in Affairs of Woman's Land Army," *Los Angeles Times,* August 7, 1918.

37. Alma Whitaker, "Woman's Land Army." *Los Angeles Times,* July 27, 1918.

38. Smith, "Battalion of Life," p. 31, in Kipp, "Women on the Land," p. 92.

39. "Soldiers Help Build Barracks for Women," *Los Angeles Times,* September 9, 1918.

40. Alma Whitaker, "Godfathers," *Los Angeles Times,* August 30, 1918.

41. *San Francisco Chronicle,* October 17, 1918, in Kipp, "Women on the Land," p. 103.

42. *Sacramento Bee,* October 10, 1918, in Kipp, "Women on the Land," p. 101.

43. "Land Army Song From Southern California," *The Farmerette* 1, no. 5 (December 1919).

CHAPTER 13: HORTENSE POWDERMAKER IN MARYLAND

1. Hortense Powdermaker, *Stranger and Friend: The Way of an Anthropologist* (New York: W. W. Norton, 1966), p. 22.

2. Ibid, p. 23.

3. U.S. Food Administration, Collegiate Section, *Food and the War: A Textbook for College Classes* (Boston: Houghton Mifflin, 1918).

4. "Alarming Facts About the Farm Labor Situation," *Baltimore Sun,* February 28, 1918.

5. "What Is Holding Up Food Production?" *Baltimore Sun,* March 16, 1918.

6. Report of the Women in Industry Committee of Prince George's County, Maryland, Women's Committee, Council of National Defense, Reports of State Activities, RG 62-13a, National Archives.

7. Women's Committee, Council of National Defense, Reports of State Activities, Report of Maryland, RG 62-13a, National Archives.

8. *Report of the Maryland State Council of Defense for 1918* (Annapolis, 1919), p. 261, appendix Q, Maryland Historical Society.

9. Ibid.

10. Ibid.

11. "Help for Truck Farms," *Washington Post,* March 31, 1918.

12. "3rd Camp of Nat'l Service School to Train Farmerettes," *Baltimore Sun,* March 3, 1918.

13. "Girls to Train as Practical Farmers in Third Encampment," *Washington Post,* March 3,

1918.
14. "3rd Camp of Nat'l Service School to Train Farmerettes."
15. "Khaki Girls in Camp," *Washington Post*, April 23, 1918.
16. Ibid.
17. "3rd Camp of Nat'l Service School to Train Farmerettes."
18. "N. B. Baker Gives Ingleside as Farmerette Headquarters," *Catonsville Argus*, April 27, 1918.
19. "Farmerettes Get Recruits," *Catonsville Argus*, June 22, 1918.
20. "Farmers Shy at Farmerettes," *Catonsville Argus*, July 6, 1918.
21. "Governor Harrington to Address Catonsville Farmers," *Catonsville Argus,* June 29, 1918.
22. "Governor Calls on Women to Join Land Army," *Baltimore Sun,* June 11, 1918.
23. "Campaign to Enroll Men a Failure So Far," *Baltimore Sun*, May 31, 1918.
24. "Conn Urges Farmers to Be Patient With Boys," *Baltimore Sun*, May 30, 1918.
25. "Catonsville Farmer Says Farmerettes Are Worth $2 a Day," *Catonsville Argus*, July 13, 1918.
26. "Catonsvillians Vie in Entertaining Farmerettes," *Catonsville Argus*, July 20, 1918.
27. Besides *Stranger and Friend,* Powdermaker's anthropology books include *Life in Lesu: The Study of a Melanesian Society in New Ireland* (1933), describing her fieldwork on a South Pacific island; *After Freedom: A Cultural Study in the Deep South* (1939), analyzing race relations in a Mississippi town, which became essential reading during the Civil Rights movement years later; and her most celebrated work, *Hollywood, The Dream Factory: An Anthropologist Studies the Movie Makers* (1950).
28. "Goucher's Fallston Unit," *Goucher College Weekly*, October 1918, Goucher College Archives.
29. "Catonsvillians Vie in Entertaining Farmerettes."
30. "Vacation Farmers," *Catonsville Argus*, June 1, 1918.
31. "Goucher's Fallston Unit."
32. "St. James' Farmerettes," *Goucher College Weekly,* November 1918.
33. "A Farmerette," *Washington Post,* October 6, 1918.
34. Letter of Stella Rothschild (Moses) to Lester Levy, June 23, 1918, postmarked from Woman's Land Army, Fallston, Maryland, Lester Levy Collection, Jewish Museum of Maryland, Baltimore. With thanks to Dr. Jessica Elfenbein, who brought the letter to the author's attention.
35. Ibid.
36. "Farmerettes Do Good Work," *Catonsville Argus*, August 27, 1918.
37. William Mc.C Hillegeist, "Another Slant of the Labor Problem," *Maryland Farmer*, October 4, 1918, Maryland Room, Special Collections, Enoch Pratt Free Library, Baltimore.

CHAPTER 14: CULTIVATING THE SOOTHING WEED

1. Minutes of Executive Committee, Woman's Land Army, Connecticut Division, April 23, 1918, RG 30, Connecticut Council of Defense, Women's Division, Box 375, Folder T 59.2, Connecticut State Archives.
2. Biographical details about Grace Schenck from the Schenck Family Files in the History Room of the Wilton Library, CT.
3. Grace Schenck to Corinne Alsop, April 8, 1918, Correspondence, Connecticut WLA, RG 30, Box 375, Folder T 59.2, Connecticut State Archives.
4. Memo from Mr. Chandler to Miss Ruutz-Rees and Miss Corwin, January 24, 1918, Correspondence, Connecticut WLA. RG 30, Box 375, Folder T 59.2, Connecticut State Archives.
5. "Women to Plough Fields and Milk Cows at $2 a Day," newspaper clipping, unidentified Connecticut newspaper, n.d. (late Winter–early Spring 1918). In files of Connecticut WLA, RG 30, Box 375, Folder T 59.2, Connecticut State Archives.
6. Ibid.
7. Schenck to Alsop, April 8, 1918.
8. "For the Clergymen," typescript, signed by Grace Schenck, State Chairman, Connecticut

WLA, RG 30, Box 375, Folder T 59.2, Connecticut State Archives.

9. From materials in the Connecticut College Archives, New London, CT.

10. Biographical details on Daisy Day and her diary of work as a farmerette in New Milford from Virginia McLoughlin's "Hoeing Smokes: A New Milford Connecticut Unit of the Woman's Land Army, World War I," *Connecticut History* 40, no. 1 (Spring 2001): 32–60.

11. Instructions to Farmerettes and Registration Card, Connecticut WLA, RG 30, Box 375, Folder T 59.2, Connecticut State Archives.

12. Quoted from Daisy Day's diary, excerpted in McLoughlin's "Hoeing Smokes." Day's diary is in the possession of McLoughlin, her niece.

13. Typescript of interview with Jeanne Schenck Erskine, daughter of Grace Knight Schenck, July 21, 2000, by Bob Russell for the Wilton Bicentennial Celebration. Schenck Family Files, History Room, Wilton Library.

14. Schenck to Alsop, April 8, 1918.

15. Schenck to Alsop, September 10, 1918. Correspondence, Connecticut WLA. RG 30, Box 375, Folder T 59.2, Connecticut State Archives.

16. Minutes of the Executive Committee meeting, WLA Connecticut Division, April 23, 1918. RG 30, Box 375, Folder T 59.2, Connecticut State Archives.

17. Ibid.

18. Schenck to Alsop, June 13, 1918, Correspondence, Connecticut WLA, RG 30, Box 375, Folder T 59.2, Connecticut State Archives.

19. Later in the season Schenck faced accusations from farmerette Evelyn Lowenstein that she had been passed over for promotion to captain of the Greenwich unit "on account of race prejudice." Schenck refuted the charge. See Schenck to Leo Korper, September 13, 1918, Correspondence, Connecticut WLA, RG 30, Box 375, Folder T 59.2, Connecticut State Archives.

20. Day diary entries, July 3 and July 6, 1918, in McLoughlin, "Hoeing Smokes."

21. "Connecticut's Tobacco Crop Saved by Girls; Army," *Hartford Courant*, September 29, 1918, Newspaper Room, Library of Congress.

22. John H. Davis, *The Guggenheims—An American Epic* (New York: William Morrow, 1978). Eleanor Guggenheim described changing her name during her Land Army stint in an interview with Davis in 1976.

23. Day diary entry, July 8, 1918, in McLoughlin, "Hoeing Smokes."

24. Ibid., July 24, 1918.

25. "Farmerettes a Success," *New Milford Gazette*, August 15, 1918, New Milford Public Library.

26. "New Milford Farmers Laud Women Who Come to Help Them," *Hartford Courant*, August 31, 1918, Newspaper Room, Library of Congress.

27. "Farmerettes and Connecticut Farmers," *Hartford Courant*, October 20, 1918, Newspaper Room, Library of Congress.

28. Day diary entry, August 9, 1918, in McLoughlin, "Hoeing Smokes."

29. "Will Women Workers Solve Connecticut Farm Labor Problem?" *Hartford (Sunday) Courant*, June 2, 1918.

30. "Farmerettes and Connecticut Farmers."

31. Day Diary entry, August 7, 1918, in McLoughlin, "Hoeing Smokes," p. 55.

32. "Farmerettes a Success."

33. Ibid.

34. Schenck to Alsop, July 24, 1918, Correspondence, Connecticut WLA, RG 30, Box 375, Folder T 59.2, Connecticut State Archives.

35. Ibid.

36. "Farmerettes and Connecticut Farmers."

37. Day diary entry, July 19, 1918, in McLoughlin, "Hoeing Smokes."

38. "Farmerettes a Success."

39. Interview of Mr. Robin Stacks by the author, at the New Milford Historical Society, October 2003.

40. Schenck to Alsop, April 8, 1918, Correspondence, Connecticut WLA, RG 30, Box 375, Folder T 59.2, Connecticut State Archives.

41. "Simsbury Farmers Not Enthusiastic Over 'Patriots,'" *Hartford Courant,* August 18, 1918.

42. Ibid.

43. Minutes of the Executive Committee, Connecticut WLA, April 23, 1918.

44. Schenck to Alsop, June 29, 1918, Correspondence, Connecticut WLA, RG 30, Box 375, Folder T 59.2, Connecticut State Archives.

45. Report of the Connecticut Branch of the Woman's Land Army of America, October 18, 1918. Connecticut State Archives.

46. Schenck to Caroline Ruutz-Rees, April 11, 1918, Correspondence, Connecticut WLA, RG 30, Box 375, Folder T 59.2, Connecticut State Archives.

47. Margaret T. Corwin to John E. Luddy, Manager, Connecticut Leaf Tobacco Association, June 26, 1918.

48. Schenck to Korper, July 24, 1918, Correspondence, Connecticut WLA, RG 30, Box 375, Folder T 59.2, Connecticut State Archives.

49. Schenck to Alsop, August 5, 1918, Correspondence, Connecticut WLA, RG 30, Box 375, Folder T 59.2, Connecticut State Archives.

50. Schenck to Alsop, August 27, 1918, Correspondence, Connecticut WLA, RG 30, Box 375, Folder T 59.2, Connecticut State Archives.

51. Ibid.

52. Schenck to Alsop, August 5, 1918, Correspondence, Connecticut WLA, RG 30, Box 375, Folder T 59.2, Connecticut State Archives.

53. "Women Presented With Brassards," *Hartford Times,* August 21, 1918. RG 30, Box 375, Folder T 59.2, Connecticut State Archives.

54. "Brassards Given to 24 'Farmerettes,'" *Hartford Courant,* August 22, 1918. Newspaper Room, Library of Congress.

55. Schenck to Alsop, August 27, 1918, Correspondence, Connecticut WLA., RG 30, Box 375, Folder T 59.2, Connecticut State Archives.

56. Schenck to Alsop, September 10, 1918, Correspondence, Connecticut WLA, RG 30, Box 375, Folder T 59.2, Connecticut State Archives.

CHAPTER 15: LIBERTYVILLE

1. "Training Girls to Farm," *Prairie Farmer,* July 13, 1918.

2. Margaret Day Blake's entry in R. L. Schultz and A. Hast, eds., *Women Building Chicago, 1790–1990: A Biographical Dictionary* (Bloomington: University of Indiana Press, 2001), pp. 89–91.

3. "Taft's Daughter to Enlist Army of Farmerettes," *Chicago Daily Tribune,* February 23, 1918.

4. "Bifurcated?" *Chicago Daily Tribune,* March 8, 1918.

5. Report of the Illinois Training Farm for Women, in the final report of the Illinois State Council of Defense, 1919, pp. 115–26, Illinois State Archives, Springfield, Il. Unless otherwise noted, all descriptions of the Libertyville farm experiment attributed to Margaret Day Blake are taken from this report.

6. Katherine Jellison, "To 'Lessen Her Heavy Burdens': The Country Life Movement and the Smith-Lever Act," in *Entitled to Power: Farm Women and Technology, 1913–1963* (Chapel Hill: University of North Carolina Press, 1993), chapter 1.

7. Report of the Illinois Training Farm for Women, p. 121.

8. Ibid.

9. Ibid.

10. The McCormick family of Chicago (who also owned the *Chicago Tribune* newspaper) owned

International Harvester, and several McCormick clan women took an early interest in the Land Army. Mrs. Medill McCormick sat on Margaret Blake's Illinois WLA board and was a generous sponsor to the Libertyville farm. Katherine Dexter McCormick, married to an insane and confined McCormick heir, did her best to support the Woman's Land Army from her position as head of the Food Production Committee of the Women's Committee of the Council of National Defense.

11. Report of the Illinois Training Farm for Women, p. 117.

12. List of Firms Contributing House and Farm Equipment to Libertyville Farm in "Illinois Training Farm for Women—Report for Six Months," typescript, Illinois State Archives.

13. Ibid.

14. Report of Illinois Training Farm for Women, p. 117; and "Report for Six Months."

15. "Report of Publicity Activities," Illinois Training Farm for Women, typescript. Illinois State Archives.

16. Report of the Illinois Training Farm for Women, p. 118.

17. Ibid.

18. Ibid.

19. "Farm Life as Lived and Extolled by Girl Workers," *The Literary Digest*, October 25, 1919, p. 68.

20. Edith Franklin Wyatt, "The Illinois Training Farm for Women," *Kimball's Dairy Farmer*, April 15, 1919.

21. "Training Girls to Farm," *Prairie Farmer*, July 13, 1918.

22. "Women Trained for Farming," *Orange Judd Farmer*, September 1918.

23. Report of the Illinois Training Farm for Women, p. 122.

24. "Farm Life as Lived and Extolled by Girl Workers," p. 68.

25. "Overalls Are Gowns for Girls of Graduating Class at Farm School," *Chicago Daily Tribune*, September 18, 1918.

26. "Governor Sees Army of Women Labor on Farm," *Chicago Daily Tribune*, September 18, 1918.

27. "Professor Holden's Tribute to the Woman's Land Army of America, September 17, 1918," typescript, Illinois State Archives.

28. "An Address Delivered by Hon. Frank O. Lowden, Governor of the State of the Illinois at the Illinois Training Farm of the Woman's Land Army, September 17, 1918," typescript, Illinois State Archives.

29. "Farmerettes' Taboo Thrills," *Chicago Daily News,* September 18, 1918.

30. Article from an unspecified Chicago newspaper, reprinted in *The Farmerette*, December 1918.

CHAPTER 16: GIRLS WHO THOUGHT POTATOES GREW ON TREES

1. Alice Holway, oral interview by the author, Putney, VT, 1980.

2. Biographical information from Mildred B. Smith's ninetieth birthday video recording and Mildred Buller Smith Papers A-49, Box 2, Schlesinger Library.

3. Biographical information from Elizabeth Clarke Papers, A-C597, Schlesinger Library, Radcliffe Institute, Harvard University.

4. Report for Massachusetts, New England Branch of the Woman's National Farm and Garden Association, 1918, WNF&GA Papers, B-4, Box 7A, Folder 51, Schlesinger Library.

5. Ibid.

6. WLA Physician's Certificate, Woman's Land Army, Connecticut Division, RG 30, Connecticut State Council of Defense, Women's Division, Box 375, Folder T 59.2, Connecticut State Archives.

7. Woman's Land Army of America Enrollment Card, Connecticut WLA, RG 30, Box 375, Folder T 59.2, Connecticut State Archives.

8. Holway, oral interview.

9. Mildred Buller Smith, journals, in Mildred Buller Smith Papers, Schlesinger Library.

10. John Anthony, "Raising Certified Seed Potatoes—How a Painstaking Vermonter Does It," *New England Homestead,* October 21, 1922, Mildred Buller Smith Papers, Schlesinger Library.

11. "Potato Growing Science at Bradford, Vt.," *Boston Sunday Globe,* August 10, 1924, Mildred Buller Smith Papers, Schlesinger Library.

12. Julian Dimock, "Women Better Than Men," *New England Homestead,* September 10, 1921, Mildred Buller Smith Papers, Schlesinger Library.

13. Mildred Buller Smith journals, Mildred Buller Smith Papers, Schlesinger Library.

14. Bess M. Rowe, "Bringing Back the Old Trees," *The Farmer's Wife,* September 1922, Mildred Buller Smith Papers, Schlesinger Library.

15. M. Holbrook, "The Woman's Land Army of Vermont," publication circa 1919, University of Vermont archives, Burlington, Vermont.

16. Holway, oral interview.

17. *Wellesley College News,* September 26, 1918. Wellesley College Archives, Wellesley, MA.

18. Charlotte E. Wilder, "A Farmerette's Day," August 1, 1918, typescript. War Collection, Farm Work, Mount Holyoke College Archives and Special Collections, South Hadley, Massachusetts.

19. "Smith Farmerettes Hoe and Harvest," *Daily Hampshire Gazette,* August 31, 1918. Smith College Archives, Northampton, Massachusetts.

20. Laurence L. Winship, "Objectors for Farm Work," *Boston Globe,* August 1, 1918.

21. "German Prisoners Raising Big Crops for Our Soldiers at Devens," *Boston Globe,* August 4, 1918.

22. Holway, oral interview by the author, Hemlock Hollow Farm, Putney, Vermont, 1980.

23. "Woman Plods 1,000 Miles a Season, Inspects 1,000,000 Potato Plants," *Boston Globe,* July 22, 1923, Elizabeth Clarke Papers, Schlesinger Library.

CHAPTER 17: THE FARMERETTE IN WANAMAKER'S WINDOW

1. Fund-raising letter, WLA New Jersey Division, March 1918, Josephine Perry Morgan Papers, Princeton Historical Society, Princeton, NJ.

2. Letter to Josephine P. Morgan from Mrs. Hack, Oakridge Place, n.d. (Spring 1918), Josephine Perry Morgan Papers, Princeton Historical Society.

3. Josephine P. Morgan, Chairman, State Finance Committee, to Mrs. Francis G. Lloyd, Treasurer, New Jersey Division of the WLA, April 11, 1918, Josephine Perry Morgan Papers, Princeton Historical Society.

4. Report of the Organization and Work of the New Jersey Division of the WLA, August 1, 1918. Josephine Perry Morgan Papers, Princeton Historical Society.

5. Laura Patterson, Report of the YWCA Polish Land Army Unit of Holmdel, New Jersey, October 21, 1918, Land Service Committee, YWCA Papers, Sophia Smith Collection, Smith College.

6. Ibid., p. 2.

7. Ibid., p. 1.

8. Ibid.

9. Ibid., p. 3.

10. Ibid., p. 4.

11. Ibid.

12. Final Report—Land Service Committee, October 8, 1918, YWCA Papers, Sophia Smith Collection, Smith College.

13. Patterson, Report of the YWCA Polish Land Army Unit, p. 2.

14. Final Report—Land Service Committee.

15. Minutes of the Executive Committee of the YWCA Land Service Committee, March 12, 1918, YWCA Papers, Sophia Smith Collection.

16. Ibid., July 23, 1918, YWCA Papers, Sophia Smith Collection.

17. Report of Mrs. Thos. J. Levery, chairman for Burlington County, July 26, 1918, in Report of the Organization and Work of the New Jersey Division of the Woman's Land Army of America, Josephine Perry Morgan Papers, Princeton Historical Society.

18. Report of the Publicity Committee in Report of Organization and Work of the New Jersey Woman's Land Army, August 1, 1918, Josephine Perry Morgan Papers, Princeton Historical Society.

19. Plan of the Publicity Committee of the Woman's Land Army of New Jersey, n.d., Josephine Perry Morgan Papers, Princeton Historical Society.

20. Elizabeth Devery, Chairman, Burlington County Branch of the Woman's Land Army of America, to Mrs. Morgan, September 30, 1918, Josephine Perry Morgan Papers, Princeton Historical Society.

21. Sarah Fuller Preston to Mrs. Morgan, October 2, 1918, Josephine Perry Morgan Papers, Princeton Historical Society.

22. Western Union Telegram to Mrs. Junius Morgan from Carolina D. Nixon, October 7, 1918, Josephine Perry Morgan Papers, Princeton Historical Society.

23. Elizabeth Devery to Josephine Morgan, September 17, 1918, Josephine Perry Morgan Papers, Princeton Historical Society.

24. Program, Mt. Holly Theatre, October 2, 1918, Josephine Perry Morgan Papers, Princeton Historical Society.

CHAPTER 18: GEORGIA COTTON

1. Gerald Shenk, "Race, Manhood, and Manpower: Mobilizing Rural Georgia in World War I," *Georgia Historical Quarterly* 81 (Fall 1997).

2. "Augusta Women Form 'Land Army', Will Pick Cotton and Gather Crops," *Augusta Chronicle*, August 25, 1918.

3. "County Agent York Endorse the Work," *Augusta Chronicle*, August 25, 1918.

4. "Augusta Woman Form 'Land Army,'" *Augusta Chronicle*, August 25, 1918.

5. "Young Ladies Go Cotton Picking," *August Chronicle*, August 28, 1918.

6. "Augusta Women Form 'Land Army.'"

7. "Woman's Land Army Held Enthusiastic Meeting Friday," *Augusta Chronicle*, September 15, 1918.

8. "Woman's Land Army Goes Out on Cotton-Picking Trip This Afternoon," *Augusta Chronicle*, August 27, 1918.

9. Ibid.

10. "Young Ladies Go Cotton Picking."

11. Ibid.

12. "Woman's Land Army Goes out on Cotton-Picking Trip."

13. "Young Ladies Go Cotton Picking."

14. "Woman's Land Army Held Enthusiastic Meeting Friday," *Augusta Chronicle*, September 15, 1918.

15. Ibid.

16. Marjorie Craig, handwritten memoir. University Archives, Walter Clinton Jackson Library, University of North Carolina at Greensboro.

17. Typescript compilation of WLA state reports, Emma L. George Papers, Manuscript Division, Library of Congress.

18. "What the Farmers Say," publication of Woman's Land Army of America, New York, 1918. Special Collections Division, Walter Clinton Jackson Library, University of North Carolina at Greensboro.

19. "Hephzibah Unit of Land Army Has Picked 13 Bales Cotton," *Augusta Chronicle*, October 7, 1918.

20. Ibid.

21. "They Are All Pushing for Pershing," *Woman's Journal*, October 12, 1918.

22. "The Girl With the Plow," *Augusta Chronicle*, September 8, 1918.

23. "Hephzibah Unit of Land Army Has Picked 13 Bales Cotton."

24. "Victory Parade Greatest in History of Augusta," *Augusta Chronicle*, May 7, 1919.

CHAPTER 19: HARSH TERRAIN

1. *The Michigan Daily* 28, no. 175 (June 1, 1918): 3, University of Michigan Archives, Ann Arbor, MI.

2. Report of Midland County Women's Committee in "Carry On," official publication of the Michigan Women's Committee (Michigan Division), Council of National Defense. Kalamazoo, MI, November 23, 1918.

3. Caroline Bartlett Crane, State Chairman, History of the Work of the Women's Committee (Michigan Division), Council of National Defense, During the World War, Bentley Historical Library, University of Michigan, p. 35.

4. R. S. Trumbull to Isabella Ferguson, August 3, 1918. Women's Land Army Letters, Collection number AC 246-P. Fray Angelico Chavez History Library, the Palace of the Governors, Santa Fe, NM.

5. Alice Corbin Henderson, "New Mexico in the Great War: The Women's Part," *New Mexico Historical Review* 1, no. 3 (July 1926): 242.

6. Martha (Patty) Flandrau Selmes, letter, as reproduced in *The Farmerette* 1, no. 3 (January 1919).

7. Corbin Henderson, "New Mexico in the Great War."

8. Photographs of Isabella Ferguson and farmerettes, Woman's Land Army of New Mexico, Photo Archives, Museum of New Mexico, Palace of the Governors, Santa Fe, New Mexico. In the 1930s Isabella Selmes Ferguson Greenway was elected to two terms in the U.S. House of Representatives from Arizona, becoming the state's first congresswoman.

9. *Touchstone*, July 1918.

10. Committee of Public Information, Division of Women's War Work, press release, May 6, 1919, Barnard College Archives.

11. "Women Asked to Enroll Saturday in Land Army," Medford (Oregon) *Mail Tribune*, May 24, 1918; and "Woman Land Army to Camp at Hollaway Orchard," *Mail Tribune*, May 14, 1918. Courtesy Southern Oregon Historical Society, Medford.

12. "Women Asked to Enroll Saturday in Land Army."

13. Ibid.

14. Minutes of the meeting of the Missouri Women's Committee, June 4, 1918, Women's Committee, Council of National Defense, Correspondence with State Committees, RG 62-13b, National Archives.

15. Ibid.

16. Report of the Utah Women's Committee of National Defense, Women's Committee, Council of National Defense, Reports of State Activities, RG 62-13b, National Archives.

17. "Volunteer Army of Women and Children Help to Save the Bumper Wheat Crop in Kansas," *Augusta Chronicle*, August 25, 1918.

18. Telegram to the president, White House, Washington, DC, from Kansas Tractor Girls' president and secretary, Salina, Kansas, August 14, 1918. Records of the Secretary of Agriculture, RG 16, Box 3129, National Archives.

19. News item in the *Topeka Capital* as reported in *Woman's Journal*, October 12, 1918.

CHAPTER 20: MISS DIEHL AND THE WELLESLEY EXPERIMENT STATION

1. Biographical information on Edith Diehl from the files of the Southeast Museum, Brewster, NY; the Brewster Public Library; and the Wellesley College Archives. The author is indebted to the

research of Deborah Rafferty-Oswald on Diehl and to the personal reminiscences of Melissa Fitzgerald, Diehl's great-niece, who now owns Diehl's home, "Our Acre," and allowed the author access to Diehl's library and papers there.

2. Diehl's blueprint for Red Cross workroom, in Diehl's personal library at Our Acre, Brewster, NY. Also "Call for Bandages Has Quick Response," *New York Times*, April 29, 1917; and "Miss Edith Diehl, Bookbinder, Dead," obituary, *New York Times*, May 13, 1953.

3. "Wellesley College Adopts Military Life," *Boston Traveler*, September 10, 1918; and "Land Army Girls in Daily Drills on Wellesley Campus," *Boston American*, n.d. (late August–early September 1918), Woman's Land Army files, WNF&GA Papers, Schlesinger Library.

4. "Report—Wellesley College Training Camp and Experiment Station for the Woman's Land Army of America, Edith Diehl, Director," 2nd ed., 1919, 95 pp. Reproduced in "History of Women" Microfilm Series (Woodbridge, CT: Research Publications, 1976), Reel 931, no. 7840.

5. "Women Organizing Immense Army for Farming Next Year," *New York Tribune*, August 21, 1918. Edith Diehl Files, Southeast Museum, Brewster, New York.

6. Wellesley Camp notebooks of Carol Maynard, WNF&GA Papers, B-4, Box 7a, Schlesinger Library.

7. Elene Foster, "A Feminine Plattsburg," *New York Tribune*, n.d. (early August 1918), in private papers of Edith Diehl, Our Acre, Brewster, NY. Courtesy of Ms. Melissa Fitzgerald.

8. *Brewster Standard*, August 9, 1918.

9. All of Edith Diehl's descriptions of the Wellesley Camp's operations, unless otherwise noted, are from her "Report—Wellesley College Training Camp."

10. "Wellesley College Training Camp for the Woman's Land Army of America—List of Graduates," typescript. Wellesley College Archives.

11. "Wellesley College Adopts Military Life," *Boston Traveler*, September 10, 1918, In private papers of Edith Diehl at Our Acre, Brewster, New York. Also "Land Army Girls in Daily Drills on Wellesley Campus," *Boston American*, n.d. (late August 1918), WNF&GA Papers, Schlesinger Library; and "What Hoe! What Hoe! Wellesley Is All Ready to Rake the Enemy," *Boston Sunday Post*, September 15, 1918, Edith Diehl Files, Southeast Museum.

12. Frank B. Gilbreth Papers, Manuscript Collections, Library of Congress.

13. Wellesley Camp notebooks of Carol Maynard.

14. Ibid.

15. Ibid.

16. Grace Schenck to Corinne Alsop, September 4, 1918, Council of Defense, Women's Division, RG 30, Box 375, Folder T 59, Connecticut State Archives.

CHAPTER 21: TILLER, PLANTER, GLEANER

1. "Soldiers Aid Land Army," *New York Times*, September 29, 1918.

2. "Woman's Land Army Begins Ten-Day Drive," *New York Times*, September 19, 1918.

3. "1,000 New Farmerettes," *New York Times*, September 22, 1918.

4. "Woman's Land Army Begins Ten-Day Drive."

5. "Mrs. Whitman in Land Army," *New York Times,* September 3, 1918.

6. "Need Workers for Land Army Drive," *New York Times*, September 15, 1918.

7. "The Woman's Land Army," editorial, *New York Times*, September 28, 1918.

8. "New York Farmers Break All Records," *New York Times*, September 8, 1918.

9. Report of the Committee to Adjust Relations Between the Public Employment Bureaus and the Woman's Land Army (Virginia Gildersleeve, Spring 1918). Barnard College Archives.

10. Virginia Gildersleeve, handwritten notes, May 27, 1918. Barnard College Archives.

11. "The Work of Farmerettes," *New York Times*, July 24, 1918.

12. *Club Worker*, publication of the National League of Women Workers, New York, July 1918.

13. "Soldiers Aid Land Army."

14. "Miss Ogilvie Addresses Students," late Fall 1918, typescript, Barnard College Archives.

15. Alice Campbell, "Masters of Agriculture," *The Thermometer*, July 17, 1918, Vassar College Archives.

16. "NY Farmers Break All Records: Farmerettes Declared to Excel Men," *New York Times*, September 8, 1918.

17. "Farmerettes Declared to Excel Men Under Agricultural Labor Conditions," *New York Tribune*, August 21, 1918.

18. "Women on Farms Prove a Success," *New York Times*, September 22, 1918.

19. "Women Organizing Immense Army for Farming Next Year," *New York Tribune*, August 21, 1918; and "Miss Diehl Says Women Should Wear Breeches," *Albany Argus*, August 21, 1918, Edith Diehl Files, Southeast Museum.

20. "Soldiers Aid Land Army."

21. "Mrs. Whitman in Land Army"; and "Governor's Wife Will Lead Drive to Aid Land Army," unidentified New York City newspaper, September 3, 1918, Edith Diehl Files, Southeast Museum.

22. Membership Enrollment Form, New York State Woman's Land Army, Felton Family Papers, Special Collections, State University of New York at Plattsburgh.

23. "Woman's Land Army Begins Ten-Day Drive," *New York Times*, September 19, 1918.

24. "English Farmerette Will Be Speaker at County Fairs in N.Y.," unidentified New York newspaper, September 4, 1918, Felton Family Papers, State University of New York at Plattsburgh.

25. "Soldiers Aid Land Army."

26. "Gerard Speaker for Land Army," *Albany Argus*, August 20, 1918.

27. "Miss Diehl Says Women Should Wear Breeches."

28. Ibid.

29. "Albany's Land Army Rally," *New York Sun*, August 21, 1918.

30. "Women Organizing," *New York Tribune*, August 21, 1918.

31. Program of the Up-State Conference of the New York State WLA, Felton Family Papers, State University of New York at Plattsburgh; and "Miss Diehl Says Women Should Wear Breeches."

32. Ibid.

CHAPTER 22: MARRIAGE OF CONVENIENCE

1. U.S. Employment Service Bulletin, July 23, 1918, Records of the U.S. Employment Service, RG 183.3, National Archives.

2. "British Land Army to American Sisters," *Woman's Journal*, August 24, 1918; and "Felicitation Received From Land Army of Britain," *New York Times*, August 12, 1918.

3. "Ideas for a Motion Picture Showing the Work of the Women's Committee of the Council of National Defense: Picturesque Ideas," typescript scenario, Division of Films, Committee of Public Information, July 1918, Records of the Secretary of Agriculture, RG 16, National Archives.

4. Breen, *Uncle Sam at Home*, pp. 124–26, 132–33.

5. Ibid., p. 135.

6. Secretary Baker to Anna Howard Shaw, June 22, 1918, Council of National Defense, Woman's Committee, RG 62.5.1, Correspondence of Anna Howard Shaw, National Archives; and Breen, *Uncle Sam at Home*, p. 177.

7. Anna Howard Shaw to the Secretary of War, Chairman, Council of National Defense, June 26, 1918, Records of the Secretary of Agriculture, RG 16, Box 3129 "Women," National Archives.

8. Anna Howard Shaw to Mabel Potter Daggett, September 6, 1918, Correspondence of Anna Howard Shaw, Council of National Defense, Woman's Committee, RG 62.5.1, National Archives.

9. Shaw was awarded the Distinguished Service Medal for her service during the war. She died less than a year after the armistice, in July 1919, while on an exhausting speaking tour on behalf of America's entry to the League of Nations.

10. *South Norwalk* (Connecticut) *Sentinel*, May 22, 1918, Connecticut Council of Defense,

Women's Division, RG 30, Box 375, Connecticut State Archives.

11. Grace Schenck to Corinne Alsop, July 24, 1918, Connecticut Council of Defense, Women's Division, RG 30, Box 375, Connecticut State Archives.

12. Grace Schenck to Leo Korper, July 24, 1918, Connecticut State Archives.

13. "U.S. Praises Farmerettes," unidentified New York City newspaper clipping, August 19, 1918, Edith Diehl Files, Southeast Museum.

14. Mrs. Edward P. Davis to President Wilson, September 5, 1918, Records of the Secretary of Agriculture, National Archives.

15. Woodrow Wilson to David Houston, September 7, 1918, Records of the Secretary of Agriculture, National Archives.

16. Secretary Houston to President Wilson, September 18, 1918, Records of the Secretary of Agriculture, National Archives.

17. Woodrow Wilson to David Houston, September 20, 1918, Records of the Secretary of Agriculture, National Archives.

18. Ida H. Ogilvie, "Agriculture, Labor and Women," *Columbia University Quarterly*, October 1918.

19. Grace Schenck to Corinne Alsop, July 24, 1918, Connecticut Council of Defense, Women's Division, RG 30, Box 375, T 59.1, Connecticut State Archives.

20. Ibid.

21. "Outline Draft of Federal Program Concerning Woman's Land Army" and "Outline Showing the Function of the Private Organization and the Federal Organization of the Woman's Land Army of America," typescript memorandums, Connecticut Council of Defense, Women's Division, RG 30, Box 375, T 59.1, Connecticut State Archives.

22. Fall Conference of State Representatives and National Board of Directors, Cosmopolitan Club, New York City, October 23, 1918, summary minutes, Connecticut Council of Defense, Women's Division, RG 30, Box 375, T 59.1, Connecticut State Archives.

23. "Women Farmers Are Recognized," *Christian Science Monitor*, October 25, 1918.

CHAPTER 23: A HUNGRY WORLD

1. Mrs. Otto Eichel, "The Future of the Land Army," *Woman Citizen*, May 17, 1919.

2. *Call to the First Annual Convention of the Woman's Land Army of America*, January 1919, Wellesley College Archives.

3. "Outlook Reviewed by Administrator Hoover," *Wall Street Journal*, November 13, 1918.

4. Ibid.

5. "Feeding Germany," *Wall Street Journal*, November 19, 1918.

6. "Will Send Food to Germans," *New York Times*, November 14, 1918.

7. "German Women Ask Food Help," *New York Times*, November 15, 1918.

8. "Reasons for Feeding Our Beaten Foes—Not Merely Humane, but Expedient," *New York Times*, November 17, 1918.

9. Ibid.

10. Ibid.

11. Katherine C. Steward to Chairmen of State and Land Service Committees, WNF&GA, n.d., Records of the WNF&GA, Schlesinger Library, Radcliffe Institute, Harvard University.

12. "Food Question Most Important," *Wall Street Journal*, November 15, 1918.

13. Foster, "A Feminine Plattsburg," in private papers of Edith Diehl, Our Acre, Brewster, New York. Courtesy of Ms. Melissa Fitzgerald.

14. "A Woman's Land Army for Peace Times," *The Survey*, July 13, 1918.

15. "Women and the Land," *Christian Science Monitor*, December 6, 1918.

16. Editorial, *New Republic*, January 11, 1919.

17. "The Outlook," *The Farmerette*, December 1918.

18. F. C. Walcott, U.S. Food Administration, to Helen Fraser, November 13, 1918, Helen Fraser Papers, Suffrage Collection, Museum of London Archives. Helen Fraser was among the first women candidates to run for Parliament. She campaigned for a seat in the House of Commons in the 1922 and 1923 elections (unsuccessfully) and was nominated again, but did not run, in 1924. She continued her active participation in civic affairs in Britain and later in Australia.

19. Memorandum for the Secretary, U.S. Department of Labor, from. J. B. Densmore, Director-General, U.S. Employment Service, December 12, 1918. Josephine Perry Morgan Papers, Princeton Historical Society.

20. Delia West Marble, *The Farmerette,* December 1918.

21. Reconstruction Plans of the Illinois Training Farm of the Woman's Land Army, State Council of Defense, press release. Illinois State Archives.

22. "Join the Incubator Class," clipping from unknown newspaper, early 1919. Illinois State Archives.

23. Eichel, "The Future of the Land Army."

24. *Call to the First Annual Convention.*

25. Editorial, *The Farmerette,* December 1918.

CHAPTER 24: CARRY ON

1. Louisine W. Havemeyer, "The Prison Special: Memories of a Militant, Part II," *Scribner's,* June 1922.

2. Ellen Carol DuBois, *Harriot Stanton Blatch and the Winning of Woman Suffrage* (New Haven, CT: Yale University Press, 1997), pp. 208–9. While Blatch intended to report on the opportunities the war had opened for women in Europe, the actual situation of devastation and poverty she encountered shocked her and caused her to radically rethink her attitude toward war. She became a pacifist. The book she wrote, *A Woman's Point of View: Some Roads to Peace,* which was published in early 1920, emphasized war's futility. She was the Socialist Party candidate for the U.S. Senate from New York in 1926 and ran unsuccessfully for several other elected positions. She died in 1940 at age eighty-three.

3. Dorothy Hubert, WLA, to Stella H. Webb, WNF&GA, December 12, 1918, WNF&GA, Schlesinger Library.

4. Juliet Morgan Hamilton to Josephine Perry Morgan, on WLA stationery, December 30, 1918, Josephine P. Morgan Papers, Princeton Historical Society.

5. Grace Elizabeth Paine to Josephine Morgan, April 2, 1918; and Maude Truesdale to Mrs. Morgan, June 15, 1918. Josephine Perry Morgan Papers, Princeton Historical Society.

6. Anne MacIlvaine to Joseph Tumulty, the White House, September 20, 1918, Records of the Secretary of Agriculture, National Archives.

7. Joseph Tumulty to David Houston, September 25, 1918, Records of the Secretary of Agriculture, National Archives.

8. Loss of confidence in MacIlvaine is described in Dorothea Miller Post to Josephine Morgan, n.d. (Fall 1918), Josephine Perry Morgan Papers, Princeton Historical Society.

9. "Illinois Unit Quits Woman's Land Army; Find Aims Conflict," *Chicago Daily Tribune,* January 10, 1919.

10. Ibid.

11. Anne MacIlvaine, handwritten statement, Josephine Perry Morgan Papers, Princeton Historical Society.

12. Ibid.

13. "Suffragist to Marry," *New York Times,* September 17, 1916.

14. "Costumes Rejected by the Farmerettes," unidentified news clipping, January 16, 1919, Emma L. George Papers, Manuscript Division, Library of Congress.

15. "Farmerettes Vote Against Uniforms," *Philadelphia Public Ledger,* January 16, 1919, Newspaper Room, Philadelphia Free Library.

16. "Report of the W.L.A.A.," an account of the Philadelphia convention, in *The Pharetra,* Wilson College, Chambersburg, PA, March 1919, Wilson College Archives.

17. Ibid.

18. "Propaganda Moving Picture Produced," *New York Times,* February 2, 1919.

19. "Program of New York State Woman's Land Army for the Season of 1919, Possibilities of Future Developments," typescript, Felton Family Papers, Special Collections, State University of New York at Plattsburgh.

20. Ibid.

21. Unidentified New York newspaper, early 1919, in Woman's Land Army files, Barnard College Archives.

22. Eichel, "The Future of the Woman's Land Army." At around this time, the *Woman's Journal* changed its name to *Woman Citizen.*

23. Ida H. Oglivie, "The Spirit of the Land Army," *The Farmerette,* 1, no. 1 (December 1918).

24. "Farmers Consider Land Army Plans," n.d., clipping from unidentified Philadelphia newspaper in Mabel Potter Lewis Papers, Pennsylvania Historical Society.

25. Ibid.

26. Ibid.

27. Clipping from unidentified Philadelphia newspaper, Winter–Spring 1919, Mabel Potter Lewis Papers, Pennsylvania Historical Society.

28. Editorial, *New Republic,* January 11, 1919.

29. Alice Graydon Phillips, "California's Woman's Land Army," *New Republic,* March 1, 1919.

30. Josephine Morgan, handwritten draft of solicitation letter, Winter 1919, Josephine Perry Morgan Papers, Princeton Historical Society.

31. Elizabeth Packard to Mrs. Junius Morgan, n.d. (Winter 1919). Josephine P. Morgan Papers, Princeton Historical Society.

32. Ibid.

33. "U.S. Employment Service Curtailed," *New York Times,* March 14, 1919.

34. Ibid.

35. Vera P. Lane to Mrs. Junius Morgan, March 6, 1919, Josephine Perry Morgan Papers, Princeton Historical Society.

36. "Official Uniforms for Field and Street" brochure, Barnard College Archives.

37. Contract for Uniform of Woman's Land Army of America, Inc., Josephine Perry Morgan Papers, Princeton Historical Society.

38. "Miss Ihlseng in the South," *The Farmerette* 1, no. 3 (January 1919).

39. "Woman's Land Army Training Camp of University of Virginia" brochure, Emma L. George Papers, Manuscript Division, Library of Congress.

40. Edith Diehl to Ellen F. Pendleton, May 13, 1919, Wellesley College Archives.

41. "Land Army to Continue," *Los Angeles Times,* February 13, 1919.

42. Ibid.

43. "State Budgets," March 20, 1919, prepared for special meeting of the Board of Directors of the Woman's Land Army of America, Inc., March 21, 1919.

CHAPTER 25: FARMERETTE REDUX

1. "New York Land Army Seeks Funds," *New York Times,* April 12, 1919.

2. "Need Labor on Farms—Rally for Farmerettes," *Washington Post,* March 9, 1919.

3. Minutes of WLA Board of Directors Meeting, May 7, 1919, Josephine P. Morgan Papers, Princeton Historical Society.

4. Ibid.

5. Ibid.

6. Nellie Jones, Wisconsin WLA, to Mabel Potter Lewis, May 29, 1919, Mabel Potter Lewis

Papers, Pennsylvania Historical Society.

7. WLA progress report, June 1919, Mabel Potter Lewis Papers, Pennsylvania Historical Society.

8. Ibid.

9. Omaha newspaper clipping, unidentified, n.d. (June 1919), RG 183, Records of the Federal State Director of the U.S. Employment Service, Omaha, Nebraska, RG 183, National Archives, Central Plains Region, Kansas City, MO.

10. Kathleen O'Brien, Superintendent, Women's Division, U.S. Employment Service, Omaha, to Mrs. William H. Hubert, National Director, WLAA, July 12, 1919. Records of the Federal State Director, U.S. Employment Service, Omaha, RG 183, National Archives, Central Plains Region, Kansas City.

11. J. D. Richards, Martin, South Dakota, to Miss O'Brien, Omaha, July 7, 1919, National Archives, Kansas City.

12. Kathleen O'Brien to J. D. Richards, July 12, 1919, National Archives, Kansas City.

13. Kathleen O'Brien to Mrs. William Hubert, July 12, 1919, National Archives, Kansas City.

14. May Kemp, Wilton, New Hampshire, to Federal Labor Bureau, July 14, 1919, National Archives, Kansas City.

15. Typescript. Emma L. George Papers, Manuscript Division, Library of Congress. The article never appeared in the paper.

16. "New Jersey Land Army Opens Cooperative Farm to Train Women Workers," press release, typescript. Emma L. George Papers, Manuscript Division, Library of Congress.

17. Woman's Land Army of America, Virginia Division, pamphlet, Virginia Historical Society, Richmond.

18. Woman's Land Army Training Camp of University of Virginia, brochure, Emma L. George Papers, Manuscript Division, Library of Congress.

19. WLA Progress Report, July 1919, Josephine Perry Morgan Papers, Princeton Historical Society.

20. Ellen Fitz Pendleton to Edith Diehl, May 15, 1919, Wellesley College Archives.

21. Edith Diehl to Ellen Fitz Pendleton, May 21, 1919, Wellesley College Archives.

22. Edith Diehl to WLA State Chairmen, May 15, 1919, Mabel Potter Lewis Papers, Pennsylvania Historical Society.

23. Diehl resumed her successful career as a bookbinder. Twenty-five years later, when she wrote her celebrated two-volume opus on the history and craft of bookbinding, she composed the first draft, in pencil, on the back of her old Wellesley Camp stationery. Diehl's handwritten pages, draft of *Bookbinding: Its Background and Technique*, in Edith Diehl Miscellany Collection, Pierpont Morgan Library, New York.

24. *Lodi Sentinal*, July 31, 1919, in Kipp, "Women on the Land," p. 120.

25. "Girls Recruit for Farm Work," *San Francisco Examiner*, August 20, 1919, Newspaper Reading Room, Library of Congress.

26. "Peace, All Triumphant, Blooms," *Los Angeles Times,* January 2, 1919.

27. "New York State Land Army Camps," report dated June 26, 1919, typescript, Emma L. George Papers, Manuscript Division, Library of Congress.

28. August Bulletin, New York State Woman's Land Army, 1919.

29. "Extracts from Address of Governor Smith on Governor's Day," July 25, 1919, Felton Family Papers, State University of New York, Plattsburgh.

30. Bulletin, New York State Woman's Land Army, August 1919, Felton Family Papers, State University of New York, Plattsburgh.

31. Josephine P. Morgan to Mrs. Carroll Bassett, June 21, 1919, Josephine Perry Morgan Papers, Princeton Historical Society.

32. Josephine P. Morgan to Commissioner Lewis T. Bryant, June 21, 1919, Josephine Perry Morgan Papers, Princeton Historical Society.

33. Notice of special meeting of the New Jersey WLA, July 8, 1919, Josephine Perry Morgan

Papers, Princeton Historical Society.

34. WLA Progress Report, August 1919. Josephine Perry Morgan Papers, Princeton Historical Society.

35. "Statistics: Reports for 1919," *The Farmerette* 1, no. 5 (December 1919).

36. "No Farming Jobs," *Smith College Weekly*, May 28, 1919, Smith College Archives.

37. Memorandum of Work Done by New England Branch, WNF&GA, 1919, WNF&GA Papers, Schlesinger Library.

38. WLA Progress Reports for July and August 1919, Josephine Morgan Papers, Princeton Historical Society

39. "World's Fourth Today," *Washington Post*, July 4, 1919; and "Washington Farmerettes and Girl Scouts Perform in 'The Call of the Land,'" *Washington Post*, July 5, 1919.

40. WLA Board of Directors Meeting, minutes, July 7, 1919, Josephine Perry Morgan Papers, Princeton Historical Society.

41. Ibid.

42. Bulletin, New York State Woman's Land Army, August 1919, Felton Family Collection, State University of New York, Plattsburgh.

43. WLA Board of Directors Meeting minutes, August 5, 1919, Josephine Perry Morgan Papers, Princeton Historical Society.

44. Ibid.

45. Ibid.

46. J. B. Densmore, Director General, U.S. Employment Service, to Mrs. William H. Schofield, August 27, 1919, Wellesley College Archives.

47. "Camps for Farmerettes," *New York Times*, August 28, 1919.

48. Reports of Olga Ihlseng, WLA National Field Secretary, on New Jersey units: July 31–August 20 and August 23–September 15, 1919, Josephine Perry Morgan Papers, Princeton Historical Society.

49. WLA Board of Directors Meeting minutes, September 9, 1919, Josephine Perry Morgan Papers, Princeton Historical Society.

50. Ibid.

51. "Princess Mary With Land Girls," *Times of London*, November 28, 1919; and *The Landswoman*, December 1919. Imperial War Museum, London.

52. Special Meeting of the WLA Board of Directors, September 26, 1919, Josephine Perry Morgan Papers, Princeton Historical Society.

53. "Women Disband Land Army," *New York Times*, February 3, 1920.

54. Virginia McComb to Mabel Potter Lewis, September 22, 1919. Mabel Potter Lewis Papers, Pennsylvania Historical Society.

55. Ibid.

56. Edith Ellicott Smith to Land Army Workers, September 20, 1919, Mabel Potter Lewis Papers, Pennsylvania Historical Society.

57. "Recommendations of the Committee on the Land Army Future," Pennsylvania WLA. Mabel Potter Lewis Papers, Pennsylvania Historical Society.

58. Recruitment brochure, Land Army Committee, League of Women Workers, Mabel Potter Lewis Papers, Pennsylvania Historical Society.

59. *The Farmerette* 1, no. 5 (December 1919); and *The Farmerette* 1, no. 6 (May 1920), New York State Library, Albany.

60. *The Farmerette*, May 1920, New York State Library, Albany.

61. "1,229 Volunteer for Farms," *New York Times*, March 21, 1920.

62. "Land Service Sends. . . ," *New York Times*, September 12, 1920.

63. Bureau of Advice and Information to Commonwealth Fund, August 2, 1921, Commonwealth Fund Archives, Series 18, Box 9, Folder 85, Rockefeller Archive Center, Pocantico Hills, NY.

64. "Room for 30 Girls in Farm Camps," *New York Times*, June 18, 1922.

65. "Where Does the Land Army Go From Here?" *Woman Citizen*, March 26, 1921.

66. Juliet Wilbor Tompkins, "The Two Benjamins," *McCall's*, August 1918.

67. Claire Chapman, *The Farmerette* (Boston: Arthur P. Schmidt Co., 1921), Performing Arts Reading Room, Library of Congress.

68. John Laurence Seymour, "The Farmerette, A Modern Opera-Bouffe in Three Acts," opus 15, Performing Arts Reading Room, Library of Congress.

69. "Prince to Buy Tractors," *Los Angeles Times*, August 22, 1920.

70. Ethel Puffer Howes, "Accepting the Universe," *The Atlantic Monthly*, April 1922; and "Continuity for Women," *The Atlantic Monthly*, May 1922. Also, "Institute to Coordinate Women's Interests Launched," *Christian Science Monitor*, October 22, 1923; and "College Expands to Reach Wives," *New York Times*, November 1, 1925, found in the papers of Laura Puffer and Ethel Puffer Howes, Schlesinger Library. See also the records of the Institute for the Coordination of Women's Interests in the Smith College Archives.

71. In faulty hindsight, the images of the farmerette and the flapper sometimes became comically commingled. The Broadway musical *Guys and Dolls,* based on Damon Runyan's tales of 1920s New York, featured scantily clad "Farmerettes" singing "I Love You, a Bushel and a Peck."

72. Judy Barrett Litoff and David C. Smith, "To the Rescue of the Crops: The Women's Land Army During WWII," *Prologue: Quarterly of the National Archives*, Winter 1993, p. 349.

73. "Farms to Need Women, First Lady Predicts," *Washington Post*, November 25, 1941.

74. Ibid.; and also *New York Herald Tribune*, November 25, 1941, as quoted in Litoff and Smith, "To the Rescue of the Crops," p. 349.

75. "Land Army," *Time*, April 27, 1942.

76. Ibid.

77. "Women Asked to Replace Drafted Farmers," *Washington Post*, January 15, 1942.

78. Dorothy Thompson, syndicated column, "Collegians Begin Back-to-the-Land Drive on Own Hook," March 12, 1942. Also Esther M. Colvin, "Another Women's Land Army?" *Independent Woman*, April 1942; Stephanie Ann Carpenter, "Regular Farm Girl: The Women's Land Army in WWII," *Agricultural History* 71, no. 2 (Spring 1997); and Florence Hall, "They're Getting in the Crops," *National Business Woman*, July 1942.

79. "Vassar Girls Aid in Harvest—Farmerette Labor Returns," *Poughkeepsie New Yorker,* September 22, 1942, Vassar College Archives.

80. Colvin, "Another Women's Land Army?"

81. "British WLA Is Visited by First Lady," *Washington Post*, November 8, 1942; and "Women's Farm Unit Gains Backing Here—First Lady Supports It," *New York Times*, December 10, 1942.

82. Dean Albertston, *Roosevelt's Farmer: Claude R. Wickard in the New Deal* (New York: Columbia University Press, 1961), as cited in Litoff and Smith, "To the Rescue of the Crops."

83. "Will Head Women in New Crop Corps," *New York Times*, April 13, 1943; and "Land Army Launched," *New York Times*, April 18, 1943.

84. "Land Army Described," *New York Times*, May 11, 1943.

85. "1943 and 1918—Women's Land Army Garb," *Christian Science Monitor*, April 17, 1943. Photograph in the Farm Security Administration and Office of War Information Collection, Library of Congress.

BIBLIOGRAPHY

ARCHIVAL COLLECTIONS

Academic Institutions

Barnard College Archives, New York City

Berry College Archives, Mount Berry, Georgia

Bryn Mawr College Archives, Bryn Mawr, Pennsylvania

Columbia University Archives, New York City

Columbia University, College of Physicians and Surgeons Archives, New York City

Connecticut College Archives, New London, Connecticut

Cornell University Alumni Records, Kheel Labor Archives, and Kroch Library, Rare and Manuscript Collections, Ithaca, New York

Georgia State University Special Collections, Augusta, Georgia

Goucher College Archives, Baltimore, Maryland

Hollins University Special Collections, Roanoke, Virginia

Hood College Special Collections, Frederick, Maryland

Hunter College Archives, University of the City of New York

Iowa State University Rural and Farm Women Collection, Ames, Iowa

Massachusetts Agricultural College Archives, University of Massachusetts, Amherst

Mills College Archives, Oakland, California

Mount Holyoke College Archives and Special Collections, South Hadley, Massachussettes.

Oberlin College Archives, Oberlin, Ohio

Oregon State University Archives, Corvallis, Oregon

Radcliffe Institute Archives, Cambridge, Massachusetts

Rutgers University Archives and Special Collections, East Brunswick, New Jersey

Arthur and Elizabeth Schlesinger Library on the History of Women, Radcliffe Institute, Harvard University, Cambridge, Massachussettes

Simmons College Archives, Boston, Massachussettes

Smith College Archives, Northampton, Massachusetts
Smith College Archives, Northampton, Massachusetts
State University of New York at Farmingdale, Archives
State University of New York at Plattsburgh, Special Collections
Sophia Smith Collection, Smith College, Northhampton, Massachusetts
Teachers College of Columbia University Archives, New York City
University of California at Berkeley Library, Special Collections
University of California at Los Angeles Library, Special Collections
University of Cambridge Reading Room, Cambridge, England
University of Chicago Special Collections and University Archives, Chicago Illinois
University of Colorado Archives, Boulder
University of Michigan Bentley Historical Library, Ann Arbor
University of North Carolina at Greensboro Jackson Library, Special Collections, and University
    Archives
University of Vermont Bailey/Howe Library Special Collections, Burlington
University of Virginia, Special Collections, Joseph M. Bruccoli Great War Collection and University
    Archives, Charlottesville
Vassar College Archives, Poughkeepsie, New York
Wellesley College Archives, Wellesley, Massachusetts
Western Michigan University Archives and Regional History Collection, Kalamazoo
Wilson College Archives, Chambersburg, Pennsylvania
Winthrop University Archives, Rock Hill, South Carolina

Public and Private Repositories

American Association of University Women Archives, Washington, D.C.
Athenaeum of Philadelphia, Pennsylvania
Augusta History Museum, Georgia
Bedford Historical Society, Bedford, New York
Brewster Public Library, Brewster, New York
British Historical Manuscripts Commission, London
California State Archives, Sacramento
Catonsville Public Library, the Catonsville Room, Catonsville, Maryland
Chester County Historical Society, West Chester, Pennsylvania
Colorado State Archives, Denver
Connecticut State Library and Archives, Hartford
Enoch Pratt Free Library, Maryland Room, Baltimore, Maryland
Free Library of Philadelphia, Pennsylvania
General Federation of Women's Clubs Archives, Washington, D.C.
Historical Society of Pennsylvania, Philadelphia
Illinois State Archives, Springfield
Imperial War Museum Archives, London

Indiana State Library, Indianapolis

Iowa Historical Society, Des Moines

Jewish Museum of Maryland, Baltimore

Kansas State Historical Society, Topeka

Kansas State Library, Topeka

Library of Congress, Main Reading Room, Manuscript Collection, Newspaper and Periodicals, and Performing Arts Reading Rooms, Prints and Photographs Collection, Washington, D.C.

Library of Virginia—State Library and Archives, Richmond

Madison County Historical Society, Oneida, New York

Marine Corps Historical Reference Service, Quantico, Virginia

Maryland Historical Society, Baltimore

Missouri State Historical Society, Columbia, Missouri

Mt. Kisco Historical Society, New York

Museum of New Mexico, Palace of the Governors, Fray Angelico Chavez History Library, Santa Fe

Museum of the City of London, Suffrage Collection, London

National Archives and Records Administration, Central Plains Region, Kansas City, Missouri, Records of the Federal State Director, U.S. Employment Service

National Archives and Records Administration, College Park, Maryland; National Archives, Northeast Region, Boston, Massachusetts

National Archives and Records Administration, Record Groups of the Department of Labor, U.S. Employment Service; Department of Agriculture, Food Administration; Council of National Defense, Women's Committee, College Park, Maryland

National Grange Headquarters, Washington, D.C.

New Jersey State Archives, Trenton

New Milford Historical Society, Connecticut

New York Botanical Gardens Archives, Bronx

New York City Municipal Archives

New York Historical Society, New York City

New York Public Library, Manuscripts and Archives Division, New York City

New York State Archives, Albany

New York State Historical Society, Albany

Peterborough Historical Society, New Hampshire

Pierpont Morgan Library, New York

Princeton Historical Society, Princeton, New Jersey

The Rockefeller Archive Center, Sleepy Hollow, New York

Shelburne Museum, Shelburne, Vermont

Sheldon Museum of Vermont History, Middlebury, Vermont

Smithsonian Institution, National Museum of American History, Archives Center, Washington, D.C.

Smithsonian Institution, Prints and Photographs Collection, Washington, D.C.

Southeast Museum, Brewster, New York

Southern Oregon Historical Society, Medford, Oregon

South Hadley Historical Society, Massachusetts
Vacaville Historical Museum, California
Wellesley Historical Society, Massachusetts
Westchester County Historical Society, New York
Wilton Public Library, Connecticut

WOMEN'S LAND ARMY OF AMERICA PUBLICATIONS

Advisory Council of the Woman's Land Army of America. *Women on the Land*. New York, January 1918.
Call to the First Annual Convention of the Woman's Land Army of America. New York, January 1919.
Camp Standards Committee of the Woman's Land Army of America. *The Farmerette*. New York, 1918.
First Annual Report of the Women's Agricultural Camp. Bedford, NY, 1917.
National Board of the WLAA *Handbook of Standards for the Woman's Land Army of America*. New York, April 1919.
Prospectus of the Woman's Land Army. New York, March 1918.
Report of the Wellesley College Training Camp and Experiment Station for the Woman's Land Army of America, advance edition. New York, 1918.
What the Farmers Say About the Work of the Woman's Land Army of America in 1918. 2nd ed. New York, 1919.
The Woman's Land Army in 1918, 2nd ed. New York: Army March, 1918.

BOOKS

Blatch, Harriot Stanton. *Mobilizing Woman-Power*. With a foreword by Theodore Roosevelt. New York: Woman's Press, 1918. Reprint, Whitefish, MT: Kessinger Publishing, 2004.
Blatch, Harriot Stanton, and Alma Lutz. *Challenging Years: The Memoirs of H. S. Blatch*. New York: G. P. Putnam's Sons, 1940. Reprint, Westport, CT: Hyperion Press, 1976.
Breen, William J. *Uncle Sam at Home: Civilian Mobilization, Wartime Federalism and the Council of National Defense, 1917–1919.* Westport, CT: Greenwood Press, 1984.
Clarke, Ida Clyde. *American Women and the World War*. New York: D. Appleton, 1918.
Daggett, Mabel Potter. *Women Wanted: The Story Written in Blood Red Letters on the Horizon of the Great World War.* New York: George H. Doran Company, 1918.
DeBauche, Leslie Midkiff. *Reel Patriotism: The Movies and World War I.* Madison: University of Wisconsin Press, 1997.
DuBois, Ellen Carol. *Harriot Stanton Blatch and the Winning of Woman Suffrage.* New Haven, CT: Yale University Press, 1997.
Farwell, Byron. *Over There: The United States in the Great War, 1917–18.* New York: W. W. Norton, 1999).
Fraser, Helen. *Women and War Work*. With an introduction by H. N. MacCracken. New York: G. Arnold Shaw, 1918.
Gilbreth, Frank B., and Ernestine Gilbreth Carey. *Cheaper by the Dozen*. New York: Thomas Y. Cromwell, 1948.
Gildersleeve, Virginia Crocheron. *Many a Good Crusade*. New York: Macmillan, 1954.

Greenwald, Maurine Weiner. *Women, War and Work: The Impact of World War I on Women Workers in the United States.* Ithaca, NY: Cornell University Press, 1990.

Hurley, Edward N. *The Bridge to France.* Philadelphia: J. B. Lippincott, 1927.

James, Bessie Rowland. *For God, for Country, for Home, the National League for Woman's Service: A Story of the First National Organization of American Women Mobilized for War Service.* New York: Putnam, 1920.

Jellison, Katherine. *Entitled to Power: Farm Women and Technology.* Chapel Hill: University of North Carolina Press, 1993.

Karetsky, Joanne. *Mustering Support for WWI by the Ladies' Home Journal.* Lewiston, NY: Edwin Mellen Press, 1997.

Kennedy, David M. *Over Here: The First World War and American Society.* New York: Oxford University Press, 2004.

Lloyd George, David. *War Memoirs.* Boston: Little, Brown & Company, 1933.

Martelet, Penny. "The Woman's Land Army, World War I." In *Clio Was a Woman: Studies in the History of American Women,* edited by Mabel E. Deutrich and Virginia C. Purdy, 136–46. Washington, DC: Howard University Press, 1980.

McLaren, Barbara. *Women of the War.* London: Hodder and Stoughton, 1917.

Millis, Walter. *Road to War—America, 1914–1917.* London: Faber and Faber, 1935.

Powdermaker, Hortense. *Stranger and Friend: The Way of an Anthropologist.* New York: W. W. Norton, 1966.

Rogers, Emma Winner. *The Journal of a Country Woman.* New York: Eaton and Mains, 1912.

——— *The Women's Land Army.* London: Michael Joseph, 1944. 2nd ed. London: Imperial War Museum, 1997.

Sackville-West, Vita. *Poems of the Land Army: An Anthology of Verse by Members of the Women's Land Army.* London: 'The Land Girl,' 1945.

Surface, Frank M., and Raymond L. Bland. *American Food in the World War and Reconstruction Period: Operations of the Organizations Under the Direction of Herbert Hoover, 1914–1924.* Palo Alto, CA: Stanford University Press, 1931.

Trask, David F., ed. *World War I at Home: Readings on American Life, 1914–1920.* New York: John Wiley & Sons, 1970.

Twinch, Carol. *Women on the Land: Their Story During Two World Wars.* Cambridge, UK: Letterworth Press 1990.

Van Voris, Jacqueline. *Carrie Chapman Catt: A Public Life.* New York: Feminist Press, 1987.

JOURNALS AND THESES

Dumenil, Lynn. "American Women and the Great War." *OAH Magazine of History* (Organization of American Historians), October 2002.

Kipp, Catherine Gabriel. "Women on the Land: The Woman's Land Army, California Northern Division, 1918–1920." Master's thesis, Sacramento State College, 1960.

Litoff, Judy Barrett, and David C. Smith. "To the Rescue of the Crops: The Women's Land Army During World War II." *Prologue, Quarterly of the National Archives,* Winter 1993.

McLoughlin, Virginia. "Hoeing Smokes: A New Milford Connecticut Unit of the Woman's Land Army, World War I." *Connecticut History* 40, no. 1 (Spring 2001).

Ogilvie, Ida H. "Agriculture, Labor and Women." *Columbia University Quarterly,* October 1918.

Shenk, Gerald. "Race, Manhood, and Manpower: Mobilizing Rural Georgia in World War I." *Georgia Historical Quarterly* 81 (Fall 1997).

"War-time Industrial Employment of Women in the United States." *Journal of Political Economy,* October 1919.

Newspapers and Periodicals

The Atlantic Monthly
Albany (New York) Argus
Augusta (Georgia) Chronicle
Baltimore News
Baltimore Sun
Boston Globe
Boston Herald
Boston Sunday Advertiser
Boston Sunday Post
Brooklyn Eagle
Chicago Tribune
Christian Science Monitor
Country Life
Farm and Garden Magazine
Farmer's Wife Magazine
Forum
Ladies Home Journal
Life Magazine
Literary Digest
Living Age
Los Angeles Times

McCall's
McClure's
New Republic
New York Herald Tribune
New York Sun
New York Times
New York Times Magazine
Overland Monthly
Puck
San Francisco Examiner
Scientific American
Scribner's
St. Nicholas
Sunset
The Survey
Time
Touchstone
Wall Street Journal
Washington Post
Woman Citizen
Woman Journal

Interviews

Fitzgerald, Melissa. Correspondence and interviews. McLean, Virginia, and Brewster, New York, 2002.

Holway, Alice. Interviews. Putney, Vermont, 1979–80.

Oswald, Deborah Rafferty. Interview. Brewster, New York, April 2002.

Starks, Robin. Interview. New Milford, Connecticut, October 2003.

Street, Barbara Weaver. Interview. New Milford, Connnecticut, October 2003.

Index

ABOUT THE AUTHOR

Elaine F. Weiss grew up in New York City, the daughter of a school librarian and a U.S. Post Office clerk. She learned to read by helping her father sort mail. She received her first article rejection letter at age ten, when *Reader's Digest* declined to publish her submission, but undeterred, she has made her career as a journalist and writer for more than three decades. A graduate of Kirkland and Hamilton College, she holds a master's degree from the Medill School of Journalism at Northwestern University. She has worked as a congressional speechwriter, a Washington correspondent, a freelance obituary writer, a Public Radio reporter and producer, a magazine editor, university instructor, and on the staff of CBS Television in New York. Her articles have appeared in the *New York Times, The Atlantic, Harper's Magazine, The Boston Globe,* and *The Philadelphia Inquirer*, among other publications, and her radio reports and documentaries have aired on NPR's *All Things Considered, Morning Edition*, and other programs. Weiss was also the associate editor of *Warfield's Magazine,* an award-winning monthly publication that covered business, politics, and cultural news in the Baltimore-Washington region. Her writing has earned awards from the Society of Professional Journalists, the Association for Education in Journalism, and a MacDowell Colony Fellowship. She is currently a features correspondent for the *Christian Science Monitor.*

Weiss lives in Baltimore, Maryland, with her husband, Julian Krolik, a professor of astrophysics at the Johns Hopkins University. Their two children, Teddy and Abigail, have become careful readers and sharp-eyed copyeditors with loving patience for a distracted mom on deadline.